*Cambridge Studies in Oral and Literate Cu*

*READING AND WRITING*

*Literacy in France from Calvin to Jules Ferry*

*Cambridge Studies in Oral and Literate Culture*

*Edited by* PETER BURKE and RUTH FINNEGAN

This series is designed to address the question of the significance of literacy in human societies; it will assess its importance for political, economic, social and cultural development, and examine how what we take to be the common functions of writing are carried out in oral cultures.

The series will be inter-disciplinary, but with particular emphasis on social anthropology and social history, and will encourage cross-fertilization between these disciplines: it will also be of interest to readers in allied fields, such as sociology, folklore and literature. Although it will include some monographs, the focus of the series will be on theoretical and comparative aspects rather than detailed description, and the books will be presented in a form accessible to non-specialist readers interested in the general subject of literacy and orality.

*Books in the series*
1 Nigel Phillips: *'Sijobang': Sung Narrative Poetry of West Sumatra.*
2 R.W. Scribner: *For the Sake of Simple Folk: Popular Propaganda for the German Reformation.*
3 Harvey J. Graff (Ed.): *Literacy and Social Development in the West: A Reader.*
4 Donald J. Cosentino: *Defiant Maids and Stubborn Farmers: Tradition and Invention in Mende Narrative Performance.*

This book, originally published in French in 1977 by Les Editions de Minuit, is published in English as part of the joint publishing agreement established in 1977 between the Fondation de la Maison des Sciences de l'Homme and the Press Syndicate of the University of Cambridge. Titles published under this arrangement may appear in any European language or, in the case of volumes of collected essays, in several languages.

New books will appear either as individual titles or in one of the series which the Maison des Sciences de l'Homme and the Cambridge University Press have jointly agreed to publish. All books published jointly by the Maison des Sciences de l'Homme and the Cambridge University Press will be distributed by the Press throughout the world.

# READING AND WRITING

## Literacy in France from Calvin to Jules Ferry

FRANÇOIS FURET

and

JACQUES OZOUF

CAMBRIDGE UNIVERSITY PRESS

*Cambridge*

*London   New York   New Rochelle   Melbourne   Sydney*

EDITIONS DE
LA MAISON DES SCIENCES DE L'HOMME

*Paris*

Published by the Press Syndicate of the University of Cambridge
The Pitt Building, Trumpington Street, Cambridge CB2 1RP
32 East 57th Street, New York, NY 10022, USA
296 Beaconsfield Parade, Middle Park, Melbourne 3206, Australia
and
Editions de la Maison des Sciences de l'Homme
54 Boulevard Raspail, 75270 Paris Cedex 06

Originally published in French as *Lire et écrire: L'alphabétisation des français de Calvin à Jules Ferry* by Les Editions de Minuit, Paris, 1977, and © Les Editions de Minuit 1977.

First published in English by the Maison des Sciences de l'Homme and Cambridge University Press, 1982 as *Reading and writing: Literacy in France from Calvin to Jules Ferry*.
English translation © Maison des Sciences de l'Homme and Cambridge University Press 1982

Printed in Great Britain at
the University Press, Cambridge

Library of Congress catalogue card number: 82-9502

*British Library Cataloguing in Publication Data*

Furet, François
Reading and writing.—(Cambridge studies in
oral and literate culture)
1. Illiteracy—History—France
I. Title        II. Ozouf, Jacques
III. Lire et écrire. *English*
306'.4    LC149

ISBN 0 521 22389 X hard covers
ISBN 0 521 27402 8 paperback

ISBN 2 901725 54 6 hard covers France only
ISBN 2 7351 8039 1 paperback    France only

TP

# CONTENTS

# MAPS, GRAPHS AND TABLES

## Maps

**Graphs**

**Tables**

# PREFACE

This book presents the findings of a research project which we have undertaken, in the form of a seminar, at the Centre de Recherches Historiques of the Ecole des Hautes Etudes en Sciences Sociales, between 1972 and 1975. The majority of the participants are members of the C.R.H. Marie-Madeleine Compère, Chargée de Recherches at the Commission de l'Histoire de l'Education, was closely involved throughout. Our colleagues P. Butel, G. Mandon, J.-P. Poussou (of the Université de Bordeaux III) and P. Lévêque (of the Université de Dijon) added their contributions to the project; for which we owe them many thanks. J.-P. Coulier and W. Sachs, researchers at the C.R.H., worked out the statistical procedure and established the necessary programs for the calculations in the book. These calculations have been based on statistical data on teaching in France in the nineteenth century, put on tape thanks to the Inter-University Consortium of Ann Arbor, Michigan. The cartographical work was done, under the supervision of Jacques Bertin, by the remarkable team at the Laboratoire de Cartographie of the E.H.E.S.S. Lastly, Cécile Dauphin played a central role in coordinating the various projects.

The financing of the research has mainly been supported by the C.R.H. The remainder of the funds came from the Commission d'Histoire de l'Education at the Ministry of Education – thanks to the support of the late Recteur Bayen – and from a contribution by the E.R.A. 446 of the Centre National de la Recherche Scientifique. The first volume of the work presents a general summary of our research. The second includes the main monographic studies on which the first volume draws.

FRANÇOIS FURET
JACQUES OZOUF

## Note on the English edition

The present volume is a translation of the first part of *Lire et écrire*, published by Editions de Minuit, Paris, in 1977. Readers are referred to the French edition for the regional studies in the second volume.

*ix*

# INTRODUCTION

The history of literacy has aroused fierce passions in France. This is because it has been studied not for its own sake, but rather in order to furnish ammunition in the political debate over education which until recently constituted one of the major lines of cleavage between left and right. Consequently, it became intimately bound up with the crucial issues and values of French political life. The reason 19th-century republicans struggled so obdurately for elementary education and for free schooling was their determination to defend what they thought of as one of the fundamental legacies of the Revolution, namely the emancipation of the people through education. The *Ancien Régime*, in their view, had accomplished nothing in this sphere: 1789 had been the start of everything. If indeed anything had existed prior to this, this something had been in the hands of the Church and was therefore obscurantist, designed to form subjects, and hence to deform man. By its very nature the school was a factor for emancipation, since it held aloft the light of instruction: therefore it had to be republican, and could only have been born in 1789, or perhaps even in 1793.

To this simple reasoning, based on any number of unspoken assumptions, the partly of clerical conservatism replied with its own, no less simple, counter-proposition: it was the Church which had taught the French to read and write through the proliferation of local elementary schools under the *Ancien Régime*; and the Revolution had destroyed this achievement, or at best halted it in its tracks, in destroying the Church. Far from having founded public instruction, it had wrecked it.

We shall have to recapitulate our 19th-century political history in order to be able to follow the thread of this key controversy. The controversy flared especially vigorously, for instance, at the end of the July Monarchy and under the Second Republic, when the schoolmaster and the parish priest led the opposing camps in village politics. It flared up once again, sharper than ever, over the question of the *ordre moral*, when the introduction of free compulsory education became one of the fundamental themes of republican vengeance and reconquest. Although unaware of the fact, the two parties shared a striking number of ideas in common. Conservatives and republicans alike attached great importance to schooling as a means to literacy, which both declared necessary. Conservatives and republicans also agreed in regarding this as a vital factor of national cohesion and strength: nobody sought elsewhere for the causes of the 1871 defeat in the Franco-Prussian war, and for both camps educational reform became a priority. Of course, the republicans wanted to see the schools inculcating greater freedom, while the conservatives wanted them to teach more obedience. But this disagreement as to the aims of the institution did not prevent consensus as to its rôle in promoting national progress.

It was this consensus, moreover, which accounts for the ease with which political controversy spilled over into empirical research. Once the debate could be broken down into two aspects – the school and literacy, with the former leading to the latter – it became possible to study their history. Hence the wealth of historiography relating to elementary education under the *Ancien Régime* which appeared in the latter half of the 19th century, especially in the 1870s and 80s, when the political debate over the school was at its height. Historians, particularly conservatives, and even more particularly the clerical ones – as they were under pressure to come up with proof – threw themselves into the quest for evidence about the elementary schools under the *Ancien Régime*, drawing up systematic inventories of them, *département* by *département*, diocese by diocese. But it was not enough for them to identify these schools and prove that they had existed in considerable numbers; they still had to demonstrate what constituted, for themselves as for their opponents, the end product of this schooling, namely literacy. This gave rise to the surprising (at the time) discovery of the old French parish records, which have been put to such intensive use in the past twenty years in the cause of historical demography. The first use to which systematic analysis of these imposing tallies of marriage signatures was put one hundred years ago, however, was as an indicator of literacy. This should serve to illustrate the observation that while the existence of sources makes history, it is the shifts in intellectual curiosity which, by creating the objects of history, constitute the sources that enable us to study them.

The brilliant culmination of this fertile polemic, this immense labour, was the inquiry conducted by the *inspecteur d'Académie*, Maggiolo, in 1879–80. We shall be referring frequently to this survey and it is fitting that the name of its author be inscribed at the threshold of this investigation. Present-day historians of literacy are his legatees.

Grateful heirs they may be, though hardly faithful ones. What interested Maggiolo and his contemporaries, after all, in the history of schooling and literacy, is by no means the same as what concerns us today: while the great political debate of the 19th century remains vivid in people's minds, it is no longer focused with quite the same acuity on the school, and we can scarcely credit now that passions so fierce could have worn themselves out so quickly. Far from appearing to us to be indispensable for the teaching of rational behaviour to human beings, nowadays on the contrary the entire school system is under attack, from primary school to university. Attempts to transpose the western European educational model, lock-stock-and-barrel, to other parts of the world, to the third world in particular, through colonization and later decolonization (their effects have been identical in this respect), have all too often ended in failure. This has been so much the case that the schooling→literacy sequence which was an article of faith in the 19th century – and which people still regarded as self-evident twenty-five years ago – is now under growing suspicion when isolated from other social conditions. In any case, even supposing the school did manage to teach people to read and write, we now know that the generalization of education and universal access to reading and writing do not in themselves guarantee a more fraternal community life. The great upheavals of the 20th century bear ample witness to that! The type of rationality that school learning introduces into people's minds can hardly be said to plumb the depths of contemporary civilization; at best it adds a little to our painful awareness of our condition.

It is possible that this type of rationality, and the model of social behaviour which it implies and commends, fits ill with the traditional process of individual socialization as this occurred – and still does occur – in institutions far older than the school, such as the family, the village group, leisure or work community. Such institutions are character-ized by oral transmission of manners and knowledge, and by the infinitely less solitary (hence less anxiety-breeding) exercise of individual aptitudes. Nobody really knows all that much (although we all have our suspicions) about the psychological, cultural and social price that has to be paid when written civilization encroaches upon traditional, oral civilizations. And what society, even the most modern, has not to this day preserved immense 'reservoirs' of traditional life?

Thus history, both within each individual and in whole societies, consists of numerous behavioural strata corresponding to different layers of acculturation. Reading and writing are among the more recent of these, and are layers to which Europe since the 16th century has attached high importance. They are not, however, the most recent: for today, through radio, television and the cinema, the world is discovering forms of learning which, while perhaps lacking the qualities of interchange that characterized oral culture, at least reproduce its homogeneity and its collective character. Perhaps indeed through the very rapid spread of new media, and through the nostalgia for tradition and the revival of more ancient living patterns that is taking hold of the most 'developed' portion of humanity, the most modern and the most ancient of instruments of intercourse invented by man will ultimately link hands to reveal the relative nature and the true cost of written culture, for so long held up as the highest good and a model for all.

Today, in the second half of the 20th century, a history of literacy in France that encompasses the *Ancien Régime* and the 19th century can no longer adopt the triumphant tone it might have done twenty or twenty-five years ago. But it has probably gained in density what it has lost in clarity. What concerns us today is less to judge the controversy over the school between State and Church, or to compare their respective records in elementary education, than to describe and analyze the social and cultural phenomenon of literacy as precisely as possible. This we plan to do by reviewing the case as it was put together and disputed in the course of the 19th century, and by adding such new facts as may since have come to light. Describing means measuring, precisely establishing the pace of the process, its spread according to sex and type of geographical and human environment. By analyzing, we mean seeking to understand the chief variables that account for this phenomenon, and their possible consequences. It is clear that in Germany and Scandinavia, for example, mass literacy was achieved well before industrialization, and that it happened on a very broad scale within traditional agrarian societies. But this chronology alone cannot account for the driving force behind the process, for the forces that resisted it, or for the long-term consequences of this process of collective integration through writing.

Of all the world's peoples, the French have probably invested more heavily than any other, both socially and culturally, in schooling and literacy. But why? How? At what cost? And with what results? These are the questions we shall be asking, even if they are impossible to answer fully.

# 1

## THE SPREAD OF LITERACY IN FRANCE: A ONE-WAY RIDE

### A fresh look at a major survey

The Maggiolo survey was presented in 1957 by Fleury and Valmary in a now classic article.[1] At the end of a career devoted to teaching and the history of teaching, Maggiolo decided to spend his retirement conducting a retrospective survey of the spread of literacy in France. He ended his career as *recteur de l'Académie* at Nancy in 1871 and carried on his research into teaching and literacy in Lorraine,[2] but in 1877 the opportunity arose of extending the scope of his survey to France as a whole. Taking advantage of the fact that education was currently at the centre of political controversy, he persuaded the Ministry of Education to commission him to conduct a retrospective survey of literacy in France.

The administrative aspects of Maggiolo's life are recorded in his final pension statement in the French National Archives. Born in 1811 in Nancy to a father who was himself a school headmaster, Maggiolo was already teaching an elementary class at Lunéville secondary school in 1830, at the age of 19. Subsequently, he rose steadily through the French *classes de grammaire* (elementary classes of the French secondary school system. Transl.): 1st form master in 1832, 2nd form in 1833, 3rd in 1836, 4th in 1837, and 5th in 1842. He married in 1841, and in 1844 he presented his two theses at the Strasbourg Faculty of Letters. His Latin dissertation was on the transformations undergone by the Senate in Ancient Rome, his French thesis on 'Petrarch's moral philosophy'. His dissertations earned him the following encouragement from the dean of the jury: 'Please continue, Sir, to see that all your work bears this same stamp of wisdom, high morality and religion.'

The doctorate seems to have accelerated his career, for in 1846 the master of the 5th form at Lunéville became principal of the 'collège' (almost certainly the local school) at Pont-à-Mousson. After seven years' dynamic headship, as the annual reports of his superiors attest, he was appointed *inspecteur d'Académie* at Châteauroux in 1854. This was but a brief interlude before returning to his native east in 1856, first to Bar-le-Duc, and later to Nancy, in 1861. He unsuccessfully applied to Victor Duruy for an inspector-generalship in 1866. However, he did become acting *recteur de l'Académie* at Nancy in 1868 and full *recteur* in 1869, two years before his retirement.

5

Louis Maggiolo's administrative record is filled with the annual reports of his superiors, and these bring to life the character of this official, at once conformist and highly original. He was conformist in his social life, in those weekly soirées spent in the company of his colleagues from the magistrature and the administration, their careers a succession of long-desired and patiently worked-for promotions. But he was also unusual, with his altogether Italianate fluency and agitated manner, his 'slightly gushing affectedness' with which one of his superiors reproaches him, and his passion for educational administration which drove him to harass his subordinates with questions and questionnaires. Depending on whether or not he was appreciated by his superiors of the moment, he was by turns dedicated and energetic, or else obsequious and agitated.

His enforced retirement in 1871, at the age of 60, was probably the Republic's way of punishing an over-loyal servant of the Empire. Maggiolo complained, in 1877, that he had been 'unfairly dealt with by the Revolution'.

On the history of his ministerial mission, file F(17) 2986(2) in the national archives sheds some light, even though the key document – Maggiolo's initial request and description of his project – is missing. His application was made on 16 July 1877; the competent commission in the Ministry turned down the project and sent the dossier on to the *Direction de l'enseignement primaire* (primary schools division), which suggested to the honorary *recteur* that he conduct an unpaid survey, i.e., with official blessing but no money. Maggiolo accepted, and the ministerial decision charging him with this task was published on 6 September.

The previous day, before he had been informed of the decision, Maggiolo wrote to the Ministry, out of growing impatience, a letter which reveals more of his plans:

> On 10 July last, I had the honour of asking you to entrust me with a mission, whose purpose was to search the archives of the different *académies* and *départements* for documents relating to the state of primary education before 1798. By dispatch dated 14 August, you offered me an unpaid mission; this I have accepted and I have continued to carry out my investigations at my own expense. However, I am still awaiting official notification of your offer.

From this it is clear that the initial project was far wider in scope than the survey of signatures. The final outcome did not exactly match the original hopes, and this may account for the laconic comments.

Rarely has a ministerial survey proved so providential for historians. Yet nothing in it was new: enthusiasm for the history of education and schooling goes back to the Restoration and persisted throughout the 19th century. As early as 1827, the Saint-Simonian Baron Dupin had published, in his admirable work on the *Forces productives et commerciales de la France*, a map of school attendance in France. Very early on, therefore, this historical approach was accompanied by a concern for measurement and the use of statistical procedures. The idea of measuring instruction according to ability to sign one's *acte de mariage* (marriage contract) entered French general statistics in 1854,[4] and from this year onwards these signatures were systematically recorded by *département* and by sex. The political situation provided *recteur* Maggiolo with the means to expand this method, not to invent it.

Where he does deserve credit, and in good measure at that, is for the chronological depth of his inquiry, attested by four successive surveys, and for the idea of employing voluntary assistants, who turned out to be particularly motivated. Maggiolo asked each village schoolmaster to record all marriage signatures in his village for four five-year periods: 1686–90, 1786–90, 1816–20 and 1872–76. The response was terrific, with close on 16,000 schoolteachers compiling village monographs to make up the final picture. Contemporary historians may have some misgivings about the dates selected. Why did he not thrust more boldly back in time, right back to the beginning of the 17th century? Did Maggiolo realise that while it was common practice for husbands and wives to sign the *acte de mariage* this only became generally compulsory in 1667?[5] Was he afraid of poorly-kept records or of problems in deciphering them? Was he trying to adhere to a kind of chronological balance on either side of the French Revolution: a century before, and a century afterwards? He never vouchsafed the reasons for his choice, and today we are prisoners of it. Probably, though, the last suggestion is closest to the truth. *Ancien Régime*, or Revolution? That was the basic question.

This was probably not such a bad thing. Compared with the historiography of the period, dominated as it was in this sphere by the clash between royalists and republicans and by more or less manichaeist interpretations, Maggiolo's inquiry comes as something of a belated echo of the problem that Tocqueville had spelled out for the previous generation: did 1789 signify continuity or break? Maggiolo's was the only attempt made to test both views empirically, in a precisely circumscribed field, on the basis of measurable and comparable data, over a period of 200 years upstream and downstream of the Revolution. One hundred years later, the very design of this research project demands that we pay tribute to its modernity.

The findings were published on two occasions. Once by Maggiolo himself, in an offprint[6] which, in addition to the data produced by the four chronological surveys (in aggregate figures and in percentages, both by *département* and by sex), contains figures for 1866 taken from government statistics (*Statistique générale de la France*). They were also published in a general chart, presented in slightly different form, in volume II of the *statistique de l'Enseignement primaire* in 1880:[7] a certain number of mistakes in the calculation of percentages were rectified here, national averages were computed for each column of percentages, and the document only contains the surveys for the first three periods, 1686–90, 1786–90 and 1816–20. The authors of the volume doubtless thought that as marriage signature figures had been published annually from 1854 onwards, and were in any case more accurate than the ones compiled by Maggiolo's schoolteachers for the last period (1872–76), there was little point in cluttering up their retrospective chart with data easily available elsewhere. They rightly focused on the irreplaceable aspect of Maggiolo's inquiry, namely the three surveys of the pre-statistical era, from Louis XIV to Louis XVIII.

The final surprise produced by this great historical study is that neither its author nor the statisticians who republished it made any serious effort to comment on it. Maggiolo confines himself to a few lines on the methods adopted; he indicates in a footnote that the tables presented were taken from an 'Exposé général de la situation de l'Enseignement primaire en France, avant 1789' (General outline of the state of primary education in France prior to 1789). But this outline was never written, even though Maggiolo survived another ten years or more after having presented the raw findings. It is hard to fathom just why this tireless and intelligent historian whose sympathies, to judge from his other writings, rather tended on the conservative side, never managed to exploit a body of evidence not altogether unfavourable to the *Ancien Régime*. He was ageing, but still active, and he continued to publish into the 1880s.[8] The answer to this minor mystery doubtless lies in the object of Maggiolo's curiosity. As the title he intended to give his general book indicates, he was chiefly interested, like his contemporaries, in the school; literacy was for him simply a sign of schooling, an indicator of scholastic and pedagogic activity, these being the central themes of his research. In this, Maggiolo kept within the bounds of the problem as it concerned his age: for the Revolution or the *Ancien Régime* to be guilty or rehabilitated it was essential to build one's central case on tangible signs of the voluntary activity of people, such as schooling, and not on objective processes, such as the spread of literacy. But the task of preparing the brief is endless, and even today we are still not in possession of all the evidence. There is a history of literacy, but there is no history of schooling. Maggiolo died with a book on his hands for which he lacked the material, and he had been unable to shift its focus accordingly.

As for the statisticians publishing in 1880, their discretion is more astonishing. The Statistical Commission for Primary Education was for the most part made up of militant anti-clericals.[9] Yet these people, despite the social utility that their work might have had at the height of the battle over the school, were content mainly to collect data and figures and to comment on them briefly, without even bothering to interpret them. Of course, they did scatter the odd line or two here and there, proudly noting the achievements in the education of the French in the 19th century, but that was all. Just as positivist history, for its part, neglected statistics, so this approach confined itself to recording data of only marginal intellectual legitimacy. This gives us another explanation of Maggiolo's silence: he was too modern for his traditionalism, and too traditional for his modernism.

But it is these 19th-century silences which lend to the survey its present-day freshness. As we find it today, a full century after its compilation, it fits the historian's curiosity miraculously. It is numerical, serial, homogeneous, allowing us far more than a simple comparison of the respective schooling merits of the kings of France, the Church or the Republic. What it in fact permits is an analysis of one of the crucial phenomena of modern civilization, namely the access of an entire society to written culture. What was marginal, or at any rate secondary, in Maggiolo's eyes, has become central. The problem is literacy. Schooling is but one means to this, and it took almost a century for a shift in the nature of the problem to turn an almost unknown 19th-century scholar into the pioneer of the statistical history of literacy.

Before going on to explore this great legacy, it would be advisable to clear up a point of method. The first statistical data on literacy rates in France, collected by the French government, date from the 19th century: from 1827 for the educational level of conscripts; from 1854 for marriage signatures; and from the 1866 and 1872 census returns for the educational level of the French people.[10]

From 1827 onwards, systematic records were made of the educational attainments of young men in each age-group 'included in each census list and in each list for call-up by lot'. The Ministry of War published these figures annually, both for the nation and for each *département*, in the *Compte rendu sur le recrutement de l'armée pendant l'année* (Annual report on army recruitment). This information on the educational level of recruits was drawn from answers given by the conscripts themselves to questions asked them, or even from declarations made by mayors to the army recruiting board; no explicit mention is made of any kind of examination. In 1864, however, Victor Duruy did decide to verify the information he was receiving and conducted a number of spot-checks, as can be seen from a footnote to the *Statistique des cours d'adultes* for 1865 (p. 6):

> In order to check the exactitude of the figures thus submitted annually, the Minister of Education persuaded Monsieur le Maréchal, the Minister of War, at the end of 1864, to order a thoroughgoing investigation to be undertaken at the moment of

induction of young recruits into the army. This check was carried out scrupulously in nine *départements* which between them supplied 3,750 conscripts, namely Ardèche, Ariège, Cher, Dordogne, Finistère, Indre, Morbihan, Saône-et-Loire and Somme. It applied to conscripts belonging to the class of 1862 and called up in 1863. It was found that, 'except for a handful of minor discrepancies, the declarations made at the moment of induction of these young people into the army have been found to be exact'.[11]

This method of observation appears to have been favoured until the 1920s. However, the *Statistique de l'enseignement primaire* for 1902–1906 (vol. VIII, Paris, 1908) suggests that this may, theoretically at least, have been modified before 1914:

> A more serious examination of young recruits is conducted once they have been incorporated into the army. They are given a dictation of ten lines or so, and four arithmetic sums to do; their answers are then corrected. This examination naturally yields a figure for illiterates or barely literates rather higher than that produced by the young men's simple declarations to the recruiting board. It would be interesting to have results of this examination by *département* and for the country as a whole, but they have yet to be centralized and published by the War Ministry.

For the post 1914–18 War period, the review *l'Education nationale,* in its issue of 23 June 1955, published a rectification (signed L. Vignau and entitled: 'l'Ecole publique sous la IIIe République') establishing the figures relating to the level of instruction of conscripts. This article emanated from the 'Centre national de documentation pédagogique', and was based on information supplied by the Institut National de la Statistique et des Etudes Economiques (I.N.S.E.E.): 'It should be noted', says the article,

> that until 1924 statistics concerning illiterate recruits were compiled as follows: at the moment of recruitment young conscripts were questioned as to their level of education ... But while statistics based solely on the declarations of the persons concerned may furnish useful indicators of educational progress, they can in no way be regarded as reliable. Since 1924, however, the illiteracy rate has been calculated on the basis of tests administered to recruits at the time of their induction.

For periods prior to the 19th century, the historian is obliged to rely on marriage signatures as his sole indicator, as Maggiolo had realized when taking this procedure devised by statisticians in 1854 and extrapolating it into the past. But nobody had ever seriously examined the significance of this index.

However, the editors of the *Statistique de l'enseignement primaire*[12] did raise the question in 1880 when noting that the number of conscripts able to read and write was regularly lower than the number of husbands signing, a few years later, their *acte de mariage*: 'It is quite possible', they point out, 'to learn to trace the letters of one's name for the purpose of some special occasion, without having received any real instruction, and it is assuredly easier to sign than to read. We could repeat this observation for every one of the years in the series 1854 to 1857.' The problem is in fact more complex, in as much as reading and writing were not taught simultaneously. The classic syllabus of primary education for a long time consisted of a series of successive learning tasks: reading first, then writing, and finally arithmetic.[13] Since each stage lasted several years, and since school attendance and teaching methods in the old-style school were highly uneven, it is extremely difficult to measure the possible benefits of schooling against a single yardstick. Furthermore, it was possible to acquire a minimum of instruction from institutions other than the school – the family, the Church – although we have little idea of which kind of minimum literacy received priority in each of these: reading, signing, writing? The traditional hierarchy of school learning has led Roger Schofield[14] to suggest that ability to sign is an intermediate indicator between ability to read and ability to write, the number of people able to sign being fewer than those able to read, but more than those able to write.

To what level of literacy does ability to sign one's name correspond? The French data enable us to test this relationship from the second half of the 19th century onwards, or, to be precise, from 1866 onwards.[15] The first population census containing data on education was made in that year. The population of France, excluding the under-5s, who were assumed to be illiterate, was divided into four categories: those unable to either read or write; those able to read only; those able to read and write; and finally those who did not reply to the question. The last are a negligible quantity compared with total population: 450,000 out of 38 million inhabitants. *Département* and national percentages were broken down according to sex, after children under 5 and the non-respondents had been subtracted. They thus allow us to overcome the tricky problem of the relationship between ability to read and full literacy, which includes ability to write as well.

In addition to this document we possess, for the same year and for the same geographical categories (national and by *département*), two other sets of statistics on French education. The first is the one shown in Maggiolo's tables, which was probably taken from the *Statistique générale de la France*.[16] Since 1854, as we have already noted, the Ministry of the Interior had kept an annual tally – taken from civil records – of the number of husbands and wives signing their *acte de mariage*. All that was needed therefore was to look up the relevant figures for 1866 in the *Statistique*

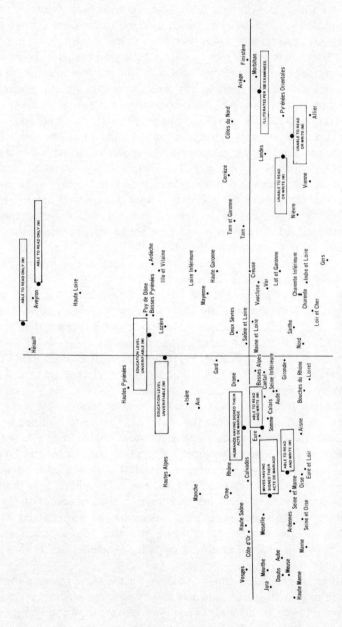

*Graph A*  Factorial analysis 1 (men and women separately)

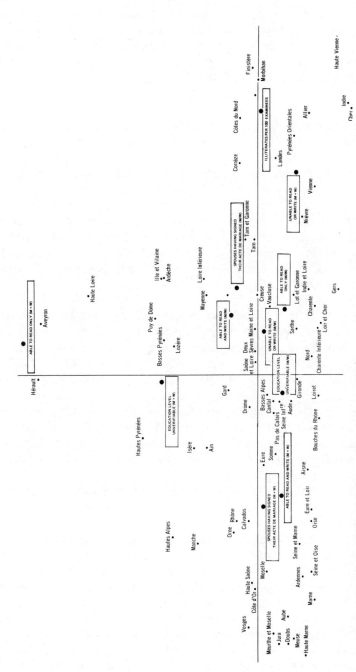

*Graph B*  Factorial analysis 2 (men and women together)

*générale de la France*: they are there in full, broken down by *département* and by sex, in the retrospective volume brought out in 1880.

Lastly, we have the set of data reporting the educational level of conscripts, which had been systematically asked of each age-group annually since 1827. In the 1860s this level began to be classified in four categories: those able to read; those able to read and write; those able neither to read nor to write; and finally men absent, whose level of education could not be verified. These data are given for each *département*.

So we have three different, yet convergent sources. Data sources 1 and 3 (general population census and conscripts) are compiled by the same method, namely statements by the individuals concerned, and are broken down into identical categories. The additional distribution by sex in the census allows us to compare male educational levels (since the conscripts were, by definition, male). Since the populations under consideration are not the same (conscripts constitute a single age-group, whereas the census data give us the educational level of all French males over the age of 5), the discrepancies in the scores are obviously attributable to these differences. The 1872 census, in which the level of education may broadly be divided into three separate age-groups (under 6, 6–20, and over 20), shows, as was to be expected, that the older generations were less literate than the younger ones – which accounts for the fact that in 1866 the census figures were lower than the conscription ones. Source 2 (marriage signatures) is different in kind: here we are dealing not with people's answers to questions put by the government, but with an objective indicator, namely their signature of the *acte de mariage*. Age-groups are mixed here, although they must in the main be fairly close to school age, since late marriages may be regarded as statistically exceptional. Obviously, the most interesting comparisons are to be sought between data sources 1 and 3, on the one hand, and source 2 on the other: this is a fundamental test of the signature's validity as an indicator.

We have reviewed all the data available on French educational levels in 1866 from these three sources, submitting them to factorial analysis, which has produced the two graphs A and B.

The first graph (Graph A) shows the following variables by *département*: men who are unable to read or write; women who are unable to read or write; men able to read only; women able to read only; men able to read and write; women able to read and write; men whose educational level was unverifiable; and women whose educational level was unverifiable. In addition, the graph indicates men having signed their *acte de mariage*; women having signed their *acte de mariage*; and lastly the illiteracy rate among conscripts. The graph shows that 75% of the information supplied by the different sources lies along a horizontal axis, while only 15% lies along the vertical one, which makes for a first pleasant surprise. It reveals, moreover, the spectacular proximity of the variables 'ability to sign the *acte de mariage*' and 'able to read and write', for both men and women. The two female variables lie more markedly to the left than their male counterparts: in as much as the level of education increases from right to left along the horizontal axis, this means that high female literacy constitutes a most significant score in this respect.

The word 'score', which suggests some sort of superiority, calls for some remarks on our part. This book on the history of literacy in France is intended, in particular, to take a critical look at the complacent tone adopted in the history of this subject in 19th-century republican ideology. We have made a point of avoiding any kind of value judgement regarding written culture or its gradual spread at the expense of oral culture.

Inevitably, though, the language we use is not neutral, in so far as the data we are analyzing constitute a classification of French *départements*. We have of course done our best to substitute the vocabulary of growth for that of progress – the latter being the more immediately and more spontaneously attuned to a traditional history of education. This has not, however, freed us from value judgements as much as we should have liked, for the concept of growth implies an unconscious reference to biology (to a serene biology, what is more, free of pathology or crisis) and leads to the assumption that growth is better than decline. Nor does discarding the vocabulary of growth in favour of hierarchy help matters much: to speak of a *département* as 'bringing up the rear', of a town 'marking time', of an *arrondissement* 'running out of steam' or of another one as 'coming out on top' unavoidably evokes a distribution of prizes. In any case, even supposing we did manage to expurgate all competitive or sporting metaphors from our account, confining ourselves to noting that a given region stands 'at the top' of our tables while another lies 'at the bottom', we should still be tangled up in our unthinking axioms of top and bottom. Having thus satisfied ourselves that it will never be possible completely to neutralize our language, we would ask readers to bear in mind all that it conveys in spite of all our efforts and to read the words 'score', 'performance', 'lead' or 'lag' in their most relative senses, and to accept – since classify we must – that there will have to be a 'first' and a 'last'. But these firsts and lasts, *in the order of written culture*, in no sense entail, to our way of thinking, any hierarchy of civilization whatever.

At the other end of the horizontal axis, it is the illiterate conscripts who bring up the rear, which is to be expected, since illiteracy in a male sample still close to school-age constitutes a rock-bottom performance. But the 'unable to read or write' variable, which refers to the proportion of male illiterates as a percentage of the entire population, remains very close to this.

Not surprisingly, therefore, we find the different *départements* of France strung out along the horizontal axis from left to right in decreasing order of literacy. On the far left lies north-eastern France, Haute-Marne, Jura, Vosges, Meurthe, Doubs, Meuse and Aube; on the far right lie Brittany, the western slopes of the Massif Central, and a handful of *départements* in the Midi; Côtes-du-Nord, Pyrénées-Orientales, Allier, Landes, Cher, Ariège, Morbihan, Finistère and Haute-Vienne.

Two variables in the series do not lie along this horizontal axis: these are the two categories contained in the 1866 census, namely men and women 'able to read only', and men and women whose 'educational level is unverifiable'. This accounts for 15% of the information and lies about a vertical axis whose significance would seem to be ability to read only (men and women). There is no correlation of this intermediate skill between total illiteracy and total literacy (reading and writing) with other indicators, and especially not with the marriage signatures indicator. It is independent of the others, because it is probably governed by other rules, is dependent on other factors, and establishes a different hierarchy among the *départements*.

A second graph (Graph B) has been compiled from a further factorial analysis, this time reviewing all the data from the three sources, though in a different form. Here, the men and the women have been treated as an aggregate, on the one hand, and following this we have established the relationship between male percentages and female percentages. This gives us: unable to read or write $(M + W, M/W)$; able to read only $(M + W, M/W)$; and able to read and write $(M + W, M/W)$, etc. This second graph contains a horizontal axis (79% of the data) arranging literacy performance in ascending order from right to left, and organizing the different indicators very distinctly: men and women able to read and write are very close to couples having signed their *acte de mariage*. At the other end, we find conscripts lying not very far from illiterates of both sexes counted in the census: however, the presence of women in this last group makes the correlation less distinct than in Graph A.

In addition, the $M/W$ ratio constitutes a set of close and relatively central variables: by and large, the phenomena described by these variables contain identical men/women proportions, and in particular a remarkable correlation between ability to read and write $(M/W)$ and signature of the marriage register $(M/W)$. Finally, as in the first graph, the 'able to read only' and 'educational level unverifiable' variables $(M + W)$ are spread along a second axis (13% of data), particularly sharply so for the first of these variables.

The main significance of these analyses is that they do establish the close correlation between signature of the *acte de mariage* and full literacy consisting of both reading and writing. This is confirmed by calculation of

*Comparative education scores in 1866*

| | 1866 Census | | | | | Maggiolo Sources | |
| --- | --- | --- | --- | --- | --- | --- | --- |
| | Scores relative to total population | | Scores relative to populative aged over 5 (less non-replies) | | | | |
| | M | W | M | W | M + W | | |
| %unable to read or write | 35.79 | 42.52 | 29.00 | 36.89 | 32.84 | — | — |
| % able to read only | 8.63 | 11.77 | 9.73 | 13.21 | 11.47 | — | — |
| % able to read and write | 54.40 | 45.00 | 61.31 | 49.90 | 55.64 | — | — |
| % indeterminate | 1.18 | 1.22 | — | — | — | — | — |
| % marriage signatures | — | — | — | — | — | 71.79 | 55.48 |

the coefficients of correlation between the 1866 signatures and the four variables contained in the census of the same year:

$+ 0.91$ between signatures and ability to read and write.

$- 0.90$ between signatures and inability to read or write.

$- 0.21$ between signatures and ability to read only.

$- 0.01$ between signatures and unverifiable cases.

The first two scores are the only ones to have a positive significance, indicating the positive and negative sides of the correlation. The third clearly shows that there is no correlation, contrary to one plausible supposition, between ability to sign and ability to read only.

These results do not show, however, that the percentages of people able to sign their own name and those able to read and write in 1866 were identical. They could not have been, since the data from which they are derived are not comparable and since there is no relationship between couples marrying in any given year and the total French population. In fact, as the following table shows, these percentages differ according to the divisor selected. What factorial analysis and computation of correlations do show is not that the figures are identical, but that these different factors vary in step with each other: the signature variable and the reading and writing variable both arrange the *départements* of France along the same axis and in the same rankings. Ability to sign one's name thus does indeed refer to what we now call literacy, which in turn means reading and writing.

Is this equally true of earlier periods, or did the school separate the two learning processes in time? We have no evidence with which to test this. But the successful trial to which the 1866 signature indicator has been submitted does lead us to a favourable prognosis regarding its application to previous periods.

So, the signature is a good test of literacy. But how reliable are the figures compiled by Maggiolo? They were criticized in 1957 by Fleury and Valmary, who identified three kinds of gap or shortcoming in the original study: its incompleteness, the unevenness of the departmental samples, and the under-representation of urban populations.

Twelve *départements* are constantly missing from Maggiolo's statistics: Moselle, Bas-Rhin, Haut-Rhin, Territoire de Belfort, Savoie, Haute-Savoie, Alpes-Maritimes, Corsica, Vaucluse, Dordogne, Lot and, lastly, Seine. The first three were either totally or partially in German hands at the time of the survey, while Territoire de Belfort was a very recent creation. The three following ones had become part of France definitively only in 1860 and had thus kept proper French records only sporadically up to that time. The same was true of Corsica and Vaucluse, even though they had been part of France for a longer period of time: their records under the *Ancien Régime* had not profited from the benefits of French regulations. Maggiolo even mentions, at the foot of his table, post-dating Corsica's attachment to France slightly, that the *départements* annexed since 1789 are not included in this table. As for Seine, we know that the Paris records were burnt in 1871 along with the Hôtel de Ville. Dordogne and Lot complete this list of omissions, the most likely cause of their absence being local shortcomings. The omissions are very few, all said and done, even when to these twelve missing *départements* we add temporary absences of Indre-et-Loire, Aveyron and Lozère (from the first survey in the inquiry), and Morbihan for the period 1816–20.

The problem of the statistical base for the samples by *département* is a tougher one. In a collective survey of this kind, Maggiolo was dependent on the good will of his correspondents; for the 78 *départements* covered by the inquiry, containing between them roughly 32,000 towns and villages, he received answers from 15,928 schoolteachers. But the *départements* did not contribute equally to this excellent overall performance, and responses were very uneven from one *département* to the next. Even in aggregate figures the discrepancy between samples is quite striking: 11,732 marriages for Eure at the end of the 18th century, and over 17,000 for each of the later surveys, compared with 95, 131 and 157 for Ariège, for example. But the representativeness of each sample is dependent on the marriage rate in each *département*, which can roughly be deduced from its population. Comparing Maggiolo's samples with data taken from the 1801 census, Fleury and Valmary were able to rank *départements* on the basis of their responses to the survey: top of the list came Eure, Somme, Ardennes, Loir-et-Cher, Allier, Haute-Marne, Ain, Isère, Saône-et-Loire, Aube, Haute-Vienne, Indre, Aisne, Haute-Loire. At the end came Nord and Pas-de-Calais, Marne, Manche, Sarthe, two Breton *départements* (Côtes-du-Nord and Finistère) and a large portion of Occitania (Charente-Inférieure, Tarn, Hautes-Pyrénées, Gers, Hérault, Ariège, Aveyron). This apparently random distribution probably reflects nothing more than the greater or lesser enthusiasm for historical research to be found among the schoolteachers of the infant Republic, but it should be borne in mind when subjecting the table drawn up by Maggiolo to detailed scrutiny.

Two things, however, tend to establish its overall credibility. The first of these is the scores reported by the schoolteachers, for the same localities as in the previous periods, in 1872–76. These scores may be compared to the (complete) figures calculated by the *Statistique de l'enseignement primaire* in 1880 for 1871–75, i.e. a virtually identical period. The differences between the two are negligible, which would tend to validate all of Maggiolo's percentages, even the ones derived from the thinnest samples. Moreover, Fleury and Valmary also compared the departmental map of male literacy in 1816–20, as built up from Maggiolo's figures, with the one drawn by Angeville on the basis of the number of conscripts able to read and write in 1830–33. From this it emerges that out of the 78 departments covered by Maggiolo's inquiry, 69 produced very similar percentages; only 10 gave evidence of a significant discrepancy, generally to the detriment of the conscripts.

Even on a national scale this difference was noticeable: 54.3% of men were able to sign in 1816–20, according to Maggiolo, whereas the figure for conscripts able at least to read in 1830–33 was 52.6%. This discrepancy – which crops up in varying degrees throughout the 19th century–is hard to explain. Fleury and Valmary[17] produce the following hypothesis:

> [The 1833 statistics] refer to recruits at a time when only a certain proportion of national-service-age men were actually called up and when those who were 'unlucky' in the draw were – if they belonged to the better-off classes – able to 'pay' for someone to do their military service in their place. Under these circumstances, it is quite possible that the proportion of recruits able to read and write could have been reduced markedly.

This explanation is not altogether satisfactory, for two reasons: firstly, reports on recruitment deal with the level of instruction for the entire age-group, and not just for the recruits actually incorporated into the army after having been drawn by lot and after taking replacements into account: and secondly, the educational level of young men actually called up is given separately and, contrary to what might have been expected to ensue from this practice of replacement, tends generally to be slightly higher than for the age-group as a whole, by around 2–3%.

In 1880, the editors of the *Statistique de l'enseignement primaire* noted this slight distortion, but hesitated before suggesting that one could 'learn to write the letters of one's name for some special occasion without having received any proper education, and [that] it is assuredly easier to sign than to read'.

The last, incurable, weakness in Maggiolo's table is the under-representation of the towns. It is true that the work of going over the civil records in large towns is more complicated and more time-consuming than in rural areas, and the records are also less readily accessible than in the country. This consideration must have weighed heavily with the school-teachers as they went about their work, and Maggiolo seems to have realized this, moreover. He refers to this, in his typically modest and discreet fashion, in two short notes at the bottom of his table: 'For Marseille, I was unable to obtain figures for couples in parishes where there were schools: the general average would have been higher. This obser-vation applies to a great many *départements*.' And immediately below, he has this to say about Haute-Garonne: 'The average for 50 localities in the Toulouse *arrondissement*, which from a statistical viewpoint best sums up the 130 localities making up this *arrondissement*, comes to (1872–76) 56%, giving 67 for husbands and 46 for wives, instead of 45.33, which is the figure given by the communes of Haute-Garonne taken together.'

The most recent investigation of the reliability of the data collected by *Recteur* Maggiolo's voluntary schoolteachers was published in an article by M. Jacques Houdaille[18] when this book had already been completed. This investigation took as its starting point the signature count made by the Institut National d'Etudes Démographiques (I.N.E.D.) in the course of its survey of the French population between 1740 and 1829. It reveals the I.N.E.D.'s agreement with Maggiolo's figures, particularly for northern France: the percentages established in 1879 are just a little over the ones produced by the I.N.E.D. survey of rural France only, regularly below those for France as a whole, towns included. Comparison thus confirms that more rural schoolteachers than urban ones complied with Maggiolo's request.

South of the line running from Saint-Malo to Geneva, on the other hand, Maggiolo's figures were consistently (9–10 points) above the I.N.E.D. ones, towns included, which leads one to wonder whether urban teachers in the south in 1879 may not have been more active than their northern colleagues. Anyway, this is impossible to prove either way, since the data have disappeared.

The problem, then, is clear: the departmental averages put forward in Maggiolo's table conceal the representation of the towns in two ways.

Firstly, because precisely in the places where these results do incorporate town figures, the massive preponderance of the rural population smothers the specificity – and the lead – of the towns in the departmental score. Secondly, and more importantly, because, owing to the difficulty of scrutinizing urban records, teachers undoubtedly covered the towns less throughly than rural localities. To elucidate this problem would require microscopic analysis, village by village or canton by canton.

Unfortunately the primary data from which Maggiolo constructed his departmental map seem to have been lost. Did he destroy them? Or did he keep them, only for someone to have mislaid them subsequently? This is the ultimate secret of this secret man: not a trace of them remains, which only adds to the mystery. What ought perhaps to be noted in this respect is, once again, the strange under-utilization of the information by its own author. As can be seen from the brief commentaries cited earlier in connection with the Toulouse *arrondissement*, Maggiolo not only aggregated his data for each *département* but also took care to examine the figures from a number of different angles, and even in the smallest areas. But he never published anything on this subject, and he never even bothered to take steps to preserve his precious material for future use. It was as if the monument to French literacy erected – at his instigation – by 16,000 schoolteachers had had no other object than to figure in his four-page table! What a slap in the face for figures, in an age when narrative was king . . .

What has been undone cannot be put together again: today we would lack the national élan, the compulsion to prove a point, the complicity of an entire corporation, to embark upon such an enterprise. But it has been necessary to retrace, on a reduced scale, at least part of the road initially travelled a hundred years ago, because the only really reliable test of Maggiolo's data lies in the compiling of local and departmental monographs on literacy, which would reconstitute the lost elements of the dossier.

A certain number of such monographs have indeed been produced, and the second volume of this book contains their main findings. However, it is worth presenting here and now, in tabular form, the comparison between the new data which they have turned up, and the departmental percentages calculated by Maggiolo. On the whole this comparison redounds very much to the credit of the former *recteur* of Nancy, and bears out what had already been established by a certain number of studies conducted by local scholars at the end of the 19th century, namely that the percentages derived from the samples surveyed by these volunteer schoolteachers stand up to thoroughgoing examination of the evidence. Michel Vovelle[19] too has noted this more recently, in a study of 18th-century Provence using wills as sources. He confirms the contrast between an illiterate lower Provence and a relatively educated upper Provence; he shows moreover the gradual downhill slope of literacy rates from towns to large villages, and from the latter to the countryside – the very countryside that had bred Maggiolo's own figures.

The new percentages, derived from surveys conducted in Haute-Normandie, Champagne, Brie, Poitou and Languedoc,[20] point in the same direction. They match those of Maggiolo pretty well, provided the specifically urban scores are subtracted from the departmental averages. The match is almost perfect for Seine-et-Marne, where the gap between the two sources never tops 4 points – and where, at the same time, one can see the towns' lead over the countryside. The same holds for Vienne, after deducting the figures for Châtellerault, the only town in our sample. The only notable discrepancy concerns female literacy at the end of the 18th century: 6%, compared with Maggiolo's 9%. In both cases, Maggiolo's sample comprises roughly 3,000 marriages, neither particularly large nor particularly small. In Champagne, astride the *départements* of Marne and Ardennes, our survey also gives scores very close to those shown in the 1880 table, even though Maggiolo's sample for Ardennes is very broad (6,000–10,000 marriages), while his Marne sample is poor (1,000–1,500).

The case of Haute-Normandie (Seine-Inférieure and Eure) is less clear-cut. These are *départements* where schoolteachers responded in substantial numbers to Maggiolo. Seine-Inférieure had a good overall match, except for women at the end of the 17th century: our sample shows that 7 or 10% (depending on whether one counts villages in with the countryside) were able to sign, compared with over 16% in Maggiolo's. This phenomenon is even more marked in Eure, but this time for both periods: 6% of women able to sign compared with 18% at the end of the 17th century; 37 or 40% as against 53% a century later. As the gap between the two sources tends to shrink in the intervening period, one possible explanation that springs to mind – although this cannot be verified – is that, as experience has shown, it is the bride's signature or mark that is hardest to identify in the earlier periods. Thus it would be in this respect, and especially for the late 17th century, that the figures produced by Maggiolo's teachers may on occasion be suspect.

That leaves Languedoc, for which we have two good samples, much superior to those of Maggiolo, for Hérault and Gard. Here, the discrepancies are quite sharp, and particularly so for Hérault at both ends of the 18th century and for both sexes: Maggiolo seems to have underestimated the real percentages quite seriously, above all for the first period, since our own come out close to double his figures! True, Maggiolo's sample here was one of the poorest in the national table: 304 marriages at the end of the 17th century, and 295 at the end of the 18th. M.-M. Compère's sample is better, but it does include the towns, and one can quite well imagine that in an ancient urban region such as the Midi the town/country literacy gap must be particularly clear-cut. As for Gard, where Maggiolo's sample was better, male scores are comparable; female scores are closer than for Hérault, but there is still a distinct discrepancy, especially for the second period: could this be due to a powerful female upswing in the towns in this *département*, Alès and Nîmes?

What this comparison shows is that, on the whole, the departmental data used by Maggiolo were astonishingly reliable when one considers the circumstances in which they were collected. However, they may only be regarded as *representative* of the rural areas. Everything points to the conclusion that urban scores, in practically every case substantially higher than those recorded in the countryside in the 18th century, were not included in the calculation of departmental averages, because they had not been collected. Villages, on the other hand, may be regarded as having been covered by the inquiry, if one accepts that literacy rates in them were closer to rates in the countryside than to urban ones.[21]

As such, at the cost of a few minor adjustments, the document is not merely usable, it is positively priceless. No other source on literacy in France has cast its net so wide in time and space, covering the whole of France over a period of two centuries. From the second third, and especially for the second half of the 19th century, the historian has available to him a series of comparable – and more systematically collected – data: conscripts, followed by marriage signatures, and lastly the two censuses taken in 1866 and 1872. So he is able to compare them with, and even, in the case of marriage signatures, substitute them for Maggiolo's dossier. This is what we shall be doing.[22] But for ancient France before the Revolution, one is obliged to turn to this goldmine, which is still far from having been worked out.

## What Maggiolo's figures tell us

What are the lessons for us contained in these figures? Let us begin with the statistician's reaction, as he speaks the language of the evidence:

> This essay in retrospective statistics surely tells us nothing about the quality of the teaching given in village schools prior to the contemporary era; but it does prove that France was not entirely lacking in instruction, even at the end of the 17th century, since close to a third of the men and an eighth of the women were already able to sign the marriage register. It shows too that progress was gradual; that on the eve of the 1789 Revolution, the level had not yet reached the point it had attained by the beginning of the Restoration, after which time the series of documents on the level of instruction of conscripts supplies us with a rather more

precise measurement of literacy. It shows finally that, as we have noted on several occasions, the regional differences are attributable to a variety of causes, but deep-seated ones which we recognize, for the most part, even if we delve back two centuries into the past. The regions that were most advanced then, and those that were least, are more or less the same as the most advanced and most backward *départements* in Baron Dupin's map and in our own statistics.

After these observations, a good word for the 19th century:

> If we compare the ratios derived from this essay with current statistics on marriage couples, we find that within the space of a century, from 1690–1790, there was an 18% improvement for men and a 13% rise for women; that in the following century, from 1790-1875/77, this improvement was 34% for men and 44% for women. It is hardly surprising that a century that made greater efforts to spread education should have achieved better results.

This commentary lacks intellectual as well as technical refinement. It confines itself to the prevailing explanation for the growth of literacy – the school – without even attempting to produce one iota of proof. It overestimates the permanence of the geographical distribution of literacy over two centuries for want of a dynamic analysis of growth. Furthermore, it compares Maggiolo's retrospective data, which were essentially rural, with the 1875/77 figures, which cover all marriages contracted, including those in towns. All it establishes, moreover, is a rate of arithmetical progression, by simply subtracting the point of departure from the point of arrival. It does, however, put forward two ideas that still remain fundamental to analysis of these retrospective figures:

1. While the point of departure at the end of the 17th century is not nil, literacy expanded steadily throughout the two following centuries; it did not grind to a halt between the end of the *Ancien Régime* and the start of the Restoration, but it did tend to speed up in the 19th century.

2. The geographical distribution of literacy in France corresponds to a profound and very ancient cleavage.

To these two ideas we should add a differential analysis of literacy according to sex: in the view of the 19th century, women were merely belatedly following the men, whereas in fact the two growth rates are more complex than that, depending on the period and *département* in question. Spatial distribution, chronological distribution and distribution by sex of the spread of literacy: these are the three central concepts on which a systematic description of the data in Maggiolo's table may be based. They will inevitably be interwoven at each stage in the description, since they are in permanent interaction; but we shall be taking each one in turn as our principal point of reference (Maps 1.1–1.4 and Graph C).

### Spatial distribution

For each survey period in the inquiry, Fleury and Valmary have established a corresponding statistical map. For each of these periods, from the end of the 17th century to the second third of the 19th, the Saint-Malo – Geneva line divides France in two from a literacy standpoint. On the one hand we have a northern and north-eastern France, characterized by fairly high percentages of couples able to sign their *acte de mariage*, while on the other we find the west of France (Brittany), the Massif Central and the entire south, Aquitaine and the Mediterranean, with very high illiteracy rates. By definition, though, these maps which reflect the persistence over two centuries of a cultural contrast tell us nothing of how this persistence evolved. They tell us nothing about the dynamics of the phenomenon inside these different chronological cross-sections and over the period as a whole, nor about the way this may have affected the relative geographical spread of literacy: a *département* could very well catch up with the rest while remaining within the predominantly illiterate zone. It is in order to answer these questions that the data collected by Maggiolo have been processed statistically in such a way as to measure the spread of literacy by *département*.

1. The distribution of the growth of literacy by period, from one end of the inquiry period to the other, is obtained from a very simple calculation: if we call the years 1686–90 period 1, 1786–90 period 2, 1816–20 period 3 and the year 1866 period 4, we may then carry out the following operations in turn:

$$\frac{\text{period 2 score} - \text{period 1 score}}{\text{period 1 score}}$$

$$\frac{\text{period 3 score} - \text{period 2 score}}{\text{period 2 score}}$$

$$\frac{\text{period 4 score} - \text{period 3 score}}{\text{period 3 score}}$$

and finally,
$$\frac{\text{period 4 score} - \text{period 1 score}}{\text{period 1 score}}$$

This will give us the distribution of literacy growth rates by *département* in the 18th century, then between the end of the 18th century and the early 19th, between the first and last thirds of the 19th century, and lastly between the end of the 17th century and the end of the Second Empire.

When mapped (Maps 1.5,1.6 and 1.7), the results reveal a number of new things: firstly, that in many *départements* in the Midi, male literacy began to catch up, relatively, back in the 18th century. Of the 19 *départements* which more than doubled their percentages between the end of the 17th century and the end of the 18th, 12 lay below the famous Saint-Malo – Geneva line: Ariège, Pyrénées-Orientales, Basses-Pyrénées, Rhône, Lot-et-Garonne, Haute-Garonne, Haute-Loire, Corrèze, Ardèche, Finistère, Var and Hautes-Pyrénées. Very broadly, the map of these growth rates in relative percentages over the 18th century forms a crescent along the eastern and southern borders of the kingdom, from Lorraine to the eastern fringe of the Massif Central, then Cévennes to the Pyrenean and Languedoc marches.

This phenomenon was accentuated during the Revolutionary period, between 1786–90 and 1816–20. All the *départements* with the highest increases in relative percentage in fact lay to the south of the 'Maggiolo' line: Landes, Ariège, Haute-Garonne, Saône-et-Loire, which at least doubled their scores; followed by Ain, Cantal, Charente, Creuse, Indre, Indre-et-Loire, Loire, Tarn, Tarn-et-Garonne, Vaucluse: the pace of this rudimentary acculturation affected the Massif Central in particular. As was to be expected, this catching-up model became general in the course of the 19th century.

From the 18th century onwards, female literacy grew faster than male literacy. This is quite marked in the national averages, since women more or less doubled their score (from 14 to 27%) while men only increased from 29 to 47%. But an examination of *départemental* data yields a good many deviations from this national rule: 23 *départements* (over a quarter) show male literacy growth rates outstripping female ones. Generally speaking, more-than-proportional growth in female percentages is particularly clear-cut in those *départements* with the highest male literacy rates in absolute terms: Vosges, Doubs, Manche, Meurthe and Moselle.

2. But clearly the preceding scores, calculated in relative terms (proportional increase in the percentage of literates) favour those *départements* whose point of departure in 1786–90 was particularly low: Nord, for example, top of the league for relative growth in the 18th century, pushed its male literacy rate up from 10% to 51%, whereas Doubs, with an increase from 30% to 80%, achieved a relatively slower growth rate even though its final score was much superior; and the gap between the two *départements* was greater at the end of the 18th century than at the start.

We must therefore also map absolute literacy growth rates, by *département* and by period. A time-lag gradually asserts itself in the 19th century (Maps 1.8,1.9 and 1.10). The greatest increases in the 18th century, both male and female, remain concentrated north of the St. Malo-Geneva line – with, for men only, an extension describing an arc from Lyon to

Bayonne. During the following, shorter, period (which explains why scores were lower), the advances, at least for the men, had shifted distinctly to the southern half of France, while stagnation in the 'bocages' of western France begins to produce a triangular map of illiteracy very different from the 18th century pattern. Women continued to perform well mainly in the east, in the front-runner regions, but they also started gaining ground beyond the Maggiolo line. Lastly, process of catching up become much more marked in the course of the first half of the 19th century, and this is particularly clear in the case of men.

This second analysis confirms the first one but with added complexity. It advances the decisive moment at which the south began to catch up in absolute terms, to the end of the 18th and the very beginning of the 19th centuries. Chiefly, though, it points to a new east/west cleavage in the country, dating from that time and blurring the Maggiolo line. With this new line, the illiterate portion of France now lies within a triangle whose base is the Atlantic coast from Brittany to Landes and whose apex is in the heart of the Massif central. What in fact happened was that the 19th century gradually erased the old Saint-Malo – Geneva line, which had seemed so ineradicable to the statistician in 1880. In its place it substituted another one which lifted the age-old curse from the Rhône corridor and the Mediterranean, but left it lying upon the whole of Brittany and its fringes, the bleak lands of the western Massif Central and the whole of Aquitaine.

### Chronological distribution

Average national percentages (men and women) have been recalculated on the basis of Maggiolo's figures, between 1686–90 and 1816–20, after which they have been established on the basis of figures contained in the *Statistique générale de la France*, for much narrower time periods, from 1854 onwards. The resulting curve shows that while the growth of literacy was spread over two centuries, the rate at which it grew was nevertheless faster in the 19th century. The annual percentage gains – always assuming that they were evenly distributed throughout each time-period – increased constantly from 1816–20 onwards, especially for women, who gradually reduced the men's lead. The phenomenon also needs to be seen in the light of changing national annual growth-rate trends for the different periods under consideration: a slow rise throughout the 18th century, slowing down between the end of the *Ancien Régime* and the Restoration, and gradually gathering speed in the 19th century, this being especially noticeable among women.

A careful look at these figures shows clearly that the Revolution neither halted nor even slowed down the overall process; all that changed was its geographical spread. True, more *départements* suffered falls in literacy rates than in the 18th century (11 for men, 4 for women, as against 3 each for the

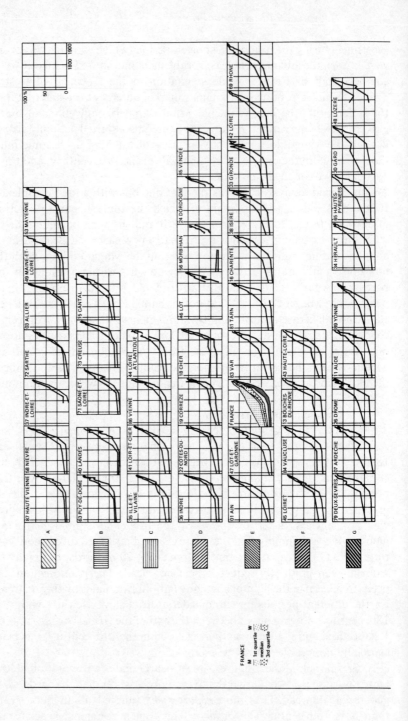

FRANCE
M W
1st quartile
median
3rd quartile

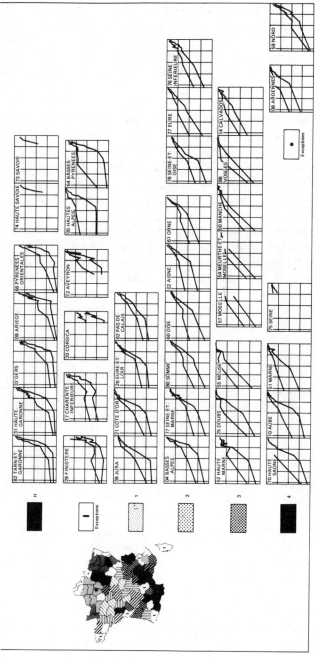

*Graph C* Evolution of literacy by *département* (end of 17th to end of 19th century)

previous period), which proves that, locally at least, the phenomenon denounced by royalist historiographers did indeed occur, particularly in the civil war zones such as Cévennes (Lozère, Gard, Ardèche), where Protestants and Catholics were in conflict. Conversely, annual growth rates in the leading *départements* in the periods 1786–90 and 1816–20 were substantially higher than under the *Ancien Régime*. In the 18th century only 6 *départements* (Nord, Haute-Saône, Ariège, Pyrénées-Orientales, Vosges and Basses-Pyrénées) had male growth-rates in excess of 1% p.a.: between 1.6% for Nord and 1.04 for Basses-Pyrénées. Four *départements* in the next period achieved annual rates of over 2% (a record of more than 4% for Landes, Haute-Garonne, Ariège, Saône-et-Loire); while 24 of them topped the 1% mark! This trend gathered strength in the middle of the 19th century, when, in the third period, at least 33 *départements* achieved this statistical threshold.

We may compare and contrast scores of men and women in like fashion: annual growth rates were generally higher for women than for men, and the gap widens with the passing of time.

Thus the gradual catching up of the south with the north, and of women with men, was not just a compensatory movement; it also involved a speed-up in literacy growth trends in many of the backward *départements*, from the late 18th century onwards. Barring local circumstances, the Revolution, far from obstructing this forward motion, actually seems to have nudged it on its way. Republican historians at the end of the 19th century were surely wrong in underestimating the vast development of lower-class culture (in rural areas especially) that had occurred in the last century of the *Ancien Régime*: but they were right, on the whole, in seeing the Revolution as leading to the cultural advancement of the lower classes overall.

Obviously, this process encompassed a wide range of departmental curves (Graph C). These reveal a handful of relatively clear-cut patterns, if we take as our two chief criteria the difference between male scores for the first two periods and the absolute level at the end of the 17th century.

1. The no-growth, or low-growth *départements* in the 18th century were, primarily, those in the north-western corner of the Massif Central (Vienne, Haute-Vienne, Allier, Creuse, Cher). Nearly all these *départements* had, at the end of the 17th century, either low or very low starting figures, which remained more or less unchanged up to the French Revolution. Cher, which started out from a slightly higher level (28% of men signing their *acte de mariage*), actually slipped back to join its neighbours at the end of the *Ancien Régime*. We encounter this stagnation of the 18th century in the *départements* of Brittany and its marches, as well as in Aquitaine (Gers, Landes). In some cases the literacy process got under way between 1786

and 1816 (Creuse, Landes), but more usually after 1816, and sometimes not until 1854 (Cher, Haute-Vienne).

Alongside these laggards under the *Ancien Régime* we must mention another *département* with an extremely low literacy growth rate in the 18th century, but this time from a particularly high starting point. In 1686–90 Hautes-Alpes had the highest score of all the *départements*. 64% of its men signed their *acte de mariage* under Louis XIV, but only 74% under Louis XVI. Women's scores remained stationary at 27%. The *département* only resumed its forward progress in the 19th century.

2. The high-growth *départements* in the 18th century mainly consisted of the north-eastern group: Vosges, Doubs, Meuse, Ardennes, Marne, Aisne, and the *départements* of Normandy: Calvados, Manche, Seine-Inférieure, Orne. This region forms the precocious side of the hexagon, all these *départements* enjoying a sound springboard at the end of the 17th century, as the threshold of 30% (and in many cases even 50%) had already been reached at that time. The spectacular growth of literacy in the countryside in the 18th century here was merely a continuing trend from the previous century. The interesting thing, in practically every case, was the long pause stretching from the end of the 18th century to the middle of the 19th, from Louis XVI to Victor Duruy. It was as if very early on – perhaps too early? – they had achieved a kind of temporary ceiling, through which it proved very hard to pass: in many cases it took a century to whittle down the remaining 10 or 20% to the point when everybody could sign his name. It was almost as if the front-runners had deliberately been holding back so that all the *départements* could sweep up the home straight abreast. Among the fliers there was a handful of outstanding performances, starting out from rather lower baselines but with finishing scores, for men at least, in excess of 50%, such as Nord and Basses-Pyrénées.

3. That leaves us with a mass of *départements* lying between the two extremes just defined – between an 18th century in which nothing happened at all, and one in which the better part of the battle was already won. The baseline in this intermediate category was low – around or below 20% for men – and they were still a long way off the 50% post at the end of the *Ancien Régime*. In other words, their progress was close to the national average, between 10 and 20% during the course of the century. Such was the case of the south-eastern group of *départements* in the Massif Central: Loire, Haute-Loire, Ardèche. The lower the starting point (as in Hautes-Pyrénées and Pyrénées-Orientales), the higher the growth-rate, but the finishing zone was roughly comparable, giving a range of between one-quarter and two-fifths signing. Depending on the *département*, growth really began to pick up either from 1786–90 or from 1816–20 onwards.

**Breakdown by sex**

The foregoing analysis obviously needs to be examined in the light of changes in men's and women's literacy scores over the entire period.

Generally speaking, as we have already noted, women's annual literacy growth-rates often exceeded those of men very early on – this phenomenon becoming general in the 19th century. This was already happening in 28 *départements* in the 18th century, most of them in the developed regions of France – Normandy, the Ile de France, the north and the north-east – whereas of the 23 in which the position is reversed,[23] 20 lie below the line that marks off the backward regions of France from the rest. This regional distribution points to the time-lag between male literacy trends and female ones: where male literacy got off to a good start in the 17th century, women began to catch up by the 18th; but where male literacy rates remained low, female ones were practically non-existent and hence there was no momentum to carry them along. This interpretation is borne out when we examine this relationship for subsequent periods: as we advance further into the 19th century higher female growth-rates increasingly become the rule. This was the case in 58 *départements* between 1786–90 and 1816–20, and in virtually all the *départements* after 1820. Creuse and Haute-Vienne were the only two in this period (1816–66) where male growth rates remained substantially higher than female ones. These were extremely backward *départements*: both sexes were almost totally illiterate at the start of the 19th century, and real progress began to be made only in the second third of the century, men showing the way. Even so, it is worth pointing out that in many comparable cases, in Brittany for example, or in the neighbouring *départements* of Vienne, Allier or Indre-et-Loire, rearguard *départements* all, the backwardness of the men did not prevent women from making up lost ground during the same period.

Even so, by focusing attention on the lowest starting scores, calculations of annual growth rates distort the actual catching-up rates. Closer examination of the overall differences between the performances of each sex for each period shows that the gap widened during the 18th century: 14 points in 1686–90, 20 in 1786–90, and a little more up to the beginning of the 19th century, when it reached its maximum, i.e. 21 points. After this it slowly fell until the middle of the century (17 points in 1854–55). Nationally-speaking, women only made up the ground separating them from the men under the Second Empire and the Third Republic.

The evolution of absolute differences in each *département* can be read off from the curves described earlier. On the whole, the gaps were rarely reduced in the course of the 18th century, and when they were reduced on a significant scale, as in Normandy (Eure, Manche) or in the Ile de France (Seine-et-Marne, Seine-et-Oise), the gain was relatively small: 8 points at most in the two most 'feminist' *départements*, Eure and Manche. The rule throughout the 18th century shows a general widening of the gap, particularly in certain *départements* in the east (Doubs, Jura, Haute-Marne, Haute-Saône) and in Hautes and Basses-Pyrénées.

This widening in the 18th century reflects a phenomenon that also occurs in the national averages: earlier growth in male literacy and a growth time-lag between the two sexes. It is easy to verify this by cross-checking, moreover: in the *départements* with zero or near-zero male growth rates, there was little change in the gap between the scores of the two sexes: it remained small, below the national average, and often tended to shrink slightly. There arose a kind of equality through shared ignorance.

So the men's score had to rise for that of the women to follow. But this occurred only on certain conditions. It is clear, for example, that a poor start to male literacy in relative terms – and still more in absolute terms (i.e. with a low finishing score at the end of the 18th century) – was generally inadequate to spur progress among the women. What it did produce was an increase in the gap between men and women, since the male improvement, however limited, was not matched by the opposite sex. This can be observed from the curves for several *départements* in the Massif Central (Corrèze, Nièvre, Haute-Loire, Loire, Tarn), for Isère and Pyrénées-Orientales.

In fact it was in *départements* where male literacy was relatively high at the start of the 18th century and continued to grow throughout the century that women either followed suit or even caught up: this is clear in Normandy (Calvados, Seine-Inférieure, Orne, Manche), in the north-east (Ardennes, Aisne, Marne, Meuse, Moselle) and in the Paris Region (Seine-et-Marne, Seine-et-Oise), i.e. in the 'developed' portion of France. While this group does contain some exceptions that might appear curious at first sight, such as Basses-Pyrénées, and even more so Haute-Marne, Vosges, Doubs and Jura, we shall find on closer examination that the *départements* where the gap between men and women widened greatly in the 18th century had ended the 17th century with scores below those cited above. Apparently, a good 18th century for women presupposed a good 17th century for the men: it took a few generations for literacy to percolate through from one sex to the other.

What happened at the close of the 18th century was that this time-lag underwent a spectacular contraction, as if this sluggish drive-mechanism had suddenly raced out of control. In many backward *départements* the female literacy curve swings upwards from 1786–90 at the same time as that of the men. Henceforward women were either catching up on men fast, in *départements* where male literacy was substantially accomplished under the *Ancien Régime*, or else were progressing faster than (although alongside) men in the developing regions. The two curves are pretty closely aligned and when, as in the Cher, they waited until mid-19th century before taking off, they did so in unison. In the history of literacy, one of the great contrasts between the *Ancien Régime* and the 19th century was this levelling-up of the rates at which men and women gained access to written culture.

## Looking beyond Maggiolo's figures

The Maggiolo survey thus furnishes us with a good set of figures describing the progress of literacy in France over two centuries. It sets the backdrop to the picture: the regional scenery, chronological trends, and male and female patterns. The facts it states are too overwhelming to be open to doubt. But they are also too overwhelming, in another sense, to be able to supply material for a more detailed, local, analysis. Their biggest drawback lies in the rigidity of the sample areas: the *département*, and nothing but the *département*. The arbitrariness of its boundaries distorts statistical aggregates and necessarily permits only the crudest of regional contrasts.

This is a well-known problem, referred to as the 'ecological fallacy' in Anglo-Saxon literature.[24] In our own study, most of the global data (i.e. concerning the entire area) are available for each *département*. Since all (or nearly all) the statistical methods employed use linear correlation in order to measure relations between variables or between subjects, the following occurs:

1. We can observe a similarity between two variables in cases where their *départemental* distribution is represented by parallel curves and hence where their profiles – again in terms of *départements* taken as a whole – are analogous. The independence of two variables (zero correlation) is observable in cases where simple (linear) correlations do not enable us to deduce one of the variables from our knowledge of the other for all the *départements*.

2. Similarly, the resemblance or dissimilarity between two *départements* is determined by whether or not it is possible to deduce their profiles, in terms of all the variables taken together, by simple arithmetic.

A number of objections – some of which we share – have been raised to the use of the *département* as the base unit. For a start, the *département* is merely an administrative district, and departmental boundaries do not coincide with the frontiers of historical, cultural, religious or economic regions. Consequently, the use of the *département* precludes insights into microphenomena while permitting only the crudest delimitations of the major regional groupings. In other words, we could greatly enhance the precision of our investigations by picking on a smaller basic unit, such as the *arrondissement*, the canton or the commune.

But to overcome this type of objection entirely we would have to draw a number of different regional boundaries, depending on the problem we wished to examine. This not only raises tricky methodological problems but would also entail a very small basic unit (ideally the individual, the household or the commune), thereby considerably increasing the mass of information to be gathered and processed, and making the cost of the operation prohibitive.

Our own experience has shown that the *département* is quite adequate for analyzing 'national' phenomena, identifying broad regional differences, although it does not allow us to plot frontiers with precision nor to determine whether these frontiers are clear-cut or blurred. Monographs provide at least some of the answers to these questions.

However, mention should be made of the advantages deriving from the use of the *département* as the base unit in preference to some smaller area. For one thing, *départements* are sufficiently numerous, and their geographical spread sufficiently 'reasonable', for us to be able to work statistically. On the other hand, there are sufficiently few of them for us to be able to know them all, and hence to add to the information contained in the matrices under investigation the immense wealth of information supplied by the 'érudits', and statistical data drawn from tables, maps and graphs. This is an important aspect of our study: we wish to avoid a narrow technical approach, and refuse to attach importance to anything that lies outside our data. In our view, if we were to examine a much wider range of subjects it would simply become impossible to analyze our tables 'manually'. And then there is the financial aspect of the matter: the cost of information retrieval is proportional to the number of subjects, and the same goes for the cost of computer printouts.

The impossibility of breaking out of the departmental administrative framework, owing to the absence of the primary data used in the survey, prohibits a comparative analysis of the different types of community and human environment. It is in this sphere that our own surveys, now that they have been used to test Maggiolo's departmental data, can be used for their own sake, independently of the national document. Certain pieces of the puzzle, however fragmentary, ought to enable us to pinpoint the discrepancies and variations masked by the averages.

For the developed, literate portions of France, the north and north-east, we have three surveys: Normandy, Brie and Champagne (Graph D). These are confined to the 18th century, or to the first two periods in Maggiolo's survey, but with an additional 'leg' in mid-century. The 18th century merits special attention in this privileged corner of France, since it was then, and not in the 19th century as for the backward regions, that literacy spread to the whole population.

This was a modern, buoyant 18th century, with a vigorously developing cultural level. True, the point of departure was high – between one third and one half of marriage partners were signing by the end of the 17th

**LANGUEDOC**

Category groups (bottom to top): FARM WORKERS · TEXTILE WORKERS · ARTISANS, SMALL HOLDERS · NOTABLES · NOTABLES, MERCHANTS · MERCHANTS · EXCEPTIONS

- HERAULT département — 150 L
- GARD département — 149 L
- CEVENNES farm workers — 20 L
- NÎMES PLAIN farm workers — 7 L
- LANGUEDOC farm workers — 26 L
- NÎMES PLAIN fisheries — 6 L
- LANGUEDOC textile (average) — 29 L
- CEVENNES textile workers — 23 L
- ANDUZE-GANGES textile workers — 17 L
- CEVENNES smallholders — 21 L
- MONTPELLIER textile workers — 3 L
- CEVENNES artisans — 28 L
- LANGUEDOC artisans (average) — 28 L
- ANDUZE-GANGES artisans — 16 L
- NÎMES PLAIN artisans — 9 L
- NÎMES PLAIN smallholders — 8 L
- LANGUEDOC smallholders (average) — 27 L
- GARRIGUE artisans — 15 L
- GARRIGUE smallholders — 14 L
- NÎMES PLAIN merchants — 1 L
- LANGUEDOC notables (average) — 31 L
- CEVENNES notables
- ANDUZE-GANGES notables — 5 L
- MONTPELLIER notables — 2 L
- GARRIGUE notables — 15 L
- LANGUEDOC merchants (average) — 30 L
- NÎMES PLAIN notables — 4 L
- MONTPELLIER merchants
- CEVENNES merchants — 24 L
- ANDUZE-GANGES merchants — 18 L
- GARRIGUE farm workers — 13 L
- MONTPELLIER farm workers
- MONTPELLIER artisans
- NÎMES PLAIN textile workers — 10 L

**SEINE-ET-MARNE**

Category groups: 1 GATINAIS · 2 BRIE FRANCAISE OVER 30 · 1 BRIE POUILLEUSE · 3 BRIE FRANCAISE, TOWNS · 2 RURAL, UNDER 25 · 1 BRIE FRANCAISE · 2 PEASANTS · 3 TOWNS, EMPLOYEES, ARTISANS · NOBLES, BOURGEOIS · RURAL, PEASANT EMPLOYEES, ARTISANS

- SEINE-ET-MARNE département — 15 S
- DIAN Gâtinais — 36 S
- RURAL Gâtinais — 38 S
- PALEY Gâtinais — 37 S
- AGED OVER 30 rural — 171 S
- CHATRES Brie Française — 41 S
- BAILLY Brie Française — 39 S
- PERTHES Brie Pouilleuse — 34 S
- CHARTRETTE Brie Pouilleuse — 32 S
- RURAL Brie Pouilleuse — 35 S
- LA ROCHETTE Brie Pouilleuse — 33 S
- SEINE-ET-MARNE rural — 49 S
- AGED UNDER 25 rural — 169 S
- COUBERT Brie Française — 42 S
- RURAL Brie Française — 46 S
- BRIE-COMTE-ROBERT Brie Française — 47 S
- SEINE-ET-MARNE towns — 48 S
- GRISY-SUISNES Brie Française — 45 S
- CHAMPEAUX Brie Française — 40 S
- PEROLLES-ATILLY Brie Française — 43 S
- PEASANTS towns — 164 S
- EMPLOYEES towns — 166 S
- GRETZ Brie Française — 44 S
- ARTISANS — 162 S
- NOBLES towns — 156 S (M-W)
- BOURGEOIS towns — 158 S (M-W)
- MERCHANTS towns — 160 S (M-W)
- NOBLES rural — 157 S (M-W)
- BOURGEOIS rural — 159 S (M-W)
- MERCHANTS rural — 161 S (M-W)
- PEASANTS rural — 165 S
- EMPLOYEES rural — 167 S
- ARTISANS rural — 163 S
- AGED OVER 30 towns — 170 S
- AGED UNDER 25 towns — 168 S

**NORMANDY** (EXCEPTIONS)

- SEINE-MARITIME département — 154 N
- EURE département — 155 N
- SEINE-MARITIME rural — 83 N
- ROUMOIS — 81 N
- EURE rural — 84 N
- VEXIN — 80 N
- SEINE VALLEY below ROUEN — 79 N
- BAQUEVILLE — 86 N
- PAYS DE CAUX — 76 N
- PICARDY BORDER — 77 N
- SEINE VALLEY above ROUEN — 82 N
- BRAY — 78 N
- EU — 87 N
- GOURNAY — 89 N
- BOLBEC — 85 N
- RURAL — 92 N
- PONT-AUDEMER — 90 N
- LE TREPORT — 88 N
- QUILLEBEUF — 91 N

**CHAMPAGNE**

Category groups: 1 SMALL TOWNS, REGIONAL AVERAGE, UNDER 25 · 2 PARISHES, WEAVERS, FARMERS, OVER 30 · A PARALLEL EVOLUTION M and W · B DISPARATE EVOLUTION M and W

- MARNE département — 153 C
- ARDENNES département — 152 C
- HAUTVILLERS wine-growing Champagne — 51 C
- WINE-GROWING CHAMPAGNE (average) — 50 C
- AY small towns — 65 C
- ATTIGNY small towns — 68 C
- CHAMPAGNE POUILLEUSE (average) — 55 C
- SIGNY-L'ABBAYE small towns — 66 C
- LA VENCE VALLEY — 62 C
- AGED UNDER 25 — 69 C
- SAVIGNY-SUR-AISNE Aisne Valley
- LA VENCE VALLEY weavers — 75 C
- GRANDPRE small towns — 67 C
- VERSY wine-growing Champagne — 54 C
- VILLE EN SELVE Forest of Rheims — 60 C
- MONTAGNE DE REIMS woodcutters — 74 C
- ISLE SUR SUIPPE Champagne Pouilleuse — 58 C
- BAZANCOURT Champagne Pouilleuse — 57 C
- AGED OVER 30 — 70 C
- CHAMPAGNE POUILLEUSE farmers — 72 C
- WINE-GROWING CHAMPAGNE wine-growers — 71 C
- VITRY-LES-REIMS Champagne Pouilleuse — 56 C
- CUMIERS wine-growing Champagne — 53 C
- CONDE-LES-VOUZIERS Aisne Valley — 64 C
- VERZENAY wine-growing Champagne — 52 C
- GERMAINE Forest of Rheims — 61 C
- AISNE VALLEY Champagne Pouilleuse — 59 C
- LA VENCE VALLEY manual workers — 73 C

Legend: 1800 / 1700 — men / women

*Graph D* Sex, occupation, region: the uneven pace of literacy century – so the process had got under way before the start of the period covered by our survey. But by the end of the 18th century, the percentage was closer to 75, both in Normandy and in the eastern part of the Paris Region. Maggiolo had already indicated this. What his table also says, which is borne out by these surveys, is that the gap between men and woman at the start of the period was considerable. Indeed, roughly one man in two was literate under Louis XIV, whereas only one woman in four or five (in Champagne and Brie) was able to sign her name. These are good examples of the phenomenon noted above, in examining the respective growth-rates for men and women in the 18th century, that growth during this period in these three regions was essentially female growth. While men continued (sometimes slowly) to make progress in a direction in which they were already fairly advanced, women positively surged forward: mass female literacy in these zones really dates from the 18th century.

The existence, in our three examples, of an additional check at the mid-century mark makes this phenomenon easier to describe and to date. In Champagne, rural male literacy only made slow progress in the first half of the 18th century (57–63%), speeding up slightly in the second half (63–76%), whereas that of women (25%, 28% and 48%) increased more rapidly and more steadily. In Brie, male progress was evenly spread over the two halves of the century, but it was relatively slow and reached a plateau at the end of the *Ancien Régime* that was to last until the Restoration. Women's literacy, in contrast, marked time, and even slipped a little, at the start of the 18th century; take-off really occurred in the second half (they doubled their score from 17 to 34%), and the pace remained lively into the early 19th century. The case of Haute-Normandie is clear-cut also: the men turned in a creditable performance (from around 40% to around 75%), but it was the women's take-off that was really spectacular, since they were more or less illiterate at the end of the 17th century (less than 10% signed), but multiplied this rather poor performance by 5 or 6 in the course of the century! Also, whereas the men's progress was often unsteady, with occasional backsliding in the second half of the century (in the Caux district and on the borders of Picardy), the women, as in Champagne, surged forward powerfully and steadily, unaffected by local hesitations among the men.

These examples suggest that in the relatively literate regions of France under the *Ancien Régime*, where almost one man in two was capable of signing by the end of the 17th century, the men continued to progress, though rather more slowly on the whole, in the 18th century. This century, on the other hand, was the age of the take-off of female literacy *par excellence*. In other words, the two trends were linked, in the sense that a certain degree of male literacy was required to start the women along the road. But this also means that the two trends were broadly autonomous;

once the women's trend had taken flight, it ceased to be affected by the frequent dips that occurred in the male curve even before the end of the 18th century.

Several more detailed analyses inside these three regions confirm these twin notions. For example, in the Forest of Reims, in Champagne, the only sector in which male rates were low at the outset of the 18th century, only 7% of the men of the village of Germaine were capable of signing! Male literacy certainly accelerated during the course of the century, but women hung around at a wretchedly low level, especially in the first half of the century. The same goes for Brie Pouilleuse, where the men themselves were lagging way behind the regional average at the end of the 17th century: they made solid progress, but the women lagged behind throughout the century. In two of the villages surveyed, practically all the women remained illiterate right up to the end of the *Ancien Régime*. Conversely, in Champagne Pouilleuse, where male rates were high right from the time of the first survey period and continued to rise slowly throughout the century, from 60 to 80%, only one woman in five was capable of signing at the end of the 17th century but more than one in two could do so a century later! The village of Vitry-les-Reims is a particularly striking example of this: it was the male literacy record-holder (83%!) in the reign of Louis XIV and had the maximum female literacy spurt in the 18th century (from 0 to 60%!). One example does upset this pattern, namely the wine-growing district of Champagne. Here high male literacy scores at the beginning of the 18th century were followed by stagnation, and even regression in the middle, before once more rising to their original level towards the end of the century. And, for once, the women reproduce this sagging curve and fail to assert their autonomy, as though some outside curse weighed upon both sexes in like manner.

But this is the only such case to be found in any of our surveys. Brie and Haute-Normandie, on the other hand, both confirm the rule: on the whole, a good 18th century, with women reaping more of the final benefits than the men, although a little breathless towards the end. An examination of data for the *arrondissement* of Meaux (*département* of Seine-et-Marne), canton by canton, proves highly interesting from this point of view.[25] Surveys were conducted for two centuries (1680–1880) at twenty-year intervals, thus forming an unequalled documentary series. Only two cantons (Coulommiers and Rebais) are missing out of the nine that make up the *arrondissement*. Figures show that male literacy, which started out from a high score (around 50%), continued to spread rapidly until 1740–60, and then stabilized until around 1820. The Revolution can hardly be held responsible for this marking-time, and, furthermore, the cantons most affected tended to be the ones with the highest scores, where the phenomenon developed into a decline, as if they had come up against some impenetrable upper-ceiling. Women, who at the end of the 17th century had a much lower level (around 20%, if we exclude the more urban cantons, Meaux and Lagny), progressed very little in the first half of the 18th and then began to gather momentum around 1740–60. From then on they caught up steadily, and the process even accelerated right at the beginning of the 19th century. Even when male literacy resumed its forward march after 1820, the women continued to progress more quickly.

The fact that the spread of male literacy was beginning to lose momentum towards the end of the 18th century is clear also in the rural areas of Haute-Normandie – as can be seen moreover from a comparison between Maggiolo's scores for 1786–90 and 1816–20 for Eure and Seine-Inférieure. For certain districts, such as Caux, our own surveys even allow us to advance this date to the middle of the 18th century, in line with the lower-Normandy chronology put forward by Pierre Chaunu and his team of historians at Caen.[26] The trend worked the other way with the women: starting from particularly low scores (between 5 and 10%), which are distinctly better than Maggiolo's figures, they took off right from the beginning of the 18th century, and continued to catch up steadily, without once either slipping back or easing off the pace. The gap in the literacy scores for the two sexes, which had been very large at the start of the period, was still a considerable one at the end of it: but even so it had shrunk from 1 : 7 to 1 : 2 in the rural areas of Eure!

A series of additional surveys of these three regions also sheds some light on a problem neglected in Maggiolo's table, namely the towns. We shall confine ourselves here to describing the key data. Everywhere we find the towns enjoying a clear lead over the countryside at the end of the 17th century, and that applies to both sexes. This is particularly clear-cut in the table for Brie: 65% of the men and 42% of the women in the towns were able to sign their names at that time. Over three-quarters of the inhabitants of Meaux, men and women, were able to sign by the middle of the 18th century! Consequently, further progress was slower, for men especially, but also for women: the difference in their scores was quite a bit smaller, since the women had been catching up for longer.

The towns studied in Haute-Normandie (small though they were) also enjoyed a marked lead over the surrounding countryside, with male scores greatly in excess of 50% for the first period surveyed. As a result, male progress was slow, especially after 1750 (with a drop recorded at Bolbec). Women's literacy, on which a good start had been made by the end of the 17th century, at a time when the peasant-women were still illiterate, everywhere started out from a level below that of their sisters in the Brie towns. Progress was thus more rapid (except at Eu), but the initial and final intervals separating them from the men were relatively smaller than in the countryside. Lastly, it is worth noting that migration from the countryside to the towns does not seem to have affected literacy rates in the towns. Scores for 'natives' are indeed generally lower than those achieved by spouses born elsewhere, doubtless in the vicinity, both for men and for women. The Normandy monograph here echoes a comment already made about the town of Caen by J.-C. Perrot:[27] that the call of the town worked selectively, attracting not the least cultivated inhabitants of the countryside, but, even then, its most 'modern' offspring.

On the other side, we have backward France. The *département* of Vienne, which was already lagging at the end of the 17th century, fell yet further behind: it was in the bottom ten *départements* for literacy in 1816–20, and there it remained throughout the 19th century. Maggiolo gives the following percentage scores:

|         | M  | W  |
|---------|----|----|
| 1686–90 | 17 | 10 |
| 1786–90 | 19 | 9  |
| 1816–20 | 25 | 13 |
| 1866    | 52 | 33 |

Our own figures are very similar, if we exclude the town of Châtellerault; indeed on the whole they are slightly inferior. In the middle of the 19th century, only one in two men and one in three women, signed their *actes de mariage*. In other words, confining ourselves purely to rural areas, Vienne trailed, roughly two hundred years behind the advanced north-eastern corner of France! Moreover, Vienne is just one of a whole series of *départements* in the centre-west with more or less similar records: one has only to glance at Maggiolo's scores for Charente, Deux-Sèvres, Indre, and Indre-et-Loire to grasp the geographical implications of this backwardness.

A review of local data for this *département, arrondissement* by *arrondissement*, canton by canton, creates a picture of an almost static 18th century – even though the starting scores, albeit low, were by no means nil. One in four men signed in the *arrondissement* of Poitiers, one in five in those of Civray and Loudun. And yet these figures hardly altered at all up to the end of the 18th century, up to 1816–20 even. It was during this third period, between the end of the *Ancien Régime* and the Restoration, that differentiation occurred. In the *arrondissement* of Poitiers, male literacy remained very mediocre and it was very poor in the *arrondissement* of Montmorillon (11%). In the *arrondissement* of Loudun it actually declined, after having risen slightly during the 18th century, thereby proving that this progress was still fragile and by no means irreversible. There was a slight increase, on the other hand, in the *arrondissement* of Civray, where men improved their performance from 25% at the end of the 18th century to 30% in 1816–20, and in that of Châtellerault, from 11 to 20%. But even so, these scores are very low, and their extreme variability from canton to canton, and from one village to another, hints at their vulnerability.

In this situation female illiteracy remained the general rule. On the morrow of the Revolution and the Empire, female rates were spread very evenly, the percentages of brides signing ranging only from 8% (Montmorillon) to 13% (Poitiers). Such progress as may be observed here and there (in the *arrondissement* of Châtellerault for example), from figures as low as these, is liable to prove to be a statistical illusion. At any rate, the threshold of irreversible establishment of literacy had not been reached.

The figures show that here the decisive male take-off only really occurred in the second and third quarters of the 19th century, between 1816–20 and 1872–76. As always, there were major local discrepancies. For example, in the *arrondissement* of Civray, with an average of 62% of men signing in 1872–76, we find that the most backward canton, Availles, scores only 36%, as against 81% for Coutré and 85% for Champagne-le-Sec. But the minimum threshold of one man in three had been reached. Women followed this belated movement, but without the generation gap observed in the more precocious regions in northern France. They still did not achieve comparable scores and they took off less rapidly, but they did take off at the same time, doubtless profiting from the belatedness of male literacy. In the cantons where they lagged behind most, 30% of them signed in 1872–76. Consequently, they suffered less inequality vis-à-vis the men than did the peasant-women in northern France one hundred or one hundred and fifty years before. Nevertheless, they did not achieve full literacy until the beginning of the 20th century.

In looking at these trends, we ought to distinguish between towns and large villages. In the *arrondissement* of Montmorillon, in the east of the *département*, for example, 13%(M + W) signed at the end of the 17th century, but at La Trimouille, later the *chef-lieu* of its canton, the score was 20–25%. The average for large villages in the *département* for that period was 28% for the men and 14% for the women rising to 43 and 37% in 1816–20 – figures for the town of Châtellerault being distinctly superior to these. Thus the development of literacy in the towns, as in the most advanced part of France, seems to have been a separate phenomenon altogether.

Neighbouring Haute-Vienne provides another example of a backward *département*. This *département* lies in the heart of the wooded Limousin uplands, and was still less privileged. A series of lucky coincidences, not to mention an Archaeological Society not indifferent to contemporary history and an active and curious *inspecteur d'Académie*,[28] have left us a priceless document, a sort of Maggiolo Mark II, devised a few years later, in 1883. This takes the form of a survey (conducted over two years) carried out by all the schoolteachers in every village in the *département*, spanning twenty-five year intervals between 1650 and 1850. The results are not strictly comparable with those given in Maggiolo's table, since neither the samples nor the time spans are identical. However, the data are the same, and the periods are very similar, while the study devoted to Haute-Vienne in particular presents the twofold advantage of delving further back in time and of presenting a more closely-woven fabric of surveys.

The backwardness of Haute-Vienne was traditional. For two centuries, it was among the bottom ten *départements* of France for literacy: it was bottom of the class between 1860 and 1870. Indeed the literacy curve is particularly depressed. Thanks to the earliness of the first survey we are able to observe the first stirrings of a take-off at the start of Louix XIV's reign, when the percentage of men able to sign rose from 5.6 to 9.3, and for women from 2.6 to 6.6, between 1650 and 1675. However, the first sample (229 households) is rather too limited to be absolutely reliable, and in any case the scores are very modest, even by comparison with Vienne. Moreover they remained unchanged for almost a century, since the middle of the 18th century even reveals a slight fall. A timid advance broke the monotony of this continuous stagnation in the second half of the century, but the curve slumped once more with the Revolution and the Empire, picking up very slowly. In 1850, only one man in four, and one woman in six or seven, was capable of signing their *acte de mariage*! Decisive progress was only made under the Second Empire and the Third Republic.

Throughout this long, changeless history, the gap between male and female scores remained more or less constant at 3–4 points, from Louis XIV to Napoleon I. In other words, the gap was small, and percentages for the two sexes always varied in the same direction: a kind of egalitarianism in backwardness. The gap only began to open up in the second quarter of the 19th century, when men pushed their score up from 18.8% to 27.2% and women only from 12.1 to 15.8%. Even so the difference remained far narrower than that between men and women in the developed *départements* a century earlier, so we may speak of egalitarianism in late development too.

Looking now at the *arrondissements*, Limoges and Bellac enjoyed a marked lead by the end of the 17th century – compared with almost total illiteracy at Saint-Yrieix, with Rochechouart lying midway between them. This was probably because of the towns. In the 1700–01 survey, the only cantons to reach the – modest – score of 10% of men signing contained at least one small town: three in the *arrondissement* of Limoges (two forming the town itself, and Saint-Léonard); Bellac, Bassines, Magnac-Laval, Mézières, Saint-Sulpice in the *arrondissement* of Bellac; Saint-Julien and Rochechouart in that of Rochechouart; there were none in that of Saint-Yrieix. By the end of the 18th century, male scores for the cantons of Limoges came to 35%, those of Saint-Léonard and Saint-Julien to over 20%. Here again, these scores were diminished by the surrounding countryside; scores in the towns or large villages themselves were 40, 37 and 31% respectively. This brings us back to the classic phenomenon of the towns' lead over the countryside. In the desolate Limousin, the towns' successes often have to be set against practically total illiteracy in the rural areas: throughout the 18th century, many village communities turned in scores close to zero.

In the towns, the women followed closely on the heels of the men. We can more or less guess this from the distribution of scores at *arrondissement* level, but it becomes clearer when we study the cantonal figures. Saint-Léonard, which turned in the best male score in the period 1700–01, with 22%, also came top of the list for female literacy with a score of 18%. The other towns or small towns achieved scores of a little under 10% (around 9 for Limoges, Bellac and Saint-Junien). At the end of the 18th century, women had achieved the 10% threshold in 7 cantons, which happened, with just one exception, to be the leading cantons for male literacy also: Limoges, Saint-Léonard, Saint-Junien, Saint-Sulpice, Bellac, Aixe and Rochechouart. The gap between women and men was never very large – between 2 and 6 points only. This is an additional pointer to a constant: even in periods of male literacy take-off, the size of the town is a factor in reducing inequality between the sexes.

Thus, like those in Vienne, the women of Haute-Vienne, throughout this period, trailed less far behind the men than their counterparts in the more advanced *départements*. This is because during the 18th century they were either stuck in a climate of rural illiteracy common to both sexes, or else they benefited from the modest gains being made in the towns and large villages. Also, when the rural take-off did finally occur in the 19th century, they took part in this race to catch up.

The local monographs presented in the second volume of this book supply a certain number of useful sidelights on the national, *département* by *département*, table.

The first of these concerns the immense contrast between rural France and urban France. Literacy scores in the towns are substantially superior to those in the countryside, even if we apply the word town to relatively small agglomerations of around 2,000 inhabitants and over. There are exceptions to this rule, and we shall be looking for the reasons for them, which should at the same time help us to pin down the reasons for 'normal' behaviour. But, generally speaking, the contrast is obvious since the end of the 17th century, and the rural exodus which populated the towns under the *Ancien Régime* did nothing to change matters. So what we have here are a rural and an urban history of literacy; they are not unrelated, but they do not obey the same forces. Neither chronological distribution nor inequality between the sexes seem to be comparable in the two cases.

In the case of rural France – which lies at the heart of this chapter devoted to the data gathered by Maggiolo – we may very broadly arrange the samples presented by us around two chronological models. From the standpoint of literacy, Normandy, Brie, and Champagne had a very good 18th century. Poitou and Limousin did not; they progressed only in the 19th century. The revolutionary period, which has raised so much controversy, thus does not appear to be crucial in our data. It resulted neither in a take-off nor in a collapse; most of the time it simply prolonged a trend begun well before. What counts above all is the last century of the *Ancien Régime*, for it was then that progress was either set in motion or else failed to get under way. And it was long after the first Bonaparte had disappeared from the scene that rapid upswings occurred in most of the backward cantons and *arrondissements*.

For north and north-eastern France, by taking an additional cross-section around 1750 we may form a more detailed picture of the spread of literacy in the 18th century. It often ran out of steam around 1750–60, for the men, as if some awkward barrier had been reached and as if this growth were incapable of sustaining itself to its expected conclusion at that time. We find this phenomenon in the most advanced *départements* in Maggiolo's table also, but our own local data allow us to push the date forward a little, thereby exonerating the French Revolution. The idea of a threshold is made all the more attractive by the fact that the spread of literacy among women began later, and from a lower level, but encountered no such plateau at the end of the 18th century.

An analysis of the relative progress of the two sexes based on these examples does confirm the shape of the departmental curves established on the basis of Maggiolo's report: the older the literacy process, as in Normandy or in Brie, the greater the time-lag between men and women – two, or even three generations. Conversely, when the men start late, as in Poitou, the women follow very close behind, and the gap between the two is never as great in the 19th century as it had been in earlier periods. Male backwardness was beneficial to sex-equality.

The two centuries vital to rural literacy – in other words, to mass literacy – were indeed the ones covered by Maggiolo's survey, from the end of the 17th century to the end of the 19th. From this standpoint, the towns were more precocious; everywhere in advance of the countryside, they often attained high levels of literacy even before the end of the 17th century, particularly in northern France. The history of urban literacy begins well before the period we have attempted to reconstitute, probably in the last centuries of the Middle Ages, therefore much of it falls outside the scope of this book. Rural literacy, on the other hand, comes within it almost in its entirety: even in *départements* where it was already fairly advanced by the end of the 17th century, we feel that it is of quite recent origin, bound up with the immense proselytizing efforts of the Counter-Reformation which marked the *Grand Siècle*. Moreover such take-offs as we are able to observe at the start of the 18th century contain more than a hint as to their origins.

In all, then, we have a period of two and a half centuries, from 1650 to 1900, from Louis XIV to Jules Ferry, with time-lags that coincide with the uneven development within the frontiers of the nation. To begin with, this unevenness produces two Frances, divided by a line running from Saint-Malo to Geneva, and later gives a residual triangle of backwardness with the Atlantic coast as its base. This spatial distribution, which had already been revealed by other indicators and announced by 19th-century statisticians, finally comes as less of a surprise than the chronology of the phenomenon: are we going to have to deprive Jules Ferry and the illustrious founders of the Third Republic of the credit for having rid their country of the shades of ignorance? For the fact is that the great educational laws of the 1880s were enacted at a time when the cause of universal literacy was, if not entirely so, at least pretty well won, as can be seen from the figures. In founding the free, non-confessional and compulsory school, the laws of the Republic – far from inaugurating it – actually crowned the elementary instruction of the French people as expressed in universal literacy. These laws were the institutional expression of the consequences of literacy, not its cause. In both camps, moreover, the battle over the school reflects the deep and ancient priority accorded to education, and it would be true to say that both histories, that of the Church and that of the Republic, bear out this sentiment.

There was in fact one France that became literate under the *Ancien Régime*, and another that, on the contrary, owed its admission to written culture to the 19th century. Broadly speaking, northern and north-eastern France was able to read and write by the end of the 18th century, at a time when the other France was only just embarking on the process of catching up. It is probably this twofold time-scale that lay hidden beneath the political controversies of the 19th century and furnished historical arguments to both camps! The illusions nurtured on both sides were not the fruit of ignorance but of partisan interpretations of the process: one side credited pre-1789 literacy to the *Ancien Régime*, while the other put post-1789 literacy down to the credit of the Revolution.

In fact, though, in neither of the two typical trends that we have been able to identify in this study of the *départements* can we attribute the decisive rôle (positive or negative) to the revolutionary or post-revolutionary period. If one thing stands out clearly in all the departmental growth curves, it is that, however hard we try to take into account the time-lag between them, we can find no trace of the major political events of contemporary French history. The least we can say is that on no occasion is

it possible to verify that intimate connection between elementary education
and political régime which, a century ago, from different standpoints,
was the common creed of both parish priest and schoolteacher. True, we
can point to a pre- and post-revolutionary period in the French literacy
process, but they refer to two geographies, not to two histories. Here,
as in many other areas, the revolutionary period merely emerges on our
curves as the pursuit and acceleration of earlier trends.

There are, however, a certain number of morphological differences
between the two main periods of literacy growth in rural France – the 18th
and the 19th centuries – which call for attention. The first of these is that
growth in the 18th century, even when it reached high levels, always ended
up against a seemingly insuperable barrier. When the male literacy score
reached 70 or 80%, the curve flattened out, as if in town and countryside
alike there existed some irreducible stock of illiterates. This phenomenon
also seems to have been present prior to the 18th century, since it is
recorded in Hautes-Alpes at the end of the 17th century. The 19th century,
on the other hand, tended towards universal literacy, even though this was
not, strictly speaking, actually achieved, since even today there exists a
residual illiteracy due to physical or mental defects. But, with this
reservation aside, the scores in every French *département* on the eve of the
First World War show that young French people in general were able to
read and write. In 1906, illiterate conscripts accounted for no more than
5.1% of the total intake, and in the period 1901–1906, practically all newly-
weds signed their *actes de mariage*: 97.1% of the men, and 94.8% of the
women.

Thus the 19th century was more than just the century in which the
backward regions caught up with the rest. Formerly, even the leading
*départements* had had their apparently permanent hard-core illiterates,
who constituted the humblest strata of French society. Everywhere, the
post-revolutionary 19th century eliminated this; in other words, we may
credit it with the demand for universal literacy. This demand did not arise
from the Revolution, but it was reinforced, broadened and enshrined by its
egalitarian ideology.

This analysis may be extended to cover the question of female literacy.
As we have already seen, in the growth *départements* in the 18th century,
female literacy generally spread faster than male literacy, in relative terms,
but even so the absolute difference between the sexes was at its greatest at
the end of the century – which is also true of the national averages. During
this period, female literacy was frequently trailing male literacy by several
generations. The backward *départements*, on the other hand, reveal a
certain degree of equality between the sexes. Here, up to the end of the 18th
century and sometimes even beyond, men and women alike shared the
short commons of illiteracy: whether at the beginning or in the middle of

the 19th century, it was still together that they took their belated first steps, for henceforward the women followed hard on the heels of their menfolk. It is as if from one century to the next, and doubtless with the advent of the Revolution, there had arisen a new awareness of the need for, and the possibility of, women's cultural advancement. It was timid, hesitant and uneven, but nevertheless absolutely clear-cut on our 19th century curves. Moreover, universal literacy for women finally occurred at the dawn of the 20th century, practically at the same moment as men achieved it.

Obviously there remained at the beginning of the 20th century a residual illiteracy among the middle and older age-groups in the population. The 1901 census, which gives the educational level by age-group (in five-year intervals) and by sex shows this. For the whole of France, the 10% illiteracy rate (unable to read or write) is exceeded in the age-groups over 30 for women and over 35 for men; the 20% level over 45 for women and over 50 for men; finally the 30% level over 50 for women and over 65 for men. It should be noted therefore that the proportion of illiterates on the electoral rolls in 1901 was considerable; there were 1,900,000 completely illiterate men (close on 16% of the total) aged over 20, i.e. electors (at the same time, there were around 3,000,000, or nearly 24% of the total, illiterate women aged over 20). Although the oncoming generations were gradually wearing down these figures, regional disparities still existed. Among French people aged over 15 in mainland France, we find the following range of scores: male illiteracy ranged from 2.05% (Doubs) to 34.05% (Corrèze); female illiteracy from 3.08% (Doubs also) to 47.13% (Ariège).

So from the Counter-Reformation Church to Jules Ferry's school-teachers, it took the depths of rural France some three centuries to accede to written civilization. But they did so neither in a single thrust, nor at a uniform pace. We are thus obliged to abandon the illusion of a steady, line-abreast march towards literacy in favour of the more contrasted picture that we obtain from a close examination of trends and patterns.

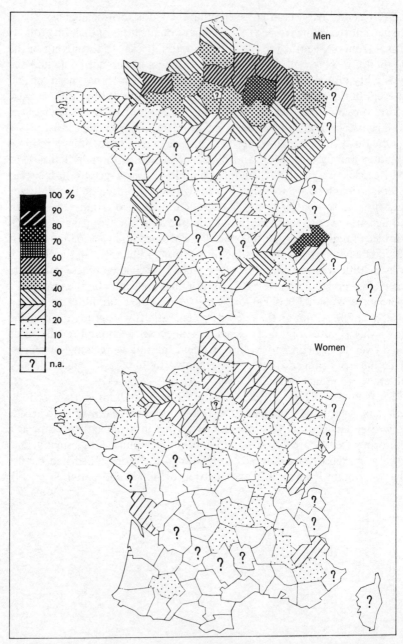

1.1   Percentage of spouses having signed their *acte de mariage* (1686–1690)

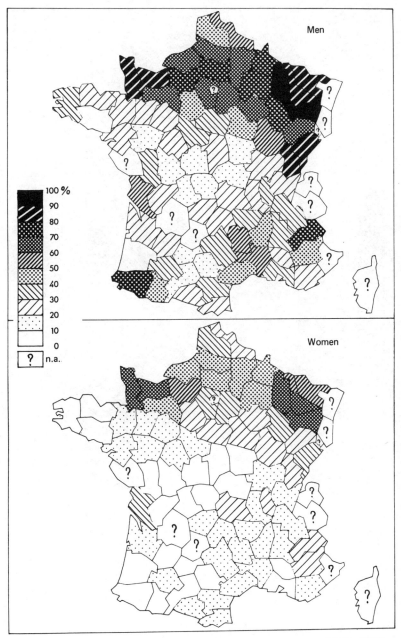

1.2 Percentage of spouses having signed their *acte de mariage* (1786–1790)

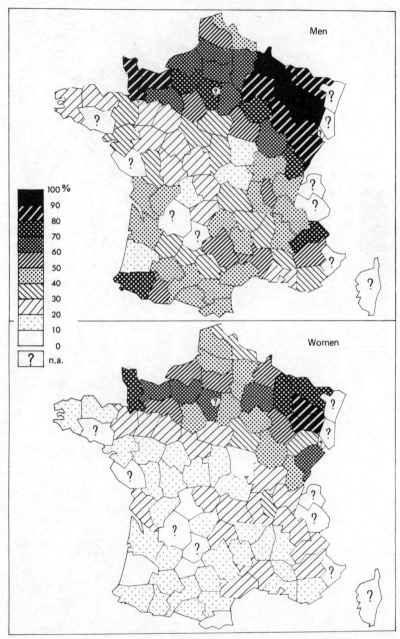

1.3.   Percentage of spouses having signed their *acte de mariage* (1816–1820)

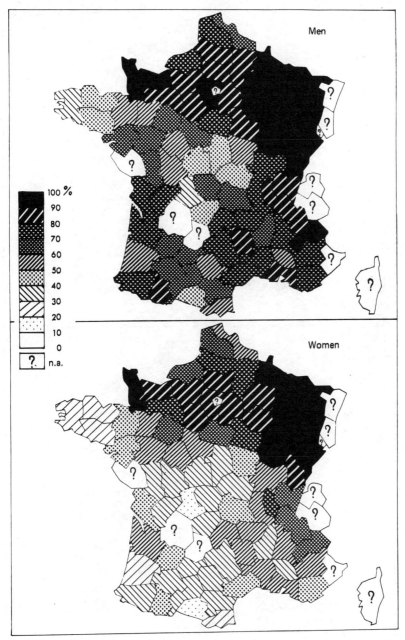

1.4  Percentage of spouses having signed their *acte de mariage* (1866)

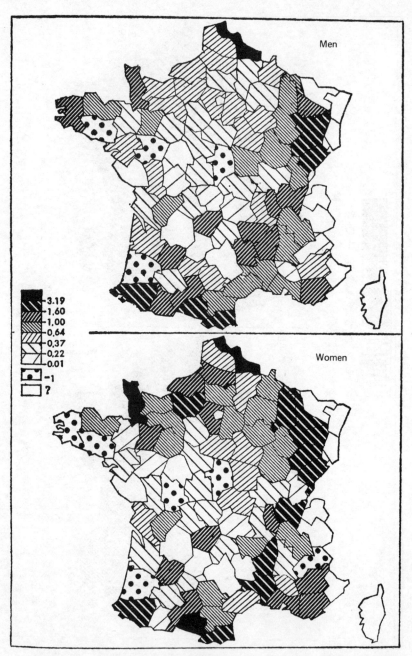

1.5   Linear growth rate of percentage differences in number of spouses having signed their *acte de mariage* (1686–1690/1786–1790)

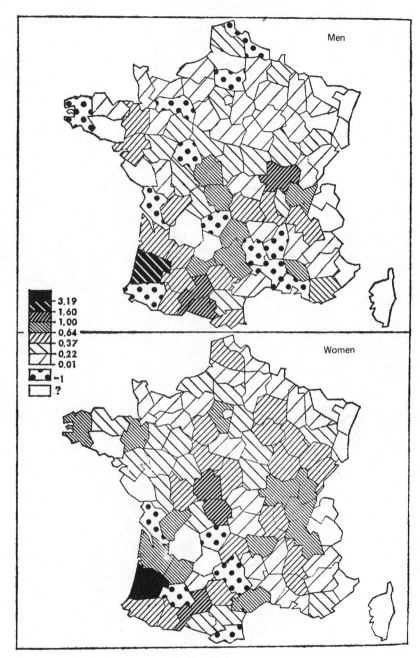

1.6 Linear growth rate of percentage differences in number of spouses having signed their *acte de mariage* (1786–1790/1816–1820)

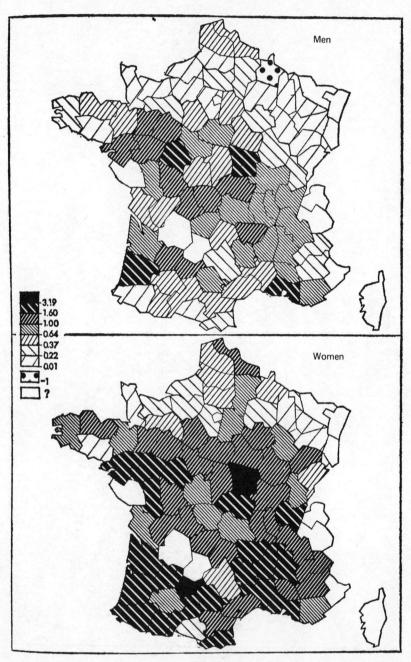

1.7   Linear growth rate of percentage differences in number of spouses having signed their *acte de mariage* (1816–1820/1866)

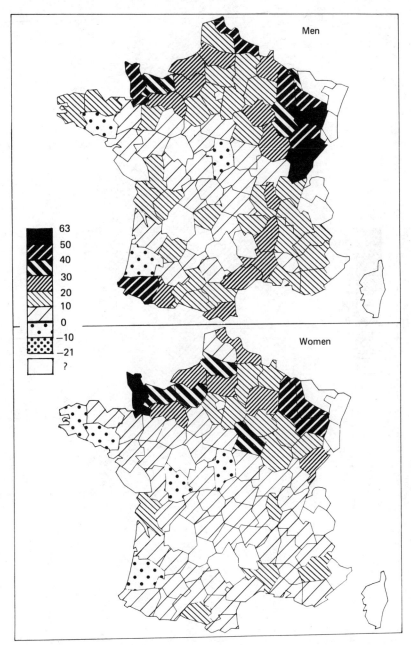

1.8   Absolute percentage differences in number of spouses having signed their *acte de mariage* (1686–1690/1786–1790)

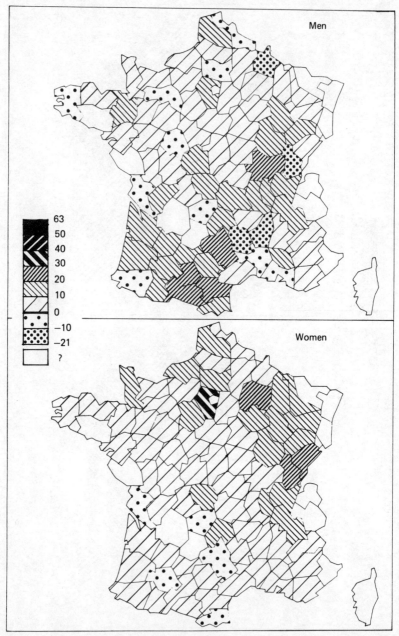

1.9   Absolute percentage differences in number of spouses having signed their *acte de mariage* (1786–1790/1816–1820)

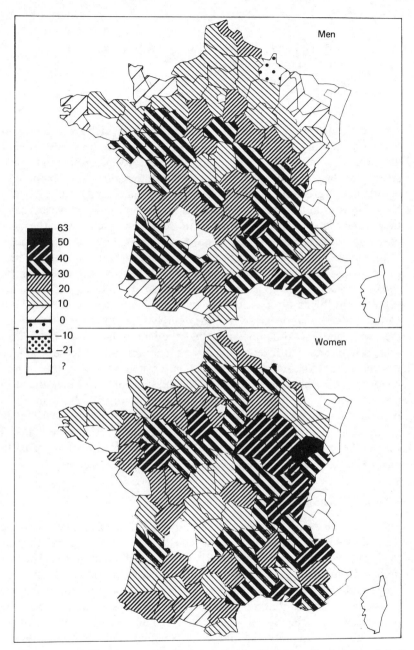

1.10  Absolute percentage differences in number of spouses having signed their *acte de mariage* (1816–1820/1866)

# 2

## THE SCHOOL, THE *ANCIEN REGIME* AND THE REVOLUTION

The great controversy over the history of the school which arose at the end of the 19th century at least settled one problem: elementary schools do not date from the French Revolution; they were already flourishing in the last century of the *Ancien Régime* and even, in some regions and communes, before that. A great many local monographs, resumed in the Abbé Allain's book,[1] have established this beyond doubt. All these works, however useful they remain to this day, focus on counting communal schools on the basis of mainly ecclesiastical sources.[2] They were obsessed by the controversies of their time, and so sought to prove their case with facts, in line with best positivist practice, i.e. by listing the number of attested schools under the *Ancien Régime*. So imbued were they, often in spite of the opinions expressed by their authors, with the republican view of the school as the test and motor of social progress, that they barely thought to look elsewhere: they were content to demonstrate that the late 19th-century republican State school had had forerunners in its sacred mission, whether these be Church school or State schools, or Church and State together. Their history of the school neglected both the question of social investment in primary education – which preceded the existence of the school and is its necessary condition – and that of its pedagogic efficiency, which they regarded as a foregone conclusion. However, the considerable material that has been amassed by their efforts does provide us with an opportunity of looking beyond the conceptual framework of their studies.

### Who wants schools?

Before schools came into existence, before they could exist, they had to be wanted by somebody, somewhere in society: at the top, by the Church or the State, or both; below, by society itself, i.e. by its communities. The two desires, from above and below, are not necessarily incompatible; nor are they necessarily interconnected. From this point of view, we could imagine a history of schools that would contrast Russia, for example, where the main, often the sole, initiative came from the State, with England, where the community assumed the bulk of responsibility.[3] In cases such as the English one, the social pressure for schooling generally intersected an identical pressure from the Church, or Churches: first, because mass education arose from the imperative of salvation – people had to be able to read the Book; and second because religious institutions were more responsive to community pressures than was the distant state machinery: they could even, as in the case of Sweden,[4] completely supplant the school in the education of believers. But in *Ancien Régime* France, the history of elementary schooling is the outcome of three interacting factors: the Church, the State and the community.

The Catholic Church: at the time covered by Maggiolo's first series of retrospective statistics, it had just seen its long struggle for reconquest against the Reformation crowned by the Revocation of the Edict of Nantes. But it did not wait for this royal sanction to turn the heretics' own weapon against them: the history of mass literacy, like that of the school, is rooted in the conflictual yet mutually-supportive confrontation between the Reformation and the Counter-Reformation.

Mediaeval Christianity had had no trouble associating the theological constructions of the *clercs* with the ancient terrors of a peasant people whose traditions were oral. The tiny ecclesiastical and urban élite which enjoyed the monopoly of written culture coexisted side by side with a multitude that clung to its images, rites and incantations. Two non-communicating worlds: the great doctrinal disputes of the universities did not filter down to the fountain or hill to which generations of peasant-women had come to worship some saint with healing powers.

The Reformation, on the other hand, confronted everyone, even the ignorant, with the problem of doctrine. Everybody was henceforth obliged to turn to the Book in place of oral tradition; each individual's relationship with God ceased to be taken for granted, or undergone passively: it now became a citizenship to which access was gained through reading, just at the very moment when the advent of printing was democratizing the book. Luther made necessary what Gutenberg had made possible: by placing the Scriptures at the centre of Christian eschatology, the Reformation turned a technical invention into a spiritual obligation. It replaced the immense body of learned, and inaccessible, commentaries on the Scriptures by the text of the Word of God itself, now made available to the faithful in their own language. It constituted both a response to a new demand and a formidable proliferation of this demand. The modern world, which was the fruit of this meeting, henceforward belonged body and soul to the written word. Europe had conquered a new memory, in which all its sons must share.

In the Middle Ages, even scholastic learning was highly oral; from the 16th century onwards, even popular culture was dominated by the written word. The *lectiones* and the *disputationes* in the great universities of the 13th and 14th centuries were exercises in memory and debating skill, taking the form of endlessly logical commentaries on texts that everybody knew by heart. The advent of the printed book, on the other hand, placed every

Christian in an individual relationship with the Book, without the compulsory mediation of age-old commentary. Learning to read ceased to be something one did by listening; now it could be done solely by reading. Everything thus conspired to place a fundamental value on this elementary aptitude: the demands of salvation, man's new relationship with learning, and the proliferation of teaching materials, all inevitably made school a social investment.

The historical literature of the 1870s on the subject of the school either masks or underestimates this crucial turning point in the 15th and 16th centuries, and it does so for two obvious reasons. This Catholic historiography was concerned to demonstrate the continuity of the Church's involvement in education from the Middle Ages to the 18th century; it was hostile to the Reformation, which it saw as the first figure in the secularization of sacred culture and the school. It was in these terms, for example, that the Abbé Allain commented on Luther's famous letter of 1524 to the towns of Germany bidding them maintain compulsory schools:[5] 'Luther invented compulsory secular education, for which discovery let us have no qualms about leaving him the credit, for we believe it to be evil, and fertile in bad results only' (p. 43). But, independently of this hostility to the Reformation on principle, what the Catholic tradition shares above all with the historiography of this period is ignorance of the cultural consequences of Protestantism: the super-eminence of written culture, the interiorization of a new rationality, the importance of education as the twin road to salvation and success. To this extent, even if the Reformation was not the sole root-cause of this transformation, it was assuredly its most spectacular symptom: a revolution in society even more than in the Church.

The proof lies in the speed with which the Catholic Church adapted itself to the changed socio-cultural conditions: in order to take up the Protestant challenge, it was obliged to wage battle on ground of the adversary's choosing, it was forced to fight the Reformation with the weapons of the Reformation. That was part of the significance of the Council of Trent, its external, sociological determination. What was at stake was not merely the need to restore order in the Church or to bring the *clercs* back under control, to establish discipline in the institution anew; the task of the Council was to adjust that great living body, the Catholic Church, to the new age of sacred communion through the written word.

Thus, the elementary school was added to the pastoral work of the parish priest. It was implied in the Decrees issued by the XXIIIrd Session of the Council on 15 July 1563.[6] Shortly afterwards, the XXIVth Session provided for the holding of periodic provincial synods, and for regular visits of dioceses by their bishops – two institutions that were to play a major role in the proliferation and progress of schools.

Another book could be written about the history of these schools from the material generated by the activity of these institutions. But the flow of educational directives and recommendations also contained in this material attests that the Church of France, faithful to the spirit of Trent, developed nothing short of an ideology of the school in the course of the 17th and 18th centuries, in which the school was regarded as inseparable from Christian education. The obsession with the school is ever-present, constantly reiterated by the diocesan authorities, in the vast printed body of synodal statutes and ordinances produced in the last two centuries of the *Ancien Régime*.[7] In 1680, Henri Arnauld, Bishop of Angers, warned negligent priests that,

> as we must consider the Church as a School of which Jesus Christ is the Master, and in which he himself deigned to teach little children, the commonest people and the poorest, they are obliged to imitate Him, since they are His Ministers, and since He shall one day demand that they account very precisely for the time that they have neglected to devote to an occupation so important.[8]

But although the Church was expected to become a school, it could not be so in a merely analogous sense, since Jesus Christ was its Master; it was also in the modern sense of the institution, according to which the child is like 'soft wax' in which evil lodges more easily than good, and to which the school is the instrument for the normalization of early acquisitions *par excellence*. Any number of texts echo the Bishop of Amiens, in the middle of the 16th century, in holding 'that there is nothing more advantageous to Christian piety, or more powerful in destroying it, then the first dye and instruction that is given to small children, whose affections being once turned towards good or evil, they acquire such strong habits that it is practically beyond human power to turn them aside'.[9]

Thus the school had a Christian and moral finality, founded on the early inculcation of discipline. It lay at the crossroads of two different ways of thought: the first, religious in nature, picked up the Protestant gauntlet and sought to root orthodox Catholic piety in instruction. The second was instrumental, being concerned to normalize social behaviour through the internalizing of a practical morality with a few simple rules: respect for one's parents, obedience towards one's masters, purity of thought and deed, turning away from evil. In all the normative writings produced by the Catholic Church during the last two centuries of the *Ancien Régime* one senses something like an anticipation of Victorian morality: a kind of socialized, secularized Christianity, reduced to the control of morality and behaviour. Groethuysen detected it in the sermons of the priests in the age of the Enlightenment;[10] but in fact its origins go back earlier, to the battle between Protestantism and the Counter-Reformation, and to the

Tridentine Church's desire for social control. Moreover, the separation – at least in theory – of the catechism, which continued to be given by
the priest in the church, from the school, which became a separate
institution with its own building and its own master, illustrates these first
stirrings of the secularization of schooling.

The job of the priest was to maintain his control over the school – and in
the first place to ensure that there was one. The schoolmaster stood at his
side, subordinate to him yet distinct, a central figure in the village. This
pair – whose break-up was frequently the central feature of local political
history in the 19th century – was conceived by the Counter-Reformation
Church as necessary to the 'policing' of the village, i.e. to its entry into
civilization. The lengthy passages devoted to the duties of the schoolmaster, to the precautions to be taken in selecting him and confirming him in his
post, made him the secular counterpart of the priest: pious, temperate,
chaste, studious, above personal quarrels, even refusing invitations: his
highly-regulated life was meant to serve as a model not only to children but
to the entire community.[11] From the very beginning, the Church invested
him with a kind of village 'leadership', under the eye of the priest. He was
much more than simply the man that taught people to read and write,
doubtless because reading and writing were far more than just that: they
were symbolic of the individual's accession to the religious and civil
community, the posthumous success of defeated Protestantism.

In the case of the State, on the other hand, we find nothing comparable to
what happened in the Church as regards elementary education: rather a
movement in the opposite direction. This had little importance in reality,
since the school was dependent on the Church. What is highly interesting,
though, for the history of ideas, is that there grew up around the absolutist
State an educational counter-ideology that was hostile to the efforts of the
Church.

A few dates to help pin down the facts: the monarchy was only interested
in the village schools from the standpoint of heresy. It intervened on
several occasions during the 16th century and early in the 17th in order to
back the Catholic Church and to confirm its educational prerogatives.[12] It
did so once again at the turn of the 17th and 18th centuries, at the time of
the Revocation of the Edict of Nantes. Article 7 of the Edict of Revocation
prohibited Protestant schools. This gave the signal for an educational
counter-offensive in which the State committed itself heavily alongside the
Church through a series of texts: an edict in 1695, which reasserted the
sovereignty of the Church over schools; the royal declarations of 13
December 1698 and 14 May 1724 laying down parental obligations to send
children to school and authorizing the raising of a special tax where
difficulties were encountered in financing schools. In all these documents,
beneath the apparent universality of the obligation, Protestant families

were in fact the real targets. Once again, more than a century after Trent, it was the Protestant threat that stirred the French monarchy into action, sealing its pact with the Church. By virtue of the fiscal provisions contained in the 1698 Declaration, the royal *intendant* was henceforth competent to intervene in matters of educational policy. As the highest authority over the towns and rural communities, he was often called on to arbitrate and settle disputes.

But this is where the paradox lies: on the whole, the 18th-century *intendant* was less concerned with elementary education than were the bishop or the parish priest. If indeed he did come to intervene increasingly in this sphere, it was more as a logical consequence of his administrative rôle and the extension of his powers than of any passion for progress. This was because the concept of elementary schooling for all rarely formed part of his modernizing vision, whereas it was central to the preoccupations of the Church.

Looked at in terms of one of the most widespread 19th-century republican beliefs, the tables are completely turned where ideas are concerned. Far from being a monolithic, obscurantist force, interested solely in keeping the population ignorant, the Catholic Church was the driving force behind a major effort in favour of elementary education; it invented and dignified the figure of the 'maître d'école', the ancestor of the teacher. Such forces hostile to education for the masses as there were under the *Ancien Régime* were generally recruited from the administrative and political élites of the kingdom, and from the Enlightenment intelligentsia. As regards the elementary school, Church and State were responding to a common factor, the Protestant challenge. But the Church derived a doctrine and a popular education policy from it, whereas the State only acted intermittently: in order to extirpate heresy, or else impelled by its genius for financial control.

The reason for this is that as early as the beginning of the 17th century a different line of advice was being offered to the king; we find this advice over the signatures of clerical deputies to the Estates[13] in 1614, and again in Richelieu's *Political Testament*:[14] namely that the unchecked spread of instruction was liable to wreck farming and trade, the true sources of the State's wealth, by attracting people to chicanery and a life of letters. This mercantilist view was accompanied moreover by threats of possible social danger, warnings that were to die hard: education would create more expectations of promotion than could possibly be fulfilled by the number of non-manual jobs available; hence the risk of wide-scale social parasitism, dangerous to the stability of a society in which an individual's prospects in life were ascribed to him at birth. The argument was initially aimed at the grammar schools, but it was quickly broadened to include the elementary schools: a report on the 'reasons and the means for the Reformation of the universities', dated 1667,[15] actually proposed to remedy the presumed inflation of the number of children in the grammar schools and universities by deliberately impoverishing the elementary curriculum, since it was this that furnished the entire system with raw material:

> In these schools, only reading, writing, reckoning and counting would be taught, and at the same time we would oblige those who are of low birth and unsuited for the sciences to learn crafts, and we would even exclude from writing those whom Providence has caused to be born in the condition of tillers of the earth, who should be taught to read only, unless there be remarked in them the dawnings of light and understanding for science for which they would merit exemption from the common rule.

This spectre of upward mobility for the labouring classes brought about by the school, a menace to society, haunted a good many *intendants* and not a few *'subdélégués'* all down the 18th century.[16] This is because this commonplace of mercantilist thought, which dominated the administration, was buttressed by Parisian 'philosophie',[17] which often contained a kind of contempt for the peasantry, even when, as with Rousseau, this contempt fed off the exaltation of 'rustic simplicity'.[18] It was as if the cultural promotion and emancipation of the towns during the 18th century had entailed a heavy dose of meritocratic investment, the resulting benefits of which were now being jealously withheld from the countrypeople, who were expected to remain unchanged, so that the rest of society could rise. The ideology was cogent enough in practice at least, if not in principle, since the urban élites were less concerned to cut the nobility down to its own level than to achieve its life-style – hence, if society was to keep going, it was essential that competition among the talents be restricted to just a few of these talents. Also, the development of philosophical anticlericalism was tending to cast a cloud of suspicion over the educational proselytizing of the Church, along with the type of education it could be expected to dispense.

This sheds light on the paradoxical conflict between the administrators and 'enlightened' philosophers on the one hand, and a supposedly obscurantist Church on the other. The former clung to a mercantilist doctrine, whose educational malthusianism they exacerbated with their élitist and secular vision of upward social mobility: society could only rise upon the vast 'savagery' of peasant labour. The Church, on the other hand, had not yet exhausted the momentum of the Counter-Reformation, whose doctrinal intransigence it gradually tempered with the teaching of a practical morality founded on the mood of the age; it was all the easier in its own mind about propagating reading and writing in that it saw these not as opening up social barriers, but quite simply as paving the way to clean living and godliness.

This opposition, slightly caricatured in our analysis, does not imply that – especially towards the end of the 18th century – there were no priests hostile to education or administrators favourable to it: R. Chartier and D. Julia cite the long complaint of the parish priest, François-Léon Réguis, against the evils of popular education, well-spring of idleness, vice and irreligion: 'All that are simplest (in our parishes), most innocent and most Christian, can neither read nor write.'[19] But this clerical tribute to ignorance, which foreshadows one of the directions taken by Catholic thought after the Revolution, is but an early warning of the supposed dangers threatening old beliefs as a consequence of the modernizing policies of the Church. It neither modified its significance nor its course.

It was the impact of the Revolution which, here as in so many other spheres, transformed people's thinking and crystallized the debate over the school in the terms to which we are accustomed – and which now seem older to us than they actually are.

But, independently of this debate about the school, which grew up between Church and State, and in cultivated society, in the 18th century, one perceives that the major force behind the development of schools was constituted by the urban and rural communities. It was from the depths of this traditional society that the demand for schools arose; it was here that value was attached to instruction, it was this section of society that was responsible for the exceptionally strong commitment to schooling, so long thought characteristic of the 19th century but in fact earlier in date.

It all began in the towns, in the 16th and 17th centuries, with the great movement of scholastic foundations, with the proliferation of pious legacies for the maintenance of schools, with the efforts of the Protestant communities, and subsequently of the societies of the militant Counter-Reformation, to develop education of the people, and for the poorest sections of society in particular. There was, throughout the *Grand Siècle*, a whole stratum of respectable urban bourgeoisie for which the individual concern for salvation was inseparable from the exercise of charity, of which schools were a favourite beneficiary: depending on the place and the people involved, this stratum ran, for example, the Company of the Holy Sacrament, or the Company of the Aa,[20] which were frequently centres of scholastic militantism. It was from this social milieu that Jean-Baptiste de la Salle came, founder of the 'Ecoles chrétiennes', scion of an urban oligarchy combining the land, trade and public office, connected with the local Church and university, with a Jansenist flavour. The urban Catholicism of the 17th century, with all its nuances, and even as a consequence of its rich variety and its quarrels, thus constituted the matrix of school development.

How this urban and patrician model 'filtered down' into rural society; at what speed, depending on the place and the people in question, it was internalized by parish communities: this problem is crucial to the history of the integration of traditional French society, in which Tocqueville saw a powerful mechanism at work, creating uniformity in minds and behavioural patterns.[21] He attributed the ambiguous merit of it to the levelling action of the monarchy; but the general spread throughout the population of a single model of sociability and culture must have been at least as decisive.

Three orders of observation may perhaps shed light on this general hypothesis. The first of these concerns chronology: as we have seen, urban literacy showed signs of running out of steam in the 18th century,[22] after brilliant performances in the 16th and 17th centuries; the 18th century, on the contrary, was the century of rural literacy *par excellence*, at least in the northern half of France. Could we not ascribe this to a slow shift of educational demand in time, from the relatively saturated towns to the countryside, aware of its backwardness – this shift being accelerated by the special efforts of the Church and the State at the time of the Revocation?

Second type of observation: we should not allow the school, in the history of literacy, to become a kind of skeleton key that explains nothing because it explains everything. In the long term, it is nothing but a product of the demand for education. Of course, a school founded purely out of individual generosity or at a bishop's initiative may produce a temporary improvement in education in a parish; but its chances of enduring and of generating far-reaching changes in cultural patterns are slim, unless it is not only accepted but actively wanted by the inhabitants. As with the history of literacy, that of the school is rooted in this primary phenomenon, which conditions the other two.

Lastly, a simultaneously religious and educational purpose such as that of the French Counter-Reformation urban élites, in the 17th century, cannot penetrate a society without being profoundly transformed itself. Between the initial project of restoring to each child the means of his salvation, and that of merely giving him access to an urban model of socialization, the school probably ceased to be a mystique to become a policy. And we should like to know just what the French, down the ages, from one social stratum to another, expected of it, and how changes in demand altered educational supply.

We do have a source which, while not permitting exact measurement of this demand, does at least permit an assessment: the contracts between schoolmasters and local communities. In the *Ancien Régime* village, the schoolmaster had to be approved by the ecclesiastical authorities (primarily by the parish priest), but he was generally chosen by the inhabitants of the village or their representatives. The only exceptions were schools founded under the terms of a bequest, endowed with a regular income, the master being appointed by the founder or his executors. All others, the more numerous, were financed by the local community in one way or another, and the master was chosen either by the assembly of the inhabitants (northern France), or by the municipal council or the consuls (southern France). This local democracy is attested by the great many leases, signed before the *notaire* by the elected master and the community, enumerating the rights and duties of each party. These help to explain how the school, which had initially emanated from the will of the Church, on occasion out of *raison d'Etat*, finally became a collective need of the French people.

The phenomenon appeared very early on in north-eastern France, which Maggiolo's figures placed so far ahead of the rest of the country. For example, in Lorraine, for which Mme de Rohan-Chabot's invaluable monograph[23] demonstrates the very early (late 16th – early 17th centuries) emergence of Counter-Reformation schools in the countryside, and even the growth of elementary education for girls; here, the inhabitants intervened actively as early as the 16th century in the choice of school *regents*, which proves that the demand for schools pre-existed the supply. In this duchy, where seigneurial tutelage over the village was weak, and where the ducal authority kept a tight rein on ecclesiastical jurisdiction, it was up to the community assemblies to hire *regents* and to set the terms of the 'treaty' and its subsequent renewal. They paid the schoolmaster's annual stipend, as specified in writing, out of their own resources, out of the tithe or by raising a special tax – as authorized by the royal texts of 1698 and 1724. The same procedure operated in the neighbouring Franche-Comté, for which numerous 'school *recteur* contracts', between the 16th and 18th centuries, have been published in the second volume of L. Borne's study.[24]

A systematic analysis of these contracts could serve as the basis for a detailed study of demand for elementary education under the *Ancien Régime*, and of the chronological continuity or discontinuity of rural schools. But this is, and is likely to remain, beyond our reach at the present time, owing to the fact that many of these deeds were simply private agreements and are difficult, or even impossible, to find. But the material already published, especially in the late 19th-century monographs, leaves no doubt as to the existence of this desire for instruction as early as the 17th century in a great many rural communities, if not earlier.

In places where this desire did not exist, or existed to a lesser degree, it was denounced by the ecclesiastical authorities: this happened for example on the occasion of episcopal visits by the bishops of La Rochelle, studied by L. Perouas.[25] A good many priests told their 'reforming' bishop, Jacques Raoul, at the end of the 17th century, that their parishioners were indifferent to the idea of instruction for their children, or else lacked the means to provide it. Which could boil down to two identical – the one frank, the other insinuating – manners of rejecting the school; the latter, though, hints at an uneasy conscience, except in cases where the parish really was too poor.

Through these examples we may perceive the outlines of a chronology and a geography of educational demand. Rural communities in Lorraine and Franche-Comté became involved in popular education as early as the 16th century, possibly even before, whereas those in Poitou and the Aunis were still reticent at the end of the 17th. So the 'supply' of education made available by the Counter-Reformation Church fell on ground of very unequal fertility. In Lorraine, it encountered such favourable conditions that it very quickly ceased to be associated with the Protestant challenge and became genuinely integrated into local life, whereas the bishops of La Rochelle had to wait until the crisis of the Revocation, and for the backing of the *intendant*, before it became possible to impose the school – from above, as a means of rooting out heresy – upon Catholic communities unmoved by the religious or civil prestige attached to instruction. The Reformation – Counter-Reformation dialectic accounts for many of the features of Church and State schooling policy; it explains, for example, why the supply of schools was more plentiful in Languedoc than in Brittany at the time of the Revocation;[26] but obviously many other factors help to account for differences in the way parishes and areas reacted to the efforts of the authorities. The school was a product of local societies before becoming a factor in their transformation.

Nor is it the sole evidence, or the only vector, of this desire for education. The region with the highest rate of literacy in the kingdom at the end of the 17th century was that of the high Alpine valleys of the Vallouise, the Briançonnais, the Queyras and Barcelonnette:[27] over two-thirds of the men signed their names in the middle of Louis XIV's reign – and yet, not a school is mentioned in the reports of the *Intendance* or in the bishops' visits! This is because these upland valleys were exporters of schoolteachers, who hired out their learning by the year to the villages of the plains; instruction was spread via non-institutionalized circuits, by itinerant teachers who spent their winters in their native region, during the long winter evenings around the family hearth. This extreme case should be taken as an additional reason for not fetishizing the rôle of the school, and for not subordinating the whole of the history of literacy to it. Even in places where it did exist, complete with master, house and contract; even in places where its presence in numbers did coincide with the spread of education; the fact remains that it was a social phenomenon before being a technical instrument: the image of an order to be created, or of prestige to be won – a symbol first, a function second – that is the secret of its ancient roots in French history.

## Patchwork school

However, we cannot ignore its function. What was the school like under the *Ancien Régime*?

Nothing predictable or standardized, as it is today. On the contrary, we find a mosaic of super-imposed, rival, complementary institutions and practices; a protean compromise between local desires, constant Church policy, occasional State imperatives; in a word, the existence and the history of the school was all the more fluid for having so long been neglected by the great unifying laws of the monarchy. It all began in the towns, with the 'little schools' of the Middle Ages, placed under the control of the cathedral church; these survived into the modern age, but only as the oldest stratum of a network that had since proliferated. The 17th century was probably the period richest in educational schemes, with scholarly foundations abounding; a profusion of congregations specializing in free elementary education for the poor, boys and girls; the active support of the Counter-Reformation societies; the 'rush' of well-born girls into socially-organized charitable work; the general mobilization of pedagogic imagination and piety, from the Ursulines to the Daughters of Charity, and from Charles Fourier to Jean-Baptiste de la Salle. But this network of teaching congregations, which covered all the towns in the kingdom at the end of the 17th century, and which was still vigorous in the next, did not prevent the growth of private schools (fee-paying), nor did it dispense with the need for master-writers, who were constantly complaining about all these rivals threatening their privileges. Nothing better illustrates the abundance of urban educational initiatives, and the democratized prestige of rapid writing, than this archaic fury of these depositees of traditional calligraphy. They started countless lawsuits against the private masters or against the Brothers of the 'Ecoles chrétiennes',[28] but even when they won, their battle was in fact lost before they entered the courts: for it was precisely against them, the guardians of an oligarchic art, that townspeople were equipping themselves with the instruments of mass education. Under the *Ancien Régime*, democracy developed along lines that were to appear incomprehensible to the following century, blinded by the Revolutionary heritage. But upstream or downstream of the Revolution, even if the institutions changed, the society at work was still the same, deploying all its resources to permit everybody to accede to the privileges of the few.

The countryside followed the example of the towns with, as we have seen, the same actors: the Church, the State and the communities. Here too, this resulted in an extremely diversified network of scholastic institutions, a sort of declension of the urban models, minus the master-writers. The central image is that of the parish school, run by a master hired by the community, with the priest's approval and the bishop's blessing or, in the 18th century, that of the *intendant*. The school might be financed out of the income from a foundation, or else paid for by the community, either by a 'croît de taille' (increase in the rates) as authorized by the 1698 royal document, or out of village revenues, out of a municipal tax, or out of rates levied at vestry meetings, or again out of 'droits d'ecolage' (schooling fees) paid by the parents, in cash or in kind: any permutation of these types of financing was possible, moreover. The 'foundation' schools, of which there were many in the 17th century, when the motives of the possessing classes were charitable, were not always free and not always open to all children. But at least they were run on a sounder footing, having been written into somebody's will, and being able therefore to count on a relatively independent income. The other factor vital to the quality of the parish school was the ability of the master. This varied greatly, depending on the existence and the density of the Counter-Reformation teaching congregations, which were a breeding ground of educational progress. Mme de Rohan-Chabot has traced this history for Lorraine, which was marked by the educational work of Pierre Fourier for boys, and the Vatelottes for girls.[29] In regions such as Brittany, where the Counter-Reformation did not manage to penetrate local society, or only managed to do so belatedly, on the other hand, the supply of schoolmasters was small, unsteady and mediocre. Where it did exist, the school was still, at the end of the 18th century, a kind of vague social practice, barely distinguishable from the rest of everyday life in the community, such as Emile Souvestre described in his *Souvenirs*:

> The *magister* in our day, housed and paid at the expense of the village, town clerk, usually a propertied man and an officer in the rural guard, can only give a very misleading idea of what a schoolmaster was like in Brittany before the Revolution. The latter did not give his lessons in a common building; the teacher went from house to house to seek out his pupils. Sometimes he would find them in a stable, whittling a stick, or else in the meadow, cutting the new-grown grass; sometimes they would be in the fields, watching their flocks. Together they would sit down on the spot, on the stone trough or on a grassy bank; the books were opened and the lesson began. If the lunch hour struck, the *magister* went and took his place at the men's table; whereas the tailor, his sworn enemy, ate later, at the women's table. His whole day was employed in this way, going from one isolated farm to the next, and on the last Sunday in each month, the schoolmaster received five sous from each family.[30]

In addition to these schoolmasters without a school, the backward regions of France also had schools without schoolmasters: even at the

beginning of the 19th century, in the Limousin, the young Martin
Nadaud's father entrusted him to a peasant who lived nearby, and who
played the part to earn a little extra money.[31] This should convey some idea
of just how different the old school could be from what we now know by
this name, since the passing of the great educational laws of the 19th
century. From the July Monarchy and the Guizot Act onwards, the process
of unification of the schools, which was actively encouraged by the State,
must have played an important part in the gradual equalization of literacy
scores, through the alignment of educational establishments on the most
highly-developed model. Before this, however, during a period of two or
three centuries, the unevenness and the diversity of these institutions more
likely served to perpetuate or perhaps even to aggravate local and regional
differences. Between the *regent* in eastern France, who often, in addition to
reading, writing and arithmetic, taught some rudiments of Latin, and the
itinerant *magister* of Lower-Brittany, barely more than a casual farm-
labourer, the schools of rural France were as diverse as its customs and its
geography.

This is why it is not possible to describe their curricula or programmes in
simple terms: the village schools of the past never had the institutional
resources to devise them. But they did sometimes seek to do so, and at least
they did share a common body of educational conceptions capable of being
analyzed: one has merely to review, from that vast body of literature on
schooling, which has been one of Europe's obsessions since the 16th
century, the portion directly written by educational practitioners. Forget
Erasmus, Montaigne, Rousseau and the rest: the history of ideas about
school is not the history of the school. Let us rather turn to all those
bishops, priests, important citizens and village *magisters* who were the
earliest educational activists, the unlikely ancestors of the 19th-century
republicans. What did they have to say? What were they looking for?

Keep the children apart, boys on one side, girls on the other. This was
more than a rule: it was an obsession. This recommendation recurs
constantly in synodal statutes, based on the highest authorities, the
councils of the Church and the kings of France. This document by the
Bishop of La Rochelle (1711) speaks for all its fellows: 'In accordance with
the decrees of the Councils, the Letters of Louis XIII of happy memory, the
Declarations of Kings and Decisions of the Higher Courts, we forbid
school Masters to teach girls with boys, and to receive them in the same
School, for whatever reason; and school Mistresses to teach boys with
girls.'[32] The corollary of this rule is: 'Schools for boys shall be run by men
only; and girls shall be instructed in a separate School by some girls or
pious women.' One last precaution: 'We likewise forbid all School Masters
to undertake, for any reason whatever, to teach any girl in private houses
without our permission; such permission we shall grant only with the

utmost difficulty, and on condition that the Father or Mother, or some
other person of acknowledged virtue, be present when the Master gives his
instruction.' Childhood was thus subjected to the same meticulous
prohibitions that governed the collective life of religious communities; it
had to be preserved not only from any occasion for, but even from any
possible thought of, sexual impurity.

The fact that these rules were reiterated in 17th- and 18th-century
synodal statutes probably means that they were not always observed: the
Bishop of Amiens' 'letter' 'concerning the schools of the diocese', in 1641,[33]
notes for example 'disorders in the small schools, by the communication of
girls and boys, who were indiscriminately admitted'. The prelate had
learned this from reports of 'certain persons of piety and zeal for the glory
of God', and one can easily imagine the bigoted clan in the village or small
town reporting failure to respect the canon instructions of the Church to
the bishop. We cannot measure the extent of this disobedience, nor its
evolution. Restif de La Bretonne, writing of his Burgundy 'schools', in the
1740s, at Sacy and later at Joux,[34] never fails to include the girls in the
class – but from what episode in his life were women ever absent?

That mixed education did sometimes occur in the schools of the
kingdom, in spite of the rule, we may deduce with greater certainty from the
cases of spectacular progress in female literacy even where there was no
increase in the number of schools for girls, as in 18th-century Normandy.[35]
But the normative aspect of this prohibition of mixed schools is perhaps
more important, from our point of view, than its practical application.
Pedagogically speaking, it reflects different conceptions of education for
boys and for girls: often, synodal regulations and episcopal ordinances
insist on reading alone for girls, accompanied by household training
centered on sewing. And the stress placed on the teaching of Christian
virtues, a horror of sins, 'especially of those incompatible with purity'
(Châlons, 1693), is still more heavily emphasized in the duties of
schoolmistresses than in those of masters. This is because the young girl, or
woman, is a mother: the image of Mary dominated this idealization, which
was inseparable from any kind of education. As the 'regulations for the
conduct of schoolmistresses in the diocese of Châlons' point out, the aim
was not to get pupils to make a vow of chastity. Of course not: but it was to
turn them into mothers, their innocence preserved.

What was being prohibited through this approach to women was
pleasure, not instruction. We probably ought to resist the anachronistic
temptation to view the Church of that time as the champion of female
intellectual inferiority. On the contrary, documents show very early on just
to what extent it churned out recommendations regarding the education of
girls, which it held as important as that of boys, and just how concerned it
was to establish communities of organized and competent school *regents*

and mistresses wherever it could. Such inequality as is perceptible (without ever being clearly formulated) in school curricula has nothing to do with the condemnation of women's intellectual powers, but betrays rather an implacable determination to keep the sexes apart. Women paid heavily for this by being shut up within the family universe, but they also gained thereby a pre-eminent dignity, which contributed to a certain symbolic equalization of social rôles. The secularization of society in the 19th century deteriorated their status.

Unmixed schooling and the segregation of women until marriage, moreover, were merely two aspects of the Counter-Reformation Church's tireless educational work to eliminate sexual matters from the world of culture. In the same compilations of diocesan instructions, regulations and ordinances laying down the law for schools, we also find a large number of passages on how children should be put to bed, or rather should not be put to bed together, or with a relative of the opposite sex, or with servant-women; on the prohibition of village festivities, which provided an opportunity for sin; on the master's dress, his hairstyle; on the morality of the Christian family, etc. Even within the boys' school, which one might have presumed to be out of temptation's way, handbooks from the age of classicism are rife with recommendations against promiscuity: boys asking to leave the classroom to relieve themselves should only be allowed to do so one at a time, so that there should never be two outside at any given moment.[36] The school was called upon to raise up the walls of its regulations and the internal censorship of language about the body, number-one suspect. The innocence of childhood was not a gift of nature, rather it was a struggle against sin, to be won by the acquisition of self-discipline. School was the place for this.

So vast an ambition implied not merely the agreement, but the collaboration of families. Through the children, the master was also educating the parents, who were expected to apply in the home the rules prescribed at school. The most revealing document in this respect, as in many others, is *l'Escole paroissiale* (the Parish School), a long handbook written by a Paris priest in the middle of the 17th century, distilling the fruit of 18 years' teaching experience.[37] 'The scope of the book', writes Yves Poutet, 'its sales, the number of editions it went into, and the fact that it was adopted by a great many diocesan officials in charge of mass education, all justify our regarding it as an ideal witness to normal practice around the period 1650–1685.' Well, the schoolmaster in the *Escole paroissiale*, whose job it is to inculcate Christian virtues, and notably chastity, also regulates family life: he must forbid children

> ever to urinate in front of others, ever to lie down with their sister, or even with their father or mother, except in extreme necessity; in

which case he shall ask parents to place them at the foot of the bed, in such a way that they shall never espy, nor even imagine what is permitted to married couples only: that if parents refused to separate their children from the servant-women at bedtime, or from their sisters or themselves, then the Master shall, after having remonstrated with them and explained the importance of the matter, expel them without further ado.

Similarly, parents were to comply with the rules of admission to the school and with the examinations conducted by the master. *L'Escole paroissiale* visibly mistrusts parents' over-indulgence of their offspring: 'All too often they are so besotted with their children that, acquiescing too freely in their disordered whims (not knowing what they ask), they thus change them easily from School to School, so that they learn nothing.' Readers of Ariès will find the observations particularly forward, and the middle of the 17th century remarkably modern. It seems as if the conjugal educational institution emerged at roughly the same time as the scholastic institution, and that they worked constantly to harmonize their rôles; the reason families invested in the school was that they had already invested in their children.

This school was moderately punitive. 16th-century documents carefully regulate the distribution of corporal punishment according to the type of misdemeanour and the character of the pupil, forbidding any gesture in anger on the part of the master, so that the justice of the punishment might be recognized by the culprit and his companions. In any case, all corporal punishment carried with it the risk of sensuality, which should lead masters to avoid over-reliance upon it. More than fear of the whip or the rod, the chief psychological mainspring of the elementary school was the same as for the Jesuit college: pride and emulation. The bad pupil was to be sent to the dunce's corner, dressed in rags, a broom in his hand and a dunce's cap on his head, 'to the jeering of schoolboys, braying like asses', while the good pupil was to change place and group in the class as he progressed, and might even be made an 'officer' of the school, i.e. assistant to the master in a whole series of extraordinarily hierarchized tasks. Here again, the aim was to get the children to internalize, as individual moral obligations, the rules governing class discipline, keeping to a timetable, and the periodic ranking of virtues and merits. As much as knowledge itself, the school taught self-control; it explicitly viewed itself, without the slightest misgiving, as the agent for the inculcation of values and proper conduct: the Counter-Reformation Church said this more clearly than did the Third Republic.

In addition to the catechism, which everybody was taught at least twice a week, the curriculum was divided into three distinct levels: reading, writing and arithmetic. In addition, in a 'régence Latine'[38] (as in the case of *l'Escole paroissiale*) or in the elementary classes of a grammar school, it also included the rudiments of Latin, in order to prepare boys for grammar school. For the ideal elementary school course was very unevenly taught from one place and one master to another. The synodal Statutes of the diocese of Angers, in 1680, complained that masters and mistresses did 'nothing but show (children) how to read', 'or if they do teach them something of the catechism, they do so in such a dry manner that it serves practically no purpose'.[39] And indeed there was an extreme diversity of standards in the elementary schools in France, prior to the introduction of uniform school legislation. But as far as the content of the teaching was concerned, this diversity always revolved around three stages which were regarded as successive: reading, writing and counting. There were masters and mistresses who taught nothing but reading, others who taught reading and writing, and yet others who added some arithmetic. This implied, seen from the other side of the barrier, that schoolchildren were liable to leave school with very different attainments, from stumbling reading to an all-round elementary education. Finally, even schools that covered the entire curriculum contained but a single class, in which all the children, of all ages and levels, were mixed together; the master taught them one by one; except for the catechism, he never took the whole class together. Even *l'Escole paroissiale*, otherwise so obsessed with putting everything and each person in its or his rightful place, only managed to distinguish the little children (as yet unable to read), from those who could read, from the 'writers', and from those writers who were taking their first steps in Latin, by assigning each group certain benches and certain tables in the schoolroom. The most general and widely-acknowledged rule in this school system – at once rigid and confused, crude yet refined – was the order of the subjects to be taught.

Reading, writing, counting. Each operation was long and difficult, and was always the prior condition for the next one. Let us take another look at our old handbook, which devotes its third part to 'what ought to be taught in the School, which is Science'. First, reading: but here, too, there are several stages to be gone through! The method of beginning by syllabizing each consonant with the aid of a vowel only began to spread, slowly, towards the end of the 17th century.[40] *L'Escole paroissiale* still starts with the learning of the letters of the alphabet, before putting them together to make syllables. The syllables were learned with the aid of a book printed in large characters, containing the Ave, the Pater, the Credo, the Confiteor and the Benedicte; when children began to spell out whole words, they turned to another book, containing the Magnificat, the Nunc Dimittis, the Salve Regina, the Seven Psalms, the litanies of the Saints. In other words, they learned to read initially in Latin. The author of our handbook makes no bones about the matter:

It is essential that in the first place, before being put to reading in French, children be capable of reading well in Latin, from all kinds of books; for this reading being the foundation of French, since it contains the same letters and syllables, if one were to show a child how to read in Latin and in French at the same time, he would give great trouble to the Master . . .

Thus Latin, as the matrix of the French language, is invested with a sort of pedagogic pre-eminence. Quite possibly it was no more foreign to many schoolchildren in the kingdom than French, enjoying as it did the advantage of being the language of worship and religious memorization. But the problems connected with differences in the pronunciation of syllables in the two languages must have slowed down the learning of French considerably. The test of a child's readiness to move on to the next stage was his ability to read a 'Civilité' (book of manners) fluently: while prayers belonged to Latin, good behaviour, 'Christian and polite', was read in French. With that accomplished, the child was ready to tackle writing.

We are inclined to forget, today, that for a long time writing was really a technical exercise, involving instruments, muscular gymnastics and a knack. Jean Meyer rightly reminds us[41] that although we now think of reading and writing as two elementary and simultaneous learning processes, they used to be culturally dissociated skills, and that historically speaking there were at least two types of written civilization, those governed by the scribe, in which writing was queen, and those of the literati, in which it was no more than manual labour. Like the rest of ancient Europe, France was in an ambiguous situation in this respect: the two kinds of skill were becoming so bound up with each other that only mastery of both of them, which was learnt in school, was regarded as defining education. But they continued to be carefully distinguished and ranked, like two unequally difficult, and perhaps unequally necessary, arts. Reading and writing rested upon the same knowledge, but the fact that writing was, in addition, a technique, entailed an extra difficulty. On another level, however, reading's original necessity – the ability to read the word of God – meant that it kept its claims to universality. It was an instrument of salvation, whereas writing ceased to be an art, to become a convenience. And if indeed it was more elementary, then it was so in both senses of the word: easier, undoubtedly, but also more fundamental. Let the poor, in fortune or in spirit, at least leave school able to read, and the Good Lord will take care of the rest. Writing, on the other hand, belonged to the 'civil' domain, as people then called it, that is to the 'civilization' of men, as people were to say in the 18th century.

What a business! George Sand gives a marvellous description[42] of the tortures her writing master, a certain Monsieur Loubens, inflicted on her in the early years of the 19th century in order to teach her to hold her body correctly: 'He had invented various instruments of constraint to force his pupils to hold their heads straight, the elbow free, three fingers held straight against the penholder, and the little finger stretched on the paper so as to support the *weight* of the hand.' To this ballet with the pen, which the *Ancien Régime* school had transmitted to the *magister* of Nohant, we have to add the choice and care of the equipment. *L'Escole paroissiale* goes on and on about tables, seats, pens, the penknives for sharpening them, ink, paper, ink-drying powder. Sharpening the quill was an art in itself, involving several pages of recommendations. When at last the pupil came to put pen to paper, according to the rules, he had to learn all about 'upstrokes' and 'downstrokes', common letters, capitals, and even the different styles of handwriting. He would write out a sample in the morning, and then recopy it in the afternoon, under the master's supervision. The material for these samples, adds the handbook, was to be taken from 'various forms of bill, bonds, farming leases, etc., lists of merchandise according to each one's vocation, so as to accustom them to the style of the practices and business of the century while learning to Write; which gives satisfaction to the parents'. What better way of indicating that, while reading belongs to the domain of religion and morality, writing is an apprenticeship in utility. It associated the school with a trade, i.e. upward mobility: which is what families were asking for.

Lastly, counting, once children had learnt to write well: 'since there are children of all conditions in a School, it is necessary to teach the sciences to give them a start in the world'. After all those years spent learning to read and write, few pupils remained – those of the best condition – for the rudiments of arithmetic, pompously dubbed 'the sciences'. First they learned to use counters, by hand, before going on to 'scribble with a pen', in other words, do their sums on paper.

Such was the full curriculum of these 'elementary schools'. But some of them, as was the case with our *Escole paroissiale*, also sought to teach their best pupils, before leaving, some elementary Latin so as to facilitate what was to become, but what in fact had already become, their 'passage en sixième' (moving up to the big school), so familiar to contemporary French children:

> Among the children in the small Schools, there are always a few in the towns, the small towns and the larger villages, who are capable and can advance in their studies. For this reason it is fitting that, wherever possible, school Masters that have studied should know a good method for teaching their Pupils the principles of the Greek and Latin languages and of making them capable of going to some good College (grammar school), into the 'sixième' (First) or

'cinquième' (Second) form, for the best of them, especially in Paris, where parents are often more careful and concerned to have them taught Latin than the Catechism and Instructions necessary for a true Christian.

Thus the chapter is devoted to the criteria (social and intellectual) for the selection of this happy few, and to a method of teaching basic Latin and Greek. The details are beyond the scope of our study. The most interesting observation, from our viewpoint, is the one that singles out children and schools in 'cities, small towns and large villages': it was unquestionably in these fairly large agglomerations that it became possible to sift out the most gifted, and the least poor, schoolboys, and to prepare them for grammar school. School standards were higher and family pressures greater in these urban and semi-urban communities.

So we must try to imagine, on the basis of this *Escole paroissiale*, a whole range of elementary schools, from the city downwards to the rural parish, with very different everyday practices, depending upon whether there was a schoolmaster, or whether the parish priest took his place; depending upon whether the pupils attended year-round, morning and afternoon (except Thursdays and Sundays), as required by the timetable of the Cantor of Paris, director of elementary schools, or whether the school was open only from All Saints' Day to Easter, as was more generally the case in the countryside, etc. This history of the school in ancient France remains to be written; what concerns us though is that, even where it is still unsure of itself, it everywhere reflects an identical need on the part of society, and the image of a uniform cultural progression on the part of the child.

A date, and an institution, do go some way towards modifying, not the need, but at least the image: I refer to the *Ecoles chrétiennes* (the Christian Schools) founded by Jean-Baptiste de la Salle at around the turn of the 17th and 18th centuries.[43] Maybe it was a sign of the times that the last great saint of the Century of Saints should have been a man identified with elementary schooling. The aim was utterly charitable: to instruct the poor townschildren, who had for too long been abandoned to the mediocre charity schools which depended for their survival on the goodwill of the Poor Offices, and which usually taught nothing but the most elementary reading. But the instrument to which this belated creation of the French Counter-Reformation gave birth was utterly modern: so modern that it partly betrayed its religious and charitable aims, often appearing to the Enlightenment bourgeoisie as the very model of the useful school. J. Quéniart[44] tells how, in the towns in the west of France, the Christian School Brothers were forced to add to their free schools (already swamped with the children of the respectable bourgeoisie) fee-paying boarding schools, in which they dispensed a proper technical education.

This alteration, or success, was no accident. On the contrary, they illustrate the pressure and the growth of social demand for a better-organized, more efficient, and socially useful school. Not that the advertized aims of the Christian Schools were any different from those laid down in earlier episcopal orders and synodal statutes: on the contrary, more than ever, Jean-Baptiste de la Salle was concerned for the glory of God and the salvation of the young souls entrusted to his Institute. But the access of poor children to reading and writing was already being thought of in terms of their insertion into society, and of the public welfare. As a result, the improvements in educational rationality embodied in the new schools offered families a better return on their investment: first of all by speeding up and improving the purely scholastic performance of boys, and secondly by turning out individuals with a better sense of work discipline and, as bourgeois wisdom was later to add, 'better equipped for life'. Thus it was that this trend towards the secularization of minds and institutions, which has forged contemporary France, occurred through the Church, and via the Church; ineluctably so because this trend was rooted in the very emergence of civil society.

The schools run by the Brothers ushered in the reign of the Norm.[45] This affected the education of the masters themselves, in the first place; henceforward they underwent a uniform training and were subject to the same rules in their everyday lives within the Institute's framework. This was to be a full-time job, no longer compatible with that of assistant to the parish priest as was the case with the country *magisters*, who rang the bells and cleaned out the church – sometimes even ministering to the dying. The Christian School Brother was fully occupied with his school and the children in his charge. As for his manner of teaching,

> uniformity must be the rule for all, without departing in any way from received practice; thus, the same signs are to be used in lessons, the same method for reading, writing and arithmetic; the same manner of coaching for the Catechism, of saying prayers and hearing them, of assembling and dismissing children; the Conduct of schools should be an unvarying rule for all. A Master shall find in his efforts to conform to it his hopes of success.

From now on, classes were held in silence, and the master expressed himself by sign language, without having to give orders to be obeyed and understood. The assiduity of the pupils was carefully recorded in an attendance register kept for each class; the system of punishments and rewards was meticulously elaborate; identical timetables were used in all the Institute's schools. On the subject of this thorough, quasi-military organization of every detail, and on the early inculcation of this consensus around abstract codes, Michel Foucault has recently written[46] brilliantly and perceptively, highlighting the operational optimization that underlay this manipulation by consent, which he calls discipline.

To this we should add the Brethren's innovations in the scholastic curriculum itself: while the order in which subjects were learned was preserved, and while pupils continued to occupy a single classroom, there were now eight orders of reading and ten distinct orders of writing, pupils being arranged in these according to their age and ability. The master addressed himself to each order in turn, as to assemblies in which every member has the same book and the same lesson: this was the beginning of the simultaneous class, and of the systematic grading of children in accordance with canonic criteria. Finally, French now took precedence over Latin in reading classes because it was the language of social utility: this was a sign that, for the founder of the Christian Schools, and probably without his being aware of it, reading itself had ceased to be the chief means of access to the word of God, becoming instead a focus of social intercourse and integration into profane society.

In pursuit of the same ideal, the Brethren introduced technical education in the 18th century: not in their ordinary schools, which had become victims of their own success, beset by a shortage of masters and money, but in boarding schools that broke with the fundamental rule of the Institute, in favour of the market-place. They were fee-paying and therefore not open to the poor. In Rouen, according to J. Quéniart,[47] 'each class in the Saint-Yon boarding school has at least two masters: the writing master who teaches French, and the mathematics master, called the figures master in the lower forms; but other Brothers teach accounting, drawing, music and modern languages. The boarders also have the use of workshops, where they may learn carpentry, metalworking or sculpture.' In Nantes, a major business centre, in addition to the basic subjects, French and arithmetic, emphasis was placed on double-entry book-keeping, foreign exchange problems, and elementary geometry.

Society thus slowly built up its school system in step with its own development. It look hold of a religious imperative and bent it to its own needs. The Counter-Reformation itself was a crucial stage in this misunderstood process in as much as it crystallized the doctrine of a mass catholicism rooted in the written word, and inasmuch as the two agents, in each village, of this vast rationalization of beliefs and behaviour – the priest and his assistant, the schoolmaster – were the Church's men. It would probably be a grave anachronism to try to dissociate the intellectual significance of the two functions too early on, in the name of a conflict born of the Revolution and the 19th century. Throughout the period of the *Ancien Régime*, during which they were associated and during which the master was subordinate to the priest, both tended gradually to secularize the morality they were teaching children and families. This drift probably did occur more rapidly in the school, but this is because, from the very beginning, the school had lain outside the realm of the sacred; because, conversely, it could not ignore the demand for educational and social profitability; and because it was therefore an ideal focus of the instrumental rationality which characterizes the government of men, and of the reforms occurring in that rationality. The Church was a modernizing force in the country; and the school was one of its tools. The family did the rest.

If one looks at that admirable account of a rural childhood, *Monsieur Nicolas*, set in the heart of Burgundy in the 18th century, how long ago the Counter-Reformation already seems! The Reverend Foudriat, brought up at Sainte-Barbe, was a disciple of Bayle, village philosopher in a dog-collar. In the school at Sacy, a reed-splitter, Jacques Bérault, taught the little children to read with the aid of a Latin spelling-book, according to the ancient custom, 'making the children precede most of the consonants with a vowel, which distorted them'. The two men in charge of educating the peasants of ancient France in Sacy were not the leading figures in the village, as far as Restif remembers. But then that was because his father filled all the rôles! It was he, Edmé Restif, procurator fiscal of the locality, who settled disputes in the community, and who meted out his patriarchal and beneficent justice to all. And what about his rôle in the family, then? He stood at the centre of everything, 'the priest of his hearth'. He would read the Bible to the assembled family, gathered round the table, giving an Old Testament interpretation of Catholicism, perhaps with slight Jansenist leanings.[48] In this background of well-to-do peasants, deeply imbued with the importance of the Book, the upbringing of children was not left to chance. Two of the sons by his first wife, Nicolas, who became parish priest at Courgis, and Thomas, schoolmaster, were both Jansenist teachers: his priest half-brother, when he was at the seminary, whipped the young Nicolas at each visit 'so as to wipe out original sin through pain'. But under the paterfamilias' auspices, the whole family was mobilized in the cause of Nicolas' schooling: he was first boarded out with his sister Anne, to enable him to attend the school at Vermenton, the nearby town; then he returned to Sacy, with master Jacques; finally, he was boarded out again, with another half-sister, Marianne, at Joux, where the school was run by Christophe Berthier, the son of Edmé Restif's own master! The fact is that the father, doubtless mindful of Nicolas' gifts – he had learnt to read French all by himself, with the aid of his school Latin, from a Latin-French psalter – had already decided that school would take his son to the city: 'I'll put my son in the city', he told Jacquot, the shepherd, 'because he's a good learner, and I think he's quick-witted.' This sentence, which the son puts in his father's mouth, already contains the ideology of the school in a nutshell: instruction, the city, becoming somebody in the world.

Historically then, literacy, and its institutional face, the school, constituted both a religious adventure and one of the forms of social modernization, at one and the same time. One is almost tempted to write: first a religious adventure, and subsequently a form of modernization, had things not been more complicated in reality; for the Reformation and the Counter-Reformation themselves, as early as the 15th and 16th centuries, grew out of the development of social communication and the relative democratization of written culture. There was constant interaction between the two processes, and it is not possible to isolate any central virtue to the advantage of one or the other. Simplifying matters somewhat, what we can say is that by substituting the necessity of knowledge of the word of God for the traditional sacred rites, the religious crisis of Christianity and the Reformation of the Church had enormously expanded the educational supply; but that this supply encountered an unevenly impatient social demand on the part of families and communities, arising out of a commitment – itself uneven – to the virtues of instruction.

It does indeed seem as if this unequal demand is what accounts for the uneven spread of schooling in France at the end of the *Ancien Régime*. The only general map available to us was compiled very late in the day, namely the one presented by Baron Dupin on the occasion of an address to the Conservatoire des arts et métiers de Paris, in November 1826, and later published in his book, *Forces productives et commerciales de la France*, the following year. As we shall see in the next chapter, Dupin's maps helped wrest the history of elementary education from the grip of religious controversy, while shifting it backwards in time in the direction of the factors that affected the social demand for education and schooling: soil fertility, farming patterns, population density, communications, types of agglomeration and types of habitat. Only a series of monographs, covered in our second volume, can provide us with a clear picture of the interplay of these factors. But the fact that very early on in French history they were working to differentiate community attitudes towards written culture and the school; the fact that they gradually transformed a necessity of salvation into an imperative of civilization, all this is already visible in Baron Dupin's map.

## Schooling for all: the dream of the Revolution

If further proof were needed of the proposition that the school, in French history, is bound up with the long maturing of social demand, independent of the evolution of institutions and régimes, then a look at the French Revolution should suffice.

The Revolution did not just transform legislation on the school; it invented an image for the school, it entrusted its own future to it: in so doing it turned it into the central issue of political and cultural conflict. But it changed nothing, or very little, in what actually went on in elementary schools; as we have seen earlier, except in a few local cases it did not modify literacy growth-rates. The reason for this was that, on either side of the Revolution, before and after, the same peasant society continued to exert its irresistible pressure in the direction of the same school, which was what it got, at the end of the day: the *magister* under the families' control, teaching a bit of catechism and lots of 'manners', the three Rs, and all with textbooks that had hardly altered. The school is a wonderful illustration of the central paradox of the Revolution: continuity and change.

As elsewhere, everything began with change: in ideas, and in reality. From the standpoint of ideas, the Revolution crystallized two major innovations destined for a long career. The first of these made instruction into a sort of demiurge, upon which the liberty of the people depended. On 4 November 1790, *La Feuille villageoise*, which combatted ignorance in the countryside, asked: 'Why did it take so long for the Rights of Man to become known?' Answer: 'Because people couldn't read, they weren't able to educate themselves, and so they were led astray by others.'[49] The school became the central figure of society's limitless powers over the happiness of the individual: under the *Ancien Régime* its job was to produce Christians, but under the new order it was expected to make men happy and free. The Revolution thereby multiplied the educational ambitions of the Church by infinity, by transforming their final purpose. As the melting-pot of new values, tirelessly pedagogic, its religion was school for everyone.

The corollary of this was to create a national school:[50] what serves the nation ought to be run by the nation. The idea had been going the rounds at the end of the 18th century; it had been caressed for example by the physiocrats, by Turgot, and by anti-Jesuit jurists such as La Chalotais, already reflecting the slow thrust of civil society towards control of an institution so important for the fashioning of the public mind. But it was the Revolution which gave it its explosive force, by democratizing it, by substituting the nation for the State, democracy for authority, and by surrounding the mission of the school with a halo of super-eminent dignity. The school was open to all and free, and it was controlled by the authorities: as early on as the Constituent Assembly, the Talleyrand Plan laid down these new principles underpinning a national system of education. They contained the seeds of what the 19th century was to call the controversy between non-confessionalism and educational freedom, which raged around a school that both sides had over-loaded with a missionary rôle. Access to written culture for all, which for two centuries had been a Church obligation, now became a Revolutionary imperative as well.

In 1789, the Constituent Assembly had transferred the Church's powers over the school to the administrative authorities; what changed the situation of the local schools, though, was far more their conflict with the

Church than this change in jurisdiction. First, there was the economic aspect: the suppression of the tithe and the subsequent sale of Church property, diminished or even cut off funds for many schools and their masters, and this at the very moment when communities, under the pressure of rising prices and uncertainty as to the future, were less and less inclined to pay. But it was the crisis that followed the civil constitution of the clergy which utterly transformed the educational situation, triggering the great conflict of values between the two schools, that of the constitutional priest and that of the refractory one: for, by virtue of the decree of 22 March 1791, schoolmasters, those traditional coadjutors to the village priest, were also obliged to take the oath. It was in that year that the two figures of the parish priest and the school *regent*, long complementary, began to drift apart in French history: the master who remained faithful to his priest, oath or no oath, did not break up the traditional village leadership; but one that asserted his loyalty to the Revolution while his priest – or his predecessor – refused to take the oath created a new character. He was already a schoolteacher.

The Revolution, in its Jacobin phase, responded to this threefold crisis affecting Church, *regents* and school with a vast programme of school legislation which cannot be dealt with in full in this book; besides, it has already been studied elsewhere.[51] It belongs more to the history of ideas about elementary education than to the history of that education itself, for this is an area where general reforms require much time and money, and the Convention's school laws, lacking both, were unable to fulfil their ambitions. These centralizing, unitarian documents, which sought to establish a single school, a single master, and the same textbooks for the entire country, are more interesting on account of the tendencies they reflect than for their success in expanding the country's school network. They made the school the focal point of republican and national integration, through the priority they gave to the French language, to the detriment of minority languages,[52] and by substituting the republican catechism for that of 'fanaticism'. But, at bottom, they were ever hesitant about the idea of a republican monopoly of schooling. Those old warhorses from the days of the Plaine[53] were shrewd enough to perceive the power of tradition and the resistance of families to the neo-spartan school of Lepeletier de Saint-Fargeau: 'In the system of compulsory universal education, you will have to contend with the pride of the aristocrats and the rich, who will long hold aloof from the national education system,' Thibaudeau warned,[54] 'you will have to contend with the powerful cry of nature in fathers and mothers of all classes; in vain you shall issue instructions: it will always be stronger than they.'

The Convention passed the law on the 'houses of equality' proposed by the martyr of Lyon, but they were to be optional. The same caution predominated some months later, in Frimaire Year II, when it passed the liberally-inspired Bouquier bill designed to unify the public and private systems under the wing of the Republic; every citizen was free to open a school, provided he could produce a certificate of good civic conduct. Finally, the 'Thermidorian' decrees of Brumaire Year III abolished the compulsory element and explicitly established educational freedom 'under the supervision of the constituted authorities'. In other words, re-volutionary legislation was constantly making concessions to a portion of the school system that lay outside its jurisdiction – because it had never ceased to belong to the local communities.

The Constitution of Year III made no bones about this abdication – or realism. In its Title X, it no longer set a minimum number of schools relative to the population, or per village; it abandoned the notion of republican pedagogy, confining itself to mentions of reading, writing, 'elementary arithmetic and the elements of morality'; lastly, the freedom to open schools was reiterated. Two months later (3 Brumaire Year IV), the last of the Revolution's great education bills was passed, weakening that of Brumaire Year III: the number of schools per canton could be reduced to a single one and teachers were no longer salaried employees of the Republic, which was now bound to supply them with premises and a garden only, but were to be paid by the parents. In addition to reading, writing and arithmetic, they were to teach 'the elements of republican morality': the epithet had been restored.

But the really important events were occurring out in the towns and villages: the clash, or rather the competition, between the two schools – the State school, which remained republican even when deprived of its Montagnard inspiration,[55] and the 'private' school, which was slightly ashamed of its true nature but was in reality traditional. At this juncture it is appropriate to attempt an initial assessment, and by chance the archives contain the requisite material.

As is quite common in French history, it was an administrative circular which gave rise to the providential document. While the Directory seems to have been relatively indifferent to the fate of schools during its early years, content to emend the fundamental decree of Brumaire, Year IV, adding two further laws in 1796 designed to facilitate the publication of new school textbooks, the situation changed entirely with 18 Fructidor 1797: the republican *coup d'état* led the victors to turn everything to account in their efforts to check the royalist revival. The school stood in the front rank of the forces to which they attributed especial importance in the fashioning of opinion, and they were accordingly anxious to win it over. Less than a month after the coup, on 12 Vendémiaire Year VI (3 October 1797), the Council of the Five Hundred, 'considering that the rising generation, which is the hope of the fatherland, can no longer be abandoned to precepts prejudicial to the State', approved a draft resolution placing all private educational institutions under the supervision of municipal authorities. On 27 Brumaire (17 November), the Directory issued an order obliging all citizens seeking 'a post of any kind whatever' to produce certificates proving that his children, if they had attained the appropriate age, attended State schools. A final order was issued on 17 Pluviôse Year VI (7 February 1798), enjoining municipal authorities to exercise strict control over private schools in general (even to the point of closing them down if the need arose), to write reports on visits and inspections, and to submit copies through the administrative channels.

But the executive had not waited upon the encouragement of the law before acting. As early as 20 Fructidor Year V, two days after the republican coup, the Minister of the Interior, François de Neufchateau, a great collector of social statistics, sent out a circular to all central departmental authorities requesting that they submit to him, at the earliest possible opportunity, a detailed and precise account of everything to do with establishments of public instruction that had either been opened or ought to have been. 'The Minister', the central authority of the Loir-et-Cher *département* commented,[56] 'wishes us to set about giving satisfactory answers to a series of questions, these answers being intended to assist him in presenting the Directory with a general picture of the progress of the Enlightenment, the state of knowledge and of social behaviour.' The questionnaire that was transmitted down from the departmental echelon to the cantons covered teaching methods, the 'spirit' – republican or otherwise – of the masters, as well as the numbers of State and private schools and their attendance figures. Then came another ministerial circular, dated 17 Prairial Year VI, this time in application of the order dated 17 Pluviôse: this was concerned in particular with counting the number of private scholastic institutions, with assessing their influence on public opinion, and with strengthening administrative control; the questionnaire, which was more 'repressive' than the previous one, was a useful adjunct. What is known as the Year VI Inquiry into primary education in fact consists of the municipal and cantonal replies, transmitted, summarized or simplified by the departmental authorities, to these two ministerial circulars. In some cases they were further enriched by a third series of cantonal reports, dating from a little later, stimulated by a new questionnaire sent out in Year VIII. Taken together, the documents available in departmental archives are too impressionistic, riddled with too many gaps, for statistical processing. In the near-unanimous picture recorded by these minor republican officials reporting to their *départements*, this body of material represents, in its own way, a plebiscite of the new French educational system.[57]

The Directory, again in its own fashion, summed up the main points in

the evidence on 3 Brumaire Year VII (24 October 1798), in its message to
the Council of the Five Hundred on the state of public instruction, which
contained a lucid appraisal of the impact of the régime upon the State
primary schools since the passage of the 3 Brumaire Year VI Act:

> The Government had barely begun to get down to work when it set
> about organizing primary schools throughout the Republic, in
> accordance with the law, this having been one of its first concerns;
> the departmental authorities were invited, urged by express
> circulars and by daily correspondence to tackle this important task
> with vigour. All promised to do so; but it can hardly be said that
> the execution was commensurate with the promises: for with the
> exception of very few *départements*, primary schools either do not
> exist, or else lead a very precarious existence. Most of the teachers
> languish in wretched need, and struggle in vain against the
> torrent of prejudice, fanaticism and superstition. While it cannot
> be said that everything remains to be done in this sphere,
> everything at least needs to be revived and to have life breathed
> into it.[58]

There follows an enumeration of the causes of 'this deplorable state of
affairs':

> The undermining of public morale and all our national institutions
> by the disorganizing fraction that was overthrown on 18
> Fructidor; the neglectfulness and ill-will shown by a great many
> departmental and municipal authorities which gave comfort to the
> schemes of the enemies of the laws and the Government; the lack
> of premises for the establishment of primary schools; the en-
> couragement given to anti-republican schools, and all kinds of
> persecutions directed against patriotic schoolteachers, the in-
> adequacy of the law in the face of these abuses; the prejudice of
> ignorance against the elementary textbooks decreed by the
> National Convention, and, more than anything else perhaps, the
> unfortunate condition of the masters, whose present means of
> existence were not assured, and who had no prospects for the
> future: such were the fatal principles which either stifled the
> primary schools at birth, or else hindered their success.

The diagnosis was detailed, respectful of the conclusions contained in the
cantonal and departmental reports compiled in Year VI, although as with
every central government, they were stretched a little for political purposes:
any republican ill-will on the part of local authorities is evidently not to be
found in the documents that have been preserved, since their purpose was,
on the contrary, to illustrate their zeal and their educational merits. But

even this discrepancy between the two analyses is of great value to us: the message of the Directory, obsessed with its crusade, lists the shortcomings of the government and the law; the local authorities, being closer to the population, are more concerned to highlight resistance encountered within society. This is what makes this whole period such an admirable historical vantage point, with the men in power, heirs to the Terror, still nurturing the revolutionary illusion of a discontinuity in time and the overriding nature of politics, at a time when civil society had already recaptured control over its own existence and reasserted the autonomy of its development, in the name of continuity. Torn between the two poles, local administrators in post-revolutionary France tempered the messianism of ideology with the realism of social observation.

At the centre of this observation, there arose a unanimous cry: the distress of the State school as compared with the competing private schools. Wherever one looked, the figures spoke for themselves. Whether the *département* or canton had a high rate of school attendance or a low one, the comparison between the two types of school was invariably greatly favourable to the latter. In Gers, where all the cantons replied,[59] there were 19 State schoolmasters or mistresses for the 53 cantons in the *département*! But inspections of private schools carried out in compliance with the order dated 17 Prairial Year VI yielded results for thirty cantons: 104 'private' masters or mistresses! In this educationally under-privileged *département*, that figure by no means implies a ratio of one teacher per village, but it does on the other hand amount to an infinitely denser network of schools than in the public sector – non-existent even in many cantonal administrative towns. In Charente,[60] where twenty-five cantons replied to the Year VI inquiry, the ratio was still of the order of ten to one: 99 private schools to 11 State ones. The signs point the same way for the more 'enlightened' areas of France, the north and the east. In thirteen cantons in Aisne,[61] there were 172 schools, of which only 23 were 'primary schools' (which, in the language of the time, meant State schools): in Bas-Rhin,[62] out of the ten cantons that listed all their schools (the others mentioned 'primary schools' only), the ratio is 138 to 23.

These data are not in themselves decisive, since they indicate only the number of teaching personnel and not pupil attendance figures. But they do give some idea of the density of the communal network, which in the case of State schools was very sparse: they mostly existed in the *chefs-lieux* of cantons, in keeping with the geometrical and economical cast of mind that had presided over the laws of Brumaire Years III and IV. The first of these had laid down a density of one primary school per 1,000 inhabitants (up to 2,000). The second spoke of establishing 'in each canton of the Republic, one or more primary schools, whose *arrondissements* shall be determined by the administration of each *département*'. A restrictive, or indolent, interpretation of the wording benefited the cantonal echelon, i.e. the large villages or towns, and not the countryside.

As it happens, the Year VI inquiry does yield, mostly for this echelon, some comparative data on State and private school attendance. But even this comparison, which by definition is favourable to the former since we are talking about large villages and towns, where they were best represented, reveals their restricted social compass. In Melun, for example, a town of over 5,000 inhabitants in the Year II, there were but two 'primary teachers', teaching only 130 children between the two of them, as against four 'private' schoolmasters and mistresses, plus two (mixed) boarding schools, totalling 226 pupils;[63] and even then one has to bear in mind the pupils receiving lessons in their own homes. Moreover, the administrators of Seine-et-Marne show signs of having minimized, doubtless in order to highlight the results of their republican zeal, the number of private institutions, and consequently the number of pupils attending them as well. At Auch, the *chef-lieu* of Gers, there was only one public schoolteacher in the Year VI, with 29 boys, compared with 7 private teachers handling 116 pupils, and 5 private schoolmistresses for 59 girls, plus a girls' boarding school with 21 boarders and 13 day-girls.[64] In Rouen, which had been in the forefront of primary education ever since the 17th century,[65] with high rates of male and female literacy,[66] a highly detailed document written in Nivôse, Year VI[67] cites nine 'primary' schools for boys, of which 'only five could be said to be run on a regular basis, three of which seemed to us to be full', and eight 'primary' schools for girls, of which 'we are forced to admit that, with the exception of that of Hilaire, attendance at the others is practically nil'. But there were on the other hand 55 private educational establishments, most of them boarding or semi-boarding schools, attended by 1,240 boys and girls. A later document, in reply to the Year VIII questionnaire for the city of Rouen,[68] mentions the 'very small number of pupils' being taught by State schoolmasters and mistresses, and the proliferation of private institutions: eleven private boys' schools and eight for girls, twenty-seven boarding schools and twenty-three semi-boarding schools for boys, thirteen and ten respectively for girls, plus 'a handful of establishments where reading only is taught to small children'. The situation of the State schools, which had not been particularly brilliant in Year VI, seems to have deteriorated less than two years later. The repercussions on public opinion, the report notes, were 'dangerous'.

The same archives[69] contain another document relating to Seine-Inférieure which sheds some light on this problem of public school attendance. This is a 'Record of pupils having frequented the primary schools of the *département* of Seine-Inférieure during the term of Vendémiaire Year VIII, drawn up by the departmental authorities and addressed to the Ministry of the Interior in Ventôse. For each of the seventy cantons (except for the six that did not send in reports) it records the names of the communes in which primary schools existed, the number of boys and girls frequenting them during the term in question (this first term in the school year was generally a 'good' one, as the country children were not required for work in the fields). However, while this document suggests a creditable geographical spread (possibly a little inflated for the good of the cause?) of State schools, present in roughly one commune in three, attendance figures for both boys and girls were mostly very low. Total school attendance for the *département* as a whole was 6,272 boys and 2,919 girls. Another source[70] indicates that in 1821 the entire male school-age population (children aged 5–15) came to around 60,000. This means that only a little more than 10 per cent of the male school-age population was attending the State school system (perhaps a bit more than that, if we take into account the six cantons that failed to send in educational reports in Year VIII); but in any case, the percentage is extremely low.

At the heart of this primary school crisis lay the dreadful conditions of the schoolteacher, which are unanimously stressed in all the administrative correspondence of the period. The Brumaire Year III Act had provided for accommodation, which was to include the schoolroom, since this was to be housed in the former presbytery, or, where this had already been sold off, in premises to be supplied by the municipality; the Act also provided the teacher with a salary, which was to be uniform throughout the Republic, albeit different according to sex: 1,200 livres for men, and 1,000 livres for women. The teacher was to be appointed by the government after selection and examination by an educational jury made up of three local family heads, and he (or she) was to be lodged in the presbytery; in the legislator's conception, he was to be the missionary of the new régime. A year later, in Brumaire Year IV, the new Act provided for a housing allowance only in the event of the Republic being incapable of providing him with premises and a garden; and even that was left to the discretion of the departmental administration. There was no more salary: the teacher henceforth lived off fees paid by the pupils, at a rate fixed by the *département*. The school was now State-run, but it remained at the mercy of the parents. The Directory lacked the means to match its policy.

Practically wherever one looked, the Republic's schoolteacher was a half-starved creature, always having trouble making ends meet for want of pupils. Give us more money! For many years this was to be the constant refrain of most local and departmental authorities. To a régime that failed to stick by its own principles, this refrain drove home the logic of the new system which turned the most insignificant country *magister* into an agent and spokesman of the State. The Seine-Inférieure dossier also contains a very fine report drafted by the administrators of the canton of Criel, near Dieppe.[71] According to the Year VIII 'Record' mentioned earlier, this was the worst canton in the *département*: there were only four schools between eighteen communes, with twenty-five pupils – girls and boys – in all; at Criel itself, a large village with a population of 1,360, the teacher had only six pupils, four boys and two girls. The cantonal authority held a lengthy discussion of this problem on 14 Brumaire Year VIII, in order to draft the gloomy educational report on Year VII which had been requested, and it wrote up lengthy minutes of the meeting.

The tone is set right from the start:

> 'The talents of our schoolteachers are doubtless unexceptional, but what right have we to expect more than this of citizens who lack for everything, who, while teaching the children of the commune, send their own out to beg a crust of bread from door to door? . . . What use is it to insist that their skills, their assiduity and their zeal for the advancement of their pupils will breed confidence, which will in turn produce a greater number of pupils, which will consequently increase the wages of the teachers? One might as well tell a day-labourer: if you are not dead of fatigue and hunger by tonight, you shall have a good supper to restore your strength.'

The entire argument flows from this:

> 'Citizen administrators, the questions you ask us as to the current state of education in our *arrondissement* [canton], compared with its state previously, might have suggested to us a workable plan, or at least a means of improving it; but one essential question is lacking, and this ought to have served as the basis for the entire edifice. Do the schoolteachers have bread? Six pupils at 75 centimes each per month gives the teacher 4.50 francs, and with that he has to feed a wife and children for thirty days. Could all the zeal in the world satisfy his real needs? Whereas 300 francs a year paid to each teacher by the government, together with his housing, together with the payment by the pupils, would nourish the master's zeal, encourage him; he would accept his condition because it would procure him an honest comfort . . . Some people have expressed the fear that there might be abuse of this comfort; but what then are rural administrations there for? Are they not the eyes through which you may see into all the parts of your jurisdiction? Has the word dismissal been banned by the republican régime? And, leaving aside the striking consideration that the 300-franc salary would make it possible to select teachers, the schoolmaster who lost his place through negligence or incompetence would surely make way for a more active, more zealous, better-educated one.'

Poor Criel schoolmaster! The authorities are almost prepared to excuse his having drunk one over the eight once in a while to drown his sorrows: no wages, no housing, no allowance, no pupils. The job cannot have aroused much envy, nor stimulated much competition! This kind of selection by default, through the wretchedness of the job, is rarely stated with such clarity in the administrative correspondence of the period; but all, or practically all, demand a salary for the teacher so as to establish his independence and his prestige.[72] In Year V, teachers received authorization to double as 'secrétaire de mairie' (town clerk), but this apparently did little to alter the situation and was never mentioned as making any useful impact. True, even if he did not have a salary, the teacher was sometimes at least housed, with classroom attached: in the former presbytery when this had not been sold off prior to the enactment of the educational laws. But while the French at this time continued to have no qualms about buying Church property that had been taken over by the State, they were often reluctant to let the schoolmaster install himself in the priest's former lodgings: what they accepted in the silence of self-interest, they opposed when it came to its symbolic confirmation. What attached them to the Revolution was the land, not hostility to the Church; one even suspects that they were all the more opposed to the Republic's usurpation of the presbytery for fear of guilt by involvement. Wherever one looks, administrative correspondence for Year VI stresses this question of the presbytery; there were even cases of teachers being driven out once they had taken possession of the premises, either by riot or by pressure of village opinion, following the return of the former priest:[73] the problem was particularly acute in the west, but it existed everywhere.[74]

Thus was society's revenge against the State clearly expressed. The municipal officials said so after their own fashion, in keeping with the constraints imposed upon them by considerations of career and revolutionary ideology, by pointing the finger at the 'fanaticism' of the population: this, together with the pinchpenny attitude of the State, was the great excuse for the mediocrity of results. In fact, the two reasons were linked. The Revolution had preserved an ideology, a government and an administration, of which now more than ever the new school was regarded as one of the pillars; but since having broken the Terror, it lacked the political muscle to impose this as the only school, supposing it had ever had that muscle: and what is more it had even abandoned the idea of favouring the State school by means of State funding. Consequently, as in the past, and perhaps even more so than in the past, when the *intendant*, and especially the bishop, had been generally active and recognized supervisory authorities, the school was back in the hands of the local community; but it was the school of the past.

For the private school, so heavily preponderant in post-Revolutionary

France, was the old *Ancien Régime* school. Patiently, painstakingly, it revived all its features, at the request of parents. It is true that in the more backward regions of France there were still *départements* where this parental demand seems to have remained weak, as in Gers for example,[75] where local officials blame the general lack of desire for education, which hampered the development of schools of whatever kind. But even where this desire did exist, it worked in favour of 'old customs': the old books, whose continued use parents more or less everywhere demanded; a minimum of scripture (catechism); and observance of Sunday and the traditional calendar in place of the republican 'décadi'[76] ceremonial, which the authorities sought to impose.

What distinguished the 'old customs' from the new, therefore, was in no way pedagogic or strictly scholastic. From this point of view, the revolutionary school was no different from the *Ancien Régime* one: it employed the same step-by-step curriculum, leading from reading to arithmetic, sometimes confining itself to reading only, or else providing an all-round education, depending on the qualities of the teacher; it had the same single-class structure, combining children of all ages and stages,[77] with same individual tuition within the class; it showed the same caution in extirpating traditional teaching in a foreign language, such as Flemish or German,[78] in spite of patriotic Jacobin instructions and the Brumaire Year III Act; it suffered the same uncertainties as to whether or not boys should be separated from girls – the Revolutionary school did maintain this separation in principle, but the rule was not uniformly observed. Despite repeated calls for improved teaching methods, it does indeed seem as if nothing had changed since the 'petites écoles'. What characterized the Republic's schools was simply that they were republican. Turning the Counter-Reformation's educational obsession with fashioning minds and behaviour against the Church, the Revolution fought to gain control of the school, not to transform it.

Hence the debate over textbooks, one of the focal points of the Year VI replies. Despite their efforts,[79] neither the Convention nor the Directory had managed to produce new textbooks for the Republic's schools; requests for them flowed in from all the local authorities, but none were forthcoming. Consequently the authorities had no option but to cite the materials that revealed the zeal of public schoolteachers: the Declaration of the Rights of Man, the Constitution of Year III, or one of those republican catechisms designed to popularize the principles of good civic conduct. Even in the private schools, when these were not overtly counter-revolutionary, it sometimes happened that the teacher, either out of tolerance or, more likely, as a precautionary measure, used one or another of the régime's credos alongside the old textbooks. Such was the case in Seine-Inférieure,[80] for example, or with the private teacher in Auch, in

Gers,[81] who gave his pupils the Rights of Man, the Constitution of Year III, the republican catechism, the Book of Imitations, the Bible, French grammar: so the teaching was republican, the local officials declared, while 'the Bible reassured parents'. But the reverse seems to have been infinitely more widespread: the State teacher, when not an extreme republican, and especially when all he wanted was just to survive, had to give plenty of room to traditional, i.e. religious, books. In Seine-et-Marne, the primary school teacher in the commune of Solers[82] lost pupils with the introduction of republican textbooks: he reacted by returning to the Catholic textbooks, explaining that 'having to earn his living, he had yielded to parental demand; that he sang at the lectern and played the serpent in church'. His neighbour, at Coubert, followed suit and placed 'books of the Catholic religion in the hands of some of his pupils'. The same was happening in Alsace, for the three religions, Catholic, Lutheran and Jewish.[83] In Charente,[84] primary schoolteachers mingled just the right ingredients of republican morality to avoid raising the hackles of the authorities and just the right amount of 'fanaticism' to retain their pupils. In short, the ideal republican schoolteacher needed to be 'right-thinking', but he also needed to know which way the wind was blowing; like a certain teacher in the canton of Gerzat, Puy-de-Dôme, whom the authorities quoted as an example, 'an ex-serviceman, discharged wounded, who has no truck with fanaticism', but who received his pupils with the schoolbooks given them by their parents.

The underlying, almost general characteristic, even in the towns, was this parental pressure in favour of the old school: it was this pressure which softened republican rigour, here and there, and which fuelled the victorious competition from the private sector. This reaction, which was the riposte of a very ancient Catholic society to the young republican messianism, was fundamentally of the same nature as the State's own educational vision, i.e. political and ideological. Circumstances did however supply it with two specifically pedagogic arguments in favour of private schools.

The first concerned the quality of the teaching. On the whole, the correspondence of Year VI, even though by definition it tended to avoid painting too 'black' a picture, was hardly brimming with admiration for the republican *magister*, who often emerges as a makeshift educator. The collapse of the *écoles normales* scheme (teacher training colleges) left the Republic with no means of training a generation of teachers of its own; the system of examination by education committees (which were far from universally effective) and appointment by the local authorities hardly presented sound professional guarantees. Career conditions and opportunities, as we have seen, were wretched, or precarious at best, and attracted few candidates. Lastly, the administration and the army at that time offered far more attractive career prospects to talented young republicans: the schoolmaster was assuredly not the pick of the rising strata. In the other camp, conversely, what an array of available skill and experience! The ex-*magister* of 1789, the ex-congregationist, the ex-nun, the former notable retired to his village ... For each married priest now teaching the republican catechism, as at Durtal,[85] how many monks and nuns that had remained faithful to the catechism *tout court*! At bottom, it was the personnel of the *Ancien Régime* school which was responsible for the proliferation of private schools, boarding schools and semi-boarding schools. Through its agency, society reworked its educational tissue, and fathers were able to give their sons the education they themselves had received.

The second technical advantage enjoyed by the private school was that it avoided the cantonal centralization that was a feature of the republican school system. The Acts of Brumaire Year III and IV did indeed give pride of place to the canton (the 'arrondissement' in Year VI terminology), although it did permit decentralization of schools in areas of particularly low population density. In fact, though, as the Year VI inquiry shows, the republican school was chiefly to be found in the *chef-lieu* of the canton. This of course gave rise to additional difficulties from the point of view of attendance, in a rural society accustomed to the decentralization of the *Ancien Régime*. This is borne out in the remarks made by the administrators of the District of Montivilliers, in Seine-Inférieure, who observed that 'the very great majority of communes that do not happen to be *arrondissement chefs-lieux* do not send their children to the primary schools':

> it is certain that the administration that is called upon to assemble a total of at least one thousand inhabitants within a radius of a half-league in order to form an *arrondissement*, will have measured its distances from church tower to church tower in calculating the population of each commune, without regard to hamlets lying outside these communes and, in certain places, cut off from them by rivers, and often by ravines and forests: obliged also to establish schools in the most central point of *arrondissements*, they [the administrations] have not been able to do the good they had hoped for and which was expected to come of the primary schools.

There follows an example:

> The muddy soil of Bray, criss-crossed in almost every direction by streams, makes communication difficult and dangerous for children throughout three-quarters of the year, cutting the scattered farms off from each other so that it is very difficult for youngsters

to assemble in order to make the journey to school together. And how can young children of both sexes be expected to journey three-quarters of a league and more to school each day, and as much to return home, along muddy, slippery paths which are almost constantly flooded in winter and in stormy weather? For all these reasons it is practically impossible for them to attend primary school during nine months in the year; they could do so, however, during the three summer months, but that is when children aged 8 to 12 are required for work in the fields.[86]

This long analysis probably accounts for one of the secrets of the private school's superiority in rural eyes: the private institutions were far more flexible, more decentralized, closer to the society upon which they depended for their existence. They were better adapted to the geographical and technical constraints of the environment, just as they satisfied more fully the parents' deep-seated desire for cultural continuity.

A good many revolutionary administrations were resigned to this failure of the State schools, and to society's response. Few followed the example of Maine-et-Loire[87] and called for closure of private schools, but then this was a region in which the clash between the Church and the Revolution had been particularly sharp. Generally, though, the diatribes against the 'fanaticism', real or potential, of private schools and their teachers, served to camouflage a more realistic assessment of the situation, which was accepted as inevitable. Plenty of *départements* could be cited in evidence of this. Let one, Charente, suffice: twenty-five rather tepidly republican cantonal administrations simply note the virtual non-existence of State schools, without further comment. At Segonzac, the nine schoolmasters and the three schoolmistresses of the Republic in Year III had, by Year VI, become private schoolteachers, 'owing to the nullity of their salary'.[88] They were all, moreover, former schoolmasters and mistresses from before 1789, plus one ex-priest. At Cognac, 'anybody who wanted to, taught, and did so as he pleased',[89] the education committee having disappeared for want of applicants to examine. At Jarnac, the schoolmaster and the mistress were both suspected of sympathy for the *Ancien Régime*, but the municipality rejected a proposal to close the school, 'owing to the state of penury'.[90] And then there was the 'parallel' school: in the canton of Aubeterre, 'there were no primary schools, but only worker or farmer citizens who taught children to read during the winter season'.[91] At Mavillon-Cauville, a group of 'honest citizens, for the most part farmers' ran the schools during winter, and they reckoned themselves better teachers than the primary school teacher at Ruffec, a former priest, whose pupils 'were barely able to read'.[92] This seasonal amateurism, in a region where educational demand seems to have been buoyant, provided the peasant-pedagogues with a small additional income, and the local children with a rudimentary education. Revived from the *Ancien Régime*, the system did not even arouse the ire of the new. It reflected the continuity of a demand that the Republic was incapable of either repressing or satisfying. Quietly, it handed the matter back to society, which restored its fabric: the old educational order had returned.

There was in the French Revolution, then, an ideology of the school and a history of the school, and the two were quite distinct. If we fail to make this distinction, we run the risk of trying to deduce the history of education under the Revolution from the Revolution's ideas about the school; republican educational historiography, which gained its credentials during this period of French history, has all too often thanked it by conceding this unwarranted privilege.[93]

In reality, we cannot isolate the French Revolution from a certain mythology of the school. It saw itself as the victory of the citizen over the humiliation of the subject, after centuries of oppression under the 'sacerdotal régime', as one of our Year VI republicans put it.[94] But the only prospect of this fragile victory's enduring lay in a constant growth in the number of citizens, especially among the younger generations: this was the task of the republican school. The more the Jacobin, and later Thermidorian, Revolution lost support in society at large, the more it placed its hopes in an educated, hence free, hence republican, man. This sequence, which both greatly simplified and confused a certain number of the philosophies of the age, substituted the school for society as depositee of the future of mankind: it was in this that the ideology of the Revolution innovated by comparison with the Enlightenment. For, after 1794, the Revolution had more or less lost its grip on society; but it did believe that it had the school well in hand.

In so doing, it was the heir – more so than it imagined – to the Church's conception of education. For the bishops and priests of the 17th – if not the 18th – century, the task of the school was to train good Catholics, if possible, with parents, if not, against them: for it was also, and above all, necessary to root out Protestantism. Indeed this notion of the child's soul as 'soft wax' can be brought in to justify any and every educational mould and even, paradoxically, the uprooting of any culture. Yet the *Ancien Régime* schools never took on that character of national priority which was later to be attributed to them by the revolutionary consciousness. The reason is that they were merely an instrument subordinate to the word of God, just as the schoolmaster was subordinate to the priest; also, because they only very occasionally and very briefly gave priority to the anti-Protestant struggle. They quickly became symbols of civilization and social mobility, approved by a broad consensus in each community.

The republican school, on the other hand, never ceased to be consubstantial with the Revolution, the triumph of the light of reason over ignorance. From the very outset it was in the thick of the battle against the Church; consequently the republicans regarded it as a crucial issue, since it was indivisibly the instrument whereby prejudice was to be extirpated and the home of the learning of liberty. As against the school of fanaticism and ignorance, it was the school of freedom and reason. Like the Revolution itself, in Year VI it was too close to its origins, and too controversial, to be divested of its metaphysical significance. In his confrontation with the priest, the schoolmaster of the Republic was far more than a pedagogue: he was the herald of the new age, mandated by the State.

Thus, it was by a misuse of words that the republican school could lay claim to embody what one document calls 'the law of tolerantism',[95] pleading its accessibility to 'citizens of all sects'. This religious neutrality concealed a defensive or a conquering secular messianism. At bottom, the French have never believed in the innocence of the school. By laying upon it a pre-eminent function, the Revolution placed it at the centre of the national political debate for over a century; the Church, being an old hand at the game, followed without the slightest effort.

But this was probably the Revolution's only major contribution to the history of the school. For the big difference, in this sphere, between Church and Revolution, was that although both had developed their own ideology of the school, the Church alone had an educational policy. The Revolution had neither the time nor the means to develop one. It was never able to follow through with its policy for a single national school for all future citizens, even though this was perfectly in line with its principles; it had always, even in 1793, and *a fortiori* in 1795, left the way clear for private schools: in other words to the local communities, which had been in the habit of choosing their own *regents* for centuries past. As a result, the battle for control of the institution, which the Republic unleashed each time it felt threatened – in 1793, in Vendémiaire Year III and in Fructidor Year VI – was a lost cause from the start. Without a national system, without a proper legal framework, without financial resources, how was one to control the teachers, how was one to control the textbooks? If one was going to leave the school to society, then one had to leave society judge of the matter. Whence the Republic's failure as reflected in the Year VI inquiry.

But there was another reason for this failure: despite its professions of faith, the Revolution had done nothing to change the elementary school. All it did was to propose a republican catechism in place of the Church catechism, not more rational and more efficient teaching methods: the only novelty it offered parents was aggression. Doubtless it further enhanced the prestige of education in the eyes of a society that was already deeply attached to it – but this was through its general message rather than its educational work. Perhaps it contributed to the encroachments of French at the expense of patois – but surely more so through the invention of a national political language than through the competence of its schoolteachers. Technically, the school of Year VI carried on from that of the *Ancien Régime.*

As with literacy, then, the history of elementary education does not seem to be subject to any revolutionary discontinuity. In confirming the kinship of the two histories, our analysis of this period suggests that they are governed by a shared logic, upon which régimes and governments are powerless to act: that of an unvarying social demand.

# 3

## SCHOOL, SOCIETY AND STATE

The inescapable conclusion to be drawn from these observations is that we ought to stop taking the Revolution as our point of reference. This is not an easy thing to do, for throughout the 19th century the French school, as it had emerged from the revolutionary decade, was time and again taken as a yardstick; and the picture drawn of it, from whatever standpoint, was black. With events still fresh in their minds, the prefects of the Consulate[1] were unsurprised when forced to reiterate the pessimism of the Directory commissioners:[2] 'non-existent', or 'practically non-existent', was how primary education appeared to them on the morrow of the Revolution. In mid-century, with the benefit of hindsight, and registering surprise as a positivist mind must at the gulf between revolutionary discourse on education and the facts, Guizot remarked acidly: 'Chimeras soared above ruins.'[3] As the last quarter of the century dawned, in the euphoria of the 4,712,000 pupils enrolled for the 1876–77 year, and to gain a better idea of the progress that had been accomplished, people looked back with commiseration to the 900,000 pupils recorded by the *Journal de l'Empire* in 1813.[4]

We do not intend to take this picture of unrelieved gloom, with its vanished schools, its ignorant schoolteachers and scarce pupils, so unvaryingly adopted as the point of departure for the history of education in the 19th century, at its face value; above all, we do not intend to turn it into a horror story of the birth of French education in the 19th century. There are two reasons for this.

The first has been made sufficiently clear in the previous chapter. By taking these 'ruins' as our starting point we would be enhancing the importance of the revolutionary episode and ascribing to those fleeting years undue influence over the long, and slow, life of the school. What actually happened was that the revolutionary parenthesis closed without making any major changes in the elementary school: it was rapidly re-established, and continued on its way in keeping with the pace and the models of the 18th century. As in the past, the Empire and the Restoration handed initiative back to society. The State refrained from intervening in either the organization, the running, or the growth of the elementary school. Depending on the time, the place and the régime, it left these tasks to the Church and the corporations of teachers, or to the national élites and local worthies, or again to private initiative and private industry. So there was no genuine State school to speak of; and genuine schoolteachers were no more numerous than in the past.

Also – and this hypothesis underpins all our research in this sphere – it is by no means certain that we may simply deduce educational standards from the density of the school network. The prefects themselves, at the close of the Revolution, were occasionally aware that these two factors were out of phase. The two accounts that follow appear to contradict one another. The prefect of Haute-Vienne notes that, at a time when the school as an institution was collapsing, the number of men able to read and write was on the increase. Acutely aware of what struck him as a contradiction, since 'it would seem . . . that the number of people able to read and write ought to have suffered a fall',[5] he felt able to affirm that 'this was an effect of the stimulus supplied by the events of 1793; each person made it a point of honour to be able to read the laws, to comment on the newspapers and to be in a position to take part in the public administration'. This meditation, of full-blooded Jacobin orthodoxy, on the acculturating benefits of political upheaval was, it should be remarked, published in 1808 'by order of His Majesty, the Emperor and King'. At that moment (1807), the prefect of Mont-Blanc, his curiosity aroused by a similar observation, preferred a rather more sober hypothesis: the reason why the number of people 'able to read and write' grew and multiplied in Tarentaise and Maurienne between 1789 and 1801 was due to purely local factors; this frontier region had served as a refuge for large numbers of clergymen, and these people had repaid the hospitality extended to them by giving instruction to the local children. What matters to us is less whether the root cause lay in clerical zeal or in civic ardour than the suggested possibility that education could increase at a time when the mesh of the school network was loosening, and that on either side of the revolutionary crisis we find the uninterrupted growth of an identical demand for education.

**The unchanging school**

The permanent nature of the school in the early decades of the 19th century is reflected, in the first place, as if by default, in the imprecision of the data (which manage to number neither the schools, nor the masters, nor the pupils); this itself being a reflection of the indifference with which the State regarded private initiative and the school in general. Consequently, right up to the end of the Restoration, little was known about the school in France.

Even so, there had been a number of attempts to gain a better understanding of the state of primary education under the Consulate and the Empire. In Floréal Year XI, Fourcroy, Director of Public Instruction, tried to get prefects to conduct a census of communes with schools and of those without.[6] In spite of a torrent of reminders, however, from prefect to sub-prefect, and from the latter to the mayors, the response to the request was poor. A new investigation was undertaken following the creation of the Imperial University in March 1809; despite the statistical ambitions of the project – 'to obtain the most exact and the fullest information possible'[7] – this too failed, since by February 1810, the Grand-Master of the University was turning to the *recteurs* and inspectors of each *académie* for information as to numbers of schoolteachers.

All through the Restoration we find similar cases of ministers, *recteurs* and inspectors of *académies* bombarding each other with requests for precise information, though harbouring no great expectations. The following letter, in which the *recteur* of Clermont-Ferrand asks the prefect of Haute-Loire to supply him with a list of primary schoolteachers in his *département*, is just one example among many:

> You would be rendering me an essential service; by this means I would emerge, I hope, from the chaos in which I still am from this point of view, and I would have a clear notion of the existence, the situation and the degree of importance of legally-constituted schools, while any clandestine school could then be notified to the appropriate authority for closure.[8]

If the results are so slender, especially in the face of this sharpening, spreading curiosity, it must be because the requests were encountering resistance somewhere. To all its recipients, the questionnaire seemed laden with potential danger. To the schoolmasters who, whether through ignorance, fear or negligence, had not taken the trouble to register themselves. To the municipalities, anxious lest the investigation prelude their dispossession: the civil administration was empowered to remove primary education from their control. Lastly to the priests, who were at that time battling to gain, or to regain, control of the school, who were concerned to obstruct attempts to satisfy a demand that did not emanate from themselves. In other words, everything conspired to put the investigatees in an uncooperative frame of mind. Many local councils refused to discuss the enquiry. Those that did respond were often confused by the enigmatic wording of the questions. Take for example the question in the 1817 enquiry, asking for the number of schoolteachers in the commune: but who exactly could claim to be a schoolteacher? There was much hesitation from one commune to the next as to the meaning of the word. The Mayor of Romagne, in Maine-et-Loire,[9] soberly replied that the commune possessed 'a schoolmistress'. But which schoolmistress? Could she have resembled the one the Mayor of La Renaudière (also Maine-et-Loire) took such pains to describe: 'Madame Lafitte, an ex-Benedictine nun, aged 72, who for the last 20 years has given free instruction in catechism, reading and writing to the young girls of the commune who wish to profit from her attention'? Or what about another commune in the same *département*, Cornillé, which possessed 'two women', who gave free lessons in reading, but whose Mayor thought that 'there was no schoolteacher'? There was 'no schoolteacher' at Gesté either, even though 'some people taught reading and writing to the children that interested them'. 'No schoolteacher', came the reply from Saint-Louis, unless, adds the Mayor, troubled by doubt, 'one means by schoolteacher the handful of poor people who go to some of the neighbouring homes or places they know to teach catechism and reading'. Another hesitant was the Mayor of Saint-Laurent-de-la-Plaine, who wrote: 'There is nobody that teaches regularly.' The Mayor of Bouchemaine, who avoids the term schoolteacher, replied that: 'the chapel priest, whenever he can, takes the time to teach whomever wishes to receive instruction'.

How, under the circumstances, was one to know who one was dealing with? In one locality, one has village schoolteachers, properly recognized, approved and qualified, who are mentioned; in another place, to these are added – although usually without specifically saying so – private teachers, clandestine or itinerant schoolteachers; in yet other places, to complete the picture, the respondent threw in all the men and women who in one capacity or another helped in teaching children to read, write or count. This imprecision, here at its peak, extended moreover to figures for pupils and schools. In most cases, the only registered pupils were boys; but replies that did mention 'mixed' schools included girls in their totals. As for schools recorded, these could in certain cases be State schools only, but it did sometimes happen that private and State schools were recorded indiscriminately. In short, there was nothing in this mish-mash to distinguish the replies from ones that could have been obtained in 1789.

What does seem to emerge, moreover, from the fragmented mirror held up to us by these partial data, is the picture of an elementary school whose underlying features remain identical on either side of the turn of the century. As before 1789, only a very small minority of children attended school; schools themselves were very unevenly spread throughout the country; and classes were only held very intermittently. The masters remained unchanged, and their methods too. The school continued to project an antiquated image of a social practice still unsure of itself.

This practice continued to affect a minority of school-age children only: in 1813, less than one million out of a total of four million; 1,400,000 in 1829. But it should be borne in mind that the pupils did not necessarily attend school regularly: summer was a closed season, from the point of view of school, in this still largely rural France. Attendance collapsed once Easter was past, and the trough lasted until All Saints Day; the school drew its sustenance from the winter slow-down in farmwork, and this was true even in the towns, on whose outskirts dwelt a whole mass of people whose lives were still governed by the rhythms of country activities. At the start of the 1830s, many summer school-attendance rates – even when calculated for an entire *département* – fell to one half, or even a third, of winter rates.

The map illustrating this under-attendance contains a surprise, for it by no means matches the one showing the poor spread of schooling (or again, the one showing the spread of literacy). The highest rates of summer attendance (calculated with reference to winter rates) were to be found in those regions where the general level of schooling was low – West Brittany, the northern borders of the Massif Central, Landes. It is as if, in these disgraced regions, the handful of parents who did make the material and moral sacrifices needed to send their children to school were even prepared to do without the additional labour of their children in the fields. The regions with high levels of schooling could afford to eschew so radical an attitude, especially in the north-eastern quarter of the country, where school-attendance rates were already often in excess of two-thirds; here, it seems, people felt able to make much more free with regularity of attendance.

This irregularity comes on top of, without affecting, the unevenness of the national spread of schools, which continued to be the chief characteristic of schooling. We may arrive at an approximate image of this for the Restoration period. The reports sent in by the *recteurs* in 1817 permit us, for example, to classify *académies* according to the density of their school network: not surprisingly, we find Rennes and Clermont at the bottom of the table (with one teacher for every 12 communes), with the *académies* of the Loire and the south-west (except for Pau), barely ahead. Among the north and north-eastern *académies*, at the top of the league, Strasbourg stands out from the rest with its 1,172 teachers for 1,045 communes. The figures supplied by Ambroise Rendu in his *Code universitaire*[10] present a comparable picture. The only overall map available, prepared by the Baron Dupin and published in a volume with the pre-marxist title: *Forces productives et commerciales de la France*,[11] once again presents an identical picture. More than a map of schools, this is really a map of school attendance. There was not much point in trying to produce a national map of such a bundle of disparate entities as the schools then were. Dupin, though unable to avoid this pitfall entirely, was nevertheless concerned to take account of the historical context and accordingly sought to weight his figures by calculating, *département* by *département*, the number of in-habitants required to send one male infant to school. This produced an extremely crude rate of school attendance, though doubtless less arbitrary than merely counting the number of schools.

But Dupin's national spread of schools, and Rendu's too, as well as that of the *recteurs*, was the same as Maggiolo's literate France. Here too there was a right side of the Saint-Malo – Geneva line: the north, with 13 million inhabitants sending 740,816 children to school, whereas in the south, 18 million inhabitants sent only 375,931 children. Where Dupin differs from Maggiolo is in the use he made of these figures: this Saint-Simonian *polytechnicien* was not narrowly corporatist in outlook; he was interested in what today we would call 'development', the expansion of public wealth. This conceptualization protected him – even though he was writing fifty years earlier than Maggiolo – from the narrowness of the simplistic sequence: school→literacy, within which Third Republic historiography was to become entrapped; for Dupin, school attendance was an indicator of development. His distribution of schools throughout France overlays that of the nation's industrial activity and its tax revenue. Literate France was indeed the same as school-attending France: but this was because – and one suspects at this point that the two variables conceal a third – the wealth of society served as the common soil for the two phenomena.

Dupin, moreover, in his 1826 address, added a remark that clearly illustrated the way his mind was working, but whose significance utterly escaped historians of the school at the end of the century: 'You will note, with me, that the most industrious part of the south also happens to be the part in which mass education is most developed.' From these oases of early schooling[12] within the otherwise educational desert of southern France, Dupin was already able to sketch a geography of the school and of development that diverged from the simple north – south cleavage. The true educationally-backward portion of France was 'the least industrious', the triangle which has the Atlantic as its base and the heart of the Massif Central as its apex. The first person to observe the under-development of western France and more generally the cultural inequality of regional communities, was Baron Dupin.

What are less easy to grasp, other than through individual accounts, are the inequalities introduced by irregularity of school attendance over time. Schools experienced the same fate as teachers: the latter might settle in a certain place, then move on a little, modify their plans and their activities, and the school would have to fit in with the whims of their personal fate. The well-known school career of Martin Nadaud, born in Creuse in 1815, gives a good illustration of the tenacity demanded of a child really determined to learn in the face of the intermittence of this whimsical early 19th-century school. Martin Nadaud's first teacher was the churchwarden of Pontarion, who took in children to teach them the alphabet and the rudiments of writing; 'from time to time', says Nadaud. The next year, Pontarion acquired a professional schoolteacher, and Nadaud enrolled in the new school. A year later, his excellent master had left Pontarion, 'gone to die somewhere around Chénérailles', and Pontarion's school withered from neglect by his replacement. Nadaud's mother then sent him off to Fournaux, 'to a man called Jeanjou', who 'agreed to teach me to read and write, along with four or five other children'. But this school too disappeared in turn, because Jeanjou took it into his head to withdraw in solitude to a house in the middle of the forest. By chance, a certain Dyprès, ex-officer of the Imperial Army, had recently opened one at Saint-Hilaire. Nadaud hastened to enroll, and then followed his master, who soon left Saint-Hilaire for Pontarion. When the master left Pontarion for Bourganeuf, the move spelt the end of Nadaud's school career.

Hundreds of kilometres away from the Marche, at the same moment, the son of the master of a Breton fishing vessel[13] was also paying the price of the educational institution's incompetence:

> Some time after our arrival in Mes Gourmelon (1818), we went to a school run by M. Préau, a customs officer at Laber . . . When M. Préau left for Camfront, we remained for some time without going to school, except for our Aunt Marie-Renée, who taught us to read. Later there came to Laber a drunkard by the name of Couër who taught us when he wasn't too plastered; he didn't stay long. Then came M. Grinet, who was an intelligent man for his time . . . When M. Grinet left for Kerhouan, that was the end of school. Finally, M. Toussaint came to Kermerrien. So we were back to school again. But this time we had to have books, paper and pens . . . Later, the would-be teacher or priest Toussaint came to Laber, and we ate at home while the children from Porspoder came to Laber. Then he too left, and that meant that the only school there was was with Aunt Marie-Renée, who taught us Latin.[14]

With so many ups and downs, and with an educational fabric as riddled with holes as that, it is easy to understand why the very notion of school remained as vague as it did early in the century. Of course, there were properly approved local schools, run by masters – lay or clerical – in possession (after 1816) of a diploma, authorized by the *recteur* with the prefect's approval, or by the bishop. But alongside these, what a mixed bag! There were schools that shifted around on the heels of the teachers that ran them, makeshift schools such as those run by the *Béates* (female religious order), private schools, clandestine ones, and so on.

The variety of clandestine elementary schools alone was infinite. In certain cases, all they were trying to do was to make up for a total absence of education. Such was the case, in 1817, with the clandestine 'schools' that existed in Maine-et-Loire: at Liré, 'several people' gave schooling; at Fontaine-Guérin, it was a 'young man', 'without qualifications', who received 15–20 sols per month from parents; at Beaucouzé, it was 'a poor woman', to whom each person gave what he could; while at Tillères we have the crudest school of all, elementary in every sense of the word – 'a person shows a few girls how to read'.[15] So, just what is a school? Certainly not a place, as is amply demonstrated in regions with scattered populations, where (illegal) itinerant teachers held classes in the children's homes, going from hamlet to hamlet.

Such was the case in the *département* of Eure, in the regions of the Forests of Conches and Breteuil.[16] In the Creuse, Guizot's inspector called them 'nomadic teachers'.[17] Sometimes this illegal practice was so widespread that prefects were obliged to act in an effort to regulate it: in 1821, for example, the prefect of Hautes-Alpes ordered itinerant teachers to carry with them 'a passbook, in which Mayors, Priests or Chapel priests of the places where they stop shall each in turn write a report on the conduct of these teachers, and on the manner in which they have discharged their duties in the course of their stay'.[18] But these 'itinerants' were mostly free-lance operators with no legal status, and they posed a serious threat to the regular teachers (who complained bitterly about them moreover). Such were the 'itinerants' in Côtes-du-Nord described by the *recteur* of Rennes in 1836:

> They go from hamlet to hamlet, from house to house, from field to field, and for 0.25 francs per month plus one meal per week they give individual lessons in catechism, reading, and less often writing, to children who cannot or who will not go to school. Always on the move, they are all over the place, but nowhere can one lay hands on them. However much trouble we go to, we have only managed to pin down 51 of them, but their numbers are much more considerable.[19]

Nor may we define the school in terms of duration. And it was an act, far more so than an activity. For there to be a school, all that was needed was a meeting between at least one pupil and a person who happened to 'faire école' (hold class). Are we not justified in reading the truth about the schools of that time into the energetic expressiveness of the term itself? 'Faire école' crops up time and again, obsessively, in the replies of these worthies when asked to make a census 'of schools'.

Clandestine schooling, moreover, was not necessarily an intermittent practice, an expedient appropriate solely to a situation of cultural poverty, but quite simply a kind of cut-price schooling by unqualified masters, competing with recognized masters by undercutting them. In 1840, the *Conseil général* of Nièvre[20] observed that many communes having approved schoolmasters also had clandestine elementary schools which admitted children for a pittance; and 'one finds a host of fathers and mothers who prefer poor teachers if they only have to pay 20 or 25 centimes a month per child'. The same 'clandestine' competition existed in Maine-et-Loire:[21] at Saint-Georges-sur-Loire, it cost one or two francs a month to send a child to the school run by an approved master, and only 50 centimes for the one run by the clandestine teacher.

One has only to take a closer look at what was going on in the regions to find clandestine schools all over the place, flourishing and diverse in form. One finds schools such as the one at Pradelles, in Haute-Loire, in 1823, which owed their existence to the predominance of the Church – and the impotence of the university – to the absolutism of a local councillor and to tax evasion.

At the request of a legal, qualified teacher, unable to obtain the approval of the mayor and parish priest, the *recteur* of Clermont drew the attention of the King's 'procureur' (attorney) to the existence at Pradelles of an illegal school, both primary and secondary. The teacher wrote:

> The Mayor said that if an application (for official authorization) was made for me, then it would have to be made for the other teachers in the town as well, which he will never do (he has let it be understood) for anybody, since he is sufficiently powerful to be able to govern the teachers without any need to encumber himself with the *académie*. For he has in fact authorized three gentlemen, none of which has ever been enrolled in any *académie*, to share in the running of the secondary school under cover of the primary, so that the secondary pupils studying the Latin language need not be obliged to pay the university fees payable to the *académie*.[22]

One comes across others, in Creuse,[23] making their living from the hostility of the priests towards the local school, which was supported by the mayor. This right-wing illegality was counterbalanced by a left-wing illegality: still in Creuse, at the end of 1846, a crowd of workers, according to the primary inspector, 'gathered during the winter, in different places, in the homes of unqualified people, in order to learn to read and write'. Summonses, police reports and even convictions were unable to put an end to these unauthorized schools before mid-century. In any case, most people were not even sure whether they were dealing with illegal clandestine schools or with plain private schools; and the mayors were often puzzled: when filling out the charts supplied by the *académie*, were they supposed to enter children attending schools not recognized in their communes as 'receiving no instruction'?

Even recognized – or merely tolerated – schools could appear in many different guises. At Chalon-sur-Saône,[24] we find schools, founded under the First Empire, teaching hordes of children for practically nothing; these establishments, humming loudly with the sound of stocking and bonnet looms, mainly taught these children to work thread, wool and cotton. Were they schools, or workrooms? One senses the same uncertainty when considering the famous *Béates* in Haute-Loire. Indeed, what were the *Béates*, for that matter? Peasant-women of modest origins, but who had been 'educated by the ladies of the "Instruction"'. 'Pious women', was how the Prefect of Haute-Loire defined them in 1816. But as they had no official status and were not bound by vows, they were not nuns, even though they were subject to the jurisdiction of the Congregation of the 'Soeurs de l'Instruction de Jésus'. As for the little establishments, the 'assemblées', which they ran, generally in their native parish: were these schools? Presumably so, since the children – girls in particular – received an elementary education there, based on the catechism and religious history, reading, and sometimes writing. But these too were workrooms, since the girls were taught lacemaking. And one could almost call them cultural centres as well, since adults went there in the evenings for prayers and meetings. The school population census returns in their own way reflect the ambiguity of the *Béates* and their 'assemblées'; sometimes they do and sometimes they do not include their pupils in the total number of children attending school. [25]

This archaic maze of school institutions did at least perform one function: before revealing to historians the French people's growing appetite for elementary education, it provided a concrete demonstration of the fact to the governing classes. What better proof could one want of the vitality of the need than the failure of this war on clandestine schools, in spite of the obstinacy of the authorities?

But, for the time being, the schoolmasters capable of satisfying this expanding demand were sufficient neither in quantity (in 1837, there were barely 60,000 schoolmasters and mistresses, permanent and temporary) nor above all in quality. We may ignore for the moment the tiny avant-garde of Brethren of the Ecoles Chrétiennes, of the Doctrine Chrétienne, and the alumni of the first teacher training colleges: the vast majority of those giving elementary instruction, even village teachers, even the qualified ones, were still part-time schoolteachers. They had to be, for the job rarely kept a man alive. Even the users understood this: a group of Angevin municipal councillors,[26] reporting in 1817 on a situation unchanged since the 18th century, summed matters up as follows: 'A primary schoolteacher could not live off the income from the fees charged to the parents; in general, teachers established in rural communes practise another profession, and their educational activities merely provide them with additional income.'

It will be recalled that the Convention, in its early days, had recommended that the State take over the remuneration of teachers; but, for want of resources, it had reverted to the school fee system on 16 Nivôse Year II.

The following is a breakdown of the income of the master in a commune in Aube (Souligny, canton of Bouilly).

In 1813: salary paid by the commune         90 francs
       right to cut firewood           25 francs
       wine donations           100 francs
       singing           90 francs
       school fees           150 francs

giving a total of 455 francs.

In 1860: salary paid by the commune       250 francs
       right to cut wood           15 francs
       clockwinding           30 francs
       town hall secretariat          50 francs
       school fees           250 francs

giving a total of 595 francs.[27]

The immediate upshot of these fees ('écolage') was that the master depended entirely on the numbers of children attending school. This meant that his activity was seasonal, since many rural schools were forced to close during the fine weather for lack of pupils: in Haute-Marne, Guizot's inspectors counted a lot of schools that only functioned five or seven months in the year – and these were proper schools, whose masters often boasted a secondary school certificate. If, during the closed season, the teacher failed to find better-paid work, either in town or one of the bigger villages – and he rarely did – he was obliged to seek additional employment in some other job. The fact of holding down two jobs seemed so obvious to Guizot's inspectors that they only bother to mention teachers that infringe the rule – such as the wretched teacher in Haute-Marne, 'exposed, in consequence, to the risk of dying of hunger'.[28] Without batting an eyelid, the inspectors reassure the reader that 'this type of work has no adverse effects on his work as schoolteacher' (discussing a weaver!), or again: 'trade not incompatible with the schoolteacher's estate' (talking about a barrel-maker!). In any case, the second job often had to accomodate itself to the demands of the former, and there was constant toing and froing between the two: the teacher at Genrupt, for instance, worked on his own vineyard in the summer, but returned to the commune each Sunday for church.

Much has been said about schoolteachers doubling as sacristans, cantors, bellringers, town clerks; and indeed additional sources of income were frequently sought in activities that were then connected with those of the schoolmaster, such as the sale of holy water which was still being carried on by schoolmasters in Eure in the 1830s.[29] But the jobs concerned were also much of the time autonomous trades, and this is worth stressing. In Hérault, where in 1833 more than a third of the schoolteachers occupied another job as well; Gérard Cholvy[30] has identified 35 barbers, 9 tobacconists,[31] 14 land-surveyors. In Creuse, we found one teacher in seven exercising another trade,[32] and close on one in five in Haute-Marne: three major occupations predominate here, namely farmers (winegrowers mainly), weavers and coopers.

One would have to be very canny to identify which, in this double life, was the real one, which was the teacher's principal 'status'. 'Cobbler, but he does little work in that capacity', notes one of Guizot's inspectors; 'mason, and works in summer according to his status', says another. The job of schoolteacher may not be a man's principal 'status'. Take the schoolmaster in Haute-Marne, a qualified one what is more: 'he claims to be a sort of farmer who, when summer is over, busies himself by teaching a dozen and a half children at most to read according to the old method'. This was because in fact there were also people who did not earn enough in their regular job, and who acted as schoolteacher in addition. The ranks of teachers thus swelled according to the state of the economy: 'Recently', wrote the *recteur* of Nîmes in 1812,[33] 'the shortage of work in the towns and the countryside has singularly multiplied the number of teachers. Those that are unable to earn a living in their ordinary job become teachers as a last resort; the number of them rises daily.' In 1815, in a single canton of Gironde, ten teachers had taken up this profession 'to supplement their means of existence; they are "spelling teachers"; among them are an ex-seaman, an ex-barrelmaker, an ex-sales-clerk, an ex-customs employee'.[34]

Teaching was thus seen as a stand-by job, but also as a last resort. There were two reasons for this. Firstly, because in the countryside the profession attracted those that were too weak or too sickly to be able to exercise a manual trade. 'He is impotent and cannot stand upright: the only suitable employment for him is teaching': thus was stated the motivation – completely negative – of the teacher at Poison-les-Grancey.[35] Secondly, after the passage of the Gouvion-Saint-Cyr Act (1818), opting for the teaching profession qualified one for exemption from military service, provided one undertook a ten-year engagement; it meant doing away with the nagging fear of turning up the 'unlucky number' on recruiting day. This reason often carried the day: Erckmann-Chatrian's assistant-master, after running through several different factors – the poverty of his family, his four brothers and sister, the high cost of living and his hard-hearted employer – finally explains what drove him to choose this profession: 'Since those entering the teaching profession were to be exempted from military service, I resolved to become a schoolmaster.'[36]

The incompetence of these schoolmasters is a commonplace. But from 1816 onwards, they were required, in principle, to produce a 'certificate of competence'. This examination, which they passed before the *inspecteur d'Académie*, or a jury appointed by him, was arranged in a hierarchy of classes: when one 'was sufficiently proficient at reading, writing and counting to be able to give lessons', one qualified for the 3rd Class; with a little spelling, calligraphy and sums, one had a good chance of obtaining a 2nd Class; grammar, arithmetic, geography and measurement permitted one to pass through the narrow portals to the 1st Class.[37]

The demands were modest enough, and yet at the time of Guizot's inquiry, many teachers were still practising with no certificate whatever: almost 13% in Creuse. At that time, the rudimentary 3rd Class encompassed the majority of teachers. So much so that in many *départements* the proportion of under-qualified (no certificate or 3rd Class only) often approached, and sometimes even exceeded, the 80% mark, as in Hérault (79%) or Creuse (81%). Even in the heart of educated France, in Haute-Marne or Côte d'Or,[38] over half the teachers lacked proper qualifications (52%). This ought to mitigate our surprise at some of the letters received from applicants for teaching posts. Here is one, for example, coupled with a request for a 3rd Class certificate (which was delivered to the author shortly afterwards, moreover):

> I, the undersigned, René Narcisse Oreau, ex-serviceman born at Baugé on 16 May 1793, beg the *recteur* to so be Kind as to having the Goodness to have Me appointed teacher in the commune of juigné sur Loire wheir My wife is schoolmistress; I beg him to having the Kineness towards a Good Soldier heving several wunds and Know pension signed at juigné sur Loire on 14 July 1831.[39]

With teachers like that, can we wonder at the failure to establish one of the few pedagogic innovations to emerge from the Revolution, namely the 'nouveau calcul', the new denomination of weights and measures, which schoolteachers were being asked to teach? Not very successfully: thirty years after the Revolution, administrative circulars were still reiterating the necessity of this change.

The fact is, the inertia of the early 19th-century school lay in its curriculum and teaching methods too. Children still learned to read before learning to write, and the two processes remained utterly distinct. Doubts on this score will be dissipated by looking up the scale – still the 18th-century one – of monthly school fees. 'Reading', 'reading and writing', 'reading, writing and sums (or counting)': the nomenclature and the rates may vary from region to region, but the steps in elementary education remain unchanged, and their discontinuity is crudely reflected in the scale of tariffs. In certain cases this could be very simple, such as the scale established by the municipal council of Bidart, in Basses-Pyrénées, for the whole of the first half of the 19th century: '50 centimes for children to read only and a bit of spelling; 75 centimes for those that are to read and write; 1 franc to read, write and do sums';[40] it could become a lot more complicated than that, depending on whether one sub-divided these three categories or not, and on whether one offered parents a more detailed 'menu'. Either way, these subtleties notwithstanding, the grading remained the same. At Jouy, in Eure-et-Loir, the school rules stipulated that:

|  | *francs* |
|---|---|
| those that read the alphabet, with a loaf, shall pay | 0.35 |
| those that bring no loaf shall pay | 0.70 |
| those that read in French, that bring a loaf | 0.40 |
| those that bring no loaf | 0.75 |
| those that read in the Psalter, Life of Jesus Christ, Civilité (book of manners), Devoir du Chrétien, who bring a loaf | 0.45 |
| those that bring no loaf | 0.80 |
| writers that bring a loaf | 0.80 |
| those that bring no loaf | 1.25 |
| those that shall do arithmetic and writing, and that bring a loaf | 1.00 |
| those that bring no loaf | 1.50 |

each fee being payable every month.[41]

The strict separation of learning processes[42] therefore governed the separation of classes and, in single classes, of divisions. The masters regarded it as financially equitable and pedagogically reasonable: the Brethren of the Ecoles Chrétiennes, who had been in the forefront of educational innovation in the 18th century, still continued to specialize their reading and writing classes strictly, and each succeeding edition of the *Conduite des Ecoles chrétiennes* (conduct of the Christian schools) emphasized the necessity for pupils to be able to read fluently in French and Latin before going on to learn to write. In answer to scattered criticism of this hierarchy of subjects, the Brethren, in 1828, added a note justifying their attitude: 'It is essential not to put children to writing until they begin to read passably, otherwise there is the risk that they shall never be able to do so. For when they are writing, not only do they have less time to apply themselves to reading, but also most of the time they lose all taste for it, as our experience has shown'. Meanwhile, J.-M. de Lamennais' Fréres de l'Instruction chrétienne at Ploermel, so innovative in other spheres, reproduced this pedagogic organization exactly: the friar in charge of the little ones handled 'alphabet and catechism', the director 'writing and counting'; not until 1868 was this division of responsibilities altered.

However, the benefits of the method were far from unanimously recognized. In 1836, the *inspecteur* for Morbihan deplored the fate of beginners in these narrowly specialized divisions; for these unfortunate children there was no lesson in writing or arithmetic, none of those 'little stories designed to fashion the heart or the intelligence', just the boredom of being 'tied to their benches for three hours, their eyes riveted to tables of letters they do not yet know'; and he notes that he had informed M. de Lamennais of the 'inconvenience and slowness of this manner of teaching'.

Ten years later, the *Journal d'éducation* reproduced this picture of childhood misery[43] and expressed astonishment that the 'brothers persist in believing, against all the evidence, that the teaching of writing is incompatible with that of reading'.

But were things any different with the lay teachers? In their immense majority (leaving aside the handful of pioneers graduating from the first teacher training colleges) they and all schoolmistresses, lay or 'congregational', split reading and writing into two separate learning processes. Even the lay-out of the schoolroom and the way the furniture was arranged reflected the undisputed character of this manner of organizing schooling. First division pupils did not even qualify for tables: they had no writing to do. Nor did they need slates or blackboards.

Compared with these stark circumstances, one can imagine just what a promotion becoming a 'writer' was. Not only was dignity conferred by learning to write, but there was also the contributing factor of the complications which the use of the goose-quill added to the everyday business of teaching. The children, once equipped with quills, had to learn to sharpen them – according to the *Conduite* this involved twelve different operations! For the teachers, there was the amount of time consumed by this delicate operation, to which they devoted every spare minute in between recitations and reading aloud. The parents baulked at the cost of exercise books and quills – this alone was enough to make writing a luxury – and often contented themselves therefore with having their children learning to read (with the accompanying lessons in catechism) and withdrew their children from school without giving them a chance to become 'writers'. Iron, and later steel pens, which made their appearance sometime in the 1830s, only very slowly undermined the prestige of writing – they too were very expensive and did little to alleviate writer's cramp: the earliest models spattered the paper, ploughed it up and even stabbed right through it.

This rigidity in the school curriculum did however admit a few exceptions, even among the Brethren. This happened in the major schools – obviously there could be no question of it in the countryside – and in special classes, with few pupils, from well-to-do families capable of paying school fees up to five francs per month. Pupils in these classes could, as indicated in the 1839 prospectus for the Brethren's school at Morlaix, 'go directly from the special class to the big class, missing out the writing class'. But one should not exaggerate the scope of such exceptions: one only pushed pupils who were obviously destined for grammar school, and these were really 'classes for young Gentlemen'.

Lastly, the final characteristic of this whole picture of scholastic inertia: the bulk of elementary education continued to be carried out according to the good old 'individual method'. The teacher got each pupil to work – reading, writing, counting, recitation – individually; the other pupils in the meantime did nothing, so one can understand the reasoning behind the chief recommendation to Erckmann-Chatrian's assistant master made by the old schoolmaster of Chêne-Fendu:

> see that bundle of hazel-Switches over there, behind the clock; I use up two or three like that every year on their backs. Don't be afraid of breaking them, you'll find all you need on the hillside. If anyone of these blighters is disrespectful, if you see him making signs with his hands, winking, or even laughing to try and get the others to laugh, just lay about him with a switch! . . . Hit him until he yells, so that when the others hear it they will think: this isn't any old Tom, Dick or Harry, he's a real assistant master!.

One can only admire this vigorous definition of an assistant master by his corrective function.

But even supposing the class was kept in order in this way, with its inevitable bonus of boredom, each pupil will only have worked a few minutes in the day. After some fastidious though reasonable calculations, an advocate of mutual teaching[44] demonstrated that, in a class lasting six hours each day, with sixty pupils, and bearing in mind the time it took for the teacher to come and go from one pupil to the other, each child would only really be occupied for roughly four minutes. The remaining five hours and fifty-six minutes of inactivity were the heavy tribute exacted by the individual method.

The simultaneous method, inaugurated back in the 18th century by the Brethren of the Ecoles Chrétiennes, also adopted by the best of the lay and congregational teachers, and the mutual method advocated by liberals ever since the earliest days of the Restoration, were beginning to compete with this old 'pointilliste' method. But very timidly so. In January 1829, four-fifths of the teaching profession were still using it, as a ministerial circular notes with regret,[45] and doubtless over-optimistically, for many teachers untruthfully declared that they had switched to simultaneous teaching, knowing that this enjoyed the favour of the university authorities.

We may contemplate this inertia, this archaism in the elementary school[46] in an invaluable, belated, but all the more revealing mirror: the results of the inquiry devised by Guizot, set in motion a month after the promulgation of his law and conducted in the summer and autumn of 1833. Guizot's investigation is a far cry from the sporadic, distant statistical curiosity of the early days in the century, when from time to time, mayors and teachers were asked to produce figures on schools, pupils, and school expenditure. Guizot's enterprise was presided over by an imperious *dirigisme* and systematic policy. His 'Report to the King', in 1834[47] paints a picture of ignorance[48] and bluntly states the purpose of the project:

in order to give fresh and fertile impetus to elementary instruction, in order to establish effectively between the authorities and the teaching profession that universal bond, those permanent links which are inscribed in the law but which are so difficult and yet so necessary to transmit into fact, it was absolutely essential that some general measure make the presence of the Central Government felt everywhere in all primary schools, that it impress upon people the force of its intentions, the spectacle of its activity and thus right from the outset and for all those concerned, carry into effect one of the fundamental concepts underpinning the law.

This general view, pretending to all-inclusiveness, overflew the thousands of French communes still lacking schools, without noticing them. What matter? That was not the point; what counted was this policy of on-the-spot investigation, in all the communal and private schools coming within the purview of the law.[49] Guizot thus bade his 490 inspectors ride forth, most of them university officials[50] (although some were lawyers, notaries, justices of the peace, doctors, but they had to be members of a Committee of Public Instruction) and he expected them to unearth what earlier statistical inquiries had concealed, namely that 'moral state of primary instruction and its results'. The subject of the study was slightly nebulous, but Guizot defined it as being the internal régime of schools, the aptitude, the zeal, the conduct of school teachers, their relationships with the pupils, parents, local authorities, civil and religious.[51] The Minister supplied a list of 34 questions, each of them subdivided, intended to provide a total of sixty-odd different items of information on each school; such was the investigators' campaign equipment.

This was to be the last photograph of the 'Ancien Régime' school, as those in charge of primary education were to call it themselves after 1833. One could have wished it better: its lens failed to distinguish girls' schools (nor did anyone bother to deduct the number of girls from the total number of pupils in mixed schools). One could also have wished the photographers more competent: in spite of their academic qualifications, hardly any of Guizot's inspectors were involved in primary education.

Out of the 490 inspectors, nine only were primary-school teachers or headmasters, while 13 were directors or professors at primary teacher training colleges. Even if we throw in the 15 'maîtres de pension' for good measure, this still made only a very tiny minority.

What was the headmaster of the Royal Grammar School at Nîmes to make of a single-class school in a wretched Cévennes village? How can we believe this inspector in Haute-Marne whose everlasting response to questions regarding the conduct of the master in school and in the village is 'no complaints' or 'no complaints lodged'? How are we to assess situations which such an assortment of men managed to describe in identical terms: 'acceptable', 'weak', 'satisfactory'?

One further circumstance should put us on our guard, the first 'print' taken from this photograph was made by one of Guizot's subordinates, P. Lorain, whom the minister had instructed to compile a *Tableau de l'Instruction primaire en France*[52] on the basis of answers to the questionnaire. Historians of primary education in 19th-century France nearly always turn to this convenient table. Yet, *ex officio* we might almost say, Lorain darkened the tones of the print: compared with so black a picture, the achievements of Guizot and his administration could not fail to appear the more brilliant.

If we bear this in mind, however, and make use of primary data as often as possible, Guizot's inquiry nevertheless remains an invaluable document. Its verdict echoes the one towards which our partial data had inclined, only this time indisputably so, because it is global in scope: namely that the primary school in 1833 had barely changed since the *Ancien Régime*. But it contains something else as well, evidence of a new age approaching: in the comments drafted by Guizot's inspectors, we can detect for the first time the upsurge of that social demand for education which was to transform the school itself. Take a look, for example, at the impressions which P. Dardenne, *régent* at the Chaumont grammar school, drew from his tour of seven cantons:

> practically everywhere one goes, communes are repairing, enlarging or rebuilding the premises where the children of their little communities assemble; everywhere one goes, schoolteachers are better paid and enjoy greater respect. There was a time when schoolteachers were regarded as keepers of children, in the way the shepherd was merely the keeper of his flock.... But ideas are improving in the countryside and if the teacher is better appreciated today, people regard him as a man who, while giving children their initial instruction, is also responsible for forming their hearts, developing their judgement, stretching their memory, and fashioning them to perform the duties of all kinds to which they will be called in later life.[53]

## Three demands for one school

'There is no longer any point in discussing today advantages and the drawbacks of primary education: in the midst of trends and practices that are springing up spontaneously on all sides, this can no longer be withheld from people; it has truly become a social need.' F. Le Play's [54] investigator saw no need to explain just who had until now 'withheld' instruction from these 'people' from whom it could no longer be withheld, nor did he explain the reasons for this demand for increased primary education – or why it could no longer be restrained. But the main point in this 1851 document, which appears to sum up a debate, is that Le Play finds no other cause for the explosion of schooling in the 19th century: the instruction of the people – by which he meant elementary instruction – had become 'a social need'; and as everyone agreed that instruction took place in schools, it was school which had to satisfy this demand.

If Le Play is to be believed, all that the inertia of the school as an institution in the first half of the 19th century had done was to conceal this rising social demand, this slowly maturing need. The first person to realize this was later, with his 28 June 1883 Act, to set in train the transformation of the French school system. Guizot made no demiurgic claims for his law; in his eyes it did not 'create', merely 'culminate'.[55]

Needless to say, outside this movement, and in opposition to it, we find the same old sworn enemies of education for the people.

Chancelier Pasquier describes these opponents of mass education in his *Mémoires*:

> To understand the price that the most active portion of the Royalist Party and the most fanatical defenders of religion placed on [the destruction of the mutual schools of the restoration] it should be borne in mind that two unshakeable ideas governed it: first, that the people have little need of instruction, that most of the time it was more dangerous than useful for a man of the people to know how to read and write, that it made him more difficult to govern; secondly, that the modicum of instruction that had to be given to the lower orders of society ought never to come to them other than through the intermediary of the clergy, that this was the only way of making sure that it would be exclusively monarchic and religious.[56]

This hostility was particularly manifest in the countryside, where it was feared that the spread of instruction would encourage the rural exodus and still more the emancipation of farm labourers. André Armengaud describes the ill grace of certain landowners in eastern Aquitaine after the passing of the Guizot Act. In the *arrondissement* of Albi, they 'watch with dismay the children of their farmer give up a portion of their time for learning. They claim that these children will one day become lazibones swollen with pride.' In the *arrondissement* of Pamiers, they see in learning a means whereby their tenant farmer may free himself of the 'absolute dependence in which they maintain him . . . whence the great displeasure that they showed to their farm foremen, going so far as to threaten non-renewal of their lease when the latter appeared to attach importance to the success of their children in school'.[57] Even in mid-century, Père Tiennon – the poor Bourbonnais peasant hero of Emile Guillaumin's *La Vie d'un simple* – notes this hostility, without being able to account for it. Anxious to send his children to school, in a commune where a certain number of places were reserved for poor children, he raised the subject with a friend of the mayor, was brusquely turned down and concluded: 'Understanding that he held something against instruction, fearing to annoy him if I persisted, I confined myself to this single attempt. And so my children did not go to school.'[58]

There now emerged a line of argument with a long and vigorous subsequent career. For a good century, a whole current of conservative thought tirelessly inveighed against the 'half-baked instruction' provided by the elementary school, inadequate to produce knowledge yet amply sufficient to fan insubordination and engender an incurable social bastardy. A cynical piece by Taine, written after the introduction of free compulsory education, demonstrates the tenacity of this conservative line and briefly rehearses this hostility, incapable of disarming:

> As between this destiny of the adult (peasant or labourer) and the fullness of his primary education, the disproportion is enormous; manifestly, his education prepares him not for his life as he will live it, but for another life less monotonous, less restricted, more cerebral, and which, vaguely perceived, will make him disgusted with his own. At least, it will go on disgusting him for a long time, and repeatedly so, until the time when his education, quite superficial, shall have completely evaporated on contact with the ambient air and shall no longer appear to him other than empty phrases: in France, for a peasant or ordinary labourer, the sooner that day comes the better.[59]

In spite of distinguished voices raised in support of it, and in spite of its persistence, those favouring the militant line were already fighting a rearguard action. Because once the religious basis of elementary education was no longer in jeopardy, a serious breach was opened in the ranks of its opponents. The existence of the primary school could provoke a clear split between partisans and adversaries; but once the discussion was restricted to its content and emphasis, the main battle had been lost. We can detect this resignation in the reply made by Cardinal Diepenbrock[60] to Eugène Rendu, who was investigating the state of mass education in Germany. Was not the spread of education among the masses liable to be ruinous to society, the latter asked? To which the Cardinal confessed: 'There is no longer any point in discussing the question; it is there before us, and on pain of death, society must resolve it. Once the waggon is on the rails, what else is there to do but to guide it?'

Now if that waggon, in this case pressure from civil society for schooling, had become impossible to halt, this was because the interests shoving at it from behind, though diverse and often contradictory, nevertheless converged in giving birth to the school as an institution. Everybody was there, helping to shape the social forces working in favour of schooling: local bigwigs, the future republican élites and, increasingly numerous, the masses themselves. All that remains is to pinpoint the motives of each of them and, where possible, to put a date on their realization of the need for schooling.

Let us take the notables – social, economic or religious – to begin with. School, for them, was first and foremost an instrument of control, designed to moralize and discipline the masses. This was not a new aim: already, in the wake of the Council of Trent, it had engendered a host of elementary schools founded more to 'moralize' the people than for their instruction proper. To this ancient idea, however, the Revolution added the fresh vigour of an image repellent to the notables. Still fresh in their memories was the vision of instruction as an unreasoning, monstrous driving force, offspring of the 'new spirit', which it was now time to rein in. As early as the Consulate, the prefects had intended elementary instruction to consolidate 'those notions so simple and so useful that a people never loses sight of them without preparing its own misfortune'; the Prefect of Lot-et-Garonne, for example, was persuaded that it would bring home to the inhabitants of his *département* 'the necessity and the advantages of a hardworking life, and just how much the preservation of the proprieties and the safety of the citizens was dependent upon the strict execution of the laws'.[61] One finds the same, slightly fevered hopes in the *conseils généraux* (departmental councils) under the Restoration. School was not there just to teach children how to read and write, but '*chiefly* to mould them by introducing them to the knowledge and practice of the religious laws, to love of and obedience towards the King': such was the definition laid down by the *conseillers généraux* of Hérault.[62] Those of Bas-Rhin were of like mind: they put forward a complete plan for the development of elementary education in their villages and, the literacy rate in this *département* being very high (barely 15% of conscripts were illiterate in 1830), they furnish additional evidence that what the leading citizens required of the school was that it should foster: 'respectable behaviour and order in the countryside'.[63]

The Restoration clergy obviously played its noisy part in this determination to turn the school into a vaccine against the plague of revolution: as in earlier centuries, it saw profane education as a means of attracting the lower classes into the elementary schools where they could be catechised. In the *Nouveau traité* (New treatise) written for schoolmasters, the future Archbishop of Paris, Abbé Affre, then Vicar-general to the

Bishop of Amiens, laid his cards squarely on the table:[64] in it, he hoped that his book would '*above all* serve to weaken the spirit of independence which our revolution has caused to germinate in so many heads'. This was because neither reading nor writing were by any means exclusively 'material operations'. The good authors one reads, the good maxims one copies out, are all so many incitements to 'order and submissiveness'. In this impregnatory view of education, in which we find once again the sensual pedagogic concept of the seal on soft wax, there is everything to be gained from keeping children in school as long as possible: which explains Abbé Affre's acrimonious attacks on methods such as the mutual teaching method, designed to cut the time taken to learn.

The best illustration, moreover, of the clergy's – and with it the priests' party's – determination to use the school to rebuild the moral fibre of the lower classes, is to be found in the proliferation of teaching congregations in the first three decades of the 19th century. Leaving behind them the accident – which was how they regarded the Revolution – the French clergy sought to revive a way of life 'signposted by the Council of Trent' (as Pierre Zind puts it)[65] and to restore the principles of stability and subordination which had been the mark of Catholic and monarchic France. The renewal of the teaching congregations, which had begun under the Consulate, gathered momentum under the Restoration: a riposte had been found to the danger, made abundantly clear by the Hundred Days, of a rapid takeover of the schools 'by a Masonic and Protestant-inspired society, armed with the mutual method'.[66]

The most systematic exponent of this conception of the school as guarantor of the existing state of society was Guizot. From the earliest, hesitant days of the Restoration, when as yet he held no political responsibility, Guizot's thinking already derived from the self-evident fact that: 'Ignorance makes the people turbulent and ferocious.' This seemed to him the very language of hard facts, made sufficiently clear by 'our deplorable Revolution'.[67] Seventeen years later, when Minister of Public Instruction, he was still as terrified as ever of 'the nasty, scant knowledge of the people, and the vague, incoherent and erroneous, albeit active and powerful, ideas with which it fills their heads'. The famous letter addressed to the schoolteachers of France on the implementation of his law resumes his thinking, and at the same time stood as the notables' creed: 'Universal elementary instruction shall henceforth be the guarantee of order and social stability.'

Any instruction whatever? Of course not. Since any faith in the action of good education obviously assumes the possibility of the reverse contagion of bad education, it was therefore imperative that the education in question be religious; not in the sense that religious instruction would henceforth figure in the curriculum, but in an atmospheric sense. There could be no question of religion being an 'exercise', Guizot stressed: it must pervade the atmosphere, 'religious impressions and habits penetrating it through and through'.[68] Should this beneficial 'influence' be lacking, the education of the people would once again become a danger: this would be tantamount, as Abbé Doyotte told his cantonal delegates as late as 1871, to building 'on a volcano'.[69]

What is more, this instruction was to be confined within the narrowest limits: 'to the simplest kinds of knowledge of truly universal utility'.[70] And in what did this cultural minimum consist? Guizot put it in a nutshell: 'the precepts of religion and morality, the general duties of men in society, and those elementary items of knowledge which have become useful and almost essential to people of all conditions, as much in the interest of the State as in that of individuals'. Above all, not a word to suggest that this elementary equipment might be expanded or added to. It is in this light that we should see Destutt de Tracy's repugnance, in Year IX, at the very idea of the term primary school. For to speak of a school as being 'primary' is to suggest that it is merely a first step, and that there are others beyond it. People may even take it into their heads that they have something in common with the *Ecoles centrales* (colleges of engineering), to which they may be a kind of ante-chamber:which would be utterly unwarranted, an error to be fought against, 'even though it has taken hold of some of our right-minded folk'.[71]

Now, in all this talk among notables of the need for a minimum of instruction, what part did economic concerns play? Was the 'people' they spoke of controlling to be regarded as a pool of labour for France's infant industry? Such was the hypothesis put forward by Pierre Vilar[72] not so long ago, for which there exist many supporting illustrations. At Le Creusot, when the Schneiders took possession of the factories there,[73] the only 'schools' were the one run by an ex-army sergeant-major, who was also church cantor, who took a few pupils, and another run by 'mère Fyot', who ran a nursery where children were also taught to read. Practically as soon as they had arrived, the Schneiders announced plans to found, at their expense, an elementary school for all children, plus a higher school for young people 'fitted to the different industries'. Even the primary school taught a wider range of subjects than in the State schools: theoretical and practical arithmetic, industrial drawing, surveying. And the Schneiders kept a close watch on the quality of their school: in 1841 they appointed a remarkable assistant master from the teacher training college at Mâcon. One finds the same train of thought among the employers at Mulhouse; back in the 1830s, the mill-owners still thought of school as a place for moral training. Twenty years later, they were entrusting it with the additional task of providing a fairly high level of intellectual and technical training. Machines needed workers capable of supervising them and adjusting them: 'There is no room for the illiterate workman in modern industry.'[74]

Yet one baulks at the suggestion that this economic objective was paramount. For even in the view of the captains of French industry, it remained subordinate to the 'moralization' of the working people, which was the fundamental aim. At no time during the 19th century – and this is sufficiently well-known for us not to have to labour the point here – did elementary education really bow to the demands of growth and the emergent industrial society: it was always one step behind industrial development, glorifying the tranquillity of the countryside, painting the worker's life, industry, and even the city itself in the drabbest colours, never bothering with the technical and vocational training of the children of the people in preparation for their lives as producers.[75]

If the elementary school did indeed develop in response to the social demand of the notables of industrial France, it did so obliquely, in the first place, under the pressure of the values – Christian initially, later lay values, but it is all the same here – which the school was supposed to inculcate in the children of the people: respect for authority, no matter what its face – family, employer, law, government. One merely has to take another look at Le Creusot to grasp this. When the general manager of the factories set to thinking, in 1868, about the 'influence of education', he did not intend the schools of his dreams to furnish technical training for his industrial labour force, but rather moral training: thanks to school there need no longer be any cause to fear

> those unhealthy aspirations to independence which destroy all respect for established organizations. . . that rumbling agitation which spreads, for no reason whatever, among little-educated workers, that discontent which comes not from within themselves, but from some leader under whose sway their ignorance places them, those easily-exploited prejudices which education alone can dispel.[76]

We may conjure up many different images of this 'leader' to whom ignorance delivers the people, bound hand and foot. The one being forged by the future republican élites most certainly contrasts with the one then haunting the nightmares of the traditional notables. Where the latter thought of the Revolution, the former thought of obscurantism. Two perils: a single remedy. For all shared a common faith in the ability of education to fashion men in its image; this fundamental consensus explains how the demand for schooling managed to find such disparate support and finally came to be satisfied. The 'social need' for school, which Le Play detected, thus reconciled – apart from their superficial quarrels – the notables with the middle classes, albeit so different in temperament. These

124    *Reading and writing*

teachers, doctors, notaries and engineers, journalists and veterinary surgeons, freemason lawyers and liberal pastors, all came together in 1866 to form the *Ligue de l'Enseignement*, advocating school as an instrument of social and political progress.

There were the humanists, who, following in Condorcet's footsteps, viewed mass education as the basis for the general progress of humanity. There were the militants, persuaded that the school would be a weapon against clerical and monarchical obscurantism, against the 'forces of the past'. Then there were the people who mingled political goals with humanist concern, in the hopes of achieving equality, now inscribed in the constitution, through education. Jules Simon puts the following words into the mouth of Jean Le Flô, the friend of his childhood in a Morbihan village, who was obliged to educate himself by his own efforts in the army before becoming ploughman, then accounts clerk, secretary to the town hall, and finally schoolmaster: 'A fine equality, written down on paper, impossible in practice! Is it not mockery to tell a man who cannot read: you shall become a deputy; or to a soldier who cannot read: you shall become a marshal? The good people who overthrew the Bastille to win that freedom for us did not dream it thus.'[77]

To tell the truth, the humanists were alone in believing that the school had a genuinely 'liberating' function, that is, in ascribing to the technical skills acquired in school – writing, reading, counting – power to liberate instantly. The others – the majority – held exactly the opposite view to that of the conservative notables. They were less concerned with the fact that the school existed than with its content. From the Revolution to the laws of Jules Ferry, they evinced a constant mistrust of a school in which they had no part. A Commissioner of the Directory in Haute-Garonne, in a disaster-laden report on the state of public instruction (one single schoolmistress in his canton, not a single schoolmaster), brazenly concludes: 'We would rather do without than have ones that are enemies of the Revolution.'[78] Three-quarters of a century later, Erckmann-Chatrian's 'assistant master' (an enlightened advocate of compulsory education and the new schools notwithstanding) declares: 'What I want to know is what all these well-paid new schoolmasters are going to teach. . . . If they are to go on teaching our children what they've been teaching them until now, the catechism and religious history, I'd almost rather there were fewer of them, for being fewer they can do less harm.'

So there was 'instruction, and instruction'.[79] Which is precisely what the conservative notables had been saying all along. Was the instruction that these future élites of the Republic were calling for so very different from their own? We could produce any number of quotations in evidence that this rising class was no more eager than the other to furnish the lower classes with the ultimate weapon of emancipation; that it too was concerned to supply the republican State with 'good workmen',[80] to turn out producers capable of developing the prosperity of the country. Consequently we may, like Georges Dupeux, conscious of the risk of 'sacrilege', describe the school as the agent of equilibrium in republican society, an instrument of pacification in social conflict, in a word, another 'opium of the people'.[81] This is not the place to discuss the grounds for this blasphemy; in any case, neither the Republic nor its school had yet established themselves at this time. The central point is to show how, paradoxically, the desire for order on the one hand, and the desire for political democracy on the other, in fact worked towards the same goal.

For such was the underlying object of the school for these new élites. Elementary education, in their view, was above all education for the suffrage. And for a restricted suffrage at that. Under the bourgeois monarchy, L.A. Meunier, the future publisher of the *Echo des Instituteurs*, at that time head of the teacher training college at Evreux, waxed indignant over the fact that many voters – numbering 200,000 in all – were obliged to have their voting slip written out by 'foreign hands'.[82] 'Without wisely graduated instruction, the power of the vote is a dead letter': such too was the verdict of the *Conseil général* of Yonne at the same moment, on the morrow of the passage of the Guizot Act.

The *Conseil général* adds:

> The right to vote implies the ability to read and write, otherwise fraud and deceit all too often divert votes to the benefit of intrigue. Consequently, a good and wise use of voting rights in the countryside inevitably entails some knowledge. That way the whole future of representative government, in the broadest sense of the term, lies; and its development, its progress, even its durability, may depend upon the instruction given to the rising generation.[83]

With the sudden advent of universal suffrage in 1848, all these people felt a 'mingling of unbounded joy and secret terror', which Jean Macé recalled.[84] Terror, because even at that time 37% of young men declared themselves totally illiterate on conscription, i.e. they could not even read;[85] more than half the men entitled to vote were also illiterate,[86] and in certain regions and *départements*, male illiteracy scores were unbelievably high. The avalanche of 'bad' elections – April 1848, 10 December 1848, 1849, the plebiscites and elections under the Empire – all gave flesh to this terror beyond their wildest nightmares. The 'Crime of 2 December' thus seemed to have been sanctioned by the 'mob of illiterates and irresponsibles'.[87] To prevent the universal suffrage from turning against those that had most ardently advocated it, it was 'therefore essential to enact a compulsory education law, as a corollary to the law on universal suffrage'.[88]

Meditation on the failure of the Second Republic inspired this commonplace of republican wisdom and stimulated the need for school. Among the conservatives, it arose from ruminations on a different failure. Later, it was yet another failure – a military one this time – that revived the demand for school education.

From one end of the 19th century to the other, the demand for schools grew out of political rancour, mingled with hopes of recovery.

But the 19th century elementary school was not born merely, as Philippe Ariès has stated in a recent book,[89] of attempts to outbid each other on the part of the clergy and the liberal bourgeoisie. There was a third character taking shape behind the two initial protagonists, and this new character was less and less content with figuring purely as an issue, a witness, or even an obstacle. To be sure the lower classes, the rural ones especially, had long been indifferent to education; still very slowly, and with many regional disparities too, they were now coming to expect two benefits at least from the school.

First, dignity: at what point does it become shameful to have to admit – to oneself as well as to others – that one is illiterate? All we can do here is to set down a few pointers. Destutt de Tracy noted that 'the indifference towards instruction which dishonours so many townsmen is indigenous in the countryside'. That was in 1794. In town, where instruction was already widespread by the end of the 18th century, people were thus aware of their own illiteracy; in the countryside, on the other hand, the illiterate in the midst of other illiterates was like a fish in a sea of ignorance.

Jules Simon expounded and explained the following law in *l'Ecole*:

> General rule: the less one knows, the less one wants to know.... In a poor commune, where no one conceives, even in his dreams, of improvement, where, from father to son, people have lived on their physical labour and routine, in the depths of ignorance, they do not think of the morrow, neither for themselves nor for others, and they feel something of the same unthinking aversion for the rich and the learned with which coarse people pursue strangers.[90]

Thus, around 1850, according to Roger Thabault, the shamefulness of being illiterate had not yet come to Mazières-en-Gâtines: 'The illiterate were too many to feel ashamed of their ignorance. And the intellectual isolation in which the inhabitants of the commune lived forbade anything resembling probing intellectual curiosity.'[91] The more illiterates there were around, the less they perceived their condition, the less they were ready to fight it, for themselves or for their children; this fecklessness was to handicap yet further the already backward regions, and singularly so in places where the social utility of the school was not self-evident. As Roger

Thabault observed for the inhabitants of Mazières: 'The semi-closed economy, and the very closed world in which they lived, made it unlikely that there would be a constant use for the kind of signs one uses in school.'

In the towns, on the other hand, things were very different. The monographs published in *Ouvriers des deux mondes* illustrate the growing difficulty a worker had when he was illiterate, and when he saw himself as such in the eyes of his neighbour. There is a description of the wife of a Paris shawl-weaver – 35 years old in 1857 – unable to read even, who 'blushes and suffers on account of her ignorance', and whose entire family feels the situation painfully: accordingly, the couple are determined to give their four children as good an 'elementary education as possible'.[92] We find the same shamefacedness, and the same consequences, at the same moment, in the household of a quarryman in the Paris region: his wife 'wishes to procure for her children the education that she herself and her husband lack, and she is eager for them to go to school, without really having much idea of what they will learn there'.[93] The fact is, here, that upward social mobility is a secondary concern: we come across a miner in the Pas-de-Calais, to whom 'his ignorance is a burden', and who wants his children to benefit from schooling, and who is yet adamant that his son shall go down the mines at thirteen.[94] What counts most is – and it was within reach in the urban areas – the desire to imitate the higher classes, which may even suggest an already quite selective, refined, form of imitation: like the laundrymen in the Paris suburbs,[95] well-to-do working men, concerned to send their sons to the best school available, which happened to be an institution in Paris. Le Play's investigator notes: 'The better-off working people sometimes yielded unthinkingly to the temptation to imitate the bourgeois class.'

In places where the model was farther off, in the countryside, it was necessary to wait until the everyday usefulness of education had been demonstrated, and at the most basic level sometimes, such as the reading of a letter. In early 1871, the two sons of *père* Tiennon – Emile Guillaumin's 'simpleton' – were soldiers, one in Africa, the other in Bourbaki's army. How was he to read their letters? And answer them?

> When the postman brought a letter, Victoire and Clémentine (his wife and daughter) ran quickly over to Roubaud's to have it read out. But he often had trouble making them out, because he was unused to reading handwriting.... Roubaud was not keen on writing the answers, excusing himself by saying he had too much to do, but in fact it was more because he lacked the skill. Clémentine would go off to the village of Franchesse to see the grocer's daughter, who knew how to write. On a weekday, because on

Sundays the grocer's customers thronged the place for the same reasons, to badger this young woman.

And *père* Tiennon summed up the situation: 'Ignorance seemed hard to bear, in those months, because we were more put out than usual.'[96]

It sometimes happened that the harshness of life made this need for education very clear very early on, as in Briançonnais: everybody feels the need of instruction, wrote the prefect in Year IX.[97] Sixty years later, the Inspector of the *Académie* of Basses-Alpes made the same observation about the mountainous areas of his *département*; people did not leave when they had education: they acquired education in order to leave: 'When a poor child of the Alps leaves his father's roof in search of better recompense for his labour and his intelligence, he rightly counts on the success of his venture if he has assiduously attended the elementary school in his locality.'[98] The upland valleys of the Pyrenees could furnish comparable cases – albeit atypical of course – of this early demand for education in rural areas.[99]

The demands made by the new society ensured its spread throughout the century. It was becoming increasingly necessary to be literate in order to read, understand and sign the swelling flood of administrative, commercial, legal, tax and notarial documents, whose embrace came to envelope even the country people, even the poor. Anxious to get his son into school, *père* Tiennon, himself illiterate, adds: 'I should like my son Jean to be able to read and write so that he may then keep our accounts.'[100] For traditional crafts were growing more complicated: the master-fisherman from Etretat, who could neither read nor write, and was accordingly incapable of keeping his 'catch logbook', forced at least regular school attendance on his sons.[101] The steel-tool assembler at Hérimoncourt[102] made a late start, but with four working women under his orders he had to keep a record of the work done, 'made the calculations needed to apply the price to the articles manufactured'. The Paris quarryman,[103] now a foreman, was obliged to turn to the boss's wife every evening in order to settle up with the quarry labourers. Nor should we forget the army, where no one could hope, without education, for promotion to corporal or sergeant; as early as 1835, the author of the *Statistique de la Drôme* pinpointed here one cause of the spread of education in the rural areas of the *département*: 'The farmer knows his son will one day have to do his military service; he knows, often from his own experience, the advantages he will gain by knowing how to read and write, and so he sends him to school.'[104]

But in addition to these necessities, which people could observe for themselves, there was also hope. Instruction came to be regarded as a kind of midsummer hay,[105] capable of sparing children the drudgery of physical labour and delivering them from a mediocre existence. With a fair hand, some ease with figures one may, the Inspector of the *Académie* of Haut-Rhin notes in 1864, find 'relatively lucrative jobs'.[106] His counterpart in Corsica assures us: the young emigrant realises that with some education, the passport to government service, industry or the army, he is not altogether venturing into the unknown.[107] Norbert Truquin, who was put out to work at the age of seven and who did not learn to read, also understood this perfectly. Picked up by the *gendarmes* at Oran for having left the family home, the idea of escaping to nearby Morocco flitted across his mind, but finally he gave up the idea: 'I thought about it', he wrote later, 'and decided that, being without instruction, I should end up a slave in Morocco like anywhere else.'[108]

Coming back to Le Play: his peasant in Basse-Provence 'unhesitatingly, and without misgiving ... spent what he had to in order to give his children [all six of them] the education required for a lucrative career'.[109] The linen-maid in Lille wanted her son to be a clerk;[110] the Paris locksmith and his wife wanted their sons to become office or shop clerk, 'a job that seemed to them more congenial and more enviable than that of the workman burdened with physical labour'.[111] If they went to school, their children would have less trouble; and they would be more respected; a twin goal that the Commentry tinsmith had already achieved by 1889: his elder daughter was a clerk in the Comptoir Parisien grocery store, the second daughter, who held an elementary certificate, a private teacher. Both had been taught at the school run by the Sisters of Saint-Vincent de Paul for the Compagnie des Forges.[112] In the people's growing yearning for education it is important to bear in mind the influence exerted by such examples as these.

Lastly, the theme of the political utility of instruction, so familiar to the radical and republican élites in the bourgeoisie, was beginning to be echoed by the lower classes, and was even being taken up by the pens of their spokesmen. A constantly recurring theme in the reports presented by the workers' delegates to the Universal Exhibition in London, in 1867 – obviously, we are dealing with the aristocracy of the working class – is the disapproval of the 'politico-radical' party's opposition to this growth of instruction; the enthusiasm aroused by universal suffrage, with its corollary, the need for civic education, hence for education *tout court*; some even went so far as to devise a proletarian definition of the aims of education, seen as a necessary instrument in the organization and struggle of the working classes, as something to be wrested from the hostile bosses.

Several reports demanded free compulsory education at once, and warmly backed Victor Duruy's policies. The coppersmiths announced that 'the day the masses are enlightened and instruction is no longer the privilege of the few shall be the last day of the power it [the politico-clerical party] wields over the minds of people'. For the leatherworkers, 'the education of the worker must progress sufficiently to enable him to know his rights and his duties'.

Occasionally someone adumbrates a 'proletarian' definition of the ultimate goals of education: 'The greatest obstacle to the social organization of the worker', the cabinet-makers remark, 'is, without fear of contradiction their ignorance.... All our hopes and plans are vain if they are not founded upon instruction.' Instruction, according to the nailworkers, 'will one day bring about that good understanding and that harmony that ought always to exist in the working class, and create within it that force against which nought can prevail.... We hold that it is through instruction alone that we shall overcome all the injustices mentioned in our report.'[113]

Documents such as these, of which many more were to follow, permit Georges Duveau to argue that the taste for instruction which he observes among his Second Empire working men stems from four basic motives: occupational convenience, desire for upward social mobility, concern to behave as responsible citizens and, lastly, hostility to the bosses who refused them this education. Here, consciousness of the obstacle adds to the prestige of the bourgeois model more than it detracts from it.[114]

The upshot of this was that working-class demand added its voice to that of the notables, conservative and liberal. However disparate these three demands may have been, we should not imagine them merely juxtaposed, each working its own furrow to hasten the development of schooling. All the élites were reconciled in the credit they accorded the school as an instrument of social control, burying in this their political divergences. As to the working classes, we may readily grasp the connection between their thirst for education and the requisites of the liberal bourgeoisie: the religion of merit, the image of individual success within a framework of never-ending collective progress; these were what produced that 'great movement for progress which excites the activity and ambition of each individual', at which the Inspector of the *Académie* of Alpes-Maritimes proclaimed himself so astounded in 1864.[115] That this alliance was a trap, and that the people ultimately bore the brunt of it, as so many recent studies suggest, is not our concern here. The poor child who succeeds, a central figure in the mythology of the 19th century school, could well, in the eyes of the bourgeoisie, have been the exception that justified the entire system, while the for the working people it stood as a collective, quasi-religious, hope. But this image survived down through the years, and even today we know how pregnant it can be, even though the evidence points in the opposite direction. What counts, if we are to understand the triumph of the school, is not the rightness of the consensus, but its solidity.

**The State steps in**

Public opinion – or rather, different sections of public opinion – went to work right from the earliest decades of the 19th century to get the development of the school institution off the ground. But it also stirred the state, and pointed to a suitable successor to itself. Between 1810 and 1830, towns and *départements* took the initiative in founding several dozen teacher training colleges, with government blessing as their sole assistance (and even that from 1828 onwards only). When, with Guizot, each *département* came under obligation to found a teacher training college, the State assumed control over their curricula and contributed to their financing. This represented a decisive change: as between the 50,000 francs that Louis XVIII paid out of his own purse in 1816 to encourage elementary instruction, and the 1,500,000 francs spent by the State in 1833 for this purpose, there is more than just a difference in proportion: there is the gulf that separates a charitable handout from a budget.

As early as 1816, moreover, Guizot fully realised the need, in popular education, to 'choose between absolute freedom and the authority of the State, between private industry and the ministrations of public wisdom'; and he hailed as one of Bonaparte's eminent merits the fact of having founded the University, whatever its political content may have been. For it embodied a principle that even the Revolution itself had failed to grasp entirely, namely that *'public instruction is the job of the State*, in other words, that it is for the State to provide education in public establishments to those that wish to receive it therefrom, and to supervise it in establishments where it is the object of private speculations'.[116]

Thus we find the State engaged in completing the construction of an institution grown to national proportions. What came of this was the gradual 'massification' of the primary school. By taking it more and more under its wing – administratively and financially – the State also worked to establish uniformity within it.

Examples from abroad played a major rôle in the discovery by the representatives of the French State of the need to transform the school and in their discussions of the means to achieve this. As early as 1808, Charles de Villers required but a 'glance at the universities and the methods of instruction in Protestant Germany'[117] to observe the abundance of primary schools, the quality of their teachers, the interest shown in them by authorities, and to note that the absence of philosophical or religious sectarianism in no way robbed teaching of its moral character. These observations which had already, in the upheavals of the Revolution, been gathered haphazardly, were henceforward organized in systematic enquiries. The calibre of the names connected with them – Georges Cuvier,

Victor Cousin[118] – gives the measure of the solemnity with which these fact-finding tours were undertaken and makes their concluding reports especially interesting. These documents are now very well known, and here we shall confine ourselves to that part of them which has inspired the educational policy of the French State. What was it that drew Cuvier's admiration right from the first primary school visited in Holland? The fact that one master, with two assistants, handled roughly 200 pupils; the fact that pupils were asked questions in the course of their exercises, the fact that boards with movable letters were used for reading, and slates with talc pencils for writing. In terms of its productivity, its lively teaching methods and technical gimmicks, this was indeed the last word in teaching if we compare it with the teaching being provided in French schools in 1811. To this we should add the quality of the teacher: Cuvier notes the guarantees underpinning the profession of schoolteacher in Holland.[119] In Germany too, this was what struck him as most admirable: the training of teachers in teacher training colleges, and regular possibilities of further training. Twenty years later, this was also what struck Victor Cousin about German schools, and singularly so the schools of Prussia.

V. Cousin hoped that, as in Prussia, teachers would, in the primary school holidays, perfect their skills in a teacher training college, there receiving, in one branch or another, 'lessons appropriate to their needs'; that, on graduation from teacher training college, candidates would be appointed as assistants to a schoolmaster; that each *département* would appoint an inspector of primary schools; that France would imitate the *Bürger-Schulen*, 'that advanced level of primary instruction', a kind of 'intermediate school' (which was to be embodied in Guizot's stillborn 'advanced primary schools').

From England came yet another example: Lancaster's monitorial system, Bell's mutual tuition, the guiding lights of mutual education. This method had been advocated in France, at the end of the 18th century, by the chevalier, Paulet, and by Canon Cherrier, obscure forerunners (though invaluable for their pride) of the 19th century French 'mutualists', who sought to 'naturalize' their initiative. In fact it was the revival of Anglo-French relations, after a ten-year interruption, which proved decisive: the First Restoration allowed French travellers to see the new teaching methods at work in England for themselves;[120] it allowed representatives of the Lancastrian British and Foreign School to come to France, and to leave again with a number of guests, young men designated by the Protestant consistories in southern France;[121] even the military occupation of France played a part in this exchange of men and ideas – French notables were able to observe the mutual method at work in several of the English regiments. Out of these contacts and exchanges, and out of the activities of the 'Société d'encouragement pour l'industrie nationale', was born in spring 1815 the 'Société pour l'instruction élémentaire' (Society for elementary instruction), with the blessing of Lazare Carnot, Commissioner for Education during the Hundred Days. This was the first of a spate of French societies devoted to the propagation of elementary instruction, and it was to play a major rôle in adapting the mutual method to France.

Having children taught by their fellow pupils, or by monitors picked from the best among them: it is hard to believe that this unprepossessing principle (which is what the countless variations on the method boil down to) could have become the centre of raging controversy, on both pedagogic and political grounds. What interests us is less the arguments put forward than the educational novelties proposed – and ultimately imposed – in their nation's schools by the French disciples of the English monitorial school.

First among these was the combination, right from the lowest form or section in the school, of reading with writing, which both the traditional individual schools and the simultaneous school of La Salle's Brethren had neglected. The method was held to be so revolutionary that the 'learned man' who taught it to Edgar Quinet, his sole pupil, in 1808, was taken for a madman, even by the perceptive Mme Quinet.

> He taught both to write and to read, either in the sand in the garden, or else with chalk on his big blackboard, without my ever seeing a book, nor paper, nor pen, nor ink. I thus knew how to write long before knowing how to read, and that threw my mother into singular alarm; for she never tired of asking my teacher if he sincerely believed that I could learn to read. To which he replied, with much reason it seems to me, that there had been many people unable to read, but that no one had ever come across a person who, able to write, had not ended up learning how to read.[122]

Ten years later, the *recteur* of Cahors expressed amazement at the time it had taken for such a simple idea to sink in, 'learning to write the letter at the same time as learning its name'.[123]

This discovery also made it possible to keep all the pupils busy at once. Like that other novelty, the widespread use of the blackboard in place of books. Or yet another, teaching children to write first of all by tracing letters in the sand with a finger, and subsequently with a schist stylus on a slate. Even the way the school was now organized bears witness to this desire to get everybody working at once: pupils were henceforward separated according to ability in eight homogeneous sections – forerunners of the form,[124] whose profile was constantly shifting. They all worked together in the same room, supervised by 'monitors': more advanced pupils, either appointed by the master or else elected by their fellow-pupils, entrusted with the task of guiding their movements, keeping order, and teaching.

What a host of advantages, in the eyes of the method's advocates! The savings it entailed: assisted by his monitors, a single teacher could, in theory, handle several hundred children, and, now removed from individual hands, school supplies – the famous group 'blackboards' – would have a longer useful life. Then there was the improved teaching: the rudiments were learnt more rapidly than under competing methods, progress was flexible, and evaluation was continual, since it occurred every fortnight or once a month, enabling pupils to transfer from one section to another in mid-year and thereby avoiding repeated years. The system was fair, too, for the monitor doing the evaluation was himself subject to evaluation: 'The discipline upheld in each division by one of the pupils cannot be too strict, and must always be fair, because it is exposed to the judgement of those that are subjected to it.' Such was the comment of the Prefect of Basses-Pyrénées, who had compiled a list of all the method's advantages and come down in favour of its benefits in terms of integration:

> It disposes children to obey merit, to show no surprise at seeing authority placed in the hands of their equal or even their inferior, to respect this authority no matter who its repository may be, an invaluable habit which ought to have the most salutary influence in the future, by preparing loyal subjects for the King, and useful citizens for the State. The goal sought is to make teaching easier and in consequence more widespread; and this goal, far from turning away from that religion without which there can be no public morality nor private morality, draws closer to it, on the contrary, since it leads men to knowledge of all the useful truths.[125]

Prefect, Baron d'Haussez, wrote in particular:

> In a school [based on] mutual teaching, the teaching is subject to well-defined rules and methods; it does not vary according to the capacities or inertia of the teachers; the pupils naturally rank themselves of their own accord, according to their aptitudes or level of attainments; although given simultaneously to several pupils, the lesson is nonetheless specific to each individual, since each division is made up of subjects of equal ability; the attention is constantly sustained by the methods employed in the teaching and, when this shows signs of flagging, a movement ordered by the master impresses upon the minds of the children some new activity.[126]

Such testimonials had their usefulness, for, in spite of State support and basking as it was in the blessings of prefects, the mutual method did not lack enemies. It was a novelty imported from heretical England, introduced into France by Protestants, during the dread 'Hundred Days' and under the patronage of 'Carnot the regicide': one look at its visiting card was enough to drive ultras and clericals into each others' arms to do battle against it.[127] And it smacked of heresy in yet another way, for in it the school hierarchy depended on merit: on this criterion alone were the monitors appointed, which accounts for the distress of the better-off parents 'seeing their son forced to obey a beggar's son, if he was a monitor'.[128] Whence arose a general suspicion: surely the mutual school was concerned less with social control than with 'progress' through instruction – nothing short of denial of the generally accepted values.[129] Some even questioned its educational standards, for to function properly it organized pupils' activities along military lines, although these were euphemistically dubbed 'regular conduct'.[130] Long before Michel Foucault saw in it a machine for breaking in bodies,[131] many educationalists had attacked the timetable of the mutual school, as laid down in Sarazin's handbook, evenly divided up by its two hundred commandments and executed to the rhythm of its mechanical exercises.[132]

Justified or not, let us leave these objections at that. The mutual school never represented more than a tiny fraction of the French school system: 4.4% of all elementary schools in 1834. For us the main point lies elsewhere: in the manner in which the mutual school stirred the schoolmasters slumbering in the archaisms of individual teaching – which meant practically all the lay teachers – or in the routine of that creaking novelty, the simultaneous method – the Christian Brethren. What interests us is the introduction of new procedures into the school system (what finally prevailed, in fact, was a 'mixed' method, borrowing from both the simultaneous and the mutual schools). What also concerns us here is an innovation of crucial importance to the subsequent history of literacy, namely the simultaneous learning of reading and writing. Lastly, what interests us here is the way the mutual school boosted school enrolments. It spread primary instruction to groups hitherto neglected or excluded: adults and soldiers, orphans and convicts. Above all, by virtue of the very danger that it posed in the eyes of the Church, it stimulated the development of the teaching congregations. Jean-Marie de Lamennais laboured to establish a Christian Brethren's school in response to each mutual school. Government officials had perceived the beneficial effects of this rivalry from the outset: the sub-prefect of Toulon, inaugurating the mutual school in his town in 1819 remarked: 'The competition, the happy rivalry even between this (mutual) method with that of the "Frères de la Doctrine Chrétienne" (brethren of the Christian doctrine), whose schools are also shortly due to open in Toulon, will be a factor which, in the eyes of impartial judges, cannot but turn out for the good of public instruction in general.'[133]

In the legislative sphere, this 'good of public instruction in general' covered half a century. It took fifty years, from 1836 to 1886, to build the State school. We shall obviously not attempt to trace this history, but we shall clearly have to outline its salient features, in the relevant documents and in its institutional principles.

In the beginning, there was Guizot. And, on either side of the 23 June 1833 Act, a positive stream of regulations, executive orders and decisions. Three obligations stem from these in the first place: for all school-masters – congregationalists included – to obtain a certificate of competence delivered by a departmental commission; for every commune with a population over 500 to maintain a primary school, to provide the master with a living – a fixed wage of F 200 at least – and a roof – somewhere to live; for each *département*, to maintain a primary-teacher training college for men. Next, with the 'Statute' of 1834, came the first attempt at putting some order into the teaching in elementary schools; the executive Order of 1835 set up a permanent corps of primary school inspectors; that of 1836 foreshadowed the development of girls' schools.

The second high point – meanwhile the Falloux Act had made it compulsory for all communes with over 800 inhabitants to establish a special school for girls – came with Victor Duruy.

Victor Duruy's education policy contained an unmistakably political element. In a letter to the Emperor on 6 February 1865, he wrote:

> From a political standpoint, it is urgent that we act: against the *Orléanists*, by using the 1865 Act to counter the 1833 Act which they never stop citing; against the *clericals*, who live off shadows, by letting there be light; against the *republicans*, by wresting a weapon from their hands. Baron de Seebach, Minister of Saxony, heard Arago's son saying: 'Free, compulsory education . . . the Emperor would never allow it: he isn't liberal enough for that; but if he did do so, he would strike a blow at us from which it would be hard to recover.'[134]

Decisions, circulars and instructions blossomed again around a major Act passed in April 1867. The chief progress here was the extension of the obligation to maintain a special school for girls to communes with a population of between 500 and 800. This was accompanied by a host of measures stipulating the material conditions of schoolmasters and – which was a great novelty – schoolmistresses and to encourage, for want of anything better, the communes to extend free schooling, to set up a school library service, to revive adult courses, to create new *caisses des écoles* (school finance boards) and also to improve their educational structures.[135]

Table 3.1 *Timetable for 'elementary primary schools' as laid down in the 25 April 1834 Statute*

| | First division (age 6–8) | Second division (age 8–10) | Third division (age over 10) |
|---|---|---|---|
| Moral and religious instruction | Prayers and pious studies | Religious history | Christian teaching |
| Reading | This exercise shall graduate in turn, from the alphabet, through spelling and reading proper, to the reading of manuscripts and Latin. | | |
| Writing | This exercise shall graduate in turn from the slate to the blackboard, and lastly to paper, in small and big letters, in the three kinds of handwriting (bastard, running and round). | | |
| Arithmetic | Mental arithmetic | Written numbers, and the first four rules of arithmetic. | Ordinary fractions and decimals; legal system of weights and measures. |
| French language | Correct pronunciation; memory exercises | French grammar. Dictation for spelling | Rules of syntax. Grammatical and logical analysis. Composition. |
| Geography and history. Line drawing. Singing | | | General geography and history. Geography and history of France. Line drawing, Singing. |

Lastly came the time of the 'lois fondamentales' (basic laws), the elaboration of the measures establishing the 'Ferryist' school, over a period of ten years. The presiding principles were proclaimed and put into effect: free, compulsory education; loopholes in the legislation were closed: the obligatory opening of teacher-training colleges for women, for instance, or the obligation to build schoolhouses in communes and hamlets. Above all, though, this period represented a new phase in the development of the school: with secular schooling, and with a secularized teaching corps in the primary system, a whole new era of history was dawning.

From this vast mass of documents that went into the building of the school as an institution let us linger a while over two issues closely related to the subject of our inquiry: the new teachers, and the school curriculum, taking the latter to begin with, as figured by Guizot's Act and the 1834 Statute. In its opening article, the Act pronounces the following apodictical judgement: 'Primary instruction necessarily embraces moral and religious instruction, reading, writing, the rudiments of the French language and arithmetic, the legal system of weights and measures.' The component parts of this necessity were laid out horizontally, without prejudging the order in which they were to be learned. On this point the 1834 Statute sheds some light (Table 3.1). Children, henceforward, were to be introduced to three types of handwriting only: bastard hand, running hand, and round hand; italic and copperplate, still required of masters until 1853, were dropped from the pupils' syllabus. This was the start of an irresistible trend towards simplification, blunting the glory of the traditional schoolmaster.[136] Henceforward, too, children were to begin to learn to read and write in French and no longer in Latin, something La Salle and the mutual school had already called for (by becoming a fact, it relegated Latin to a position *behind* the alphabet, spelling and reading in French). Again, as the Brethren and the mutual school had wanted, pupils were separated into several divisions, 'based on their age and the subjects with which they are to be occupied'. But we should not imagine that this concern for a hierarchy of ages and activities necessarily led to a strict distribution of subjects along a vertical axis. For the most original feature of the Statute – the one that can claim exclusive descent from the mutual school – runs counter to the strict linear progression of subjects and upsets the picture: each division or class is no longer confined, as with the Brethren, to the study of a single principal subject. In each class pupils are taught all the subjects at once: in addition to exercises in piety – prayers and talks – beginners are introduced to mental arithmetic and French; and without going as far as Michelet would have liked,[137] i.e. standing the old curriculum on its head and putting writing before reading ('much harder'), and by putting 'the drawing of living objects' before writing, at least children were now taught to read and write at the same time.

One consequence of this simultaneity was that ideas about the order in which subjects ought to be taught remained muddled. And so they did for the next three decades; subsequent Acts of Parliament and administrative measures[138] are no more specific as to the correct distribution of subjects among the three divisions, nor moreover do they make the application of the Statute compulsory: it was necessary to reckon with the inertia of an institution in which the vast majority of schools in 1850 still had but a single schoolmaster. Nevertheless, the new curriculum gradually spread outwards from Paris and the big cities. In 1867, Duruy added the history and geography of France. Gréard, principally, systematized it by filling in the blank spaces in the 1834 Statute[139] (Table 3.2). To be sure he still says that each pupil should be introduced to each subject in each division. But he divides each subject into a series of precise steps for each age-group. This truly can be called pedagogic 'organization', the principle being to eliminate improvisation from the school curriculum. In principle: because for the time being it is merely recommended,[140] only becoming a necessity with the advent of Ferry.[141]

The reason is that to put Gréard's sophisticated prescriptions, or even the modest pointers in the 1834 Statute, into effect, schools needed resources, both human and material – and these they did not have, by any means. Article 9 of the Statute, for instance, suggests that it would be a good idea if all the pupils in a given division had the same books. This requirement alone revealed a state of penury which Montalivet, Guizot's predecessor, had observed in 1831.[142] Three years later Guizot listed, for the benefit of the *recteurs*, the measures taken in the intervening period: a million *Alphabet ou premier livre de lecture*, 250,000 *Petit catechisme historique*, 55,000 *Petite arithmétique raisonnée*, distributed free in the *départements*.[143] Among these consignments in 1831–33, which were the unmistakable legacy of mutualist influence, figured 10,000 reading charts: a massive improvement, since this time it was 10,000 schools – and not just 10,000 pupils – that would benefit. Soon, moreover, Michel-Auguste Peigné's forty-six *Nouveaux Tableaux de lecture* (new reading charts) were to perfect the process[144] and to win general acceptance for it, wearing down the resistance of the traditional schoolmasters and above all – but only in 1847 – that of the Brethren.

School furniture also began to change. Mere application of the 1834 Statute entailed expenditure by the communes: henceforward even 'infants' needed slates, blackboards and tables, something they had never had before. Traditional schoolhouses too came to seem less and less suited to the new teaching methods. Although it was not until 1883 that each commune was obliged to have its own schoolhouse, many had felt so obliged well beforehand. Mazières-en-Gâtine had had its own since 1857; it had been built with State aid, and with a spaciousness – large classroom, three-room

Table 3.2  *Timetable of the local schools of the Seine 'département' after Octave Gréard (July 1868)*

| Subjects taught | Elementary course (6–8) | Intermediate course (8–10) | Advanced course (10–12) |
|---|---|---|---|
| Religious instruction | Prayers and shorter catechism. Rudiments of religious history. | Catechism and Gospel. Religious history | Catechism – Old and New Testament. |
| Reading | Alphabet, spelling, reading in a book. | Reading exercises in books and handwritten exercise books. | Reading from books and handwritten exercise books, with commentary. Reading in Latin. |
| Writing | Rudiments of writing. | Running, large, medium and fine | Running, round and bastard hands. |
| French language | Elementary spelling exercises – Simple dictation | Spelling exercises – Dictation in exercise books. | Reasoned application of the rules of grammar to classic texts. Simple exercises in composition. |
| Arithmetic | The principles of numbers; practical exercises | Exercises in the four rules (whole numbers and decimals). | Reasoned study of arithmetic (whole numbers and decimals, ordinary fractions) Application to practical operations. |
| Metric system | Names and uses of metric measures. | Practical exercises in the different measures. | Application of the metric system to the measurement of areas and volumes. |
| Lessons in observation | Learning by looking (wall maps, pictures geometric solids blackboard reproductions). | — | — |

| | | | |
|---|---|---|---|
| History of France | Talks and tales of leading figures and events. | Events continued, from earliest times to our own times. Main dates. | Brief recapitulation of principal events up to the Hundred Years' War. More detailed history from the Hundred Years' War to our own times. |
| Geography | Notions of general geography, definitions. | Brief notions of the five parts of the world, and of Europe in particular. | Physical, political, agricultural, industrial and commercial history of France |
| Drawing | — | Rudiments of line drawing. | Line drawing and decorative drawing. |
| Singing | — | — | Principal pieces for unison or choir singing. |
| Exercises in memory | Fables or very simple verse or prose. | Selections from the classics. | Selections from the classics. |
| Sewing | Introduction to sewing. | Practical sewing work. | Practical sewing work. |

lodgings for the teacher, woodshed, playground, large garden – that immediately impressed the villagers that here was a 'palace' of education.[145]

All these changes took place very slowly, meeting with resistance of many kinds. One just has to think of the obstacle to implementation of the new curriculum created by the tradition of paying the teacher according to the subjects learned.[146] This was not brushed aside until the 1850s.[147] So it would be all too easy to turn up examples of outmoded teaching practices right up to the end of the century. Let a single one suffice: in 1880, an Inspector-General noted that in the Breton *Académie* he had just visited, reading could still go without writing: 'Many masters,' he mourned, 'think that children should only learn to write when they have learned to read and, putting this piece of nonsense into practice, they let a whole year pass before beginners have an opportunity of holding a pen or a pencil'. It is worth noting that the man who speaks of this 'piece of nonsense' is not an educational pioneer but a government official. The main point, in all this education boom, is that the State was now playing an active rôle, not merely by issuing edicts from afar or by handing out a few thousand francs here and there, but also by offering permanent encouragement and through the provision of increasing amounts of material assistance.

This State intervention can be seen at its fullest extent in efforts made to establish the human conditions needed for the new school: the Guizot Act institutionalized training colleges for primary-school teachers and thus provided for the training of schoolteachers capable of applying innovations made in curriculum and methods.[148] These training colleges did not just spring out of thin air. Before them there had been the mutual teacher training courses of the liberal Restoration, and before that, as early as 1810, the famous 'Classe normale des instituteurs du Bas-Rhin' (Training class for schoolteachers in Bas-Rhin), the first 'genuine' teacher training college.[149] Gradually, by degrees, towns and *départements* began to imitate Strasbourg – the Meuse taking the lead, followed by the Moselle; all over the place, departmental and *arrondissement* councils began to call for the same thing; and, even before Guizot, the State began to back the trend. Vatimesnil devoted several circulars to praising the Strasbourg teacher training college, recommending that the example be followed, even going so far as to promise financial assistance.

'I can hardly recommended too strongly', wrote Vatimesnil to the *recteurs*, 'that you work to set up, in one of the principal communes in your *Académie*, a teacher training class in imitation of the one that has been so successful in Strasbourg'.

Teacher training colleges proliferated in the four years straddling the July Revolution: fifteen in 1830, and close on forty at the end of 1832. Their burgeoning was rapid, though as yet very uneven. Anything was possible in these new teacher training colleges: teacher training classes annexed to the royal colleges; mutual training courses resuscitated by July; congregational boarding colleges; special training classes opened in some good existing primary school; elementary schools where the master took on one or two trainee-teachers. Such was the case with the minimal teacher training college in Cantal: opened at Salers in 1831 – for the space was available! – this was in fact a mutual school, beginning with a single trainee-teacher and joined in 1832 by a handful of companions.[150]

Guizot's desire for institutional homogeneity was to put an end to this patchwork. The 1832 'Règlement' (regulation) sought to standardize the teacher-training colleges: two years' study in principle, ending up with six months' practical work; a standard timetable; a ten-year contract for students; and a supervisory board. Until then strictly departmental, the training colleges now became State establishments, dependent upon the central government for their Statutes, their regulations and their senior staff. Now all that remained for Guizot to do was to turn them into a 'public and legal, ... general and compulsory institution'.[151] With the 1833 Act,[152] this became an accomplished fact. On paper at least, for State intervention by no means put an end to anomalies in the establishment of this new institution overnight: in Troyes, the first director of the teacher training college was a young man of twenty-five; in Melun, they appointed the headmaster of the municipal mutual school; in Rodez, there was a veritable local feud between the *recteur* and the prefect: the minister handed down an exotic choice in the form of a boarding school headmaster from Saône-et-Loire (!), a man of 'excellent principles' at any rate.[153]

In spite of these unorthodox origins, the spread of teacher-training colleges – there were 72 by 1848 – was the chief factor in the transformation of the primary-school teaching corps. To begin with, the masters they now started supplying to the elementary schools were professionals, trained for the job they were about to perform. In 1838, six years after the founding of the Evreux teacher training college, Primary-school Inspector Gadebled counted the fifty-six genuine teachers trained by it and already running big schools; and he described with satisfaction the irresistible rise, in the communes of Eure, of the peaceful, beneficial tide of these missionaries of a new kind. The new-look teachers did indeed have wide-ranging talents, enabling them to perform a 'great variety of functions': 'to back up the administration and individuals in their work, to teach children in their classes, to fashion more and more enlightened, and harder working, men'.[154] By 1848, in Drôme, over a quarter of all elementary-school teachers were teacher-training-college graduates; a little later, in 1869, the figure for Bas-Rhin (champion, as was to be expected) was close on three-quarters. For France as a whole, out of fewer than fifty thousand elementary-school teachers in 1846, 9,200 were teacher-training-college graduates.

Furthermore, what is equally significant, is that the teacher training colleges began retraining the '*Ancien Régime*' – i.e. pre-1833! – teachers still teaching.[155] This was a huge task, for it involved not only 'fortifying the knowledge they already possessed', but also 'teaching them to apply the improved methods': this meant a considerable wrench for them. In many teacher training colleges, the first students were precisely these older masters, experienced teachers returning to school for a few weeks – in Gap, for example[156] – and the task of retraining preceded that of training. In most cases, however, training and retraining went hand in hand, as at Aix-en-Provence,[157] Troyes[158] or in Manche.[159] As early as 1833, in Eure, the inspector of primary schools felt able to announce that more than half the teachers currently active had attended retraining courses, which he described as second birth: they had become like 'new masters'.[160] Sufficiently so, in certain cases, to take charge of retraining their colleagues themselves.[161]

Still, the teacher training colleges were not the answer to everything.[162] First, because many ex-training-college students, rather than becoming elementary teachers in localities where they could not hope to earn much, preferred to take up jobs in private schools while awaiting more important, more lucrative jobs. In 1840, the Conseil général of Nièvre noted that a quarter of training-college graduates in its *département* had done this.[163] One also had to reckon with training-college graduates who did not remain elementary-school teachers, taking up posts elsewhere in the education system: at the Vesoul teacher training college, between 1835 and 1900, roughly 10% of former students followed this course.[164] Lastly, the number of places available in the teacher training colleges quite often exceeded the number of candidates.[165] Although it had become a little steadier, the teaching profession was not much more lucrative than before, and its status only improved slowly. As elsewhere, though, State intervention here helped to improve the present and provide for the future. The 1833 Act guaranteed teachers decent lodgings and a fixed minimum wage; it provided for the payment of school fees by mayoral mandate, and no longer directly by the parents. Shortly afterwards, when setting up the corps of primary-school inspectors, Guizot was presumably thinking both of the need to supervise the teachers, and, doubtless, of the need to establish their social position in the commune too: henceforward they would be in direct contact with a State official. Less wretched, trained for their occupation, possessors of knowledge, teachers now in addition gradually came to be seen as wielding a small portion of the power of the State.[166]

Schoolmistresses had yet to achieve this by a long chalk! Although prudent, the provisions of the Guizot Bill relating to girls had been dropped; the 1836 Order, in which they were included, made them optional only. This is because, while social pressure for boys' education was growing rapidly, education for girls left everyone indifferent, people and leading citizens alike. The time-lag in demand led to a corresponding time-lag in the intervention of the State. Nor was this time-lag restricted to the three years that elapsed between Guizot's entirely masculine Act and the 1836 Order on girls' schools, for the content of the latter only really came to be applied in the aftermath of Duruy's 1867 Act. Even then, one of its key measures, the obligation laid upon each *département* to establish a teacher training college, was only extended to include women in 1879, forty-six years after the men! In the meantime, the State left the bulk of education for girls in the hands of the congregations. The first women's teacher training college, the one at Argentan, was not founded until 1838, a generation after the first schoolmasters' training college, and the number of establishments grew only very slowly. In 1863, Duruy listed no more that eleven (there had been forty-six for men as early as 1833, even before Guizot's Act made them compulsory); to be sure there were in addition some fifty-odd 'teacher training courses' for schoolmistresses, although not subject to State control and with no guarantee as to their educational standards. By and large, training for lay mistresses was only dispensed with great parsimony.

So poor were the material conditions of lay schoolmistresses in most rural communes in general (far worse than for their male counterparts at the same date) that in any case it was hard to recruit them: 'Even were we to open an excellent teacher training college in the chief town of each *département*,' wrote Jules Simon in 1865,

> we wouldn't be able to find the students to fill them. One-third of all elementary-school mistresses earn 90 centimes per day all told; that is hardly, readers will agree, a great incentive. . . . Lacking money, lacking promotion, does the schoolmistress in her wretched school enjoy security and dignity at least? Not a bit of it: she is dependent on everyone, the mayor, the priest, the inspector, the parents. The priest has no need even to call for her dismissal: a mere word from him can compass her downfall, or he may call in the nuns, and that's the end of the lay school.

As a result, the control of the women's teacher training colleges themselves lay in the hands of the congregations, who thereby controlled the training of the lay schoolmistresses. The congregations owned and ran three out of every four training colleges, and four out of every five training courses.[167] And when, under the Second Empire, public schooling for girls began to develop in the wake of the Falloux Act, the congregational schoolmistresses flocked to the girls' schools armed not with a certificate of competence but merely with a letter of obedience. In 1863, at a time when the local schoolmasters were 85% 'lay' – i.e. not congregational – (and 88% had certificates),[168] 70% of the local schoolmistresses were congregational and 69% of them had no certificate:[169] over two-thirds of the schoolmistresses could show no document attesting to their qualifications as teachers.

Not to mention the clandestine schoolmistresses: 'Yesterday, at Saint-Avé, near Vannes,' relates the Inspector of the *Académie* of Morbihan in 1880,

> I surprised a clandestine girls' school run by a sort of *Béate*, without qualifications, needless to say; there were 42 or 43 children aged between 3 and 13 in a single room. . . . Under the auspices of the priest, this *Béate* teaches in this hovel nothing but the Breton catechism, and books and prayers in Breton; no, that is wrong: she also teaches reading in a Book of Psalms in Latin. Apart from that, neither writing, nor arithmetic, and not a word of French.[170]

So, until the passage of the republican laws, the new 19th century school was a masculine one. Not even necessarily because fewer girls attended school, indeed the figures for 1863 show 2,070,000 girls enrolled compared with 2,266,000 boys. But because private education, beyond the control of the State, was only really important for girls (35% of girls attending school in 1863, as against 9% of boys), and above all because, in the State system, it was only the male teaching corps that had been transformed by State intervention: there were 'new schoolmasters', but no new mistresses. It was not until the republicans took over the Republic that a Minister of Education – Jules Ferry, in August 1879, speaking before the Senate – could dare to cry out: 'And I say, gentlemen, that the education of girls, as with all education, belongs to the State, is the job of the State!'[171]

By the time the Ferry Bills came up for discussion, the battle for schooling may be regarded as having been won: in 1876–77, out of 4,500,000 children aged between 6 and 13 (i.e. of school age), we find 4,716,000 pupils in elementary schools of all kinds. This gives us a rate of 105%: which is comprehensible because there were also children aged under 6 and over 13 in these schools, artificially inflating school attendance figures.[172]

This gives some idea of how swiftly schooling had expanded in mid-century: in 1850, the number of children attending school represented only 73% of the 6–13 age group. In the twenty-five years intervening, one of the major inequalities in French education – inequality between the sexes – had almost disappeared. Thanks to the Falloux, and later the Duruy, Acts there were now almost as many girls in the primary schools as boys.[173] Regional disparities, so blatant at the beginning of the century, had also narrowed a great deal. Disparities between *départements*, too, shrank considerably: most of the laggards[174] were areas of low population density, where local discrepancies further sharpened the contrasts: for children in outlying hamlets, the village school was hard to reach, especially in the closed season on the farms. Even so, there now remained but these ten or so *départements* to blush at their under-90% school attendance rates.

These triumphant figures refer, it is true, to children *enrolled* in school. They say nothing about how long children kept up their attendance, or how regularly they attended throughout the year. In this respect, there was still much to be done at the dawn of the Republic. But one of the chief obstacles to attendance, the monthly school fee, had already been substantially overcome by the Duruy Act, which provided communes with the means to facilitate free schooling.[175] In 1876-77 there were 2,200,000 non-fee-paying pupils in the elementary schools, i.e. roughly 58%.

So, even before the passage of these basic laws, the French elementary school was, on the whole, a mass school. It was also a much more uniform school. From the earliest days of the Empire, the 'departmental regulations for State schools', modelled – barring a few minor shades of terminology – on the 1851 national Regulation, worked towards a standardization to which everything was in any case contributing at once: the growing importance of the teacher-training college graduates – with their identical cultural background – within the teaching profession; the spread of Gréard's *Organisation pédagogique* and the use of standard time-tables;[176] the spread of lectures on teaching methods for teachers; and the considerable growth of educational periodicals.[177]

We need not conclude from all this normative standardization that the institution had thereby achieved uniformity: there were still poverty-stricken schools and overcrowded classes;[178] incompetent masters and – still more so – mistresses; poor-quality teaching, failing to instil the rudiments even. A primary-school inspector was astonished to see to what extent teaching standards had failed to keep pace with progress in other areas. While everything else was improving, the art of teaching marked time: 'Ought we not', he wrote, 'to be struck by the crowd of children who have been attending school for the last two or three years and who still cannot read or write, ignorant even of the most elementary things that less than half a century ago could have been learned in the bosom of the family?'[179] This pedagogic lethargy, attested to a hundred times over,[180] explains why, from Duruy's time onwards, people began to take an interest in 'unteachable' children, i.e. children who attend school but gain nothing from it: in 1865, the *Statistique de l'enseignement primaire* estimated that close on 100,000 children had left school for good, able neither to read nor to write, or else able to read only: in other words 16.4% of school-leavers.

In addition, Duruy reckoned that those who left school only able to read and write – unable to count even – had an educational level so low and so uncertain that they must surely quickly forget what they had learned, and that they too must be included among the 'unteachables': in 1865 they numbered 124,000, or 19%. In all then, over a third of school-leavers were regarded – strictly from the point of view of literacy – as 'unteachables'.

The overall picture was thus rather disturbing, and those apparently attenuated regional disparities return once more in full force.[181]

We now see more clearly just what can be ascribed to Jules Ferry. First of all, he made up the deficiencies in school attendance in three areas at least: he expanded schooling for girls where it was still scarce (in the west and the centre); he had schools set up in every hamlet; and he improved regularity of school attendance by making it compulsory and free. Furthermore, he made the elementary schools more efficient by providing them with money, premises and schoolmasters. Masters above all: hence the generalization of teacher training colleges for women and the introduction of a compulsory certificate of competence for schoolmistresses, and so on.

To this aspect of Ferry's educational policy, immediate political concerns added another: along with the extension of the content of elementary education, the secularization and the republicanization of the school. But that does not concern us here. What our inquiry has shown is that, at the end the 1870s, the vast majority of French boys and girls were already attending – though the actual length of time spent in school and regularity of attendance varied – some sort of (more or less suitable) school, and that in the vast majority of cases, they were attending a State school.[182] When we contemplate the battle that raged about the Ferry Acts, it seems hard to believe that all this was already an accomplished fact, in the absence of any form of compulsion. The most likely conclusion to draw from this, as in so many other domains, is that it is only when a change is almost completed that it becomes the centre of vehement, acrimonious controversy.

# 4

## THE PEASANT: FROM ORAL
## TO WRITTEN CULTURE

If indeed the school is not the substance or the heart of the literacy process but merely its form, we must seek the social pressures in favour of it; who in the old French society wanted instruction, and why?

Who? Well the rich to begin with, the established families, the notables. The literacy process is quite simply the story of how an élitist cultural model penetrated throughout society. From the top downwards, from the upper to the lower classes, so much so that very early on in our history instruction came to be taken as synonymous with social superiority, whereas in fact it was merely its corollary. From its ability to modify the fate of individual people, some concluded that it had the power to transform society as well, when in fact it was on the contrary governed by the prior distribution of opportunities. In this respect, the history of the literacy process is a crystal-clear refutation of meritocratic illusions: the influence of social stratification is here a fact of life. Only the socio-occupational structure appears to correlate constantly with the ability to sign one's name.

This proves that while, ever since the 16th century, universal literacy was a religious imperative, selective literacy was also rooted from the outset in the division of labour and the social hierarchy. The formidable boost given to it by Protestantism and the Counter-Reformation proved an inadequate countervailing force against the inertia of society, i.e. against inequalities of craft, status and prestige. Created to furnish all men with a single means of communication with God and among themselves, reading and writing first of all served to strengthen the existing divisions in society, between rich and poor, the educated and the unlettered, town and country. For if all men *had to* learn to read and write, then those who persisted in their ignorance are marked by an additional lack of public esteem. The religious need for instruction, when caught up in the mesh of social reality, blended with the secular demands of craft, rank and prestige. It reflected them, at the same time adding to them a symbol of modernity: henceforward, there were bumpkins, who could not read, and the rest.

Put more crudely still, there was the town and there was the country. Not that all the townsfolk could read and write, nor that all countrypeople were illiterate. But we have seen the time-lag – a century at least – that separated urban literacy from rural literacy: it was the town which dominated and directed the entire process. It was the centre for the administration – ecclesiastical or royal – of men, and of trade. Now the

Church, the centralized State and the local market were spreading written civilization; they were the foci of the process; their agents served as models. It was in the towns that the bishop, the canon, the *intendant*, the judge, the merchant, artisan and shopkeeper lived; it was from the towns, frequently, that the drive for schooling emanated, or at any rate the example. The disparities between town and country, where literacy was concerned, were in the first place the product of its specific socio-occupational structure: even though under the *Ancien Régime* the town still housed a good many peasants within its walls, commercial, administrative and intellectual activities were nonetheless over-represented there. The above-average literacy of the towns reflected their more advanced social development, and their influence – real and symbolic – over the surrounding countryside.

Let us look at the map showing the percentage of the population engaged in agricultural pursuits – the 19th century was in full swing – *département* by *département* (Map 4.1). Even so crude a social indicator as this – for want of better – once more reveals two Frances, separated by the Saint-Malo–Geneva line (provided we exclude the big cities of the Midi, Gironde with Bordeaux, the Lyons region and the Mediterranean and Provençal coast around Marseilles). The map of below-average literacy coincides accurately with one socio-occupational map at least, that of the peasantry.

This is not to suggest that within rural France the law that binds literacy with social status functions less rigorously. For there were non-peasants living in the villages; and then there were peasants and peasants. The figures contained in the *Statistique générale de la France* are too coarse for this kind of analysis, but all the monographs, without exception, base their literacy ratings on socio-occupational groups. In the Normandy countryside,[1] in the second half of the 18th century (figures by occupation are not available prior to this date), the 'notables' had long been 100% literate, the landowning peasants or farmers were almost all literate too, though presumably more recently. More than three-quarters of the merchants, and just about three-quarters of the artisans signed their *acte de mariage*, and more than one weaver in two even. Only a single social category failed to cross the threshold of 50% in 1750, the agricultural day-labourers who, with the weavers, though more so than they, constituted a pool of humanity long impervious to the progress of literacy – except in the region of Bray. For example, in Caux, it is through the scores of the day-labourers, the weavers and the seamen, either static or declining, that a kind of plateau of literacy emerges to characterize the second half of the 18th century. The same analysis holds good for day-labourers in Vexin or on the fringes of Picardy. One gets the impression that, in its conquest of society, literacy comes up against some kind of obstacle around the bottom of the social ladder, having once reached a certain level, though this might vary from region to region. Like growth, stagnation was socially selective: we may observe this once again in Normandy, among women, since the big gains in literacy in the 18th century were due to the daughters of farmers, merchants, and of artisans as well, whereas figures for the daughters of day-labourers indicate a relative stagnation. The spread of literacy reflects the growing awareness and the demand exercised by the social milieu; the rural France that was learning in large numbers to read and write in the 18th century was that of the rural middle and lower-middle classes, the farmers, small tradespeople and artisans.

By the beginning of the 19th century, in that France, both geographically and socially speaking, the cause had been won: witness Eure-et-Loir, a *département* straddling natural regions as diverse as Perche and Beauce, for which we possess a chart showing the educational level of conscripts for 1835–37, by canton and by trade.[2] At that date, the artisans and crop-growers – at least those in this age-bracket – in the *département* were to a very large extent literate, even in the canton of Nogent-le-Rotrou, where 55% of crop-growers could read and write. But two social categories continued to lag behind: day-workers on the land and shepherds who, even in Beauce (the canton of Chartres), were just about 50% educated, whereas in Perche (canton of Nogent-le-Rotrou) they scored 25% and 17% respectively. The Perche crop-grower was better-educated than the Beauce day-labourer: which shows that social inequality was greater still than regional inequality.

The same phenomenon was at work, naturally, in the backward France, though at a later date. In Vovelle's Provence,[3] neither notables nor peasants 'budged', where literacy is concerned, in the 18th century: the former because they were already literate by the beginning of the century, the latter because they remained totally illiterate. The tiny increases visible on the general curves are due to the progress of the artisans and tradespeople. The peasants of Provence only began their take-off in the 19th century and, as always, the crop-growers led the day-labourers. In the most backward *départements* the standstill of the poorest strata was unremitting: in Vienne at the beginning of the 19th century, only 7% of day-labourers were able to sign their name!

It would be pointless to cite further examples of a mechanism that was everywhere at work and that recurs in all the monographs in this book. Mediaeval society was a restricted literacy society, where the handling of the written word was left to a body of specialist clercs. In modern society, which in this respect begins with printing and the Reformation, literacy is supposed to be universal, since it is simultaneously a means to salvation, a training in social order, in good manners, and an instrument for the generation of social intercourse. Hardly surprisingly, from all these viewpoints, it quickly gained recognition as not only useful but also exemplary, and slowly spread downwards throughout the body of society, under pressure ascribed to example, the necessity granted to utility, or the resistance of habit: in other words, depending on the different groups and classes' representations and social practices. It took several centuries for written civilization in its most rudimentary form to filter down from the notables in the towns to the day-labourer in the countryside.

## Open-field versus 'Bocage' (Mixed woodland and pasture)

Nevertheless social stratification cannot account for the fact that at a given moment in time the Provençal tradesman was more likely to be able to read and write than a Norman tradesman, or a Limousin peasant less likely than his Lorraine colleague. This is because in the old France the literacy performance of an individual was governed by two principles. As we have just seen, it is closely bound up with social background. But in this highly diversified society, still barely integrated into the State and still financing its own schools, individual performance also reflects geographical disparities in cultural development. Everywhere, for instance, or almost everywhere, the towns are ahead of the countryside; but in the diversity of their scores they inexorably reflect the precociousness or backwardness of the surrounding countryside. Wherever one looks within a given *département* or region, peasant smallholders are more literate than day-labourers; but an early-19th-century Beauceron day-labourer is more literate than a Limousin smallholder. Social determinations are thus not the sole factor at work: we all know, in any case, just how vague occupational labels could be in the old society, either concealing the exercise of several trades at once, which is common in the country, or because a single word could be used to designate different types of farm from one province to another, or again because different words ('ménager' in Provence, and 'closier' in Normandy) could refer to situations that were similar yet difficult to distinguish and relate exactly. The extraordinary constancy of socio-occupational determination thus far from dispensing with a region-by-region analysis actually points in that direction.

The simplest thing would be to begin with the departmental figures contained in the *Statistique générale de la France* around the middle of the 19th century, from 1851[4] onwards, at a time when facts about agriculture began to flow abundantly and systematically. Simplest perhaps, but the trouble with these national snapshots of figures selected more than a century ago for other purposes is not hard to spot. They come a little late in the day for one thing: by the mid-19th century, the country was well on the way to becoming literate, even in most of the regions that had been backward in this respect, and such connections as there may be between them and the facts of rural civilization tell us of an irreversible, already largely self-sustaining phenomenon. But above all it is the departmental breakdown of the figures which sheds little light on comparison: the *département* is an administrative unit that cuts across natural regions, cultivation patterns, types of farm and habit. Aggregating figures at this level – whether by Maggiolo or by the statisticians responsible for the *Statistique générale de la France* – is liable to lead attempts at correlation either into the 'ecological illusion'[5] or, alternatively, to an artificially negative picture.

Indeed, factorial analysis of agricultural variables and literacy figures in the *Statistique* in the mid-19th century[6] does produce disappointing results. The only correlation with the literacy axis (which covers only 28% of total information) to emerge is a negative correlation with the proportion of share-croppers in relation to farmers (Map 4.2). In the mid-19th century, the average proportion of farms run by share-croppers was 12%. But the map of this type of management reveals particularly high concentrations in the centre-west and the south-west, with share-croppers representing 58% in Haute-Vienne, 45% in Cher, 27% in Corrèze and 54% in Landes, and so on. Outside this region, one only finds extensive share-cropping in Aude (30%) and Bouches-du-Rhône (39%). Although not entirely absent in north and north-eastern France, it was uncommon. Leaving aside Bouches-du-Rhône (whose literacy figures are swollen by the presence of Marseilles), it is clear that not all the backward *départements* (from the point of view of literacy) were share-cropping *départements* (cf. Brittany), but that on the other hand the share-cropping *départements* all had a very high percentage of illiteracy, although not necessarily occupying the same rankings on the two scales. More than a strictly socio-occupational curse – since Brittany, so educationally backward, does not suffer from it – this is more likely a sickness of a more general order: rural poverty, of which share-cropping is one of the more reliable indicators. Not that the status of the farm has no rôle to play, like the close dependence on its landlord which it entails; but this status and this dependence reflect a poor, backward agriculture, one that they in turn help to perpetuate.

This naturally brings to mind Emile Guillaumin's admirable *Vie d'un simple*,[7] and the account given by *père* Tiennon the share-cropper, son of a share-cropper, brother of share-croppers, father of share-croppers too, in the poor 19th-century Bourbonnais, which was a typical bastion of rural immobility and archaic peasantry. Young Tiennon, born in 1823, never left his farm, except, four or five times a year, to go to mass in the village. Before the age of seven, he was watching the flocks, rising at five in the morning, his work as shepherd being vital to the family economy. Of those around him, none could read, neither his father, nor his uncles, and the women still less. School was out of the question: 'Schools were far apart at the time, and only the semi-bourgeois could send their children to them; for the yearly fees were dear.' Tiennon's first contact with 'society', as he describes it, was the catechism, more than a league away from the farm: this was more a formality prior to communion than a pedagogic experience, since of his two years of weekly sessions with the old priest of Meillers, all the child could recall was his pranks on the way home; no trace remained of any contact with books. Tiennon is a good example of that 'red' peasantry inhabiting the Centre (he voted republican in 1848, then for Bonaparte at the end of the year), still heavily dependent on the landlord, poor, illiterate, not much cared for by the Church, and whose own 1789 was to come nearly a century late with the advent of the Third Republic and the eclipse of the rural notables. In the 1850s, 'the schools began to fill', and Tiennon had tried to put his son to school, in one of the free places for the poor; but the village councillor, a peremptory obscurantist, refused point blank to take him away from tending the flock. It was the grandson who finally learned to read and write at the same time – it was the end of the century by now – as the history of France. In this harsh land, where the gentlemen from the towns and their stewards had replaced the lords and their bailiffs, the educational opportunities available to children were a caricature of the social ladder: early in the century, the bourgeois or 'semi-bourgeois'. In mid-century, 'the village tradespeople, and the posher countryfolk'. The poor share-cropper's turn did not come until the arrival of the Third Republic.

Leaving aside agricultural variables in 1851 – we have seen how little there is to be had by analysing the correlation with literacy scores – there is one item in the 1872 census that marries fairly well with that which emerges from the Maggiolo scores, namely the relationship between urbanized population and total population (Map 4.3). This is not a question of the size of the communes, since it is quite possible to find, as in Brittany for example (Morbihan and Finistère), highly populous yet 'scattered' communes, containing numerous 'deviations'. What concerns us is the population actually concentrated in villages or small towns, i.e. village civilization as opposed to that of the hamlet – in which Siegfried saw the characteristic of the 'open-field' as opposed to the 'bocage'.[8]

Generally speaking, *départements* with a small proportion of urban population, such as Landes (20%), Corrèze (28%), Morbihan (29%), Côtes-du-Nord (31%), Finistère (31%), Haute-Vienne (32%) are also those with the lowest literacy rates. Here again we find that great triangle of cultural backwardness in France, embracing Brittany, the centre-west and the south-west. Conversely, the *départements* with the largest proportion of urban population lie precisely in that part of France, the north-east, that had achieved literacy earliest: Aube (90%), Marne (91%), Somme (91%), Haute-Marne (93%), Meurthe (94%), Meuse (95%) and Haut-Rhin (97%). It is not hard to imagine the factors working in favour of the spread of education in a civilization of concentrated villages: social contacts are easier, communication between inhabitants better, and hence cultural contagion works faster; lastly, children have less far to go to reach school, which is an important factor in making up parents' minds – remembering that school attendance was a winter activity, from November to March, when dirt tracks were muddy, or snowed under, and often practically impassible.

Like all simple hypotheses, this cultural division of France based on two different types of rural habitat is tempting. Most particularly it has the advantage of coinciding with two secular types of peasant civilization, open-field and 'bocage' and hence refers back to the old dividing line in the relative wealth of communities and individuals: the open-field peasantry usually had the best land, the best yields, and produced more systematically for the market than did the farm or the family enclosure in the 'bocage'.

Even so, the notion ought not to be stretched too far, as the example of Normandy shows. This was a zone of relatively scattered habitat, and yet the Norman 'bocage' had high literacy rates as early as the 18th century. G. Désert has devoted a monograph to school attendance in the 19th century in the *département* of Calvados.[9] This has the advantage of dealing at the same time with the Plain of Caen, an open-field area with concentrated villages, the Auge region and the beginnings of the Norman 'bocage' with dispersed settlements. Well, around the beginning of the July Monarchy, the Caen Plain and the 'bocage' *arrondissements* (Vire, Falaise, Bayeux) had high school-attendance rates, whereas the Auge area (*arrondissements* of Pont-l'Evêque and Lisieux) was lagging behind. So in Normandy, where the 'bocage' land is, to be sure, exceptionally profitable (and well used), the contrast detected on a nationwide scale is inapplicable, at least where school attendance among the rural population is concerned. And indeed, judging by the average rates paid per inhabitant, the richest areas were the two *arrondissements* with the lowest school attendance, Pont-l'Evêque and Lisieux. G. Désert concludes that the origins of disparities in school attendance lie rather in the size of commune populations, which were appreciably smaller in Auge: the smaller the population of a commune, the heavier the financial burden imposed by a school.

This is an argument often encountered in the 19th century, from the pens of the *académie* authorities. True, the map showing the proportion of communes with a population of under 500 in each *département*, in 1861,[10] divides France more or less along a line close to that of *recteur* Maggiolo. But this rough partition in turn admits of many exceptions to the rule on both sides of the line.

The wealth of a commune – since that is what we are talking about – does not depend solely on the number of its inhabitants. In his report to the King prior to the passage of his Bill,[11] Guizot also stresses this aspect of the problem when commenting on the departmental distribution of school costs; but he puts this down to inequalities in the ownership of communal forests and soil fertility:

> Whereas in some *départements* the taxes borne by the ratepayers barely exceed one centime, in many they exceed four centimes. The richest *départements*, those where primary instruction is in the most flourishing state, are those where the costs are lowest; the highest costs are borne by the poorest *départements*. This state of affairs flows from a specific set of circumstances that warrants attention.
>
> In the former provinces most recently united with France, whether by conquest or by marriage, such as Champagne, Burgundy, Franche-Comté, Alsace or Lorraine, the communes preserved their ownership of the communal forests; whereas in the old France, for a multitude of reasons which it would be tedious and pointless to go into here, the communes had been almost completely deprived of their forests. Hence, for the communes of those provinces, [came] a considerable source of income. It was with this income that they built schoolhouses, paid teachers, provided their inhabitants with the benefits of primary instruction, and thereby contributed to the great development of civilization which exists in these parts. Most of these communes having sufficient income to meet this expenditure, the *département* only had to provide a very small additional amount: consequently, the burden on ratepayers was extremely light.
>
> In other parts of France, and in fertile areas moreover, such as Calvados, Eure-et-Loir, Manche, Nord, Pas-de-Calais, Seine-Inférieure, Hérault, Gard, Lot-et-Garonne, Tarn-et-Garonne, rates being higher than in the arid areas, communes which are obliged to raise a tax to pay for expenditure on primary instruction are only rarely obliged to demand as much as three centimes; and in general they have no need to request a supplement out of departmental funds. As a result, additional rates levied for this purpose are reasonably low.
>
> But this is not so in the poor, hilly areas such as Ariège, Cantal, Creuse, Landes, Haute-Loire, Lozère, Vienne, Haute-Vienne, etc. There, rates are low because incomes are scant. The three centimes are far from sufficient to pay the teacher a minimal wage; so it is necessary to turn to departmental funds, which are also inadequate to cope with all these needs, and the State will have to give big subsidies to these *départements*.
>
> One other circumstance tends to make the spread of primary instruction more difficult here than elsewhere.

In the communes that own their communal forest, as in the fertile parts of the country, teachers received a wage paid out of the municipal budget, in exchange for which they educated all children free. Communes in infertile or hilly areas, on the other hand, were unable to pay their teachers out of municipal funds. Instruction was entirely at the family's expense, although their incomes were extremely limited; consequently they only managed with the greatest difficulty, and these areas which have until now been pointed to as being unfavourable to primary education, because no one took into account the financial situation of the communes, were in fact those in which people made the greatest sacrifices for their children's education.

According to Guizot, in this document, there were three types of communal wealth, the first based on communal ownership of the forests, the second on soil fertility and the wealth of the ratepayers, the third, in contrast, on poverty-stricken farms and people. In the first two cases, the costs of schooling are borne by the wealth of the community, while in the last they fall upon the parents themselves. The trouble with this type of analysis is its assumption that all French people felt the need for education in the same way, when so many documents suggest the reverse. Its merit is that it raises the topic of the wealth of the communities, an infinitely more fruitful concept than the variables suggested by comparative analysis of departmental statistics, whether of the structure of peasant farms, type of habitat, or the size of communes. It is clear, in fact, that the literacy or schooling processes are far too complex to be tied down to a single variable, but that through share-cropping or habitat they doubtless constantly run up against a third underlying factor: individual and community poverty.

None of the statistical overviews enable us then to dispense with closer scrutiny of individual cases, in order to shade in our general hypothesis. We are going to have to turn to the local monographs, most of which are published in the second volume of this book.

**Journey through the *départements* of France**

We shall take first one of the simplest cases, the *département* of Eure-et-Loir, for which we possess good records of the state of instruction of conscripts, according to residence, in the 19th century.[12] Eure-et-Loir contains two very different types of rural economy, corresponding to two different types of countryside, two landscapes, two land occupancy patterns: one might almost say two populations. To travel from Beauce to Perche is like changing countries. Large-scale open-field cereal farming, the vast plain dotted with huddled villages and fortified farms, gives way to hill and vale, to the characteristic enclosures of the humble 'bocage', studded with forests and ponds, with tiny peasant farms in scattered hamlets. In administrative terms, it means journeying from the *arrondissement* of Chartres to that of Nogent-le-Rotrou.

In 1835–37, 36% of the entire *département*'s conscripts were illiterate. This figure drops to 28% for the *arrondissement* of Chartres, while rising to 56% in that of Nogent; 29.5% and 59% if one leaves the two towns out of account, themselves highly unequal in this respect (15% illiteracy in Chartres, and 36% in Nogent) because they were tributary to the surrounding countryside. Concealed within the departmental average, this difference is enough to make Beauce, early in the 19th century, a relatively literacy 'country', and Perche a stronghold of backwardness comparable to a good many regions of the south of France. Figures on the level of instruction of conscripts for 1878–82 show that this inequality became less marked towards the end of the century, as education spread, but that it did not disappear completely: 4% illiteracy in Beauce, against 11% in Perche. Memories (and perhaps more than that) of it were still so vivid that an old Beauceron farmer in the village of Saint-Loup, talking to one of the authors of this book in 1973 still recalled: 'During the 1914–18 War, the Beaucerons had to write letters for the chaps from Perche to send to their fiancées.'[13] One detects in this comment a kind of ancestral sense of civilized superiority.

So sharp is the contrast between the two types of rural economy that these disparities in literacy rates encompass every social and occupational category: artisans, labourers, farmers, agricultural day-labourers, shepherds. As a region of large-scale crop-growing Beauce had more day-labourers than the small peasant holdings of Perche: but even the Beauce day-labourers were far less massively illiterate than those in Perche (49% compared with 71%), and almost on an equal footing with Perche 'farmers' (49% compared with 41%). What we have here is a gulf not just between different types of farming, but between a rich agriculture and a poor one, between production for the market and a subsistence economy: as early as 1803, a consular inquiry indicated that only 14 of the 120 communes in the Chartres *arrondissement* lacked schools.[14] At the other end of the *département* lay poverty and ignorance. Eure-et-Loir was a positive laboratory for the *académie* inspectorate (Map 4.4).

Things do not have quite this clean-cut simplicity in the case of Normandy, studied by Muriel Jeorger.[15] The former diocese of Rouen, from which the literacy samples have been taken, also contained several different types of rural economy side by side. The extreme patchwork and dispersal of farms in the Caux and Bray areas was offset everywhere else by clustered villages. But in the prosperous Normandy of the 18th century, the different types of habitat did not coincide with the disparities in wealth: like

Vexin, a vast open-field cereal-growing area, Caux was a wheat-growing region, though mingled with 'bocage', apple orchards and animal husbandry. The Roumois plateau was a mixed-farming area, as were the Seine Valley villages. Lastly, the Bray district, a region of woodland and pasture *par excellence*, a weald of clay on the chalky plateaux, had discovered its dairy vocation as early as the 18th century, supplying the Paris market: the scattered habitat and hedged meadows served here as a foundation for small-scale rural capitalism (Table 4.1).

These literacy scores show that the Bray district was ahead by the end of the 17th century, with 45% of its men signing their name, compared with the Caux's 31% and the Norman Vexin's 38%. Bray held on to its lead throughout the 18th century, thanks to constantly improving performance: from 45% to 83% for the men, and better still for the women, from 6% to 58%. This combined to give the Bray district a firm superiority (M + W) in literacy over all the other regions in the diocese of Rouen: over the Vexin and the Picardy borderlands, whose female literacy rose much less quickly, over the Roumois, where both sexes improved their scores more slowly, and above all the Caux, where male literacy seems to have marked time throughout the latter half of the century.

Indeed it is this marking-time which, *a contrario*, gives the clue to the superiority of the Bray district and to the regional ranking: for it was caused by stagnation, slippage even, in the scores achieved by the day-labourers and textile workers. The Caux, in addition to being a region of large farms like the Vexin, also had a large textile industry, which accounts for its big population of poor agricultural labourers and textile workers (men and women), which acted as a brake on the spread of literacy. In Bray, on the other hand, landholding patterns were less concentrated; the profitable dairy-farming for the market enabled the small and medium-sized peasant holdings to enjoy a fair measure of prosperity; the abundance of communal pastures, where even the poorest peasants could keep a beast or two, was an additional asset to this rural economy favouring a kind of landowning individualism. It is not hard to see – or guess, rather – which social group was the driving force behind, and the embodiment of, the spread of literacy in the countryside: it was the middling peasantry, consisting of landowners and farmers, living relatively comfortably off their marketable output and enjoying an annual cash surplus. In this agricultural Normandy in the 18th century, rich and culturally advanced, the regional literacy rankings in fact reveal, in the last analysis, the structures of rural society.

The example of Burgundy, presented by Pierre Lévêque,[16] bears out this analysis entirely. Here the study focuses on two neighbouring *départements*: Côte-d'Or, well above the average literacy rate for the nation (54% of the men signed their names on the eve of the Revolution, 69% at the

Table 4.1  *Literacy in rural Normandy by natural region and département*

| SEINE INFERIEURE | Caux distinct % | Picardy border % | Bray % | TOTAL % | Maggiolo % |
|---|---|---|---|---|---|
| **Men** | | | | | |
| Late 17th ......... | 31 | 36 | 45 | 37 | 39 |
| | [26 ⌉ 31 | [38 ⌉ 38 | [19 ⌉ 38 | [28 ⌉ 36 | |
| Mid-18th ......... | 57 | 74 | 64 | 65 | |
| | [05 ⌋ | [00 ⌋ | [19 ⌋ | [08 ⌋ | |
| Late 18th ......... | 62 | 74 | 83 | 73 | 64 |
| **Women** | | | | | |
| Late 17th ......... | 3 | 13 | 6 | 7 | 16 |
| | [12 ⌉ 34 | [21 ⌉ 30 | [20 ⌉ 52 | [18 ⌉ 39 | |
| Mid-18th ......... | 15 | 34 | 26 | 25 | |
| | [22 ⌋ | [09 ⌋ | [32 ⌋ | [21 ⌋ | |
| Late 18th ......... | 37 | 43 | 58 | 46 | 40 |
| **TOTAL** | | | | | |
| Late 17th ......... | 17 | 24 | 25 | 22 | 28 |
| Mid-18th ......... | 36 | 53 | 45 | 45 | |
| Late 18th ......... | 50 | 58 | 70.5 | 60 | 52.26 |

| EURE<br>Men | Norman<br>Vexin | Roumois<br>district | TOTAL | Maggiolo |
|---|---|---|---|---|
| Late 17th.......... | 38 | 46 | 42 | 47 |
| | [21 | [08 | [15 | |
| Mid-18th .......... | 59   38 | 54   25 | 57   32 | |
| | [17 | [19 | [17 | |
| Late 18th.......... | 76 | 73 | 74 | 75.28 |
| Women | | | | |
| Late 17th.......... | 7 | 7 | 7 | 17.96 |
| | [13 | [13 | [13 | |
| Mid-18th.......... | 20   32 | 20   33 | 20   33 | |
| | [19 | [20 | [19.5 | |
| Late 18th.......... | 39 | 40 | 39.5 | 53.43 |
| TOTAL | | | | |
| Late 17th.......... | 22 | 40 | 40 | |
| Late 18th.......... | 57 | 58 | 57.5 | 64.25 |

N.B. Figures in brackets indicate differences between literacy scores at different dates.

Restoration) and Saône-et-Loire, which was lagging a long way behind (20% and 40% respectively). Southern Burgundy continued to lag, the distance widening even, in the 1830s, as can be seen from conscription figures, at a time when Côte-d'Or had cut the figure for illiteracy to 10% of its conscripts; the gap only began to narrow again from 1845 onwards, when in ten years Saône-et-Loire reduced its illiteracy rate from 50% to 40%.

According to Lévêque, the explanation of this contrast lies in the different ways in which local populations reacted to the school and to education. Although in the 19th century both *départements* belonged to the same *académie* (area education authority) and were run by the same *recteur*, who applied the same legislation, Côte-d'Or was greatly in favour of elementary schooling – there had been elementary schools in practically every commune since the start of the century – whereas the inhabitants of Saône-et-Loire were guarded, if not hostile. In Côte-d'Or, a social threshold of literacy had been achieved even before the Guizot Act, a threshold that excluded only the rural proletariat; in Saône-et-Loire, it took the Revolution of 1830 and the passage of the Guizot Act to achieve the decisive breach in the social resistance to literacy, the earliest results of which were to become apparent ten years later.

What is this differential propensity to education? A series of maps throws some light on the regional figures and their economic and social roots.[17] The first requisite is to locate the major pockets of illiteracy, ignoring administrative boundaries. While there was indeed an overall contrast between the two *départements*, the cantonal map showing the educational level of conscripts in 1827–30 shows that, in Saône-et-Loire, the whole of the western part of the *département* was 90% illiterate (Morvan, the region around Autun, Charolais). Facing this backward Massif Central, the Maconnais and Charolais plains looked like an advanced region, even though their performances were inferior to those of Châtillonnais or the Burgundian plain between Beaune and Dijon. Lastly, to the east, Bresse once again turned in high illiteracy scores. The 1845–47 conscription map somewhat dilutes the colours but does not affect the overall picture.

Now it so happens that P. Lévêque's cantonal maps of 'rural civilization' also pinpoint with remarkable clarity the backward Massif Central zone and the less markedly backward Bresse: these were regions of 'bocage', in contradistinction to the open field of the north and the great vineyards along a north-south line; two-yearly rotation cropping predominated here, whereas a three-yearly rotation was the rule in northern Burgundy. Again, we find the same division between scattered and clustered habitat, as measured by the average number of deviations per commune. The map showing the extent of communal property, which was an essential element of the wealth of a community, also isolates two pockets of illiteracy in the east and west of Saône-et-Loire: in Morvan and Charolais, collective property accounted for less than 2.5% of the communes' total area! One final indicator: the percentage of men employed in industry and trade also points the finger at the Massif Central and Bresse as islands of rural life.

'Bocage', two-yearly crop rotation, penniless communes, low urban and market penetration thus together weave the fabric of illiteracy. Still, there were exceptions to this law of generalized backwardness: analysis of the cantons, combined into *pays* (or districts), reveals some anomalies in the literacy scores compared with the indicators of rural civilization; for instance, the Bresse 'bocage' was markedly less illiterate than the 'bocages' of the west, and even boasted one genuinely educated canton. The explanation for this difference will become apparent from a look at the comparative table for the four cantons or groups of 'bocage' cantons: two in the heart of the Massif Central, Issy l'Evêque (Autunois) and Guegnon (Charolais), the third in the transitional zone in the direction of the plain (Semur-en-Brionnais), and lastly the group of ten Bressan cantons. Of the conscripts from Issy l'Evêque and Guegnon 80% were still illiterate in the mid-19th century; only 34% in Brionnais and Bresse. Now the first two cantons stand out from the others not only by their especially scattered habitat (average number of deviations per commune), but above all by the poverty of their peasants: the rateable value per hectare was three or four times less; small estates accounted for 10% of the area (compared with 30% in Brionnais and 33% in Bresse); share-cropping was prevalent, whereas it scarcely existed at all in Brionnais or Bresse, which were largely owner-farmed. Here again we arrive at one of the conclusions drawn from the Normandy study, namely that the 'bocage' peasantry was only illiterate when it also happened to be dependent and poverty-stricken. Thus what seems to be backwardness in a civilization is in fact poverty in a society.

The same law is at work in what Maggiolo's maps show up as the homogeneous block formed by under-developed France. Analysis by canton and by commune fills in the details while at the same time helping us to grasp the social factors. Let us take a look, for example, at those *départements* in the north-west of the Massif Central which constitute precisely the area with the lowest literacy scores (Map 4.5). The Deux-Sèvres literacy scores at the beginning of the 19th century coincide with the physical geography and farming patterns of the *département*: the central and northern parts, the 'bocage' and above all the sterile marshlands (*gâtine*) had low literacy rates; the situation only brightens in the Thouars plain, in the north-east. The south, on the other hand, the Poitou marshes, living on market gardening and animal husbandry, had fewer illiterates. The best scores are to be found in the plain of Niort and Melle, an area of prosperous mixed farming, with big clustered villages; although the 'bocage' reappears in Mellois, none of these cantons had illiteracy of over 30%.

A comparable situation prevails in Vienne, which has been studied in detail by Yvonne Pasquet,[18] and in neighbouring Charente. Literacy levels divide the *département* of the Vienne along a north-south line. Whereas Maggiolo's statistics for the *département* give an impression of utter stagnation throughout the 18th century and even into the early 19th, Yvonne Pasquet's communal and cantonal figures, grouped by agricultural micro-region, show that the start-up actually began in the 18th century, in the clustered plains villages in the centre and south-west (cantons of Poitiers, Couhé Civray), in those areas with a market-oriented agriculture and an active social life – whereas the south-eastern part of the *département* was to remain prisoner of its poverty until the middle of the 19th century. As for Charente, one look at the cantonal map should be enough to single out the foothills of the Massif Central, the whole of the Confolentais (a fastness of illiteracy of up to 80% to 90%), as opposed to the wheat and winegrowing land stretching westwards from Angoulême, where illiteracy among conscripts drops to less than 35%.

Alain Corbin's work[19] at last gives us some interesting details on the three backward *départements* of Limousin in the 19th century, Creuse, Corrèze and Haute-Vienne. In mid-century, 73% of conscripts from Haute-Vienne and Corrèze were still illiterate, and 50% from Creuse. Creuse was right in the middle of its 'catching up' phase at this time, as can be seen from its scores for subsequent decades (by 1876–77, only 18% of its conscripts were illiterate), whereas Corrèze and Haute-Vienne lagged behind until the end of the century (37 and 38% of conscripts were illiterate in 1876–77). In place of departmental figures, whose disparities are already problematic enough, Corbin has substituted a canton-by-canton map of conscript literacy in 1846–50 and in 1880–84, together with a socio-occupational analysis of these data. The figures thus distributed reveal that the countryside was lagging well behind the towns: by mid-century, illiteracy had dropped to zero among the professions, civil servants and employees in trade, and was considerably less among industrial workers than among peasants. In the countryside, illiteracy was practically total among share-croppers, who were especially numerous in Haute-Vienne and Corrèze, a good deal less so in Creuse. But domestic servants and journeymen were in the same boat; and the performance of the vast majority of farmers, whether they styled themselves *cultivateurs*, *laboureurs* or *agriculteurs*, was scarcely any better: 91% of them were illiterate in Haute-Vienne. It was the whole of this poorly differentiated peasant society which was illiterate.

What then lies at the root of these rural inequalities in the canton-by-canton scores? Not just the greater or lesser frequency of share-cropping, type of habitat or land ownership, but also seasonal migratory patterns. The migrant peasant was already more literate than the sedentary one. To this prior selection should be added their long education in the towns, where these thrifty and – within reason – ambitious workers lived in digs with other members of their local community, which particularly meant that they kept up contacts with their native region. On their periodical visits to their home village, these people came as prophets and examples of urban culture in a land of oral tradition.

Take, for example, Martin Nadaud, the great 19th century Creuse republican.[20] He was born in 1815, in the hamlet of La Martinèche, in the parish of Soubrebost, in the *arrondissement* of Bourganeuf; he was the son of a 'dynamic' emigrant, one of the best workers in those parts. His family was completely illiterate, even his father, in spite of his journeys to Paris. There were no schools for miles around. In the local town, though, an old churchwarden, Père Faucher, used to take in a few children to teach them 'the alphabet and some notions of writing'. When Nadaud *père* decided, one Sunday as they were celebrating his 'return' home, to place his son there, the whole family rose in protest: 'My mother put up the stoutest resistance, claiming that she needed me to work in the fields. My grandfather agreed, as did other peasants, who wasted no time joining in the conversation. Anyway, everyone said, the things country children were likely to learn in school wouldn't be much use to them, other than to write a letter or two and take one's prayer book to mass.'

The grandfather, himself a former emigrant, was the sharpest critic of his son's obsessive plan, which he put down to the influence of the town: 'Since coming home from Paris, not a day has passed without your telling us what you'd like to do with your boy; you'd have done better to stay in Paris than come here with your plans for schooling. Not my brothers, nor you, nor myself, have ever learnt our letters, and yet we've had bread to eat all the same.'

Not my brothers, nor you, nor myself. ... Yet Martin's father must have made a timid breach in the tradition, since he bought the *Bulletins de la Grande Armée* at the market. This 'Napoleonist' peasant-worker brushed aside the curse of his environment and confided his son, for two hours a day, to the old churchwarden – except at harvest time, when the child had to spend the whole day in the fields. But the following year, on his return from his long Paris 'season', the father discovered that his son was a bit thickheaded. However, a teacher 'by profession', Rioublanc, had come to live in the town at the priest's request – this was towards the end of the Restoration. What about sending the child to him? This was the signal for a fresh rearguard action on the part of the grandfather and the mother, who this time argued that there was not enough money, and that there would be no one to watch the flock. But the father had his way, as he did each time he came home: the striking thing about Léonard's tale is the father's commitment to education in the face of the whole of peasant society; the peasant mason brought back from Paris for his son a modern ambition: 'If I'd been able to read and write,' he told his wife, 'you wouldn't be as wretched as you are, for I've not wanted opportunities of earning money; only, as I knew nothing, I had to stay a simple mate, with my nose stuck in the trough.' The obstinacy with which this avant-garde father sought to educate his son is probably not unconnected with his passion for the Napoleonic era and the songs of Béranger, which he brought back from Paris. This unlettered Bonapartist was to fashion an educated republican, furnishing an early illustration – in this backward Limousin – of the twin belief in education and the Republic. A quarter-century late, the task assigned to the elementary school by the French Revolution was beginning to materialize. Quite possibly it is no mere accident that this should have happened in the more backward rural areas, where the Church had done little in the previous century to establish schools, but which were now beginning to be irrigated by the message of the workers from the big towns.

Taken together, these local surveys thus confirm what our examination of departmental statistics had already hinted at, namely that there was no single, nor even paramount, variable in the history of the literacy process capable of accounting alone for disparities observed between *départements*, cantons, villages, and finally individuals. The most fertile concept is that of the social demand for education, collectively, and among families and individuals the propensity to seek education; but this is not directly measurable. Right up to the end of the 19th century, the greater or lesser wealth of the local community conditioned the feasibility of opening a school. But this did not depend solely on the relative size of the communal property. It was a function of the structure of rural society itself: types of habitat, land ownership patterns, cropping and land-use patterns, degree of urban (or at least market economy) penetration. Lastly, over and beyond all these different indicators, share-cropping or owner-farming, 'bocage' or open-field, three- or two-yearly rotation, what best defines the propensity to instruction was the prosperity or otherwise of the peasantry; this, together with, depending on the region or the canton, more specific factors (such as migration in Creuse or, elsewhere, the presence of some personality or an activist schoolteacher) capable of rapidly galvanizing the surrounding community. Almost until the end, rural society in France made its sons literate by its own efforts, without help from the State: not surprisingly, therefore, the history of this process, devoid of corrective mechanism, reflects the social inequalities that riddled this society.

**Reading only**

Literacy was born at the point where religion and society meet; but little by little it passed under society's sway. When the scholars lost their monopoly, reading and writing very quickly became instruments of social utility and status symbols as well. For these reasons, their spread naturally coincided with the geography of social development, itself merely the spatial expression of inequality: it is this underlying state of affairs which is reflected in Maggiolo's map, notwithstanding the crudeness of his departmental boundaries. Although one does come across islets of poverty in the rich portion of France and vice versa, the fact remains that northern and north-eastern France was prosperous, and the rest poor. Closer scrutiny by region and locality merely spells out in greater detail and refinement the longstanding intuitions of Baron Dupin.

There is however one factor in literacy that does not fit in with the general pattern of social wealth, and which for that reason deserves special attention: namely the ability to read only. As we have seen, in the old-style school, at least until the beginning of the 19th century, the processes of learning to read and write were distinct and followed one after the other; for the parents, moreover, they entailed separate items on the school bill. The complete school offered a 'menu', from arithmetic to reading, in descending order (plus, right at the top of the curriculum, Latin, in the Latin schools); writing generally cost twice as much as reading. When the school was not a complete one, it often happened that its master was not expected to offer more than the rudiments of reading; many documents even hint that in certain places this was what was wanted, not a limitation imposed by poverty, at least where the education of girls was concerned. To bear this out, Dame Charpentier, of Magnac-Laval in Limousin, drew up a will in 1689 making provision for the upkeep of a person whose job it would be to educate fifteen poor girls: to 'keep school, teach the young girls of this town to read, pray to God, the principal mysteries of our holy faith and religion, the principles of salvation, the dignified reception of the sacraments, to make their first confession and communion properly, the education and correction of behaviour and the practice of Christian virtue'.[21]

Like so many others of that time, drawn up for the same purpose, this document is filled with Catholic proselytism, with a fervent desire to achieve merit by extending to the poor some rudimentary knowledge of the Christian mysteries. In this distant township, as the century drew to a close, possibly even already with Revolution brewing, what guided the pen that wrote this will was still the Counter-Reformation, with not even a wink to acknowledge the modernity of writing. If all one wants is to make good Christians, then reading will do. To be sure, the bequest was for the education of girls; it is less common to come across clauses banning writing where boys' schools are concerned, although here too they do occur. Boys or girls, whichever, the message is clear: that the religious vocation of the school rests first and foremost upon reading, that is the basic subject to be learnt. It was quite likely that it was in this lasting conviction, a posthumous victory of ill-starred Protestantism, that the roots of this scholastic separation of reading from writing lay. Far more powerful than teaching methods or the cost of learning this or that subject, the origin of this compartmentalization of two kinds of knowledge was the gulf that divided the sacred from the profane.

Now factorial analysis of the 1866 literacy figures (chapter 1 in this book)[22] isolates a minor series of data distributed along a vertical axis, around the variable 'reading only'. The units, i.e. the *départements*, are arranged in an order that has nothing to do with the one on the horizontal axis (which concerns ability to sign one's name and ability to read and write): along this vertical axis, women precede men, and the regions arrange themselves in a very different order.

So we are going to have to analyze the ability to 'read only' separately. This is not going to be easy. Only two censuses measure this indicator for the population as a whole, those of 1866 and 1872. For earlier data we can go no further back than the 1827 conscripts, less than half a century beforehand, taking all the precautions that comparison between two such different population samples implies. It is not easy to trace the progress of literacy among men only – i.e. in this case among the least interesting category. Above all, though, the significance of ability to 'read only' in the literacy process is ambiguous.

Being able to read only is more than being able neither to read nor to write, yet less than being able to do both: so one might take an optimistic view of the situation, namely that this is a stage on the road to literacy; or alternatively a pessimistic view, taking this for a sign of cultural backwardness. For the period for which we have figures regarding this variable, one inclines to the second interpretation, especially in view of the superiority of female over male scores: since we already know that in all parts of the country completely literate men (able to read and write) outnumber completely literate women, their relative inferiority on the 'reading only' scale may be due to the fact that more of them have already reached the second category. However, the 1866 census classified the *départements* of France according to their educational level, in rising order of illiteracy: this meant counting as literate those able to read only, as well as those able to read and write. The top ten and the bottom ten *départements* were as follows:

| Top ten | Illiteracy |
|---|---|
| Bas-Rhin | 5.44% |
| Jura | 5.67% |
| Haute-Marne | 6.39% |
| Vosges | 8.93% |
| Doubs | 10.05% |
| Meurthe | 10.20% |
| Meuse | 11.07% |

| | |
|---|---|
| Aube | 11.79% |
| Haut-Rhin | 13.69% |
| Seine | 13.94% |
| Bottom ten: | |
| Vienne | 55.56% |
| Allier | 59.52% |
| Ariège | 59.82% |
| Dordogne | 60.66% |
| Morbihan | 60.76% |
| Finistère | 60.88% |
| Pyrénées-Orientales | 61.36% |
| Indre | 63.61% |
| Cher | 64.98% |
| Haute-Vienne | 66.67% |

Now, if we take a closer look at these twenty *départements*, the different literacy scores available in the 1866 census yield the following table:

| 1866 | neither read nor write | read only | read and write |
|---|---|---|---|
| Top ten *départements* | | | |
| Bas-Rhin | 5.44% | 5.65 | 88.91 |
| Jura | 5.67 | 8.70 | 85.63 |
| Haute-Marne | 6.39 | 4.98 | 88.63 |
| Vosges | 8.93 | 11.68 | 79.39 |
| Doubs | 10.05 | 7.84 | 82.11 |
| Meurthe | 10.20 | 9.38 | 80.42 |
| Meuse | 11.07 | 7.34 | 81.59 |
| Aube | 11.79 | 7.36 | 80.85 |
| Haut-Rhin | 13.69 | 7.14 | 79.17 |
| Seine | 13.94 | 2.59 | 83.47 |
| Bottom ten *départements* | | | |
| Vienne | 55.56 | 6.48 | 37.96 |
| Allier | 59.52 | 7.56 | 32.92 |
| Ariège | 59.82 | 13.59 | 26.59 |
| Dordogne | 60.66 | 9.38 | 29.96 |
| Morbihan | 60.76 | 13.14 | 26.10 |
| Finistère | 60.88 | 15.01 | 25.11 |
| Pyrénées-Orientales | 61.36 | 9.21 | 29.43 |
| Indre | 63.61 | 3.86 | 32.53 |
| Cher | 64.98 | 3.39 | 31.63 |
| Haute-Vienne | 66.67 | 5.22 | 28.11 |

Thus, if for this period we adopt a more restrictive classification of French *départements* than did the statisticians in 1866, placing our dividing line between those able to read *and* write on the one hand, and all the rest on the other, then according to the pessimistic view of the ability to read only, the distribution of *départements* is altered: in favour of Haute-Marne, Doubs, and above all Seine, at the top of the table (the Seine moves up six places); and in favour of Indre, Cher and Haute-Vienne to the detriment of Ariège and the Bretonwards *départements* at the bottom of the table.

Contemporary statisticians never bothered to analyze this distortion, and passed over the 'read only' indicator in utter silence. What this distortion expresses is in fact very simple, namely that the relation between the numbers of those able to read only and those able to read and write is highly variable. In Finistère, Morbihan and Ariège, the ratio is 1:2; it is 1:3 in Pyrénées-Orientales; 1:10 in Jura, and 1:32 in Seine! In other words, reading only may well be a step on the road to literacy, but it appears to be an independent step, with no clear relation to what went before or to what comes after. The hypothesis that might be suggested by the old elementary-school curriculum (where reading was taught before writing), namely that this intermediate score varies in the same proportions as the 'lower' and 'higher' scores does not appear to fit the facts.

Let us now take a look at the national figures for 1872, which provide us with a very rough and ready breakdown by age-group:

| | 0–6 years old | 6–20 years | > 20 years | > 6 years |
|---|---|---|---|---|
| neither read nor write | 88.85% | 23.89 | 33.37 | 30.77 |
| read only | 7.33 | 13.48 | 9.99 | 10.94 |
| read and write | 3.82 | 62.63 | 56.64 | 58.29 |

A quick glance at these figures suggests the interdependence of first and third line scores, between illiterates and 'complete' literates: the essential dividing line occurs between small children and the 6–20 age-group, and the two sets of scores evolve in opposite directions. Scores for the population aged over 20 reflect the continuing presence of older, less-educated generations. The second line – reading only – on the contrary, varies much less. The national average for French people aged over 20 comes out at 10%. But the average for children aged under 6 is only slightly less: 7.33%. And the transition from the 0–6 to the 6–20 age-group scarcely doubles the figure. This relative stability in the proportion of people able to 'read only' in each age-group is yet another way of expressing the autonomy of this cultural plateau vis-à-vis the other two. This leads us to shift our scrutiny upstream: what could be the cause of the relatively high rate of under-6-year-olds able to read? All those 19th-century children's asylums, the ancestors of our own kindergartens? Or, more likely, education at home, and in particular early readings in the catechism or the missal? Downstream, among the 6–20 year-olds, one suspects a certain number of elementary school drop-outs, who quit school before learning to write: yet by this time it had become normal to learn to read and write simultaneously. Perhaps there was no school at all, just the family or the parish priest: it is anybody's guess. At any rate, the aridity of the figures and the crudeness of the overall percentages uncover an unfamiliar story, one that seems to run parallel to the story of full literacy yet never converges with it.

Now, let us try to map these figures, by *département* and by sex, on the basis of the 1872 census. Percentages have been worked out for the population aged over 20, i.e. for the older generations. They are based on the crude figures contained in the *Statistique générale*, since no 19th-century statistician ever analysed them as such (Map 4.6).

We shall take women to begin with, since they come top of this ambiguous prize-list. Their national average: 12% (11.86% to be precise). Distribution by *département* shows that the highest scores (over 18%) all lie south of the Maggiolo line, in the trailing part of France. At first sight, one is tempted to draw a parallel between the two predominances: women and the Midi, attributing to them the same signification, namely the sign of cultural backwardness. On closer examination, though, and comparing the two 1872 maps, 'reading only' and 'reading and writing', we find that the distribution of high 'reading only' percentages by no means coincides with low reading and writing scores, quite the reverse: the backward triangle Brest – Guéret – Bayonne which emerges with growing sharpness as the heartland of illiteracy in the 19th century is completely non-existent when it comes to ability to read only.

The eighteen *départements* having the highest percentage of women able to read only (over 20%) were as follows: Lozère (40), Aveyron (34), Haute-Loire (33), Loire (23), Puy-de-Dôme (20), Ardèche (24), Cantal (26), in other words the east-south-eastern corner of the Massif Central; Hautes and Basses-Pyrénées (29 and 28); four Alpine *départements*, Savoie (23), Hautes-Alpes (22), Haute-Savoie (21), Isère (20); three *départements* either in Brittany or on its borders, Ille-et-Vilaine (24), Côtes-du-Nord (23), Mayenne (23); plus Hérault (24) and Gers (20). This gives us twelve mountainous *départements*, three in the western 'bocage' and two in the deep south. This distribution by no means matches that of the worst illiteracy: in Brittany alone, for example, it is the *départements* with the lowest illiteracy percentages (Côtes-du-Nord and Ille-et-Vilaine) which – compared with Finistère and the Morbihan – have the higher percentages of women able to read.

This analysis is borne out by the reverse map of the lowest scorers on the 'able to read only' (women below the national average) departmental indicator: these figures, indeed, furnish us with a group of *départements* spanning the entire nation like a belt, from south-west to north-east, from the Landes to the Ardennes, this time straddling the famous Maggiolo line and broadly perpendicular to it. This band of territory thus includes *départements* near the top of the literacy league (though not necessarily the best-educated, since Lorraine and that part of the north-east are absent), and *départements* at the bottom of the table, such as those in the south-west. This ambiguity maps the fact that low scores on 'reading only' may be attributable to high percentages on 'reading and writing' squeezing this intermediate population (as in the case of the north-east) or, on the contrary, to a level of literacy so low that even this elementary difference is impossible (the *départements* in the north-western Massif Central, for instance).

This reverse system of communication is perfectly illustrated, for example, by the figures for Seine and Indre. In Seine, 84% of the women are able to read and write, and 2.5% able to read only. The latter percentage is practically identical for women in Indre, only here, no more than 29% of them are able to read and write! One suspects that in the former case it is the 'reading and writing' column which pushes down the 'read only' column, while in the latter it is the 'illiterates' one which exerts the pressure. In this way the variable regains its autonomy, apparently having no systematic link with either of the other two: hence the blurring of Maggiolo's France.

The map of men's scores adds little that is new; it reproduces that of the women's scores with lower percentages. The leading *départements* (over 15%) are those on the south-eastern fringes of the Massif Central: Haute-Loire (29), Lozère (28), Aveyron (24), Puy-de-Dôme (20), Cantal (18), Loire (16), Ardèche (16); then come three Breton *départements*: Côtes-du-Nord (23), Ille-et-Vilaine (18), Loire-Inférieure (15). Lastly, Basses-Pyrénées (17) and Hérault (21) are two isolated cases. There is but one major change compared with the women's map: the disappearance of the Alpine *départements*. This is hardly surprising, bearing in mind the numerical thresholds selected, since the women's 'read only' scores in this region are barely in excess of 20%, while the men's performances are 10% less. The persistence of Brittany (where Loire-Inférieure replaces Mayenne) is due, conversely, to the fact that the men's 'read only' scores are very close to those of the women. While the departmental distribution of this indicator is very close for both sexes, as is established by the two maps of men's and women's scores above the national average, the ratio of women to men able to read only (12:8 on a national scale) is capable of substantial variations from one region to another: practically nil in Brittany, close to 2:1 in the Alps.

One last question remains, regarding the description of the data: how does this 'read only' indicator *behave*?

For this we can compare the census figures for 1866 and 1872, although the time-span is rather short. The figures are as follows:

|  | 1866<br>(population aged > 5) | 1872<br>(population aged > 6) |
|---|---|---|
| Reading only | 11.47 | 10.94 |

i.e. a half-point more in 1866, but with an additional age-group (5–6), which ought to lower the 1866 percentage artificially, since the percentage of young children able to read only was less than the national average. The percentage of French people able to read only ought therefore to have been on a downward curve in the second half of the 19th century.

However, comparison with figures for conscripts in the period 1827–30 shows a reverse trend. In most French *départements*, the percentages of conscripts able to 'read only' rose sharply between the end of the Restoration and 1872. This rise is especially clear-cut when one compares conscripts with the younger age-groups (6–20 years) for 1872, whose percentages, as we have seen, are higher than the national average. But it is clear too when we consider the male population aged over 20, or the national average.

In fact, as a general rule the departmental percentages of men able to read only tended to rise between 1827–30 and 1872. The biggest differences (equal to or more than 6 points) were to be found, as can be seen from the map, in the Breton *départements*, the Alps, the south-eastern fringes of the Massif Central, and the Pyrenees. Where percentages dropped, they did so to a lesser degree (1 to 3 points) and in thirteen *départements* only, almost all of them in Maggiolo's favoured France. As can be seen from the table below, the only *départements* within this group with low literacy scores in the first half of the 19th century were Cher, Sarthe and Vendée.

| *Départements* | Drop in percentage of<br>males able to read only<br>between 1827–30 and 1872 | Maggiolo's percentage<br>1816–20 |
|---|---|---|
| Manche | 15–13 | 83 |
| Orne | 10–9 | 59 |
| Aisne | 6–3 | 57 |
| Sarthe | 6–5 | 27 |
| Haute-Saône | 6–5 | 60 |
| Oise | 5–3 | 60 |
| Seine-et-Marne | 5–2 | 54 |
| Aube | 4–3 | 57 |
| Seine | 4–2 | ? |
| Marne | 4–2 | 75 |
| Cher | 4–3 | 23 |
| Meuse | 4–3 | 86 |
| Vendée | 3–2 | 23 |

Together, these factors suggest that a fall in the number of men able to read only was associated with a high rate of 'complete' literacy right at the beginning of the 19th century; and that conversely an increase in the ability to read only is associated with a surge in certain backward *départements*, though not in all of them.

In any event, the pattern of ability to read only in the 19th century is a problem of minor importance, since by this late stage it amounted to a sort of residual performance, affecting a relatively small number of Frenchmen. What is more important is to understand why these data are distributed so strangely compared with 'reading and writing' or 'ability to sign one's name'. This partial literacy, which coincides neither with the pattern of social wealth nor with that of poverty, and which figures a very different France from that of Baron Dupin or of *Recteur* Maggiolo, is in fact governed by a logic distinct from that of full literacy.

However, the maps that emerge from its distribution do suggest one hypothesis, for they can be compared with the map of religious observance for the same period (Map 4.7), as drawn up by Canon Boulard.[23] The two maps do not coincide exactly, of course: the map of religious observance was drawn up on a canton-by-canton basis, using data (attendance at Easter Mass and communion) almost a century later than those for literacy which we have just been discussing. But then, until 1950, patterns of religious observance evolved only very slowly, and their distribution shows relatively little change. Notwithstanding the differences in the units mapped, the overall similarity that emerges is striking: as in the case of partially literate and 'reading only' France, the parts of France where religious observance was most intense coincided with the Norman, Breton and Vendéen bocage to the west, and then eastwards with the Jura uplands, the Alps and the south-eastern Massif Central, giving us the beginnings of an arc that enfolds the Garonne Valley and takes in the western Pyrenees. The main divergence between these two maps concerns the north-east around Lorraine and Alsace, where religious observance was widespread, even though 'reading only' scores in 1866 and 1872 were less than the national average. But here, in eastern France, whose *départements* already topped Maggiolo's survey at the end of the 18th century, we may suppose that the early development of all-round education very quickly eliminated 'reading only', which is after all but a rudimentary phase of literacy.

This hypothesis, which flows from the crude superimposition of two variables on a national scale, suggests that the Catholic Church, by dispensing an education that was not only scholastic but also familial and religious, played a major rôle in the development of a kind of partial education restricted to reading only; that in the 19th century this education chiefly represented a factor in closing the cultural gap in the backward *départements* (and among women, in these *départements*), but that it might also be a belated testimony to a far more ancient specific acculturation, which by definition could leave no written evidence since it was founded upon oral, diffuse, transmission of the rules for the reading of holy texts.

What lends weight to our hypothesis, and what in our view helped breathe life into it, was the extraordinary precedent of literacy in Sweden in the 17th and 18th centuries:[24] it was then, at a time when no school institution yet existed, that every subject of the Kingdom of Sweden learnt to read (but not to write) under the control of the Lutheran pastors who, year after year, village after village, meticulously noted down their individual performance. In this school-less literacy process, where all one learnt was to read the word of God, through Lutheran eyes, the central figure seems to have been the mother. The pastor was the annual examiner, but the job of daily drilling fell to the mother. Indeed, a systematic scrutiny of the 'score sheets' of several villages show that practically all Swedish women could read fluently by the mid-18th century, being better readers of the holy books than men. Yet at the same moment, practically no one was capable of writing, of signing his or her name: writing had to wait until the introduction of schooling in the middle of the 19th century.

However, what prevents us from transposing the Swedish hypothesis to France in its pristine simplicity – i.e. from distinguishing between a family/religious education based on reading, and school learning in which writing was taught as well – is that in France the history of literacy involved the village schools from very early on, with their two-stage curriculum: first reading, then writing. This makes it impossible to dissociate family education, or the catechism, from school education proper; or to distinguish what, in the ability to read only, ought to be credited to home or Church instruction from what is merely the outcome of prematurely foreshortened school attendance. At the very late period for which we have statistical data on this basic skill, all communes in France, or nearly all, had a school, which makes it harder to identify the two learning frameworks that exist in chronological succession in Swedish history. We shall nevertheless take a handful of examples in an effort to do so.

Let us take a look at one of those *départements* in the south-eastern Massif Central with one of the highest 'read only' rates in the country in 1866, namely Aveyron. The census returns for 1866 have been preserved for two *arrondissements*, Rodez and Millau, and are available for consultation in the departmental archives.[25] They deal with the countryside only; it has not been possible to trace records for the towns (Espalion, Rodez and Millau).

The cantonal scores for the *arrondissement* of Rodez indicate the importance of 'reading only' in literacy in this part of the world, among women especially: practically wherever one looks (except in Laguiole, where the two sexes balance each other) there are far more women able to read only than ones able to read and write. When, as in the case of the (rural) canton of Espalion, this happens to be so for 45% of the women, as against 26% 'fully' literate and 29% illiterate, one is forced to conclude that we are dealing here with a rather special, and systematically partial, form of acculturation. This situation also arises, although to a lesser degree, among the men in this canton, as well as in others. Generally speaking, in five cantons out of seven, there are far more women able to 'read only' than to 'read and write' (41% compared with 13% on the Sauveterre *causse*!), while the men's scores corresponding to these skills are roughly comparable in three of these cantons. Now in all of these cantons, there was a particularly high percentage of adults attending Easter mass and communion, according to the 19th century episcopal visitors:[26] between 92 and 100% among women, and 80 and 94% among the men. The practically uniform distribution of these record scores for religious observance in all the rural communes of the *arrondissement* gives us no clue as to differences in scores for the different types of literacy from canton to canton, but it does inevitably suggest the existence of an overall correlation between the presence of the Church and the fact of learning to read (Table 4.2).

In the south-eastern part of the *département*, the *arrondissement* of Millau also had a very high rate of women able to 'read only', equal to or above the full literacy rate in three cantons out of five. But the men's scores are very distinctly lower than those in the *arrondissement* of Rodez, and throughout the *arrondissement* they are much below the figures for full literacy, which seems to have been far more widespread than around Rodez. What appears to have happened is that the systematic learning of reading only – which is attested by the very high women's percentages, and suggested, as in the case of Rodez, by the still very great intensity of religious observance – must have begun to dwindle among the men as full schooling took its place. Is there any connexion between this and the fact that the *arrondissement* of Millau was slightly more urban, judging by the social and occupational patterns of their respective populations? The example of the canton of Nant does point this way, with its truly residual 'reading only' scores, even among the women (13%), while according to the census returns 30% of the population is non-agricultural. This hypothesis is borne out by other cases.[27]

This leaves unexplained the tie that still exists in the countryside, and here in the culturally-backward, religious Rouergue, between reading and the Church in the 19th century, which may be a belated witness, a rare leftover of a type of acculturation that had gradually succumbed to the more complete education offered by the schools. The culturally distinctive

Table 4.2–AVEYRON: *Breakdown of literacy scores by canton and by sex. Social and occupational classification of males by canton (1866)*
(*The canton with the highest proportion of men able to read only is placed at the head of the list; thereafter, in descending order*)

| | Male literacy | | | Female literacy | | | socio-occupational classification | | Religious observance | |
|---|---|---|---|---|---|---|---|---|---|---|
| | % neither read nor write | % read only | % read and write | % neither read nor write | % read only | % read and write | % agric | % indust. | M | W |
| *Arrondissement of Rodez* | | | | | | | | | | |
| Canton of Espalion (rural) | 27% | 37% | 35% | 29% | 45% | 26% | 85% | 12% | 88% | 92% |
| Canton of Rodez (rural) | 30% | 35% | 35% | 40% | 32% | 28% | 77% | 15% | 90% | 98% |
| Canton of Pont-de-Sala | 33% | 32% | 34% | 43% | 39% | 18% | 90% | 10% | 94% | 100% |
| Canton of Bozouls | 31% | 29% | 41% | 32% | 38% | 29% | 72% | 16% | 94% | 99% |
| Canton of Sauveterre | 38% | 27% | 34% | 46% | 41% | 13% | 87% | 5% | 90% | 99% |
| Canton of Laguiole | 26% | 24% | 50% | 32% | 33% | 35% | 82% | 13% | 80% | 94% |
| Canton of Estaing | 34% | 23% | 43% | 39% | 32% | 29% | 91% | 4% | 95% | 99% |
| *Arrondissement of Millau* | | | | | | | | | | |
| Canton of St-Rome-du-Tarn | 32% | 21% | 47% | 39% | 34% | 27% | 80% | 14% | 98% | 100% |
| Canton of St-Sernin/Rance | 26% | 20% | 54% | 32% | 34% | 34% | 77% | 10% | 94% | 99% |
| Canton of St-Affrique | 27% | 13% | 60% | 32% | 28% | 40% | 77% | 19% | 94% | 97% |
| Canton of Millau | 23% | 13% | 64% | 25% | 36% | 39% | 74% | 17% | 77% | 100% |
| Canton of Nant | 31% | 8% | 51% | 49% | 13% | 46% | 70% | 15% | 77% | 100% |

feature of this south-eastern corner of the Massif Central, which broadly embraces, in addition to Aveyron, the *départements* of Haute-Loire, Loire, Lozère, Ardèche and Cantal – all characterized by a relatively high proportion of 'readers only' – lies not so much in poor rates of school attendance or the belated arrival of schooling (this was something that these impoverished uplands shared with Limousin, where peasants, and still more so the women, could neither read nor write): it lies in the combination of this lack of a school network with the early establishment of the militant Counter-Reformation, imported from the *garrigues* (Mediterranean scrubland) of Languedoc, scaling the *causses* (limestone plateaux pitted with sinkholes) towards the end of the 18th century. Typical of this was the example of the *Béates*, the Third Order of the 'Congregation des Soeurs de l'instruction de l'Enfant Jésus', founded in Puy-en-Velay in 1688.

These poor country girls, who took no vows but who remained under the orders of the Congregation, devoted themselves to the evangelization of the countryside, working among the girls at the famous Le Puy laceworks, dispensing the rudiments of literacy. They themselves received from the 'demoiselles' of the Congregation some form of basic education; they were less schoolteachers than humble priests' auxiliaries, caring for the sick, catechizing children, making up for the lack of schools by dispensing, in the words of one of their historians, 'a rather poor standard of education, though better than nothing'.[28] One of the monographs assembled under Le Play's direction,[29] which holds up the wise lacemakers of the Velay as an example to the loose-living Vosges embroideresses, contains invaluable information regarding the educational activities of the *Béates*. For example, one of the conditions that a village or hamlet had to satisfy before the Congregation would dispatch a *Béate* was that it should 'oblige each pupil attending the reading school, who was able to do so, to pay a fee of 50 centimes per month'. Here is a description of what this 'school' was like in the mid-19th century:

> At seven o'clock in summer, at eight in winter, the girls on hearing the bell went to the *Béate*'s house, which people still call the *assemblée*, as in the early days of its foundation. The older girls each carried their lacemaking pillow, and busied themselves solely with their work. The younger ones carried a book as well as their pillow, alternating lacemaking with reading. They read their lessons in *bardes* (groups) – simultaneous method – either out of their books or from manuscripts, which are still known as *papiers*. Right until evening, this timetable made no provision for writing: nothing but lacemaking, hymns, recitation and reading.

Strictly speaking, the *Béates* did not run 'schools', and so their *assemblées* were not included in the 19th-century school surveys.[30] And yet their auxiliary educational rôle, especially for girls and incidentally for boys, seems to have been crucial; the memory of it is still bright among the older folk in this part of the world.[31] In this impoverished rural area, as in nearby Rouergue, children were 'hired out' very young, from spring to November, and this early participation in farm work is one factor accounting for the backwardness of the school network. The diffuse, decentralized teaching performed by the *Béates*, on the other hand, sat well with the traditions of country life. Did it, anywhere, extend beyond reading only? Although certain studies do suggest as much, it is hard to see how, without a minimum of equipment, these poor nuns, themselves endowed with only a modicum of education, could have taught what was still an intricate technique at the time. And besides, the figures are clear: at the end of the 18th century, after a century of Counter-Reformation pedagogy, Haute-Loire still scored very poorly on signatures, with 32.5% for men, and 11% for women. It is only with the 1866 census that for the first time, beneath an apparently compact illiteracy, we catch a glimpse of the doubtless ancient furrow ploughed by the *Béates*.

So there was undoubtedly a specifically Counter-Reformation approach to education, aimed primarily at girls and excluding writing. It is not altogether certain that this was confined to the countryside; if we are to believe the *Notice* written by *Recteur* Dunglas in the middle of the 19th century,[32] the *Béates* democratized a 'scholastic' model that had originated in the townships:

> The 'Béates de l'Instruction' were not the only ones; there were also the women of the Third Order of Saint Dominic, of the Presentation, of the Cross, of Mount Carmel, and so on. Each locality of any importance had a religious community, often two or even three, and each such community had a free school for girls. Some had an asylum ward as well. Nowhere else were girls' schools as plentiful and cheap: so, in a manner of speaking, the communal schools would have been superfluous.

At about the same time, a report to the Prefect of Haute-Loire on the situation in his *département*, dated 25 November 1853,[33] shows just how far public education policy, right in the middle of the 19th century, resembled that of the *Ancien Régime* bishops. In the eyes of the Prefect, the *Béates*

> redeem by their devotion what they lack in enlightenment, and however slender the rudimentary instruction they broadcast, they are not the less precious in a region whose contours, lack of roads

and harsh climate prevent all communication for several months in the year, not only with the outside world but also between the various points within. The influence of the *Béates* is thus all the more salutary from the point of view of public morality. During the long winter evenings, they bring the girls together in a place known as an *assemblée*, which one finds even in the tiniest hamlets, and which serves as a school for the children in the morning, becoming a workplace for the girls in the evening. Young men are not allowed into these evening gatherings, and in certain places this separation extends to amusements and dances as well. These meticulous precautions have borne fruit. The rate of illegitimate births in the countryside is fairly low, and we may say in general that morals have retained a strictness that is all the more noteworthy for the way they contrast with the depravity, whether blatant or disguised, in the towns.

For the Prefect, the *Béates* were the incarnation of Providence in the *département*.

The scores in Rouergue were, as we have seen, roughly similar, despite the absence of the *Béates*, who do not seem to have spread as far afield as Millau or Rodez. So who filled their role?

In the *Etat du diocèse de Rodez* in 1771, published in 1906,[34] we may observe the extraordinary scarcity of parish schools, which persisted until the early 19th century. There was one exception to this, however, as can be seen from school-enrolment maps for the diocese published in Chartier, Compère, Julia:[35] as early as 1771, the district of Millau was better endowed than the rest with schools; the Reformation had gained a firm foothold in the 16th century, and the Catholic counter-offensive had been obliged to pay the price in schools. This probably accounts for the extent of full male literacy in 1866 (64% able to read and write) compared with the other cantons in the *arrondissement*, and especially in comparison with the *arrondissement* of Rodez.

But we also know that the *arrondissement* of Millau had a high proportion of women able to 'read only' in 1866; and Aveyron as a whole, like Haute-Loire next door, featured a relatively low level of literacy, a sparse network of schools, and a high level of partial literacy, female especially. This was because, like Haute-Loire, the clergy had long been thick on the ground in Aveyron. The 1771 *Etat du diocèse de Rodez* reports the importance of priestly 'brotherhoods' in many Rouergue parishes, in the absence of schools: indeed, the land around here was particularly fertile in sacerdotal vocations, and the peasant tradition of raising a son for the Church died hard. This pattern of upward social mobility which was typical of the *Ancien Régime*, and which throve until not so long ago, meant that the density of priests in this region was exceptionally high,[36] as can be observed from the 16th century onwards. This 'prodigious number of priests', mentioned in the *Dictionnaire des institutions, moeurs et coutumes du Rouergue* (Dictionary of institutions, ways and customs of Rouergue) was too great to be absorbed into the service of the parishes: 'It was not uncommon to find priests occupied as watchsmiths, bellringers, agricultural journeymen, notaries, merchants and others.' And the arrival of the Counter-Reformation in this part of the world (belated, in that it did not begin to bear fruit until the mid-18th century) must have occurred through the agency of these pre-existing clerical structures, which disseminated a kind of diffuse acculturation but not, until the 19th century, a specialized school network.

Returning to the *Etat du Diocèse* prepared at the request of Bishop Champion de Cicé, we find that while schools were very scarce outside the district of Millau, the multiform presence of the Church bred congregations and devotions more or less all over the place. The 'Soeurs de l'Union' (Sisters of Union), also known as the 'filles associées du travail' (associate daughters of labour) – a lay society founded in the 17th century, whose membership consisted of widows and spinsters – for example, were assigned the mission of evangelizing women. At Saint-Cyprien, in the district of Conques, they 'read the lesson to girls and had no fixed hours'. At Bessuéjouls, the document accounts for the absence of schoolmaster and mistress thus: 'In truth, the sisters of labour, established seven years ago, read the lesson to girls wishing to learn to read and to spin wool; but there is no fixed timetable.' Within the diocese, we find teaching-nuns – belonging to a variety of orders – at Aubin Saint-Cyprien, Etraygues, Espalion, Millau, Rodez, Agen, Saint-Antonin, Saint-Geniez, Livinhac-le-Haut and Villefranche. Down to the tiniest villages – the population was very sparse – unpaid auxiliaries spread the influence of the congregations: at Recoules, Sainte-Geneviève, Vines or Saint-Juéry d'Athun, 'good girls taught reading to the children of the hamlets'.[37]

The work of the Church only received full institutional recognition with the Restoration, in the period of reconstruction that followed the revolutionary crisis; many new religious families saw the light of day in this period, such as Lamennais' Brethren, the Marians, the Marists, the Clerks of Saint-Viateur and of the Sacred Heart, as did congregations for the education of girls. In the Diocese of Rodez alone, the Sisters of the Holy Family, of the Sacred Heart of Mary, the Dominicans of Gramond, the Dominicans of Bor, the Sisters of Saint Joseph of Clairvaux, of Estaing, and so on.[38] Towards the middle of the 19th century, this movement ultimately led to the establishment of a network of religious schools; but it also left in being, in those rural areas where children often lived far from the village and went to work outside at a very early age, the sub-system of partial literacy mainly intended for girls and dispensed by the Sisters' auxiliaries.

This was because, even when school reached all the villages in Rouergue, it did not necessarily reach the children in the hamlets, who lived too far away, and who were prevented from getting to school easily by the harsh winters of this region; school clashed, too, with the practice of hiring out, which tended to turn 10-year-olds into precocious wage-labourers and hardened illiterates. This left family education, centred around the catechism, as many witnesses still alive can attest;[39] then there was the education provided weekly by the parish priest; and lastly there was the multifarious, time-hallowed presence of the Church in this remote mountain fastness. For years, reading the catechism and the holy scriptures was probably all that the parish priest had demanded of these extraordinarily believing and practising populations (even if their Catholicism was more or less impervious to the rationalizations of the Counter-Reformation). Writing, with its individual, secretive dimension on the one hand, and the extra-familial sociability that it entailed on the other, may have seemed pointless and possibly even dangerously tempting, for girls in particular, in the eyes of this culture. This is what *Recteur* Dunglas explains in his *Notice* in justifying the reluctance of the *Béates* and their members: 'In the beginning, writing was regarded as of no use to girls, dangerous even. But it became necessary to keep up with the times; accordingly it was introduced into the houses of the *assemblées*, notwithstanding the fears and presentiments of the older folk.' And yet, census figures show that, for a large portion of this *causses* and Velay peasantry, especially the women, but men also, reading without writing remained the rule until well into the 19th century, thus reflecting a form of acculturation specific to the backward regions of France: non-scholastic, exclusively familial and religious.

The Massif Central, that stronghold of rural poverty and belated literacy, for example, presents two contrasting cultural models, still visible in present-day voting patterns. In the north-western and south-eastern Massif Central alike, in the Limousin plateaux as in the *causses*, we find unproductive land, rural isolation, communities too poor to finance schools out of their own resources: the differences stem not from two contrasting agrarian patterns but from the cultural rôle of the Church. The reason why Limousin remained practically totally illiterate until the first third of the 19th century, holding the wooden spoon in the literacy league table, was that the Counter-Reformation had never passed this way. Failing this ancient Catholic militancy, the school arrived here as a result of the progress achieved by the Republic, as a conquest of the Republic.

Rouergue, Velay and Lozère, on the other hand, had a very long tradition of Catholic presence and fidelity, where in the 18th century the Counter-Reformation, rising from Languedoc, disciplined and settled the practices and beliefs of the peasants through the agency of countless clergymen: reading, and women, along with the catechism, would appear to have been instrumental in rendering these permanent. When the school – i.e. reading plus writing – did appear belatedly in the early 19th century, it no longer arrived, nor was it viewed, as representing a break with the past, rather as a continuation, as an additional gift of the Church and, within a very short space of time, as a weapon with which to oppose the Republic.

Now, while 'reading only' does appear to be an excellent indicator of a particular, autonomous kind of cultural development, centred around religious faith, in the under-literate portion of France, it is by no means certain that the same is true of the north-north-eastern part of the country, where the demand for 'full' literacy, a network of schools, and high signature scores coexisted as early as the 18th century. For in this part of France, in the period we are dealing with, the different degrees of religious faith are liable to be concealed by the early generalization of schooling and instruction: acculturation – 'reading only' – in the Massif Central naturally becomes backwardness in Lorraine or Normandy.

This is why this indicator has been examined in a *département* in the 'developed' part of France, where full literacy scores are much higher than in Rouergue, namely Seine-Inférieure. The census returns for 1866 and 1872 are kept in the departmental archives;[40] the pastoral surveys conducted between 1876 and 1880 report the number of Easter communicants in the three *arrondissements* of Yvetot, Neufchâtel and Dieppe.[41] The data on literacy point to the relative lead enjoyed by the *arrondissement* of Neufchâtel (the region of Bray) which we have identified for the 18th century, and which persisted right down to the date under discussion. The *arrondissement* of Yvetot (the Caux region), on the other hand, was lagging behind, with over half its men still unable to read and write in 1872. However, Yvetot's 'read only' scores were higher, especially among the women. The *arrondissement* of Dieppe occupied a position in the middle (Map 4.8, and Tables 4.3–4.6).

Examination of the census figures reveals a sharp economic and social contrast between Neufchâtel and Yvetot. Bray was a completely rural region, whereas Caux was more urban, and especially more industrial, being a centre of the textile industry. But, contrary to the stereotyped view of religious observance as a rural phenomenon, it was in fact in Caux that Easter communion was the more widespread, by a long way: although this regular observance of the annual sacrament could in no way compare with the quasi-universal religious practice of Rouergue, it was at any rate far more in evidence than among the peasants in Bray. This is borne out, in a

Table 4.3

| Cantons of: | Economic activity (1) | | | Religious observance | Literacy | | | |
|---|---|---|---|---|---|---|---|---|
| _Arrondissement of Yvetot_ | farm population as % of total population | industrial population as % of total population | cotton-population as % of industrial population | % of Easter communicants in population concerned | % able to read only | | % able to read and write | |
| | | | | | M | W | M | W |
| Saint-Valéry-en-Caux | 26.1 | 61.8 | 48.9 | 72.5 | 8.9 | 11.7 | 56.2 | 51.1 |
| Caury | 34.9 | 56.4 | 54.6 | 71.0 | 8.3 | 15.3 | 46.5 | 41.3 |
| Fauville | 34.1 | 55.0 | 67.1 | 59.0 | 9.4 | 13.8 | 49.6 | 42.3 |
| Ourville | 30.4 | 66.4 | 65.0 | 68.2 | 11.3 | 16.7 | 44.6 | 36.9 |
| Yerville | 34.9 | 53.0 | 68.4 | —(2) | 7.3 | 10.8 | 51.5 | 42.0 |
| Caudebec-en-Caux | 43.8 | 40.6 | 28.1 | 54.0 | 8.6 | 10.8 | 59.9 | 51.6 |
| Fontaine-le-Dun | 32.5 | 60.2 | 66.8 | — | 8.5 | 12.8 | 52.8 | 36.2 |
| Valmont | 30.8 | 54.7 | 81.7 | — | 7.3 | 11.8 | 52.7 | 43.1 |
| Doudeville | 23.7 | 67.8 | 76.8 | — | 7.3 | 13.5 | 48.8 | 41.2 |

(1) _Source_: 1866 Census
(2) Not available

Table 4.4

| *Arrondissement* of Yvetot | % of women in the working population (1) |
|---|---|
| *Cantons* of: | |
| Saint-Valéry-en-Caux | 54.9 |
| Caury | 60.2 |
| Fauville | 61.1 |
| Ourville | 60.3 |
| Yerville | 66.7 |
| Caudebec-en-Caux | 60.4 |
| Fontaine-le-Dun | 50.4 |
| Valmont | 65.3 |
| Doudeville | 55.4 |

(1) If children are counted as 'Men', then this would reduce the number of men employed in the cotton industry accordingly.

Table 4.5

| *Arrondissement* of Dieppe | Economic activity (1) | | | Religious observance | Literacy | | | |
|---|---|---|---|---|---|---|---|---|
| | | | | % of Easter communicants in population concerned | % able to read only | | % able to read and write | |
| | farm population as % of total population | industrial population as % of total population | cotton population workers as % of total industrial population | | M | W | M | W |
| *Cantons* of: | | | | | | | | |
| Envermeu | 50.2 | 43.2 | 2.4 | 35.4 | 6.7 | 10.3 | 60.9 | 54.1 |
| Totes | 51.6 | 38.6 | 50.0 | 48.1 | 11.7 | 14.5 | 50.2 | 37.3 |
| Bellen-Combre | 53.0 | 22.3 | 18.5 | 35.7 | 7.6 | 7.8 | 53.4 | 43.5 |
| Eu | 44.1 | 49.2 | 4.4 | — | 9.3 | 12.6 | 54.1 | 55.3 |
| Bacqueville | 29.8 | 60.2 | 58.5 | — | 10.0 | 13.6 | 45.7 | 34.4 |
| Longueville | 47.4 | 39.5 | 36.4 | — | 7.9 | 13.5 | 52.0 | 40.7 |
| Offranville | 61.9 | 43.4 | 19.6 | —(2) | 9.1 | 14.0 | 51.2 | 43.3 |

(1) *Source*: 1866 Census
(2) Not available

Table 4.6

| *Arrondissement* of Neufchâtel | Economic activity (1) | | | Religious observance | Literacy | | | |
|---|---|---|---|---|---|---|---|---|
| | farm population as % of total population | industrial population as % of total population | cotton population workers as % of total industrial population | % of Easter communicants in population concerned | % able to read only | | % able to read and write | |
| | | | | | M | W | M | W |
| *Cantons* of: | | | | | | | | |
| Forges-lès-Eaux | 65.9 | 23.8 | 0.0 | 20.5 | 5.5 | 8.3 | 65.0 | 57.1 |
| Gournay | 43.9 | 24.8 | 0.0 | 12.5 | 5.5 | 5.9 | 63.8 | 59.0 |
| Neufchâtel | 68.6 | 15.6 | 0.0 | 34.0 | 6.8 | 9.7 | 66.8 | 60.2 |
| Argueil | 61.9 | 25.4 | 6.8 | 24.9 | 8.2 | 8.8 | 52.5 | 49.5 |
| Aumale | 68.8 | 25.0 | 0.0 | 24.6 | 4.5 | 5.5 | 66.5 | 64.0 |
| Saint-Saens | 60.1 | 32.0 | 9.5 | 36.0 | 5.4 | 6.7 | 57.7 | 51.4 |
| Loudinière | 60.6 | 16.5 | 0.0 | 39.6 | 7.8 | 10.0 | 62.4 | 51.8 |
| Blangy | 52.9 | 31.2 | 0.6 | 26.1 | 8.3 | 11.1 | 55.5 | 48.5 |

(1) *Source*: 1866 Census

sense, by an additional figure that emerges from the administrative surveys, to the effect that there were no regular clergymen whatsoever in the *arrondissement* of Neufchâtel.

Now, the question arises: is there any connection between different degrees of religious practice and the contrast in the 'read only' scores of these two *arrondissements*? Or does this contrast stem from differences in their structures of economic and social development that would account for the Bray region's lead in literacy? Were the latter so, then 'reading only' would simply serve as additional evidence of Caux's backwardness.

Scrutiny of the cantonal figures points in the direction of the second hypothesis. In the *arrondissement* of Yvetot, those cantons having the greatest number of individuals able to 'read only' are those having the highest percentage of industrial workers, while the intensity of religious practice apparently has nothing whatever to do with any particular type of literacy. The majority of this industrial labour was female, mostly employed in the cotton mills. Those cantons with the highest proportions of industrial workers are also those with the highest female 'read only' scores: 16.7% at Ourville, 13.5% at Doudeville, 12.8% at Fontaine-le-Dun. Simultaneously, moreover, full-literacy scores are particularly low, among women especially: 37% able to read and write at Ourville, 41% at Doudeville, and 36% at Fontaine-le-Dun. Figures on religious observance are unavailable for two of these cantons, Doudeville and Fontaine-le-Dun; but at Ourville, and wherever they are available, they seem to bear no clear relation to different types of literacy. However, the canton with the most brilliant full-literacy scores, Caudebec-en-Caux, whose 'read only' scores also happen to be low, contrasts with the rest of the Caux area in every respect: it is the least industrial, and least observant of religion, of the cantons. In this peasant Normandy, relatively ahead on literacy scores and with widespread schooling since the 18th century, this canton demonstrates that the truly significant performance is reading and writing. But all around, wherever the rural cotton industry has broken up the traditional patterns, thrusting women and children into wage labour, this performance is less frequent; and the ability to read only more likely reflects prematurely foreshortened schooling than elementary acculturation by the Church alone.

Literacy rates in the Bray region are a further illustration of this phenomenon and authorize us to generalize from the Caudebec-en-Caux pattern. For at the other end of the *département*, in the cantons of the *arrondissement* of Neufchâtel, full literacy scores are particularly high, the 'read only' percentages particularly low, religious observance too; and while the proportion of the population employed in industry in general is low, the proportion of cotton-workers is practically nil. Cantonal differences in religious observance apparently bear no relation to the ability to 'read only'. However, it is in the two most purely rural cantons, Neufchâtel and Aumale, that we find the highest percentages of men and women able to read and write. And, more generally, in all these cantons, the higher the rate of full literacy, the less likely one is to encounter individuals able to 'read only', and vice versa. The region of Bray offers us an example of a long-developed rural society, undisturbed by industry, by child and women's labour particularly, continuing throughout the 19th century the literacy process begun some hundred and fifty to two hundred years earlier. Ability to read only, as in the Caux region, is chiefly a reflection of inadequate schooling; but this was much less frequent, since the attractions of industrial employment were not present here as a permanent and massive incentive to leave school early.

That in the educated parts of French peasant society reading without writing was taken as a sign of deplorable ignorance, at best excusable, is perfectly demonstrated in the written account which an old Beauceron schoolteacher sent to one of the authors of this book.[42] Cyr Bigot was born at Saint-Prest, in the Eure Valley, 7 km. north of Chartres, in 1856, from a long line of vine-growers established in this village. His father and mother had received from a Monsieur Martin, communal schoolmaster under the July Monarchy, a well-rounded elementary education comprising, successively, reading, writing and arithmetic. But here is how our schoolteacher (who began teaching in primary schools in 1876) casts a professional eye over the family's educational record, in the middle of the last century:

> My mother very early showed 'a fortunate aptitude for reading'; when they bought her a missal for her 'communion', she was able to read the French text fluently. Her father, who passed – and rightly, I think – as more learned than M. Martin, had need of no one not only to sustain this fortunate aptitude but also to develop it. Under his supervision, she became the family reader, when there was time, the occasion or the means to read something.
>
> He did as much with arithmetic for his two daughters, but he made the mistake of neglecting writing. He himself kept regular and careful account of the household receipts and outgoings, which was then fairly uncommon in a working-class home. But he said his daughters' handwriting was too poor for him to allow them to take part in the setting out of this work, other than to get them to check the sums.
>
> Special coaching in writing would presumably have remedied this shortcoming, but such coaching could only be given in the long winter evenings, and then their mother claimed her two daughters: had they not to learn how to sew, darn, sew a patch on

a trouser-seat, iron? For want of practice, my mother gradually fell out of the habit of writing. So much so that later, when I got to know her, the need to take up a pen put her in such a state that her hand began to shake, and it became for her 'a whole business' just to put her signature at the bottom of a letter or some deed whenever the need arose.

My father had greater difficulty than my mother and was not fortunate enough, like her, to have someone at home capable of supervising his work and helping him to progress. His parents, indeed, were 'just about capable of signing their names', and they did not bear this lightly, as you may imagine. They had two sons, my father being the youngest by a few years; and they sent them regularly to school every winter so that they would not be completely uneducated like themselves. At the earliest possible opportunity, the two brothers were given the task of 'keeping the accounts' as best they were able, the eldest to begin with, as he was 'more advanced', and later the two of them together, helping each other out.

When the eldest son's time came to do his national service – for seven years – the younger one, who was exempted by the fact that his brother was already under arms, stayed behind and carried on with the task alone. Which is why, when he married, although he read only slowly and with much hesitation, he at least had the advantage over my mother of having kept up the habit of writing.

He found the pen too light in his hand, accustomed as it was to handling heavier implements. Fearing that it would drop from his fingers, he gripped it tightly and pressed heavily onto the paper, making his handwriting thick and heavy. Considered individually, the letters were not badly-shaped, but the words were disfigured by his spelling, which was frequently quite illegible, even to my mother, and she was used to it. She soon gave up mentioning it to him, because her comments used to annoy him; but he realized it himself, and when the need for a letter arose – which was very rarely, fortunately – 'he grew all gloomy about it for eight days beforehand'.

Which explains why, as soon as I was able, I was given the job of writing the few letters required by our relations with a handful of distant friends or relatives, such as to invite them to the parish feast, or incidentally, to the occasional family gathering. When I was young, these letters used to be dictated by my mother, because while my father could never 'think of what to say to them', my mother had no trouble thinking up the appropriate ideas and expressions.

The reader will no doubt excuse the length of this quotation on the grounds of its interest. For in this peasant family we find a division of cultural tasks and skills: the women read but could not write; the men wrote, but could not read. Reading was associated with communion and catechism, writing with keeping accounts and, less frequently, with keeping up with distant relations. Life gradually specialized men and women in one or another of the skills learnt in school – even though both were ashamed at not having preserved the two skills acquired in their youth. The reason is that, even in the case of small farmers such as these, rural life offered few opportunities of genuine contact with written culture. Women read out of obedience to the demands of religious education or, from time to time, to maintain the family's – but only the family's – social relations. Men wrote in order to perform the minimum bookkeeping required in a market economy. The school had as yet established only a very precarious link between the two skills, reading and writing, tenuous in that adult life soon parted them. Hardly surprisingly, then, in the west and the Midi where the school was such a long time coming, the Church, wherever present, looked upon reading, and women, as its principal missionary fields.

4.1 Farm population/total population 1866

:: 38.73 ::: 43.31 ::: 47.88 ::: 52.46 ::: 57.04

::: 61.61 ₀₀₀ 66.19 ₀₀₀ 70.77 ▒▒▒ 75.34 ▓▓

4.2 Percentage of share-croppers/total farmers

::: 3.32 ::: 6.65 ::: 9.97 ::: 13.29 ::: 16.62

::: 19.94 ₀₀₀ 23.26 ₀₀₀ 26.59 ▒▒▒ 29.91 ▓▓

4.3 Urban population/total population

::: 32.89 ::: 39.37 ::: 45.86 ::: 52.35 ::: 58.84

::: 65.32 ₀₀₀ 71.81 ₀₀₀ 78.30 ▒▒▒ 84.78 ▓▓

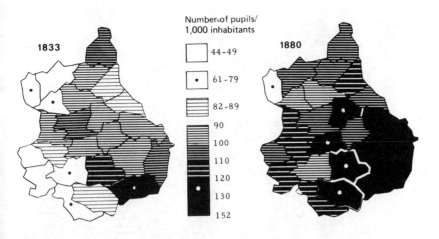

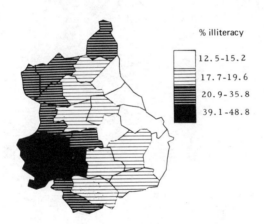

4.4   School attendance in Eure-et-Loir. Education level of conscripts (1848–1852)

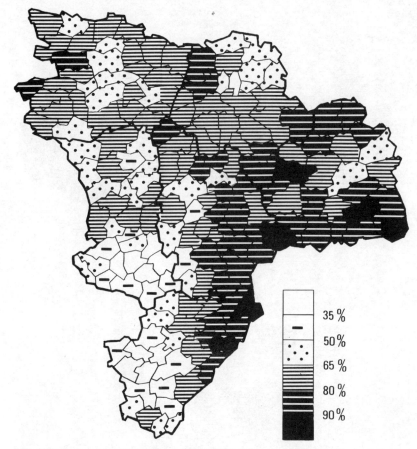

4.5   Illiteracy among conscripts, 1827–1830 (Maine-et-Loire, Indre-et-Loire, Deux-Sèvres, Vienne, Indre, Charentes)

4.7   (*opposite*) Map of adult Easter communicants by canton (for the dioceses of Marseilles, Meaux, Paris and Versailles, the base used is that of adults 'attending mass', with a corrective factor applied. The difference between Easter communicants and mass is slight. The dioceses of Metz and Nancy have been calculated on the basis of approximate data)

4.6 Able to read only, aged over 20
Men 1872

::: 3.56 ::: 5.18 ::: 6.81 ::: 8.43 ::: 10.06

::: 11.69 ::: 13.31 ::: 14.94 ::: 16.56 ■

Able to read only, aged over 20
Women 1872

::: 4.17 | ::: 6.59 ::: 9.01 ::: 11.43 ::: 13.85

::: 16.27 ::: 18.69 ::: 21.11 ::: 23.54 ■

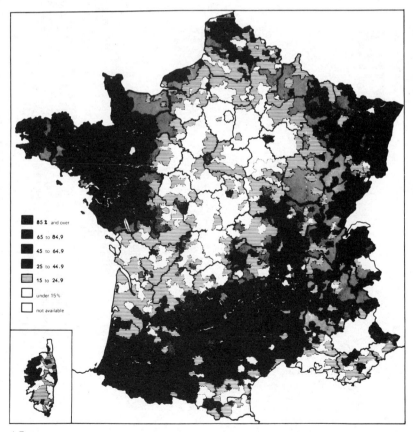

85 % and over
65 to 84.9
45 to 64.9
25 to 44.9
15 to 24.9
under 15%
not available

4.7

EASTER COMMUNICANTS IN 1873–83
(men and women)

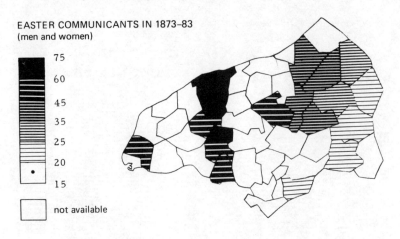

'READING ONLY'

WOMEN

MEN

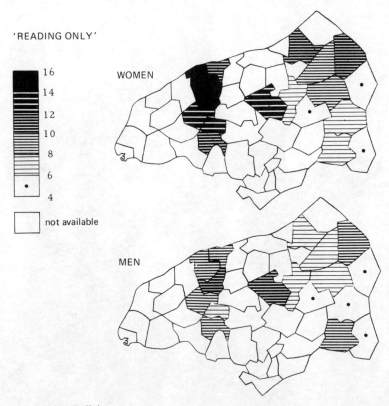

4.8   Seine-Inférieure

# 5

## CITY LIGHTS

Invited, in the Year VI, to report on public feeling in his *département*, the Departmental Commissioner of the Executive Directorate for Isère resorted to a bland commonplace: 'In this *département*, as in all the others, citizens are divided into two main classes, that of educated men, and that of the ignorant; the former is in the towns, the latter in the countryside'.[1] If he is to be believed – and at that moment, moreoever, we would turn up very similar sentiments among his colleagues labouring over the same task – the town was a form of acculturation in itself. In the reports of the Directorate commissioners, the main theme organizing the educational geography of France, then, was this very ancient definition of the town as the home of Enlightenment and Civilization, with bright urban islets standing out against a dark backcloth. The fact of living in a town, entailing a specific form of social life, was thought to be the decisive factor in the acquisition of knowledge. Far more so than social hierarchy: in these pre-statistical writings, public officials do not appear all that concerned to discriminate between journeymen, share-croppers, labourers or tillers. Throwing nuance to the winds, they subsume all under the syncretic formula 'country people'.

It comes as some surprise to see these men, nurtured on the economic, moral, medical and demographic literature of the 18th century, with its endless enumerations of city vices, now presenting city-dwelling as an indisputable form of superiority. The reason is that, with each passing day, the performance of their duties has borne away whatever nostalgic memories of pastoral life they may have cherished. When one is striving to introduce the new calendar, new measures, new fairs into the village, 'all those things that complicate life even for an educated man', one is, as the Commissioner for Cher is forced to admit, tempted to yield to discouragement: 'The stubborn-headedness of country people is unbelievable. Their minds do not seem to be moulded for the truth.' The town, by contrast, as the centre of trade, is also the centre of cultural intercourse. As if the mere agglutination of men were sufficient in itself to start knowledge and truth circulating. 'A numerous people, and for that reason less superstitious', wrote the Commissioner for Rhône. One senses, in the necessity attributed to this connection, just how much town life, in educational terms, was thought of as a second nature.

This intuitive notion of geography, according to which the centres of education coincided with the urban centres is now borne out by such a wealth of figures that there is practically no point in dwelling on it. The monographs published here and works of Jean Quéniart on Western France, Michel Vovelle on Provence, Jean Meyer on Upper Brittany[2] and others, all furnish contrasting images of a single state of affairs, namely the disparity between urban and rural literacy rates in *Ancien Régime* France, existing in both the developed and the backward parts of France.

Jean Quéniart's study, which straddles the two Frances (literate and backward), is particularly eloquent. In the late 17th century, whether in the more advanced regions (Normandy), backward (Brittany), or mixed (Maine and Anjou), towns are always appreciably more literate than the surrounding countryside. The difference between these and Maggiolo's departmental scores (which are essentially rural), may be fairly small (a dozen percentage points for Brest), considerable (between 22 and 28 points for Quimper, Saint-Malo, Nantes, Rennes and Rouen), or enormous (over 30 for Angers and Le Mans): but always in the same direction.

For literate France, J.-P. Poussou offers us the aggregate performances of 73 towns of all sizes, spread over thirteen *départements* in the south-west, for the period 1776–86: 42.2% of men were 'able to sign the marriage register', and 26.3% of women. Now, Maggiolo's figures for the same group of *départements* for the period 1786–90 are 30.9% for the men and 9.4% for the women. And even then, J.-P. Poussou warns us, Maggiolo's figures undoubtedly include urban signatures in certain *départements* at least. So we must therefore postulate a still greater discrepancy, which recurs in all of the Aquitaine *départements*, whatever their respective performances. Take Charente, for instance: 26.6% of 'Maggiolo's men' signed, whereas the male scores for Angoulême, Cognac and Barbezieux were 45.3%, 48.5% and 43.8% respectively; 9% of 'Maggiolo's' women signed, but the corresponding figures for Angoulême, Cognac and Barbezieux were 30.7%, 35.3% and 32.5%. We find the same phenomenon at lower levels of education (in Haute-Vienne, for example, where Maggiolo's scores are 10.6% for the men and 6% for the women, we find figures of 32.1% for men and 26.8% for women in Limoges), as well as at more satisfactory levels of education, as in Hautes-Pyrénées, where the men of Tarbes score 56% (Maggiolo: 42.4%) and the women 25% (Maggiolo: 9.4%).

It looks like an open and shut case for the backward regions of France: Michel Vovelle's Provençal towns (with rare exceptions such as Barcelonette), Jean Meyer's small Breton towns or the Languedoc towns studied by Marie-Madeleine Compère, all confirm the rule. Indeed, in the more backward regions, the educational superiority of the towns – as may be seen today in the under-developed countries – seems to be taken for granted.

**Urban superiority: A second look at the obvious**

Is this true of the developed part of France too? In Seine-Inférieure at the end of the 17th century, Maggiolo's scores show 39.3% for the men and 16.7% for the women. But the figures for Bolbec show men, 65%, and women, 21%; while at Eu the figures are 74 and 43% respectively, and at Gournay, 72 and 36%. This discrepancy was still in evidence at the end of the 18th century. In Seine-et-Marne, at the end of the 18th century, 60.5% of the men were able to sign their names, but at Meaux the figure was 88%. Here again, there is a heap of examples showing how towns, great and small, led the surrounding countryside.

Now, let us take a slightly more detailed look at the problem of disparities between town and country in the educated parts of France, concentrating on the *département* of Nord.[3] Nord, which in 1786–90 stood 26th in Maggiolo's rankings for marriage signatures – hence well above the national average – presents the advantage of closely interacting town and countryside, farming and industry, thereby yielding some instructive comparisons. In addition, the militant labours of a scholarly clergymen published in 1878 and contemporary with Maggiolo's survey,[4] provides us with the necessary means. Fontaine de Resbecq was concerned, like so many others, to demonstrate the grandeur of the educational accomplishments of the Church and the monarchy, and for the period 1750–90 he supplies the number of brides and grooms (men and women are listed separately) signing their names for each commune in Nord (barring a few rare exceptions due to destruction). The demonstrative character of his work detracts not one wit from his rigour since, for the *département* as a whole, his figures are comparable to those of Maggiolo.

|  | Men able to sign | Women able to sign |
|---|---|---|
| Maggiolo (1786–90) | 51.38% | 29.32% |
| Fontaine de Resbecq (1750–90) | 53.9% | 36.3% |

Note the proximity of the male scores (the slight superiority of de Resbecq's scores probably stems from his inclusion of urban figures, which Maggiolo's survey tended to underestimate: Fontaine de Resbecq thereby more than makes up for the handicap implicit in a sample covering an earlier period). But the discrepancy between the female scores is more surprising: to account for this, we would have to accept (a hypothesis demanding detailed scrutiny) that female literacy rates were particularly high (relative to male rates) in the towns – which tends to reduce the overall average discrepancy for the *département*.

In order to give positive weight to a point of detail, we have taken
Fontaine de Resbecq's figures and used them to establish the marriage
signature percentages for each commune; and we have also amalgamated
the figures for each canton, and subsequently for each *arrondissement*, on
the basis of the 19th century administrative boundaries[5] (Maps 5.1, 5.2 and
5.3). What are we to make of the respective educational situations in the
different regions of Nord in the second half of the 18th century?

---

Marriage signatures (1750–90) – Men
(at *arrondissement* level)

| Avesnes | 73.6% | Valenciennes | 54.5% |
|---|---|---|---|
| Dunkirk | 58.6% | Hazebrouck | 51.2% |
| Cambrai | 55.2% | Lille | 44.4% |
| Douai | 54.8% | | |

Departmental average: 53.97%

---

Marriage signatures (1750–90) – Women

| Avesnes | 60.7% | Douai | 33.4% |
|---|---|---|---|
| Dunkirk | 37.1% | Lille | 31.8% |
| Hazebrouck | 34.2% | Cambrai | 29.7% |
| Valenciennes | 33.9% | | |

Departmental average: 36.29%

---

Now this is an odd table. The figures in it seem to indicate a quite
remarkable exception to the rule that in 18th century France the towns
always scored better than the countryside. For these figures show that it
was the most urban *arrondissement*, Lille, which brings up the rear. And the
men especially, as can be seen from the map of male literacy rates drawn up
on the basis of Fontaine de Resbecq's data (Map 5.2): in the period under
review, Lille was lagging ten points behind Cambrai, Douai and
Valenciennes, fourteen behind Dunkirk, and thirty behind Avesnes.
Avesnes, the champion, just happens to be the most rural *arrondissement*.
What could be the cause of this anomaly?

Then comes a second surprise, again produced by the figures themselves:
whereas the disparity in male and female scores for the *département* as a
whole is over twenty points in Maggiolo's survey and over seventeen in
Fontaine de Resbecq's, it narrows in the *arrondissement* of Lille: twelve
points according to Fontaine de Resbecq. In other words, it is as if the
*arrondissement*'s laggardliness relative to the rest of the *département* were

chiefly the fault of the men. Indeed, when we look at the map of marriage signatures (women), *arrondissement* by *arrondissement*, built up from Fontaine de Resbecq's information (map 5.3), Lille moves up from the rear, its place taken by Cambrai; this time, although still scoring far less than Avesnes and Dunkirk, its literacy rate is nevertheless very comparable to those of Hazebrouck, Valenciennes or Douai, with roughly a third of the women able to sign. And indeed this was more than the national average for the time, whereas its male percentage was appreciably below average. So in this backward *arrondissement* we find a fairly good score by the women, resulting in an abnormally small discrepancy between male and female performances; as if the causes that were blocking or impeding the progress of men in this part of the *département* produced different effects among the women.

What strikes one first in the table produced from Fontaine de Resbecq's figures is the considerable disparities that are opened up between *arrondissements* and cantons, both for men and for women. The departmental average for men's signatures is 54%; yet nearly thirty points separate Avesnes (73.6%) and Lille (44.4%), and again, for the women, between Avesnes (60.7%) and Cambrai (29.7%). Among the cantons, the gaps grow wider still: between Solre and Tourcoing, for the men (79.9% and 29.1%) and for the women (77.8% and 20.1%).

The second remarkable feature is the performance of the *arrondissement* of Avesnes and *all* its cantons in the second half of the 18th century.

These are truly late-19th-century figures, a century ahead of their time. Now, in this ranking of *arrondissements* in the 18th century, the other leading *arrondissement*, for both men and women, was Dunkirk: a long way behind Avesnes, to be sure, but enjoying a clear lead over the other five. And these were the two most rural *arrondissements*, with the lowest population densities.[6]

Behind the leaders lie the three *arrondissements* of Cambrai, Douai and Valenciennes, grouped around the 55% mark for male signatures. All three were still largely agricultural, with a long tradition of urban life too, but with some newly-arrived rural textile industries. Last come the two most industrial *arrondissements*, Hazebrouck and above all Lille.

The map by cantons confirms this hierarchy. The sectors with middling literacy rates coincide with the cantons where the rural textile industries were established: Hainault, Cambrésis and the Hazebrouck-Bailleul region. Chiefly, though, the most illiterate cantons are concentrated around the periphery of the Lille industrial region, where the textile mills had recently opened up (because the regulations were less strict here than those enforced by the corporations in the Flemish capital):[7] the cantons of Roubaix (33.7% literate) or Tourcoing (29.1%). The cantons embracing the city of Lille itself chalk up less wretched figures, but even these are pulled down by the nature of their origin, mingling working-class areas with bourgeois neighbourhoods. The artificiality of the mean thus obtained (49.7%) is plain for all to see once we note the very low figures (around 30%) recorded for the working-class areas such as Faches or Ronchin juxtaposing Lille. Scrutiny of parish figures, as furnished by Cottez-Perin[8] for instance, confirms this, moreover: the well-to-do Lille parish of Saint-Etienne was 73.5% literate, whereas the others, the lower-class parishes, Saint-André and Saint-Sauveur, scored but 37 and 34.5%. Incidentally, this examination of parish figures yields some interesting information regarding the immediate consequences of industrialization – as with the first coalfields developed by the Compagnie d'Anzin (founded in 1757). In three out of four (Anzin, Vieux-Condé and Raismes), the percentage of men signing their names in the year 1789 taken in isolation was appreciably lower than the average for 1750–90; the only place that achieved any progress was Fresnes, but this was precisely the centre least affected by the spread of coal mining.[9]

The cantons in the *arrondissement* of Avesnes, on the other hand, all appear at the top of the canton league table, with the other rural cantons following immediately behind, especially those in the *arrondissement* of Dunkirk (Bergues, for example). The overall lead enjoyed by the Avesnois remains an enigma: especially when one considers that, of the four most literate cantons, two (Berlaimont and Avesnes) were overwhelmingly agricultural, while in the other two (Solre and Maubeuge), traditional rural industry played a key rôle. These observations raise a host of questions. Was it the long-established Protestant presence? Was it the lasting vigour of the communities formed by the inhabitants (careful, for instance, to ensure that schools not only existed but were well run)? Could it have been – but in that case we should have to revise our initial hypothesis – the rural character of the region, which was not incompatible with the existence of old-established, small-scale yet prosperous mining and industry?

But we should be wary of interpreting the superior literacy of the countryside as if it enjoyed some advantage over the towns and large villages. For as a general rule, if we compare town and country, we find that the former was more literate than the surrounding dependent hinterland. Thus, of the seven future *chefs-lieux d'arrondissement* in the *département* of Nord, only two (Avesnes and Hazebrouck, which were by far the smallest) were less literate than the rest of their respective cantons; only one, Hazebrouck, was less so than the rest of its *arrondissement*. Even then, this only holds for the men, as do most of the other exceptions (Quesnoy-sur-Deule, Le Cateau, Solesmes, Saint-Amand and so on). On the other hand, educational disparities in favour of towns and large villages and to the detriment of the hinterland (here, the rest of the canton), were often considerable:

|           | Men     | Women   |
|-----------|---------|---------|
| Bailleul  | + 13.9% | + 25.8% |
| Bergues   | + 18.6% | + 18.6% |
| Cassel    | + 12.1% | + 17.0% |
| Douai     | +  8.4% | + 23.1% |
| Dunkirk   | + 13.0% | + 19.5% |
| Haubourdin| + 15.9% | + 16.0% |
| Lille     | + 10.4% | + 14.0% |
| Roubaix   | +  4.7% | +  7.7% |

Population concentrations thus always appear to 'generate' literacy, compared with the surrounding countryside, in advanced[10] and backward zones alike. Whether this was due to the higher proportion of notables in the towns and townships than in the villages, or the persuasive example of the bourgeois, here visible to all, or again to better schooling than in the countryside, we ought at any rate to note that what was hampering literacy was not a specifically urban curse (Table 5.1). In keeping with the general rule established under the *Ancien Régime*, it was the cantons with the oldest-established urban populations that were the most literate. But we need to distinguish between these traditional urban areas and the more recently urbanized ones: for the laggards in each *arrondissement* also happened to be urban cantons (Roubaix, with 33.7% of its males able to sign their names; Tourcoing, with 29%!). These really are very low figures; and we find them in recently urbanized areas, which were virtually dumping grounds for unskilled workers attracted by the demand for labour in the nascent textile industry. The hypothesis that comes to mind is similar in kind to the one put forward by Michael Sanderson for Lancashire,[11] namely that not only does the modern type of industry have little need of educated labour, but that it actually has a negative effect on literacy rates.

If we now go on to consider women, we find that low level literacy is a far more widespread, more uniform phenomenon than for the men; and consequently far less sensitive to regional differences in economic activities. Indeed leaving aside the untypical (once again) case of Avesnes, we find that the disparity in literacy rates between the most literate and the least literate *arrondissements* is only half as big for the women as for the men: 7.4% (between Dunkirk and Cambrai) compared with 14.2% (between Dunkirk and Lille). As a result, women emerge in general as the neglected sex in literacy.

But this shared state of wretchedness by no means rules out regional inequalities: the more rural the district, the greater the gap between men

Table 5.1    *Town and country (1750–90)*
            *(marriage signatures)*

| | Town or large village | | Canton minus town or large village | |
|---|---|---|---|---|
| | Men | Women | Men | Women |
| Avesnes | 76.0% | 67.8% | 79.0% | 64.8% |
| Maubeuge | 77.5% | 58.6% | 79.3% | 71.1% |
| Trélon | | | | |
| (large village) | 78.7% | 65.7% | 73.4% | 60.9% |
| Le Quesnoy | 70.0% | 60.4% | 56.5% | 44.3% |
| Hazebrouck | 45.7% | 34.8% | 46.7% | 28.7% |
| Bailleul | 63.0% | 56.6% | 49.1% | 30.8% |
| Cassel | | | | |
| (large village) | 69.1% | 48.7% | 57.0% | 31.7% |
| Dunkirk | 66.2% | 43.9% | 53.2% | 24.4% |
| Bergues | | | | |
| (large village) | 75.3% | 55.5% | 56.7% | 36.9% |
| Bourbourg | | | | |
| (large village) | 62.0% | 42.9% | 55.2% | 34.9% |
| Hondschoote | | | | |
| (large village) | 60.0% | 48.8% | 53.9% | 29.7% |
| Douai | 61.1% | 48.3% | 52.7% | 25.2% |
| Orchies | | | | |
| (large village) | 55.9% | 45.9% | 45.9% | 22.3% |
| Cambrai | 55.8% | 46.5% | 52.2% | 18.9% |
| Valenciennes | 63.4% | 48.1% | 55.7% | 35.8% |
| Saint-Amand | 39.3% | 30.8% | 51.6% | 24.8% |
| Lille | 50.6% | 40.3% | 40.2% | 26.3% |
| Armentières | 52.0% | 43.5% | 47.0% | 36.4% |
| Roubaix | 35.8% | 31.0% | 31.1% | 23.3% |
| Tourcoing | 24.3% | 18.1% | 30.9% | 20.9% |
| Haudourdin | | | | |
| (large village) | 55.8% | 48.5% | 39.9% | 23.9% |
| Seclin | | | | |
| (large village) | 48.4% | 31.3% | 43.4% | 23.2% |

and women. The following table contrasts men's leads in the towns of the *département* of Nord with their leads in the surrounding countryside:

Disparities between men and women
(in men's favour)

| | town or large village | rest of canton |
|---|---|---|
| Avesnes | + 8.2% | + 14.2% |
| Bailleul | + 6.4% | + 18.3% |
| Bergues | + 19.8% | + 19.8% |
| Cambrai | + 9.3% | + 33.3% |
| Cassel | • + 20.4% | + 25.3% |
| Douai | + 12.8% | + 27.5% |
| Dunkirk | + 18.3% | + 28.8% |
| Haubourdin | − 7.3% | + 16.0% |
| Hazebrouck | + 10.9% | + 18.4% |
| Lille | + 10.3% | + 13.9% |
| Roubaix | + 4.8% | + 7.8% |
| Seclin | + 17.1% | + 20.2% |
| Tourcoing | + 6.2% | + 10.0% |

The most glaring example is that of the two cantons of Cambrai, with a mere 9-point difference between men and women in the town and 33 in the hinterland around. It is hard, when thinking of the Cambrésis countryside's poor rate of female literacy, to suppress the thought of another fact, namely that there were more than 10,000 rural textile looms in the Cambrésis at the end of the 18th century. As we can see, the countryside was poor and women and girls were constantly at work on their looms, probably making it even harder than elsewhere for girls to attend school; and, there were very few daughters of notables there. But although this was an extreme case, with rural industry making matters worse, it was by no means exceptional: whatever people's occupations might be in this hinterland, whether purely agricultural or mixed, the male – female disparity was always greater than in the main town of the locality.

A closer look at the figures for the *arrondissement* of Lille, canton by canton, would bear out this view. Here again we find that the more rural the area, as in the cantons of Pont-à-Marcq and Cysoing, the wider the discrepancy and the closer that discrepancy is to the average difference found in Maggiolo's figures. This is by no means to be taken as implying that women's literacy rates are always lower in the country than in the towns: the lowest women's score in the *arrondissement* is that of Tourcoing (20%), and the reason why the difference between male and female scores is low in that town is that the men's literacy rate is also very low.

Disparities between men and women
(in men's favour)

canton of

| | | | |
|---|---|---|---|
| Roubaix | + 6.1% | Haubourdin | + 14.8% |
| Tourcoing | + 9.0% | Lannoy | + 15.0% |
| Armentières | + 9.4% | Seclin | + 19.5% |
| Quesnoy-sur-Deule | + 10.2% | Pont-à-Marcq | + 24.5% |
| Lille | + 10.7% | Cysoing | + 25.1% |
| La Basse | + 13.1% | | |

The last two tables show that towns tend to level the performances of the two sexes, either upwards (Armentières or Lille) or downwards (Roubaix, Tourcoing). But the downwards levelling process works faster in those cantons that are both most backward and most recently industrialized and urbanized. In such cases, the discrepancies in the literacy rates of the two sexes remain appreciably greater.

One is tempted to interpret this phenomenon as a manifestation of the contrast between the traditional rural community, governed by a residual patriarchal civilization, where the women only very slowly make good their accumulated backwardness, on the one hand, and on the other the egalitarian, emancipatory influence of the town. The latter works in two ways: upward social mobility through school and culture in the ancient urban regions, and through the mingled curse and blessing of shared work and uprooting in towns that were growing up in the thick of the modern industrial adventure. In either case, women shared an increasingly common lot, although it is true that they were likely to experience deprivation more swiftly than good fortune.

What are the salient points that emerge from this detailed analysis? For one thing, that the town does have an influence on the sexual dimorphism of literacy; and secondly, that before concluding that towns are conducive to progress in literacy, we must distinguish between towns and towns.

**Urban literacy and typology**

In the literate France, under the *Ancien Régime*, the towns tended to narrow the differences between male and female literacy rates. This much we have already learnt from the example of the *département* of Nord. We shall find confirmation, moreover, if we take a look at Rouen, for example, where at the end of the 17th century there was a 16% discrepancy between men and women compared with 23% for the *département* as a whole; or at Rheims, where at the end of the 18th century the urban difference was 24%, as against a departmental average of 33%. This was because, in this developed part of France, the townswomen were taught to read and write very early on, in the 17th century even. So that we do not find in the towns the cultural chasm that all too frequently developed between men and women in the country areas.

Things are a little more complicated in the illiterate France: it is quite possible to find practically insignificant differences between men and women in the towns. At the end of the 18th century, the figure was only 4% in Limoges, 5% in Saint-Junien, at a time when the average departmental difference was 4.6%. To be sure, the explanation for this tiny disparity is to be found in the very poor general rate of literacy: at the time, the departmental average was scarcely more than 10% for the men and 6% for the women (17% and 13% respectively even in Limoges itself!)

But we also come across another kind of situation in this illiterate France: that of towns whose literacy process had been set in motion under the *Ancien Régime*. Here, according to the rule, men set the ball rolling, with the result that in the early stages the gap between men and women widened in line with the leap forwards in male literacy rates. Only if this male progress proved lasting did the townswomen, much later, follow suit; after another interval, the countrywomen joined in the movement. In Landes, for example, ignorance had been apportioned with exceptional even-handedness: 5.2% of the men and 1.7% of the women were literate, making a difference of 3.5%. But at Dax and Mont-de-Marsan, the gap reaches or even exceeds 30%, i.e. in towns where male literacy has gathered momentum. In Gironde, with a slightly higher level of education, we find a modest difference of 15.5%. But Bordeaux, the economic, administrative and intellectual capital of the *département*, yields a difference of close on 21%, the male literacy process having got under way. Agen presents a similar profile at the same moment in time.

To appreciate these figures, we need to bear in mind the national male–female differential for the years 1786–90 that emerges from Maggiolo's figures, namely 20.6%. From this we can see that, in illiterate France, a large gap between men and women is in fact a sign that the literacy process has recently got under way in towns surrounded by a countryside in which ignorance is widespread among both sexes. In the educated France, on the other hand, a low urban differential between men and women generally indicates a very high overall rate of literacy, as we have seen in Avesnes, where 76% of the men and 68% of the women were literate. Here, the urban literacy process is already an old one, and these figures are its culmination, the surrounding countryside having achieved literacy too. But it may also happen that, foreshadowing one aspect of the 19th century, very low differentials can reflect a much more 'modern' trend, such as when these figures reflect a generally very low level of literacy, as found in towns like Lille or Tourcoing which were already reeling under the impact of the industrial revolution.

208 Reading and writing

In other words, there were towns, and towns; which brings us back to the problem raised by detailed analysis of the *arrondissements* of Nord. We now have to examine the literacy process in the light of a number of variables, which have been artificially isolated for purposes of observation.

First, there is the question of the size of towns. As a general rule, within a given geographic and cultural zone, the biggest towns have the highest literacy rates for both men and women. This can be verified at departmental level, as in Corrèze between 1777 and 1786, where Brive and Tulle stand head and shoulders above Ussel, Allassac, Lubersac or Meymac.

Then comes the type of town. Towns that were traditionally given over to administrative, ecclesiastic, judicial or even university functions had a higher level of education, in the 17th and 18th centuries, than did towns that had grown up or developed more recently, towns whose activities were centred more around trade, port activities or industry. Thus in late-17th-century Brittany, Quimper was better educated than Brest, likewise Rennes than Nantes; in the *département* of Nord in the 18th century, Valenciennes and Douai more so than Roubaix and even Lille. This was the advantage that G. Cholvy, writing about the Languedoc in the early 19th century once again, terms the 'town-towns' over the 'industrial-centre-towns'. On the other hand, these traditional towns, with their solid, stable core of educated people, generally closed to outsiders, did little to make these cultural advantages available to the newcomers resulting from demographic growth, where this existed. Less, at all events, than towns with a greater diversity of activities, where the proliferation of intermediate categories prevented the emergence of a gulf between a completely educated élite and an utterly illiterate people: such intermediate strata acted as relays, creating conditions for the cultural advancement of the fast-growing lower classes.

The third urban variable that needs to be taken into account is the socio-occupational structure. For clearly those socio-occupational categories that need to be able to write – and whose members are therefore all, or almost, able to sign their names – are much better represented here than in the countryside: this includes the professions and the 'bourgeois', merchants and brokers, government officials and noblemen, all of them plentiful in the towns, and all able to sign their names, with very few exceptions, even the women. The middle strata too are over-represented: the craftsmen and shopkeepers, most of whom also signed their names. In La Rochelle, for instance, in 1777–86, more than two-thirds of the bakers could sign, while more than three-quarters of the tailors and blacksmiths could do so. Lastly, a further factor enhancing the pre-eminence of the towns was that these socio-occupational categories were better educated in town than in the country. This was the case in the backward France, such as

Brittany and the south-west for instance: like the craftsmen in 18th-century Corrèze, of whom half in Tulle were able to sign their names, while none in Lubersac could do so. In the educated France, on the other hand, at the end of the 18th century, rural literacy rates for the same categories often drew very near to urban rates: in Normandy, economically equivalent socio-occupational groups enjoyed very comparable literacy rates, with the countryside trailing very slightly. In this same France, however, the power of the town to acculturize seems nevertheless to have passed over the least privileged sections of society, and we find for instance that urban journeymen were still more illiterate than rural ones.

Lastly, there is the question of the type of immigration. It is generally accepted, without further qualification, that the slowness of the spread of literacy in towns, in the 18th century particularly, was due to the influx of new inhabitants from the surrounding countryside, most of them illiterate: a sort of immigration of economic and cultural poverty, which is supposed to have unsettled the steady growth of urban literacy. Indeed there is no lack of evidence for this view: in Brittany, for instance, where the utterly ignorant countryside dispatched hordes of illiterates to the towns, smother-ing the cultural progress being made by native city-dwellers at the same moment. Or in the south-west where, as J.-P. Poussou's figures de-monstrate, late 18th-century immigrants (women especially) were far less able than the natives to sign their names: in Bayonne, the figures were 58% compared with 77% for the men, and 17% compared with 58% for the women; in Bordeaux, they were 49% compared with 63% and 22% compared with 43%, and so forth. But one even comes across similar cases in the educated regions: in lle-de-France for instance, where Michel Lachiver[12] notes that in Meulan, in 1769–90, 65% of women making the compulsory 'declaration of pregnancy' signed the register, but that only 20% of the women from outside Meulan making the same declaration signed their names. Still, the facts will not warrant stretching this thesis to cover the whole of the developed part of France. Where the rural populations were highly educated, immigration often turned out to be a selective process, for men and women alike. In the small towns of Haute-Normandie, for instance, as well as in Rouen, the rate of literacy among newcomers was always higher than the average for the countryside they had just left behind them. To be sure, this rate was often slightly lower than among the townspeople. But not always. In Caen, in the decade prior to the Revolution, J.-C. Perrot[13] finds more educated immigrant bridegrooms than natives, and among the brides, just as many; immig-ration in such circumstances may be motivated by penury (shortage of work or low pay), but not by illiteracy.

In certain Breton towns even, in the ports, where as we have seen the immigrants from nearby were illiterate, one also comes across a highly-educated immigrant élite originating from much further away: on the eve of the Revolution, according to J. Quéniart, most of the citizens of Brest who were able to read and write not only did not hail from Brest but in fact did not even come from Brittany originally!

From the interplay of these different factors, we may deduce a geography of literacy inside the towns of the *Ancien Régime*. Classically, this would oppose a historic centre, which would also be the educated district with its parishes inhabited by the notables, to the less central areas and the suburbs where the poor dwelt in cultural poverty, mingling countryfolk, small peasants and agricultural labourers with the pariahs of urban society, the journeymen, the porters, watermen and so on.

But already in certain towns the geography of education points to the transition from a traditional society to one dominated by industrial-type employment. This is the case, for instance, in Lille or Rouen, where as early as the 18th century we find highly literate parishes and ignorant ones, the former associated with the town's traditional activities, the latter swelling with the growth of new industrial activities. In Rouen, for example, the administrative, commercial and residential districts in the town centre were almost completely literate (98% of the bridal couples signed their names in the parish of Saint-Etienne de la Grande Eglise); on the other hand, in the outlying suburbs to the north, the east and the south – the big parishes of Saint-Maclou and Saint-Vivien especially, the lower-class craftmen's and textile workers' districts – the level of education was much lower (only 37% of the bridal couples in Saint-Maclou were able to sign their names). What is more, in these districts the level of education stagnated throughout the 18th century, just when industry, that source of ignorance and misery, was developing.

### Industrial revolution and literacy

How did the decisive transition to an industrial economy, in the 19th century, affect literacy in urban society? To try to find out, let us dwell on the example of the *département* of Nord, where the situation at the end of the 18th century reveals a state of low-level literacy that is all the more surprising when set against the emergence of a modern-type economy. We shall, in surveying the developments in the course of the 19th century, adopt four benchmarks (see graph overleaf), three of which refer to young men only:

   − the educational level of conscripts in 1827–1829;
   − marriage signatures in 1866 (by *arrondissement*);
   − the educational level of conscripts in 1878–1880;
   − the educational level of conscripts in 1899–1904.

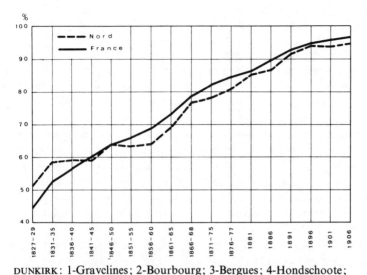

DUNKIRK: 1-Gravelines; 2-Bourbourg; 3-Bergues; 4-Hondschoote;
5-Wormhoudt. HAZEBROUCK: 1-Cassel; 2-Steenworde; 3-Bailleul;
4-Merville. LILLE: 1-Tourcoing; 2-Quesnoy-sur-Leule; 3-Armentières;
4-Haubourdin; 5-La Bassée; 6-Seclin; 7-Roubaix; 8-Lannoy;
9-Cysoing; 10-Pont-à-Marcq. VALENCIENNES: 1-Saint-Amand; 2-Condé;
3-Bouchain. DOUAI: 1-Orchies; 2-Marchienne; 3-Arleux. CAMBRAI:
1-Carnières; 2-Solesmes; 3-Marcoing; 4-Clary; 5-Le Cateau. AVESNES:
1-Le Quesnoy; 2-Bavai; 3-Maubeuge; 4-Berlaimont; 5-Solre de Chateau;
6-Landrecies; 7-Trélon.

Comparative literacy in the *département* of Nord and in France, based on
departmental figures

### The education level of conscripts in 1827–29 (Map 5.4)

A preliminary remark is called for: the departmental average for
conscripts able at least to read in 1827–29 is lower (by 3%) than that for
bridegrooms signing the marriage register in 1750–90. The drop was
particularly marked in three *arrondissements*: Avesnes, Cambrai and
Valenciennes; and low in two others: Dunkirk and Hazebrouck.
Admittedly, the figures are not absolutely comparable, but even so, it is
surprising to find fewer young men of 20 able to read in 1827–29 than men
capable of signing their names a half-century earlier.[14]

Conscripts able at least to read (1827–29)

| | | | |
|---|---|---|---|
| Avesnes | 61.6% | Valenciennes | 48.8% |
| Dunkirk | 58.2% | Hazebrouck | 48.7% |
| Douai | 57.2% | Cambrai | 46.9% |
| | | Lille | 45.8% |

Departmental average: 50.8%

Admittedly, Maggiolo had found that, in Nord, men's signatures in 1816–20 were appreciably less plentiful than in 1786–90 (48.5% as against 51.3%): he too noted a slight regression.

Was this poor start to the 19th century already a sign of the economic transformations that the *département* was undergoing? The relative position of the different regions in the educational league table may provide us with some pointers in answer to this question. To begin with it will be noted that, as in the 18th century, the leading *arrondissements* were Dunkirk and Avesnes: the development of modern heavy industry had yet to begin, either in the valley of the Sambre or in Dunkirk. The *arrondissement* of Douai also managed to worm its way into this leading group: it too lay outside the 'black country'. The *arrondissement* of Lille, on the other hand, then in the grip of textile fever, once again lagged way behind the rest.

On this point, the reader is naturally referred to Villermé's survey, which is contemporary with the 1827–29 sample of conscripts, [15] and in particular to Volume 1, under the chapter headed 'Des ouvriers manufacturiers du département du Nord, en général, et, en particulier, de ceux des villes de Lille, Roubaix et Tourcoing'. Thus, Villermé records that in 1828, according to the prefect, there were 224,300 industrial workers in Lille, 'the greater portion of them connected with the cotton mills'. With their families, this made close on 400,000 people (at a time when the entire population of Nord was under a million), 163,453 of whom were registered with the welfare boards, i.e. one-sixth of the total population, by far the highest proportion of indigents for a whole *département* anywhere in France. In Lille itself, around 1837, we find that 30% of the population was indigent.

With mediocre scores (45.8–48.8% 'able at least to read'), similar to the *arrondissement* of Lille, we find the other three industrial *arrondissements*: Hazebrouck (the decline of the textile industry in Flemish-speaking Flanders in favour of the Lille region had barely begun), Cambrai (where the rural textile industry reached its zenith under the Restoration) and Valenciennes (where the development of coalmining was gathering momentum).

The map by canton shows that the western part of the *arrondissement* of Avesnes (Le Quesnoy, Landrecies, etc.), rubbing shoulders with the largely illiterate Cambrésis, gradually lost its lead. Further, the illiterate cantons were by now less exclusively the wretched privilege of the *arrondissement* of Lille than in the 18th century: we now find them in those of Hazebrouck, Cambrai and Valenciennes. Lastly, owing to the logic of the conurbations, which tended to foster literacy, we now find that the cantons containing the chief towns (except Valenciennes) stand out as oases of greater literacy in the 'bad' *arrondissements*, as in the case of the cantons of Douai and those of Cambrai; in Lille itself, we may distinguish between south and east, where the workers lived and the level of instruction remained poor, and the other cantons, where it was much better.

### Marriage signatures in 1866 (Maps 5.5 and 5.6)

The only figures available here are for each *arrondissement*. Where the men are concerned, it should be noted first of all that the three leading *arrondissements* are also, and in the same order, the least urban and the least densely-populated: Avesnes (103 inhabitants per sq. km.), Dunkirk (143) and Hazebrouck (150). The other four are far more so, from Cambrai (194) to Lille (422). Ought we therefore to regard high population density, and especially a high density of urban population, wherever the social structures and amenities are inadequate to cope with them, as an obstacle to literacy?

Marriage signatures (1866) – Men

| | | | |
|---|---|---|---|
| Avesnes | 83.6% | Douai | 68.6% |
| Dunkirk | 77.2% | Cambrai | 68.3% |
| Hazebrouck | 70.6% | Lille | 64.0% |
| Valenciennes | 69.6% | | |

Departmental average: 69.5%

However, if we compare the departmental figures for 1866 with the average proportion of marriage signatures in 1750–90 (53.9%) or in 1786–90 (51.3% according to Maggiolo), we see just how slow Nord's progress was: + 15.6 to + 18.2%, depending on the source. During the same period, the national average gained 28 points, increasing from 47 to 75%!

Of the seven *arrondissements*, three progressed faster than the *département* as a whole: Dunkirk (+ 18.6%), already runner-up to Avesnes in the 18th century; and especially Hazebrouck (+ 19.4%) and Lille (+ 19.6%), i.e. the two worst performers in the 18th century. The *arrondissement* of Valenciennes progressed at the average rate, namely 14.5%. The other three, meanwhile, did less well than the average for the *département*: Avesnes (+ 10%), which is hardly surprising in view of the very high level already attained in the 18th century (even so, it still continued to improve), Cambrai (+ 13.2%) and Douai (+ 13.8%); all three were affected by the position – ancient or recent – of industry.

Comparison with the level of instruction of conscripts in 1827–29 is trickier, owing to the different nature of the sources.[16] Even so, it may be noted that Douai, struck by coalmining fever since the 1840s, dropped out of the leading group and now mingled with the industrial *arrondissements* with only mediocre literacy rates, level with Valenciennes or Cambrai. Lille, with its fast-growing population and urban sprawl, stayed at the bottom of the table. Hazebrouck, on the other hand, had started out on a fast upward climb. Why? Because its rural industry had been declining rapidly for some decades now? Or because, unlike the other *arrondissements*, Hazebrouck's population density did not increase (149 inhabitants per sq. km. in 1832, 150 in 1851, 158 in 1872: a relative increase of 6%, whereas the rates in the other *arrondissements* ranged between 23 and 89%)? Was it because these factors made it much easier for children to attend school and receive an education?

If we now take a look, for a moment, at women's marriage signature rates, the first thing to note is, compared with 1750–90, the poor overall rate of progress: + 19.3%, scarcely more than the figure for male signatures. This means that, in the course of a century, women made practically no inroads on the male lead. True, comparison with Maggiolo's figures for 1786–90 is more flattering: + 26%. But then, as we are aware, Maggiolo's give undue weight to rural scores which, for women, are distinctly inferior to the urban scores; and secondly, these figures too show Nord trailing: between 1786–90 (Maggiolo) and 1866–70 (*Statistique générale*), women in Nord improved their rate by only 26%, whereas the national average for Frenchwomen rose by 35.5%! For the *département* as a whole then, urban, demographic and industrial expansion impeded progress in literacy for women as well as for men.

Marriage signatures (1866) – Women

| Avesnes | 76.9% | Valenciennes | 52.7% |
|---|---|---|---|
| Dunkirk | 60.5% | Lille | 51.5% |
| Hazebrouck | 58.1% | Cambrai | 48.4% |
| Douai | 54.1% | | |

Departmental average: 55.6%

Within this generally mediocre score, moreover, we find a remarkable degree of stability in the *arrondissement* rankings for women: all, or practically all, maintained their station as though nothing had happened for a century. Even the difference between the most (Avesnes) and the least (Cambrai) literate scarcely budged: 28.5% as opposed to 31% (for men, the comparable differential – between Avesnes and Lille – fell from 29.7 to 19.6%). The two most backward *arrondissements* in the 18th century show no signs of wanting to catch up: neither Lille ( + 19.7%), nor Cambrai ( + 18.7%). Apart from Avesnes (which had already enjoyed a high rate in 1750–90), it was once more the other two leading *arrondissements* which made the greatest strides in absolute figures: Dunkirk ( + 23.4%) and Hazebrouck ( + 23.9%). This suggests that the women's performance here is attributable more to local traditions than to any other factor.

**The education level of conscripts in 1878–80 (Map 5.7)**

Here, on the other hand, there has been a change of scene since 1827–29. First, the overall progress is undeniable: +30.5%. Next, the internal hierarchy is transformed. It is hard to explain why Hazebrouck now takes the lead among the seven *arrondissements*: are de-industrialization and a static population (149 inhabitants per sq. km. in 1832, 158 in 1872 and 162 in 1891) really enough to account for this promotion ... by facilitating improved school attendance (in 1840, Hazebrouck and Lille had the lowest school attendance rates)?

Conscripts able at least to read (1878–80)

| | | | |
|---|---|---|---|
| Hazebrouck | 85.4% | Douai | 80.5% |
| Dunkirk | 85.2% | Cambrai | 77.1% |
| Avesnes | 83.1% | Valenciennes | 75.9% |
| Lille | 82.6% | | |

Departmental average: 81.3%

The *arrondissement* of Dunkirk, where industrial expansion only got under way in the 1860s and remained very localized even so, continued to make good headway and, as in the previous century, maintained its second place. Avesnes, on the other hand, for the first time slips down to third place. There are grounds for thinking that this drop is due to far-reaching changes in industrial patterns in the Avesnois. From 1830 onwards, the traditional specialized metalworking industries went into rapid decline (coke supplanted wood, and the local iron deposits had been worked out), while two major industrial centres arose: textiles at Fourmies, starting in 1823, and heavy ironmaking (the first coke-fired blast furnace dates from 1829) and metal processing in the valley of the Sambre, on either side of Maubeuge, thanks to Belgian coal.

At the same time, Lille for the first time moves up from last place, reaching fourth place in one go, overtaking the departmental average and achieving an improvement of close on 37 points compared with 1827–29. Sometime around the middle of the century, the modern industrial and urban transformation of French Flanders – for so long uncontrolled and totally unorganized – seems to have embarked upon a twin process of socio-economic rationalization and cultural modernization, enabling it to 'digest' its persistent demographic growth (between 1851 and 1891, the population density doubled from 422 to 834 inhabitants per sq. km.). Henceforward, there was a rapid surge in literacy rates: of the seven *arrondissements*, it had made the most notable progress since 1827–29.

Being now left behind by the *arrondissement* of Lille, the other three major industrial *arrondissements* made up the tail-end. Compared with 1827–29, they made only modest gains: from 24 to 30%. Valenciennes, where heavy iron foundries were added to coalmining in the 1840s, dropped to last place. Cambrai, meanwhile, remained unchanged in second-to-last position: in the absence of any urban tradition, the decline of its rural textile industries, which were being supplanted by Lille on the one hand and by the smaller local industrial centres such as Le Cateau, Caudry and so on, on the other, did nothing to further the cause of education.

The map by canton sheds some light on local patterns. First of all, we may observe here the consequences of patchwork industrialization confined to certain sectors: Dunkirk, which was where the new industrial establishments clustered mainly, sank into a mediocre category of literacy; similarly, in the far eastern part of the *département*, the canton of Trélon, which contained the town of Fourmies in particular, suffered a marked relative decline. In the *arrondissement* of Hazebrouck, the only sectors still dragging their feet were the cantons that had preserved their industries: Hazebrouck itself and, next-door to Armentières, that of Bailleul-Est. In the region of Valenciennes, the two southern cantons of the *chef-liéu* which mainly lay outside the coal basin, were considerably more literate than the others. Lastly, education took a big step forward in the cantons of the city of Lille itself: industrialization was by now a long-established process, and urban problems had grown less acute.

### The education level of conscripts in 1899–1904 (Map 5.8)

Turning, finally, to 1899–1904, given the degree of literacy achieved by all conscripts from Nord (94.3% were able at least to read), the differences from one *arrondissement* to the next were now very slight, and are therefore rather awkward to analyse. Two distinct groups do emerge, however. Four *arrondissements* exceed the departmental average (and the figure of 95%), among them the *arrondissements*

| Conscripts able at least to read (1899–1904) | | | |
|---|---|---|---|
| Douai | 96.8% | Avesnes | 92.6% |
| Lille | 95.7% | Cambrai | 91.2% |
| Hazebrouck | 95.3% | Valenciennes | 90.9% |
| Dunkirk | 95.2% | | |

Departmental average: 94.3%

of Lille and Douai, which had made a good deal of progress ( + 13% and + 16%) since 1878–80. These two *arrondissements* seem, by the end of the century, to have absorbed the consequences of the untramelled industrial and urban growth of the previous decades and to have rediscovered the advantages that organized urban life usually offers to education. The other two leading *arrondissements* were Hazebrouck, now in a good, stable position, and Dunkirk which, after a period of rapid industrial growth and poor educational progress ( + 10% only), was back in fourth place. At the bottom of the table, we find two distinct models: that represented by Avesnes, to begin with, continuing its long term relative decline ( + 9% only, and now in fifth place) and the development of heavy industry; and Cambrai and Valenciennes, which had been very backward for twenty years but had made very swift progress since. The map by canton indicates the extent of a cloud of poor literacy figures in the Dunkirk region; a similar phenomenon existed in the Sambre district too. Progress in the Douai *arrondissement*, on the other hand, was principally achieved by those cantons that lay either entirely or partly outside the coal basin; progress in the *arrondissement* of Cambrai, meanwhile, was due to the urban cantons of the *chef-lieu*.

But are these figures of any real help in understanding what fostered, and what hampered, the progress of literacy in the towns of Nord in the 19th century? The first thing to rule out is the linguistic factor: the figures themselves show that the customary use of a language other than French by no means stood in the way of literacy in the towns and large villages of the two Flemish-speaking *arrondissements*, namely Dunkirk and Hazebrouck.[17]

What about the rôle played by the school, then? Comparison of school attendance with literacy rates yields little that is certain, here. At most, we may observe that the urban *arrondissement* of Lille had a very low rate of school attendance in the 1830s, with 43.3%, coming sixth out of seven *arrondissements* (exactly the position it was to occupy twenty years later for marriage signatures).[18] We also find a sharp increase in school attendance rates ( + 12.7%) for the period observed. Should we therefore see in this surge in schooling in the 1830s the first stirrings that eventually produced Lille's rapid advances in educational levels in the last third of the century?

What is quite likely, at any rate, is that when and where towns were swamped by the demographic tide – i.e. in regions subject to sudden bursts of industrial growth – the school system would have proved inadequate and cramped, and may even have acted as a repellent. This is confirmed for example by P. Pierrard, writing about Lille under the Second Empire: he saw in these 'dreary, dingy schools. . . absolutely the last thing to attract the unenthusiastic or the truant'.[19]

The most significant distinction then, throughout the period under discussion, was between the agricultural sectors and the industrial ones (between *arrondissements* and inside individual *arrondissements*). Not until the end of the 19th century did the two most urban and industrial *arrondissements* – Lille and Douai – move (or return) to the head of the *département*. The spread, both overall and geographical, of literacy does indeed seem here to be connected primarily with the different phases of industrial development. Literacy had been dragging its feet in all the

cantons or *arrondissements* experiencing sudden, wide-scale industrialization since the 18th century and in the decades following. All the 19th-
century surveys bear this out. Take for instance the one conducted by E.
Vuillemin, in 1872, on the working population of the Nord–Pas-de-Calais
coalmining basin.[20] Going on the replies to his questionnaire sent in by
several mining companies, Vuillemin established the level of education, for
each age-bracket, of 21,426 people aged over 10 making up the 'coalmining
population' housed in dwellings owned by these companies:

Education level of working people
in the Nord–Pas-de-Calais coal basin (1871)
(over 10, able to read and write)

| Age | Men | Women |
|---|---|---|
| 10–20 | 48.7% | 47.3% |
| 20–30 | 52.4% | 41.9% |
| 30–40 | 49.0% | 32.4% |
| 40–50 | 40.6% | 24.0% |
| 50–60 | 43.4% | 20.8% |
| over 60 | 27.7% | 14.2% |
| TOTAL | 47.3% | 36.6% |

At almost the same date (the 1866 census), the entire population of the
*département* of Nord aged over *five years old* yielded the following
percentages able to read and write: male, 59.4% and female, 52.7% (this
figure was higher still in Pas-de-Calais).

National surveys of the condition of working people in Nord, conducted
in the 19th century, furnish comparable figures. All the replies to the 1872
parliamentary survey[21] emphasize the extremely high proportion of
illiterates among the workers – whether in textiles or in mining. The owner
of one wool mill said that practically all his workers were illiterate; the
Compagnie des Charbonnages d'Anzin reckoned that the proportion of
the working population aged over ten and able to read and write came to
around 50%. The Douai Chamber of Commerce reckoned that roughly
two-thirds of the workers were illiterate, and its counterpart in
Valenciennes gave its proportion as around a third, Cambrai's Health
Board replying with seven-tenths. The Lille Chamber of Commerce,
meanwhile, claimed that the educational level of its workers was 'practically nil'. The 1866 census confirms that, among the main towns in Nord,
the ones with the lowest literacy rates were the ones that were the most
exclusively working class in make-up: Halluin (21.1% 'able to read and
write' among the over-5s), Denain (40.2%) and Wattrelos (38.3%).

Certainly, the periods of 'unchecked' industrial and urban growth, going
hand in hand with spectacular population growth, meant that the school

system (like the other social amenities) in the towns had trouble keeping up with this rate of expansion.

But we cannot look upon poor school facilities as the determining factor in illiteracy. For that it would be necessary to show that existing schools were full, which was not necessarily the case, as the English experience illustrates. In Nottingham, in the mid-19th century, at the height of the industrial and demographic revolution, David Wardle points out that, following a major school building drive, the schools nevertheless stood empty to a large extent – with the exception of the infant departments, which were overcrowded because these children were too young to have a hope of finding work.[22]

The duration of this backward state varied, towns with more ancient traditions (such as Lille and Douai) catching up more swiftly than the others. Further, wide-scale child labour in industry – attributable both to the demand for labour and to the families' need of the income[23] – made the development of education an impossibility, whether in school, in the home or in church: for it was in the nature of industrial work that it kept children occupied year-round. Farm work, on the other hand, was less demanding because of the changing seasons, and throughout the months of bad weather (from All Saints Day to Easter) children were free to attend school or to learn to read and write by any other means.[24] It thus becomes easier to grasp why the rural areas provided conditions favourable to literacy.[25] An exception should nevertheless be made for regions such as the Cambrésis, where rural industrial activities were superimposed onto framework, for in such cases too there was no closed season. The three *arrondissements* of Nord in which conscript literacy was lowest in 1827–29 and where school attendance rates languished, were Lille, then in the grip of industrial and urban growth, and Cambrai and Hazebrouck, where rural industry combined with farming.

Nord, which we have presented here as an example of how industrial growth can hamper the spread of literacy in the towns, is no isolated case. We may find confirmation of this hypothesis in figures for the four cantons of Saint-Etienne,[26] for the industrial towns of Saône-et-Loire,[27] the industrial centres in the Limousin[28] or in Haute-Normandie.

But there is one specific question we cannot dodge: was it really *because* of industrialization that literacy did not spread more rapidly than it did in certain towns in the 19th century? Raymond Oberlé, who has focused on the case of Mulhouse 'in the century of industrialization',[29] believes that, in the final analysis, industrial growth must be acquitted: 'The onset of industrialization', he writes, 'did not stand in the way of educational progress.' But in that case, who is the guilty figure? It was immigration, stirred by the development of industry, which drew to the towns the *déclassés* and the wretched: families that arrived from the countryside so destitute that they were unable to have their children educated. For Raymond Oberlé, it was this wave of illiterates, newly-arrived in the towns, which accounts for the high illiteracy rate found in industrial Mulhouse in the 19th century. Indeed, in 1841 for example, when 28% of *all* conscripts registered in Mulhouse were illiterate, only 19% of those actually born in the town itself fell into this category. Better still, while, around 1840, nine out of ten conscripts in Bas-Rhin were able at least to read, only two-thirds of the conscripts born in the Bas-Rhin but now settled in Mulhouse were literate, which is further evidence of the high proportion of illiterates found among immigrants.

However, if we now examine the diachronic data on Mulhouse supplied by Raymond Oberlé himself, the picture changes radically. Between 1841 and 1871, the three decennial averages for the educational level of conscripts indicate no progress whatever – quite the reverse in fact – in literacy rates among native Mulhousians: 7.7% illiteracy in 1841–50; 9.5% in 1851–60; and 8.1% in 1861–70.[30] During the same period, illiteracy fell sharply among non-native conscripts: from 22.7 to 11.5% for those coming from the rest of Haut-Rhin; from 32.1 to 18.5% for natives of Bas-Rhin; from 34.3 to 12.2% for immigrants from other *départements*. Over this period of thirty years (crucial to the industrial and demographic growth of the town), therefore, the percentage of illiterate conscripts was at best static. To be sure, it remained lower than the figure for exogenous conscripts; but the gap narrowed considerably: in 1841–50 it was *at least* 1 to 3 (and up to 1 to 5); in 1861–70, it was *at most* 1 to 2.

It seems certain, therefore, contrary to what Raymond Oberlé writes, that the overall spread of literacy among Mulhousian conscripts from 1841 onwards cannot be ascribed to the alleged acculturizing power of all towns regardless of their rate or type of industrial development; but rather to the rapid decline in illiteracy among young men coming in from the country-side. Culturally deprived they may have been, but it would be quite wrong to present them as the *cause* of the slowdown in the process of education in the towns. Industrial growth did indeed draw to Mulhouse a flood of little-educated immigrants, but it also blocked the level of education (which was admittedly high to begin with) among the natives.

We must also give proper weight to the nature of the industries growing up in the towns, and to the specific occupational groups to which they gave rise. The literacy process is by no means indifferent to diversity – technical and human – in industry. The Chamber of Commerce surveys of 'industrial statistics', in 1847–48 first of all, and later in 1860, make this abundantly plain in the case of Paris.[31] In 1847–48, for instance, the average percentage of Parisian workers (all categories) able to read and write was 87% (this concerns men only); but in the textile trade, this figure drops to 73%; it stands at 81% in the building trade, while climbing to 95%

in 'fancy goods', to 96% among gold and silversmiths, and to 97% in printing, engraving and stationery. For female workers, to a slightly lesser degree (overall average, 79%), we find similar differences between the same activity sectors: only 64% were able to read and write in 'textiles', but 83% of the women in 'fancy goods' were able to do so, and 84% in 'furnishings'. A dozen years later, in 1860, the relative positions of the different sectors, educationally speaking, had hardly changed at all. At that date, when we try to distinguish crafts within one of the major sectors of activity, the differentials widen. In the building trade, for instance, barely 50% of the quarrymen, pavers, masons and plasterers were literate; in the 'transport' industry, water-transport labourers just about made 56%. This was at a time when certain crafts – engravers, typesetters, bronze-founders, or precision instrument makers – were fully literate.

Evidence from other 19th-century industrial towns points in the same direction. Take, for example, the four cantons of Saint-Etienne, in 1866–68:[32] the south-eastern canton, with a majority of ribbon and arms workers, was the best-educated (only 13.2% of conscripts were illiterate); in the north-western canton, where miners join the ribbon workers, the illiteracy rate rises to 16.6%; in the south-western canton, where miners, blacksmiths and ironsmiths were still more numerous than ribbon workers, the figure came to 23%; while in the north-eastern canton, where the miners outnumbered all other categories by far, 32.6% of the conscripts were illiterate: this canton ranked 27th out of 30 in the *département*! The same goes for Mulhouse, where in 1841–50 nearly 50% of the spinners, piecers and journeymen were illiterate, compared with a figure of only 7% for workers in mechanical engineering, printing and engraving; and for the Limousin, with the porcelain and glove makers of Haute-Vienne, who were far better-educated than the arms makers of Tulle or the Aubusson tapestry weavers. This shows just how powerful tradition could be in the influence that it exerted; it shows, too, just how careful one has to be when discussing the relations between 'industrial growth' and the literacy process. Just as we need to distinguish between towns and towns, we are equally obliged to distinguish between the different industries.[33]

### The national rule

In the final analysis, only the national figures will allow us to appreciate to what extent the 19th century altered the shape and the process of elementary education in the French towns. This is possible with the aid of the *Statistique générale de la France* for the second half of the century: the 1866, and especially the 1872, censuses contain figures on the educational level of the population for all *arrondissement chefs-lieux* – regardless of size – and for all towns, whether *arrondissement chefs-lieux* or not, with a population of over 10,000.[34] This means that certain towns with close on 10,000 inhabitants and growing fast, but which did not happen to be *arrondissement chefs-lieux* (in Nord and the Paris Region, for instance), were left out of this survey, whereas one finds a number of very small towns, some with under 2,000 or 3,000 inhabitants, included simply by virtue of their administrative functions.

One has no need of such refined statistics to establish that practically everywhere, in the 19th century, the towns were more literate than the countryside (Map 5.9). Where marriage signatures are concerned, the national differential is significant: according to the *Statistique*, in 1855, townsmen and women both led their country cousins by roughly 11 per cent (men: 73.7% in the towns compared with 62.4% in the countryside; women: 56.9% and 45.2%). In twenty or so *départements*, the rural areas enjoyed educational parity with the towns, or were even very slightly ahead; nearly all such cases occurred in north-eastern France, where we find that literacy rates had long been high in the countryside and that a lot of towns were undergoing rapid industrial growth. In the 1872 census, we find both the national rule and the departmental exceptions (Doubs, Meurthe-et-Moselle, Meuse, Marne, Calvados, etc.), all of them located in areas where educational levels had been high in both town and country since the *Ancien Régime*.

This brings us to a second observation. Literacy rates in the towns are always, as in the previous century, determined by the general level of literacy in the region concerned. Taking the census figures as the basis for a map of illiteracy in towns (Maps 5.10 and 5.11), we find that the general shape of the maps is in itself eloquent: whatever the size of the town (fewer than 5,000 inhabitants, from 5 to 20,000, over 20,000...), it is in the backward part of France, south-west of the Saint-Malo–Geneva line, that percentages of illiteracy in towns rise above the 30 or even the 40 mark. This rule suffers but a few exceptions, and those are mainly in the four northern *départments* (Nord, Pas-de-Calais, Somme, Aisne).

Locally, we find the equivalent – sometimes even to the point of caricature – of these regional contrasts. For instance, urban illiteracy rates are particularly high in the new industrial centres developed right in the midst of backward country areas: in Saône-et-Loire, the industrial towns that grew up in the poorly-educated western 'bocage' produced a generation of particularly ill-educated conscripts in the 1830s. Even when industrial development is not directly involved, the connection with local levels of education is still decisive: still in Burgundy,[35] illiteracy rates were higher, on average, in the small towns in the 'bocage' than in those situated in open countryside, and they were higher in the towns of the Chalons and Mâcon hill-country than in those of the Côte-d'Or vineyards.

Even so, the more backward the region, and the more recent the take-off of elementary education, the wider the gap was (or became) between town and country. As witnessed by Haute-Vienne in 1872: the illiteracy rate[36] was 37.6% in Limoges,[36] and 66.3% in the 'countryside'[37] of that *département*.[38] Or again, Finistère: 27.8% in the four largest towns (Brest, Morlaix, Quimper and Lambézellec), and 69.8% in the 'countryside'.[39] But we might suggest that here, in the towns in the (economically and culturally) backward parts of France, education – primarily through schooling – occupied a position of considerable importance in the 19th century, because it was through its agency, and through the migratory movements which it opened up, that upward social mobility (which was impossible to achieve locally, in the midst of an archaic, declining economy) occurred. In the towns of the developed regions of France, on the other hand, it was modern economic activity itself, more than the school, which underpinned the reproduction and improvement of the work force and its internal promotion, all on-the-spot.

In *départements* that, though slightly less culturally backward, still only possessed a single 'tertiary' metropolis, one may uncover differentials just as impressive. In Indre-et-Loire, for instance, between Tours (43,000 inhabitants, 21.75% illiterate) and the Tourangelle 'countryside' (47.31% illiterate); or in the next-door Loir-et-Cher, between Blois (20,000 inhabitants, 15.5% illiterate) and the Blésois 'countryside' (41.1%). Further on, in Nièvre, between Nevers (22,000 inhabitants, 23.4% illiterate) and the Nivernais 'countryside' (49.5%). Or in Pyrénées-Orientales, between Perpignan (27,000 inhabitants, 33.6% illiterate) and the Catalan 'country-side' (51.8%). And so on.

Are we to infer from this that literacy rates are conditioned by the size of towns and rise in step with this without any other form of intervention? What actually happens, as can be seen from the 1872 census, is that in a similar regional cultural context, illiteracy rates in the biggest towns are generally well below those of their smaller neighbours. Clermont-Ferrand is better-educated than Thiers, Riom, Ambert or Issoire; Montpellier better than Lodève, Sète, Béziers or Saint-Pons; Brest better than Quimper, Châteaulin or Quimperlé; Grenoble better than Vienne, la Tour-du-Pin, Saint-Marcellin or Voiron; Marseille better than Tarascon, Arles or Aix; Saint-Etienne better than Firminy or Roanne. This is due, of course, to the fact that as towns grow in size so does the range of crafts and trades, and especially the range of tertiary professions demanding at least a minimum of knowledge or even education.

Still, the rule is by no means applicable everywhere. For one thing, it is primarily valid for the biggest towns, the regional rather than the departmental metropolises. The less important 'big' towns do not always enjoy a cultural advantage over the smaller towns in the *département*. Bourg, for example, is less educated than Gex, Trévoux or Nantua; Rodez

less than Villefranche-de-Rouergue; Angoulême less than Barbezieux or
Ruffec; Laval less than Château-Gontier; Cherbourg less than Coutances;
Bourges less than Saint-Amand or Sancerre; Troyes less than Arcis-sur-
Aube, etc.

Further, even the regional metropolises may break the rule. Not only in
the backward areas of France: Morlaix scored better than Brest, as Redon
did better than Rennes; and Rive-de-Gier, Montbrison and Saint-
Chamond produced better scores than Saint-Etienne. But also – and
perhaps above all – in the educated parts of France: Besançon trailed
Pontarlier and Baume-les-Dames; Rheims scored less well than Sainte-
Menehould; Caen less than Bayeux; Rouen less than Neufchâtel-en-Bray;
Lille less than Avesnes and Hazebrouck; Dijon less than Semur and
Châtillon-sur-Seine; and Strasbourg – in 1866–was bettered by Sélestat
and Wissembourg.

What this proliferation of exceptions suggests is that, in the 19th century,
urban literacy rates depended mainly on the nature of the town's function,
economic or administrative, and hence on the socio-occupational make-up
of its population. In the beginning, at least, the surge in urban growth in the
19th century drew forth and 'sustained' an unskilled work force for which
even the most elementary education was not necessary in the way it was in
traditional urban society. Certain conditions had to be fulfilled before this
new urban population could begin to imitate the cultural behaviour of the
traditional city-dwellers: firstly, the occupational composition of the
population had to have achieved diversity and equilibrium, mingling the
'middle managers', clerks and shopkeepers with modern industrial workers
and the 'élites' of the older urban society; secondly, the town had to have
had time to 'digest' its untramelled growth and to acquire the
amenities – school obviously being one of these – they needed to catch up
culturally.

All this explains why, in the 1872 census, a great many medium-sized
towns (often ones with populations of between 10,000 and 20,000, but still
not *chefs-lieux* of *arrondissements* or *départements*) were so glaringly be-
hindhand in so far as their educational level was concerned. Examples
abound in the industrial growth areas, whether in the educated or the
uneducated part of France: Sotteville, Saint-Nazaire, Firminy,
Lambézellec, Annonay, Romans, Commentry, Le Creusot, Maubeuge,
Denain, Saint-Amand, Halluin, and so forth. A single *département*, Tarn,
offers an interesting contrast in two medium-sized towns: in 1872, Castres
had 23,000 inhabitants, Mazamet 14,000; the former was the *chef-lieu* of its
*arrondissement*, while the latter was not. In the last-named, 60.3% of the
population made its living in industry, while 6.1% of heads of household
were either *rentiers* or members of the professions; in Castres, the *chef-
lieu d'arrondissement*, on the other hand, only 36.4% of the population

depended on industry for their living, while 24.1% were *rentiers* or members of the professions. Their respective levels of education tell the rest of the tale: 15.7% illiteracy among the 'over-sixes' in Castres, compared with 37.4% in Mazamet (where however, the proportion of Protestants, reputedly better-educated than the Catholics, was a particularly high 25% compared with 5% in Castres).

In most *départements*, on the other hand, small towns that happened to be the *chef-lieu* in their *arrondissement* and to have populations of fewer than 5,000 inhabitants came top of the urban league for literacy rates, especially where male literacy was concerned. Here, in these small cities performing administrative and intellectual functions – sub-prefecture, law courts, grammar school or seminary – the importance of the literate élite was proportionally far greater than in more populous, though exclusively (or chiefly) industrial towns.

We had set out with the quiet assurance of the Directory Commissioners, who were convinced that the gathering together of men fostered the contagion of Enlightenment. Indeed, statistically speaking, our study bears out their intuition: as a rule, towns improve literacy rates. But what we have discovered in addition is that this is not everywhere, nor uniformly, so: the superiority of the towns over the surrounding countryside only becomes really impressive when the regional level of education is wretched; when the *département* as a whole is well-educated, the town – country differential shrinks, and it sometimes even happens that the countryside does better than the towns. Further, more than the size of the towns alone, what really determines literacy rates is their function (and hence their socio-occupational structure): in towns that are not the *chef-lieu* of their *arrondissement*, we tend to run into a point at which literacy begins to mark time, or even slither backwards, at around 10,000 to 20,000 inhabitants. Beyond this figure, population size once more becomes a valuable pointer to educational levels. This does however show that population in itself has no acculturating effect. It shows too that, notwithstanding the confidence of the Enlightenment, and as we have learnt from the tragic example of the towns that grew up in the industrial frenzy, to educate men it is not enough that they should simply come together.

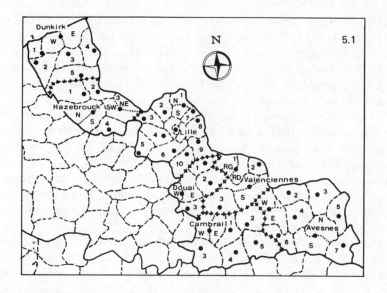

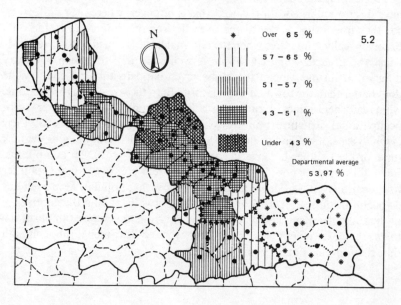

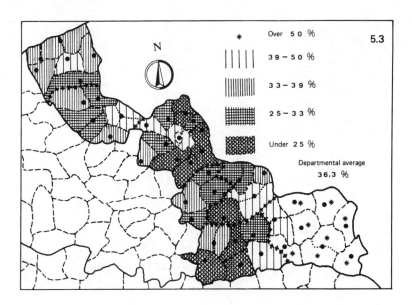

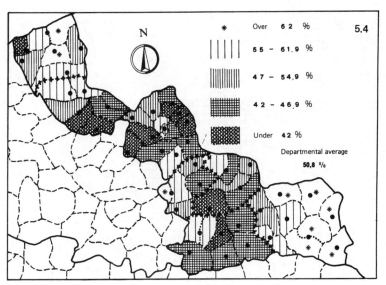

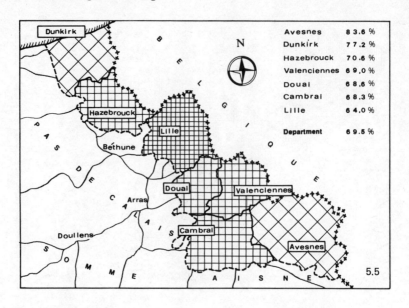

| | |
|---|---|
| Avesnes | 8 3.6 % |
| Dunkirk | 7 7.2 % |
| Hazebrouck | 7 0.6 % |
| Valenciennes | 6 9.0 % |
| Douai | 6 8.6 % |
| Cambrai | 6 8.3 % |
| Lille | 6 4.0 % |
| **Department** | **6 9.5 %** |

5.5

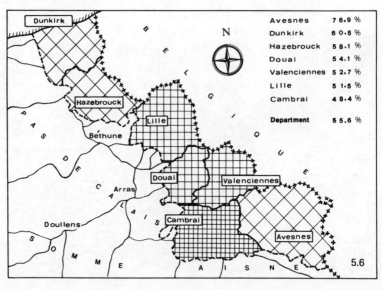

| | |
|---|---|
| Avesnes | 7 6.9 % |
| Dunkirk | 6 0.5 % |
| Hazebrouck | 5 8.1 % |
| Douai | 5 4.1 % |
| Valenciennes | 5 2.7 % |
| Lille | 5 1.5 % |
| Cambrai | 4 8.4 % |
| **Department** | **5 5.6 %** |

5.6

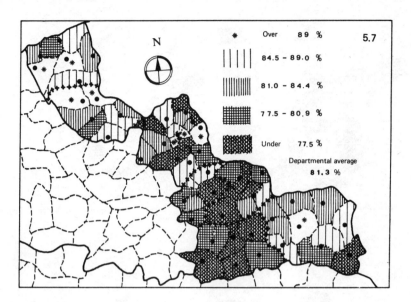

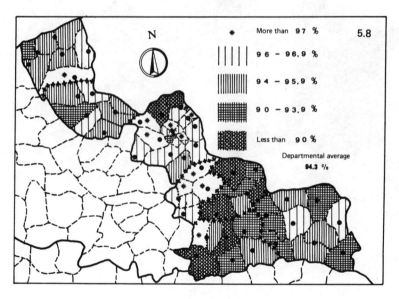

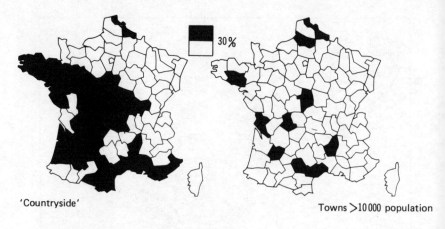

'Countryside'                                    Towns >10 000 population

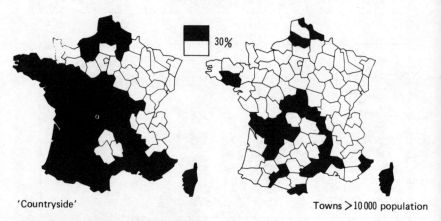

'Countryside'                                    Towns >10 000 population

5.9   Illiterate males aged over 6 in 1872
(neither read nor write)
National average 27.15%

Illiterate females aged over 6 in 1872
(neither read nor write)
National average 33.81%

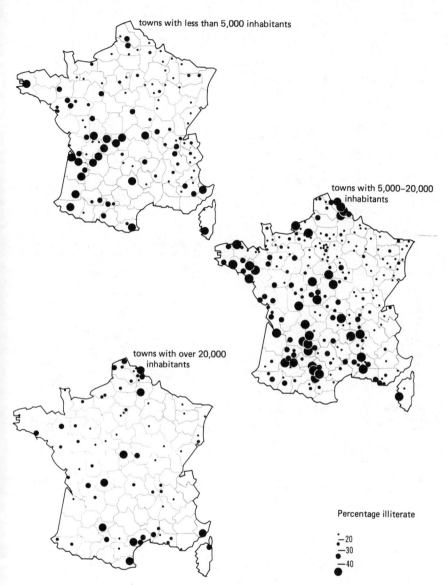

5.10   Breakdown of illiteracy by size of towns in 1866 (all towns with population of over 10,000 whether *chefs-lieux* or not, and towns with under 10,000 inhabitants where these are *chefs-lieux*)

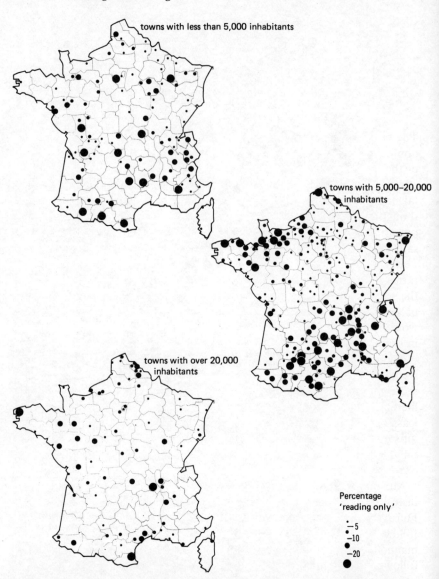

5.11   Breakdown of 'reading only' by size of towns in 1866 (all towns with population of over 10,000, whether *chefs-lieux* or not, and towns with under 10,000 inhabitants where these are *chefs-lieux*)

# 6

## THE ROLE OF THE SCHOOL: THE COMPUTER'S VERDICT

The assumption of responsibility for schooling by the State, which was the dominant feature of the 19th century, was accompanied by an acceleration of the literacy process. The parallel suggests some relation of cause and effect.[1] That literacy was the outcome and the vindication of schooling was taken for granted in all 19th-century economic, historical or political thought. Even today, when historians studying a given *département* single out an 'educated' district, this invariably happens to be the one with a satisfactory school network.[2]

It is not out of a taste for paradox that we have cast doubt on this linkage, rather it is because our review of Maggiolo's figures sounds the alarm. Can the school, and the school alone, account for the start-up of the literacy process? Can it explain the different rates observed for men and for women? Is it, finally, responsible for variations in growth rates in time and in space?

To find out, we shall have to confine ourselves to the 19th century, for want of earlier statistical data; this chronological limitation is made all the more regrettable by the fact that, as we now know, the first signs of literacy's gathering momentum are visible as early as the 17th century. At least in this enforced choice of the 19th century the precision of the information compensates for its lack of extension: from the 1830s onwards, we are able to call upon the profuse and rigorous resources of the *Statistique générale de la France*.

Most of the time, these statistical data refer to the landmarks in the history of schooling in the 19th century and to its great names, Guizot, Duruy, Ferry. The reason is that each major Act was preceded or followed by surveys which, either a priori or a posteriori justified some new manner of organizing the school system. As a result, statistical observation followed closely upon the heels of the institution as it grew up. Thus, we have no reliable series describing the state of schooling in France prior to Guizot. Between Guizot's pioneering survey and Duruy's surveys, i.e. between the 1830s and the 1860s, we have some partial indicators. Lastly, from 1876 onwards, we have the five-yearly surveys, which provide us with an overall, constantly updated, picture of the school.[3] So it is inevitably around these three major landmarks, Guizot, Duruy and Ferry (for Ferry, we have decided to study the impact of his policy around the 1890s, so as to allow it a decent interval to take effect) that our analysis will turn.

*233*

Inevitably, yet without illusion. For there is no getting away from the fact that these sources are ambiguous: they are both the product and the justification of an administration in dogged pursuit of its twin goals, namely national integration and political acculturation; their coverage of regions too distant from the capital was patchy, with occluded areas and marginal ones; above all, though, they tailor the whole of our field of analysis to the chronology of the school rather than to that of the literacy process. To remedy these drawbacks, we have tried to broaden our notion of the school as much as possible; in the first place, we have avoided reducing it merely to a matter of the density of the school network, which is the indicator conventionally regarded as a factor of literacy.

## The school network

Is the proliferation of schools in France a valid yardstick by which to measure the progress in reading and writing that was accomplished in the 19th century? This is the most traditional of all hypotheses, and therefore the first to require testing.

In 1837, the school network covered France very unevenly indeed. This was because the choices involved in founding and maintaining a school were complex ones. They were bound up with the wealth of the commune: the existence of a school might be the outcome of historical accident (as in the case of communes that had retained ownership of their forests) or of geographical accident (as with communes situated on fertile land); such choices were obviously bound up with cultural and psychological factors too. But beyond a certain threshold of wealth indifference or hostility to the school was always overcome. In the provinces of the north-east, Guizot noted, [4] the communes, with their comfortable incomes, have 'built school houses, paid teachers, granted their inhabitants the benefits of primary education', and thereby stimulated prosperity. The south-west, in contrast, was caught up in the vicious circle of poverty: barren regions, hence low communal incomes, hence educational spending borne entirely by the population, with per capita costs raised by sparse population, hence resistance to school. Those regions reputed most hostile to education were precisely those that demanded the greatest financial effort of the individual. Guizot perceived the paradox clearly: 'The richest *départements* are those in which costs are lowest; the heaviest costs are borne by the poorest *départements*.' Under such circumstances, inequalities tend to worsen rather than disappear. [5]

Rather than the number of schools per 10,000 inhabitants as proposed by the *Statistique générale de la France*, which tends to accord an illusory lead to those rural areas in which, because of the sparseness of the population, there may be more schools than in the towns; and rather than the number of schools per commune, which would reduce all 37,000 communes to the same level regardless of their size, we have preferred a negative indicator of the distribution of schools, namely the number of communes per *département not* having a school. This criterion obviously favours the highly urban regions, since the likelihood of a town having no school diminishes as its size increases. The distortion is negligible where large towns (accounting for only 11% of the population in 1836) are concerned.[6] It becomes more serious along the Mediterranean littoral, where the majority of the population was 'urban' by that time. Allowing for these reservations as to the significance of this slightly crude indicator (i.e. the number of communes having no school at all), we shall treat it as a minimum, partial indicator.

Compared with the marriage-signature maps (men and women) for 1816–20 and the map of conscripts able at least to read for 1831–35, in which Maggiolo's division of France in two is fully apparent, the map of communes bereft of schools in 1837 is rather more complicated to interpret (Map 6.1). Unsurprisingly, on the 'right' side of the Saint-Malo–Geneva line, at least three quarters of the communes are equipped with a school. On the 'wrong' side, the situation is less uniform. We find regions of shame such as Brittany and the Massif Central (except for Aveyron and Cantal), where the proportion of communes without a school is always higher: over half in Finistère, Morbihan, Corrèze and Puy-de-Dôme. But then we find regions with a reasonably good proportion of schools (above the median): the Mediterranean littoral, the Aquitaine basin and the Atlantic coastline; plus a handful of *départements* bordering on the literate half of France: Sarthe, Mayenne, Loir-et-Cher, Ain.

Thirty and sixty years later, these disparities have been wiped off the map: whereas in 1837, 18.3% of communes on average maintained no school, by 1863 this figure had dwindled to 2%; in 1896, finally, only the very smallest communes were stigmatized by the absence of a school, and they grouped together to maintain an establishment. So let's go back to the situation in 1837: we may straight away rule out any simple linear correlation between schooling and illiteracy (r = .75). We can sum this up in two ways:

### Correlation between school network and literacy

A. *Positive coincidence of two phenomena*: S and L (i.e. school and literacy). A good school network in 1837 is matched by satisfactory literacy rates at the same date. This is the case in the north-east, the Paris Basin and Normandy.

B. *Negative coincidence of two phenonmena*: Not-S and Not-L (i.e. shortage of schools *plus* illiteracy).

The shortage of schools in 1837 is matched by illiteracy at the same date and by a backlog lasting until the end of the century. This was the case in Brittany, Poitou, the north-west Massif Central and a few *départements* in the south-west: Ariège, Haute-Garonne, Tarn.

These two situations are evidence that it was possible for the two phenomena to coincide, either positively or negatively; but they fail to demonstrate the necessity of this coincidence, nor do they give any clue as to which preceded the other. This is borne out by our second configuration, which ignores any form of correlation, positive or negative, between the two phenomena:

### Absence of correlation between school network and literacy

A. The case of not-S *and* L (i.e. where a shortage of schools exists alongside literacy). A shortage of schools in 1837 is matched by good literacy rates dating back to the beginning of the 19th century. This only occurred in the southern Alps (Hautes and Basses).

B. The case of S *and* not-L (i.e , schools exist *alongside* illiteracy). A good school network in 1837 is accompanied by illiteracy and relative backwardness lasting until the end of the century. This is the case in Aquitaine, the Vendée, *départements* bordering on the literate half of France: Mayenne, Sarthe, Loir-et-Cher.

Further, still on the subject of the distribution of schools in 1837, but focusing this time on literacy rates some decades later, we find that identical situations in the second half of the century (literacy makes rapid progress) may spring from very different initial conditions. Here, as for the Mediterranean littoral, the south-east and the heart of the Massif Central, there was already a good school network by 1837, yet this coexisted with a poor level of education. Elsewhere, as in Lozère, Haute-Loire or Puy-de-Dôme, a skimpy network of schools and poor educational standards had both been made good by the end of the century. The process of catching up conceals these disparities. But for us they are crucial, since they suggest yet again that progress in literacy cannot be ascribed exclusively to the school as such.

It should also be remarked that we have so far dealt with the distribution of schools as a global factor, disregarding the issue of sexual dimorphism. Admittedly, the absence of a school in a commune penalizes the girls as much as the boys, but the existence of a school, on the other hand, does not necessarily have the same implications for girls as for boys: it may be mixed, or it may be an exclusively boys' or girls' school.

It was only in 1836 that Guizot recommended modelling the girls' schools on those that already existed for boys.[7] Were we systematically to catalogue all the different measures taken in favour of schooling for girls throughout the course of the 19th century, we could find that the passage of legislation observed an unvaryingly canonical pattern: first the boys, then

the girls. The disadvantages from which girls suffered can be inferred from
the very silence of the figures. Counting girls' schools was for years the last
of the authorities' worries. Guizot's survey, in 1833, was concerned with
specifically boys' schools and mixed schools; true, it was concerned to find
out whether the school was open to both sexes, but few inspectors took the
trouble to report the proportion of girls in the school-going population.

However, as regards the subject under discussion, the real handicap
under which girls laboured was probably not the lack of schools especially
reserved for them. It so happens that the regions with the highest
proportion of exclusively girls' schools in 1837 were Brittany, Lower
Normandy, the eastern part of the Massif Central, Languedoc and
Provence, Gironde and the *départements* of Jura and Doubs (Map 6.7).
And that it was precisely in the privileged north-eastern region that the
single village school, for boys and girls alike, was most widespread: more
than half the schools here were mixed in 1837 (Maps 6.4, 6.5 and 6.6). The
existence of exclusively girls' schools may indeed have been a sign of some
degree of under-development. This constitutes an additional reason for not
being satisfied with an examination of the school network and for
henceforward concerning ourselves less with the existence of schools and
more with their essence or attributes.

## The school-goers

Obviously, the mere existence of a school is no guarantee of proper, regular
attendance, nor even that people actually learn to read and write there.[8]
After all, a school is just a building. Which is why we would do well to go
and take a look inside; and first of all to count the pupils:

| | | | |
|---|---|---|---|
| 1832 | 1,939,000 | 1865 | 4,436,000 |
| 1837 | 2,690,000 | 1866 | 4,515,000 |
| 1840 | 2,897,000 | 1872 | 4,722,000 |
| 1843 | 3,164,000 | 1875 | 4,809,000 |
| 1847 | 3,530,000 | 1876–77 | 4,716,000 |
| 1861 | 4,286,000 | 1881–82 | 5,341,000 |
| 1863 | 4,336,000 | 1886–87 | 5,526,000[9] |

The term 'scolarisation' (in the French) refers to enrolment in school, not
to actual attendance. Generally speaking, we find that enrolments outnumber those present owing to absenteeism, and above all to two or three
enrolments in a single year: a pupil may leave school and re-enrol several
times in the course of the year. Other errors stem, especially around the
1870s (when school registers were modified), from confusion between the
school and the calendar years.

School enrolments rose quite spectacularly in the space of half a century.

Comparing these figures with the total school-age population (taking this in a very broad sense, for want of more precise statistics for the period 1850–70: we are dealing here with children aged 5 to 15),[10] the percentages turn out to be equally significant:

47.5% in 1850 (50.7% of boys, 44.1% of girls)
70.4% in 1867 (73.1% of boys, 67.7% of girls)
93.5% in 1896 (94.4% of boys, 92.5% of girls).

In the early period, the number of pupils obviously grew with the founding of new schools. The end of the July Monarchy, which coincided with the completion of the school network, brought a fresh influx of pupils into the schools (Jules Ferry's compulsory education Act tended rather to prolong the effective length of schooling than to increasing actual school enrolments). Even so, what is true for the nation as a whole needs to be qualified when we examine the regions individually.

Not surprisingly, it is north-eastern and south-eastern France that show up in full on the map of children's school enrolments in mid-century (Maps 6.8 and 6.11). What does come as a surprise is to find how ill this map fits the one showing 'communes with no school' (in 1850 also, Map 6.2). In other words, where there are few schools, the rate of school enrolments is, a fortiori, low too; however, a good distribution of schools does not necessarily entail a high rate of school attendance. If we add together these 'exceptions' we obtain practically one-quarter of all *départements*: the only thing that they have in common is that they all lie south of the 'Maggiolo line'. To understand this distortion, visible at a glance, let us take a look at the coefficients of correlation.

The coefficient of correlation, which is a measure of dispersion, evaluates the angle permitting observation of the maximum information contained on two axes (i.e. two variables). When the coefficient is equal to $+$ or $-1$, all the points observed (in this case, the *départements* of France) lie along a single straight line, known as a regression. In this case, the two arms of the angle of observation are superimposed. In our example, the literacy rate for each *département* would be exactly proportional (or inversely pro-portional: negative correlation) to the rate of school enrolment. Where the coefficient of correlation is nil, the points observed are scattered in a 'cloud' about the two perpendicular axes. In that case, the distribution of *départements* would be completely random. Between absolute correlation (positive or negative) and absolute non-correlation, we obtain intermediate values whose significance increases the closer they are to unity.

The square of the coefficient gives us an estimate of the percentage of information contained in the angle of observation. For example, a coefficient equal to 0.90 is significant for 81% of the sample. A coefficient equal to .70 would be significant for 49% of the sample, and so forth. It is common practice to accept that a coefficient is significant when it is equal to .80 or more. Diagnosis will depend largely on the nature of the phenomena under observation.

It should be borne in mind that the coefficient of correlation is a linear measure of relations between two variables, although this is hardly a feature of social phenomena.

We begin with a synchronic cross section:[11]

| MEN | Conscripts | Signatures | Communes with no school |
|---|---|---|---|
| Signatures | .992 | | |
| Communes with no school | .267 | .344 | |
| Boys enrolled in school | .994 | .987 | .274 |

| WOMEN | Signatures | Communes with no school | with no girls' school |
|---|---|---|---|
| Communes with no school | .255 | | |
| With no girls' school | .779 | .559 | |
| Girls enrolled in school | .986 | .234 | .775 |

A look at this table shows that we shall have to discard the parameter 'communes with no school' from our factors of literacy. The only factor that coincides with the literacy rate is the proportion of children enrolled in school.[12]

If, on the other hand, we look at the variables chronologically, interpretation becomes much more complicated, as can be seen from the accompanying table. The first thing to note – whether on account of inertia brought about by backwardness or of accumulated handicaps – is the permanence of the profile of literacy between 1854 and 1896, as indicated by the signatures, in whichever diachronic section we happen to choose. We ought also to note, alongside this, the stability of the picture of boys' and girls' school enrolment between 1850 and 1867 (Maps 6.9 and 6.12). This time, however, the picture changes between 1867 and 1896 (Maps 6.10 and 6.13), illustrating how the Saint-Malo–Geneva line has slipped towards that residual triangle of under-development, Britanny, the Massif Central and the western Pyrenees. Maggiolo's France was no more.

Let us now try to correlate school enrolments with signatures (Table 6.1): once again, these new figures turn up a number of surprises. We would

Table 6.1—Signatures – Schools – Enrolments (coefficients of correlation)

| Men | | Bridegrooms' signatures | | Communes with no school | | | Boys enrolled in school | | |
|---|---|---|---|---|---|---|---|---|---|
| | | 1866–70 | 1896 | 1837 | 1863 | 1896 | 1850 | 1867 | 1896 |
| Husbands' signatures | 1854–55 | 945 | 767 | 691 | 350 | 079 | 829 | 773 | 349 |
| | 1866–70 | | 835 | 739 | 396 | 052 | 853 | 805 | 377 |
| | 1896 | | | 632 | 336 | 038 | 701 | 733 | 433 |
| Communes with no school | 1837 | | | | 440 | 036 | 685 | 664 | 242 |
| | 1863 | | | | | 313 | 336 | 302 | 260 |
| | 1896 | | | | | | 104 | 153 | 166 |
| Boys enrolled in school | 1850 | | | | | | 427 | 897 | |
| | 1867 | | | | | | | | 462 |

| Women | | Brides' signatures | | Communes with no school | | | Girls enrolled in school | | |
|---|---|---|---|---|---|---|---|---|---|
| | | 1866–70 | 1896 | 1837 | 1863 | 1896 | 1850 | 1867 | 1896 |
| Brides' signatures | 1854–55 | 942 | 705 | 647 | 398 | 119 | 828 | 780 | 504 |
| | 1866 | | 797 | 702 | 405 | 080 | 875 | 839 | 539 |
| | 1896 | | | 610 | 392 | 086 | 745 | 810 | 591 |
| Communes with no school | 1837 | | | | 440 | 036 | 731 | 731 | 474 |
| | 1863 | | | | | 313 | 427 | 377 | 358 |
| | 1896 | | | | | | 094 | 141 | 136 |
| Girls enrolled in school | 1850 | | | | | | | 913 | 545 |
| | 1867 | | | | | | | | 591 |

expect to find that school enrolments in 1850 (our reference date for comparison) are correlated with literacy rates in 1866–70 (i.e. when the infants in school in 1850 would be of marrying age, hence in a position to sign the register). And this is indeed what we do find. More unexpected is to find that this correlation *already* existed in 1854–55 (i.e. before these school enrolments had had time to produce their effects); and that it had ceased to exist by 1896. Here again, we are witnessing the unravelling of a linear relation of cause and effect.

So we have tried to stand our hypothesis on its head to see whether the traditional sequence ought not rather to be read as *Literacy—School enrolment*, in other words, starting with bridal couples able to sign their names and leading to future schoolchildren. However, literacy, as measured by signatures in 1854, gives us no hint as to school enrolments forty years on, in 1896. On the other hand, it is (weakly) correlated with school enrolments twenty years after (1866–70); above all, it is powerfully correlated with school enrolment in the same period (1854).

These two series of remarks, which stress the ties between literacy and school enrolment at a given moment in time, upset our expectations of a deferred correlation in which the French would have achieved literacy through schooling, with a time-lag of around fifteen to twenty years. Nor do they help us to determine which of the two phenomena preceded the other. What they do suggest is some kind of circular relationship. We may therefore hypothesize that the spread of literacy in the 19th century did indeed occur through schooling, but on condition that there already existed a literate core population, in other words a certain cultural threshold that could only be crossed under certain circumstances: among them, the formation of a social élite, the growth of an administrative structure, and the breakdown of cultural insulators. In that case, the school would merely act as a catalyst in what was in any case a favourable environment.

To refine our hypothesis, we have adopted a departmental framework to compare a given generation between the moment at which it is supposed to have been in school in 1850 (when the children in question would have been aged between 8 and 12) and the moment at which it would be of marriageable age (24 and 32 years old between 1866 and 1870). Can we 'predict', from the level of school enrolments in 1850, the percentage of marriage signatures between 1866 and 1870?

Among the twenty *départements* coming at the top of the table both for school enrolments and for literacy, we find the entire eastern region, plus Manche, Oise and Hautes-Alpes (for men only) (Maps 6.17 and 6.18). Never has a frontier been drawn so cleanly. The *département* of Manche stands witness to a Normandy which, though brilliant in the classical era, had failed to withstand the test of modernization. It alone had preserved the benefits, regarding schooling and literacy alike, of Normandy's former leading position. As for the *département* of Hautes-Alpes, whose atypicality has come to our notice on several occasions, it was also champion in the sexual dimorphism league: women had made huge strides since the 18th century, although they had yet to catch up with their husbands (80.3% compared with 93.0% were able to sign in 1866–70), whereas we find practically as many girls as boys on the school benches in 1850 (78% and 84%, ranking third for both sexes). Oise, lastly, lying close to the 'cultural front', bears witness to the east – west march of 'Enlightenment'. Only three *départements* figure among the top twenty for school enrolments without also appearing among the twenty most literate ones. Once again, though, the coincidence of the two phenomena, in the 19th century, gives us no clue as to their causal sequence: it so happens that these same regions were already the most literate in France at the end of the 18th century, when the school network was obviously more loose-knit.

At the other end of the table of *départements* the champion truants in 1850 were rarely able to sign their *actes de mariage* when their turn came, in 1866–70: as in Brittany and the Vendée, on the north-western fringes of the Massif Central, in Landes and Ariège. This suggests a picture of husbands unable to sign their names, between 1866 and 1870, because they had not been to school – or scarcely – in 1850. But here again, we cannot really interpret this merely in terms of cause and effect, for we might then suppose, conversely, that the parents of 1850 did not send their children to school because they themselves were illiterate. But in fact most of the communes, even in the most backward *départements*, had at least one school (albeit recent, one should point out)[13] at this date. So, whether we consider the leading *départements* or the tail-enders, closer scrutiny suggests, therefore, that school enrolments were not boosted, *ipso facto*, by the existence of the school network and that, *a fortiori*, they are no help in indicating literacy rates.

This was because people's mentalities took time to adapt to school. The mere existence of the means to acquire education was not enough in itself. For education was long more or less dimly perceived as a break with the established order.[14] With the social order: since the possibility of upward social mobility through schooling and the triumph of the meritocracy undermine the social hierarchy. With the natural order: in that the school diverts women from their maternal and domestic 'vocation', the ploughman from his land and the smith from his anvil. With the political order: the democratization of knowledge and power worried the notables who until now had wielded knowledge and power. Thus instruction contained within itself the risk of a kind of silent revolution: so it took more than a generation for opinion to become penetrated with the social utility of writing.

It may be objected that our field of observation, the 19th century, lies too far downstream of the two phenomena – literacy and schooling – that we are comparing. We have thus tried to push back our investigation a few years by examining, with caution, the 'number of children enrolled in school per 10,000 inhabitants in 1837'.

This variable ignores the age structure of the population and only very approximately accounts for girls attending school. What is more, the figures for 1837 and 1850 are clearly not directly comparable, since the school enrolment figures for 1850 are expressed in terms of the total number of school-age children and not of the population as a whole. Still, in the absence of alternative statistics, this does constitute an invaluable indicator.

The analogies that this new map (Map 6.14) presents with the map of school enrolments in 1850 (Maps 6.8 and 6.11) are quite striking. Whether one compares school enrolment rates with the total population (as in 1837) or with the school-age population (as in 1850), the profiles obtained are identical: to be sure, all *départements* made progress between these two dates, but their rankings remain astonishingly stable at a time when, thanks to Guizot, the school network was growing everywhere more close-knit. So the spread of schooling did not harmonize school enrolment rates. Not only did inter-departmental inequalities subsist, they actually widened: at the top of the table, the north-east was literate and attending school by 1850, whereas those bringing up the rear were only just making contact with literacy and the school.

Although this retrospective view does not delve far enough back into the past, it does confirm our hypothesis of a minimal cultural threshold without which the school cannot play a positive rôle in the literacy process. One might almost speak of a kind of 'scholastic entropy', born of local resistance and consequently a factor of inertia. During the time it takes to run the new machine in, the school places a heavy financial burden on those who support it while producing low returns.

Another point to bear in mind, obviously, is that these schooling figures are rather ambiguous in that they refer to *enrolments*, frequently of fictitious pupils. For one thing, because registers may have been kept sloppily, leaving pupils out, or on the contrary counting some twice or more (through re-enrolments in the course of a single year, or through confusion of the school year with the calendar year).[15] And then again because in any case they tell us nothing about attendance itself: regularity, seasonal attendance and number of years' schooling. Indeed, there are no reliable figures to measure the amount of time actually spent in school. We do know that, depending on the teaching method used, the time taken to learn to read and write might vary between two and six years or more. Because of the expense of schooling, big families often chose to send only some of their children to school, or else sent them all, but alternately. From their tenth year onwards, earlier sometimes, the factory and the fields often claimed children from the schools. Without dwelling here on other obstacles, climatic or geographic, one can readily comprehend how, thus nibbled away on all sides, the amount of time actually spent in the classroom could easily dwindle to the point where learning the most rudimentary skills became something of an achievement.

Can we nevertheless establish some kind of relation between actual attendance and enrolment registers? The relevant figures are very piece-meal. Generally, a high percentage of school attendance in summer is taken as a sign of a good attendance score, and we can determine how many of the pupils enrolled in winter also attend school in summer: on average, 61.5% in 1837, with a standard deviation of 19.3%

79.1% in 1866, with a standard deviation of 8.3%
91.6% in 1896, with a standard deviation of 9.9%.

So, even before the advent of Jules Ferry, parents sacrificed to schooling the help in the fields in summer that they would otherwise have had from their children: these figures eloquently illustrate how custom had stolen a march on the law.

The maps (Maps 6.20 to 6.23) reflecting these percentages nevertheless contain a number of surprises: we find neither the Saint-Malo – Geneva line, nor the contrast between town and country. This is because a good summer attendance score may conceal a variety of situations in real life. Sometimes it merely reflects the low degree of winter attendance: this is the case in regions of widely scattered habitat and bad roads, where the return of fine weather brings the children out of their 'hibernation'. Sometimes it reflects poor overall attendance throughout the year, as in Drôme (where only 30.5% of pupils attended school for ten months in the year 1865), Loire (23.6%), Tarn-et-Garonne (29.5%), Ille-et-Vilaine (35.9%) and Finistère (35.5%); yet these *départements* came top of the league for summer attendance.

Conversely, one also comes across poor summer attendance figures in *départements* where children attend school for more than the average number of months (over 35% for at least ten months). This was the case in several advanced *départements*: Pas-de-Calais, Oise, Marne, Meuse and Aube, all hit by harvest-time absenteeism.

Lastly, it may also happen that the summer attendance rate varies in the same direction as the annual rate (either *both* good, or *both* poor). But the *départements* that illustrate this coexistence are as likely to lie in the south as in the north: Maggiolo's line blurs once again (Map 6.19).

Summer/winter attendance less than 80% and annual attendance less than 45%:

| South of the Maggiolo line | | North of the Maggiolo line | |
|---|---|---|---|
| Loire-Inférieure | Lozère | Eure-et-Loir | Haute-Marne |
| Deux-Sèvres | Aveyron | Yonne | Haute-Saône |
| Vienne | Cantal | Côte-d'Or | Doubs |
| Charente | Hautes-Alpes | | |
| Puy-de-Dôme | | | |

Summer/winter attendance over 80% and annual attèndance over 55%
South of the Maggiolo line

| Var | Tarn |
|---|---|
| Gard | Vendée |
| Gironde | Creuse |
| Allier | |

We may examine another criterion of attendance through some of the statistics published in 1876–77, at least in so far as the State schools (or those doing office as such) are concerned. This criterion measures regularity of attendance *per se*, i.e. the number of children present throughout the entire term (a semester, for there were two terms in the school year, Trans.) compared with the average number of children enrolled for that same term. This comparison reveals no marked difference in regularity between boys and girls: 89.36% and 90.98% for the first term (winter); 87.75% and 86.63% for the second term (summer). Average absenteeism relative to total numbers enrolled turn around the 10 to 15% mark, which seems rather low for the pre-Ferry period. This residual truancy was fairly evenly spread among all the *départements* except for Ariège, and Basses and Hautes-Pyrénées, where regularity fell to around 80%.

What are we to make of all this? This tentative approach to the issues of attendance and regularity of attendance slightly alters the shading of the picture painted by school enrolments, but not to the point of upsetting our hypotheses regarding schooling. In certain regions where school was still a rarity or a novelty, only a minority of children enrolled; once enrolled, though, these children appear to have been more regular in attendance than in regions better provided with schools; there, the majority of school-age children enrolled but did not attend school steadily throughout the year. Which explains why we find *départements* south of the Maggiolo line heading the assiduity league table (it will be recalled that these assiduity scores only refer to enrolled children, i.e. a minority in the west/south-west triangle, and the great mass of children in the north-east and south-east). In the final analysis, Maggiolo's France experienced two types of schooling, one democratic, with occasionally mediocre rates of assiduity, the other élitist, though more assiduous.

It is tempting, in conclusion, to sketch two models of literacy: the first rests chiefly on the village community, which invented the school prior to State intervention and distributed the rudiments of learning 'horizontally' to all strata of the community more or less. The roots of this movement can be traced back to the 17th century, or further still into the history of agrarian structures and landscapes. The second model keeps time with the history of the school itself, as a centralized institution controlled by the State, 'parachuted' at great expense as part of a grand design of cultural and political integration. Finally, this process came to play a more élitist rôle around the beginning of the 20th century by, for example, creaming off those generations of 'white-collar workers' heading for the capital.

## The quality of life in school

Just as there were pupils and pupils, there was teaching and teaching. In raising the issue of teaching standards it is not our intention to embark on a chapter on the content of education, still less on its ideological, denominational or political ramifications. All we are concerned with here is reading and writing, rudimentary enough in itself, yet vital to any further intellectual attainment. In discussing the quality of schools, therefore, we intend merely to examine the practical conditions that are indispensable in any kind of learning process. In other words, what does the teacher know? What are the teaching methods available to him? In what material conditions does he perform his task? And is there any demonstrable connection between these factors and what the children actually learn, i.e. the literacy rate?[16]

To speak of teaching methods in the early 19th century, attempting to itemize them and appraise their effectiveness, may seem rather a bold undertaking. How many teachers can have been aware of applying a specific method? There is something distinctly theoretical in the very notion of a method, suggestive of gilded pedagogues. Ingenuity, patience and intuition must do service in its place most of the time.

However, we do know what methods were in use at the time. The mutual method (Maps 6.30, 6.31 and 6.32), which had just introduced a crucial innovation, namely the simultaneous learning of reading and writing, and played a decisive rôle in the pedagogic awakening, was in fact not very widely used, as we have seen, and it does not seem to have played much of a direct rôle in the literacy process. The old individual method persisted throughout the entire first half of the century; graphic illustration (Maps 6.33, 6.34 and 6.35) of its extent (associated with a higher proportion of private schools) conveys a rather pessimistic view of its effectiveness, for the map reproduces the backward triangle, except that Brittany is absent this time, being replaced by the Alps where – and this is exceptional – the individual instruction provided by itinerant teachers had triumphed over illiteracy. The simultaneous method, lastly (Maps 6.36, 6.37 and 6.38), is very clearly associated with better literacy scores. It is this method which coincides best with the maps of the State school system (Map 6.3) and of school enrolments and literacy. That leaves us with the question of whether the adoption of a given method was not itself governed by the existing standard of teaching.

The progress of schooling in the 19th century was due also to the specialization of the place in which it took place. The itinerant teachers in the Alps, who managed to teach children to read and write in their own homes, were the exception to this. What could we expect, after all, to come of lessons given in a bar, an attic or by the roadside? The novel feature of the schoolhouse was not that it solved the problem of finding a roof and accommodation for children (so many schoolhouses were wretched, cramped hovels, scarcely worthy to be called shelters!), but that it established a place especially for the purpose of learning and isolated it within the community. Thus the process of learning to read and write gradually abandoned homes and inns, presbyteries and makeshift rooms, and was housed in a place especially set aside for this purpose.

> Schoolhouses rising up everywhere, everywhere drawing the attention of the inhabitants, inspiring in them that powerful interest in primary education that springs from the sense of ownership and the prospect of duration; let them (those who were reticent) imagine not only all the consequences of such a fact for the rapid and effective progress of popular education, but also its influence on the moral inclinations of the population, and let them judge whether the grandeur of the outcome does not infinitely outweigh the sacrifices made.[17]

Once again it is to Guizot that we owe the first national census of schoolhouses; unfortunately it is restricted to buildings that communes either owned, rented or were planning to acquire, and thus excludes private schools. At first sight, the part of France that was covered with schoolhouses (Map 6.24), is by and large the literate north-eastern region, which is hardly surprising since these were State schools which happened to be concentrated in the same region. This map does however contain a number of exceptions worth closer scrutiny: first, the advanced part of Normandy, where most of the schools were State-run (83.9% in Manche, 79.2% in Seine-Inférieure, 73.6% in Calvados, 69.8% in Eure and 57.8% in Orne), showed little concern to acquire or maintain schoolhouses.[18] Second, the Mediterranean south, which had achieved literacy in the early years of the 19th century despite the absence of the material conditions upon which the literacy process seems otherwise to depend: there the majority of schools were private. When a school was State-run, its building was rented, not bought by the commune and even that was true of only four *départements*, Var, Vaucluse, Gard and Hérault. Leaving aside these special cases (which can only be accounted for by local history), it does indeed look as if the settling of primary education in a specialized, 'public', place was an essential factor in the literacy process.

> A class, after all, is a small society, it should not be conducted as though it was a mere agglomeration of independent subjects. Children in the classroom think, feel and behave differently from when they are separated from each other. In the classroom there occur phenomena of contagion, collective demoralisation, mutual over-excitement, healthy stimulation, which the teacher must be able to discern in order to prevent or repress, or take advantage of, whichever the case may be.[19]

The school building, that first bastion of written culture, was also the realm of books, the blackboard, slates, exercise books and pens. We must therefore, as for schoolhouses, look to see whether there is some relation between school facilities and literacy.

This new variable – which we shall obviously have to interpret against the background of the reference population, in this case the total school-age population in the north-eastern regions, and only a minority in the south-west – seems to be decisive: how is one to learn to read without a book, or to write without a pen? And yet the maps derived from the 1833–34 statistics (Maps 6.25 and 6.26) do not indicate this causal link. Certainly, school facilities seem to be better in the educated part of France; but in the ignorant portion of France, there coexisted *départements* that were under-equipped (Côtes-du-Nord, Ille-et-Vilaine, where only one out of four or five schools was adequately equipped) and *départements* that were well-provided for (nine out of ten schools in Haute-Vienne had proper facilities). As with assiduity earlier, school facilities seem to play a secondary rôle in literacy. What counts, for a commune, is to have a schoolhouse and to put its children through it. These factors bring us back to the issue of communal revenues and, above all, to the population's reactions to written culture.

Lastly, does the fact that a commune provides a livelihood for its schoolteacher (symbolic of the transition from individual to collective learning) allow us to predict a good rate of literacy? Guizot deserves credit for having perceived the problem with great acuity when, in his 'grand design' for education, he provided for the housing and remuneration of teachers. And indeed, the regions in which communes did either house their teachers or at least paid them a housing allowance and a decent wage (Maps 6.27 and 6.28) also happen to be those with the best literacy rates (Normandy apart, once again miserly with its communal resources: it did provide housing for its teachers, but withheld from the fixed wages paid to teachers in the north-east; apart too from the Mediterranean south, which grew increasingly well-integrated into the literate portion of France as the century wore on but furnished neither housing nor fixed wages for its teachers).

However, although it does bear witness to collective attitudes in favour of primary education, the payment of a fixed wage to schoolteachers is in itself a rather crude indicator of their teaching abilities. For this fixed wage was a guaranteed minimum, but not necessarily the actual amount paid (Map 6.29), which communes determined in the light of their resources. The better-off communes therefore attracted the more able teachers, while the less-gifted or less lucky teachers drifted off to those communes that were either unable or unwilling to pay them their just deserts. This further aggravated regional disparities: Paris and her 'crown' of surrounding *départements* creamed off the most enterprising, most ambitious, or perhaps simply the best, teachers, through the twin attractions of wages and prestige. The teachers rotting in the depths of the countryside and in the remoter provinces were often half-vergers, half-peasants, often paid in kind. Guizot's introduction of a minimum wage, which alleviated the lot of many teachers, could not therefore in itself alter a situation which in fact depended on the wealth of the communes: some spontaneously paid more than Guizot's minimum, while others left it to the parents to top up the teacher's income.

This helps us to grasp the ambivalence of the extension of free schooling even before the Ferry laws made it compulsory: for while giving relief to family budgets, it ate into teachers' income without any compensating mechanism. Above all, the touchstone of mercantile society is the demand for 'something in return for one's money', in the sense that the price paid for a service obtained indicates the value of that service. The *Académie* inspectors questioned by Duruy were unanimous on this score:[20] 'In the countryside, as in the towns, the value of things is reckoned according to the price paid. totally free (education) generally produces deplorable consequences, for both master and pupils.' Their grounds? The Inspector for the Aube gives his:

> In the four communes in the *arrondissement* of Nogent-sur-Seine where schooling is entirely free, the schools in three of them have the lowest attendance records of the entire *département* and produce the worst results. Two communes in the *arrondissement* of Bar-sur-Aube where schooling had been free have now abandoned

this, practice having shown that children came to school less
regularly than when they had to pay fees.[21]

Still, we should not generalize: reactions to free schooling differed between
town and country, according to whether it was paid for by the commune or
by some foundation or other (generally religious).[22]

One lesson does emerge from this passive resistance to free schooling,
namely that simple economic calculation did not automatically bring
improved attendance. So the rôle played by free schooling in the literacy
process is therefore more theoretical than real: once more we come back to
the attitude of the population towards schooling, thus underlining the
importance of mentalities.

## School results

So far, we have tried to measure the deferred effects of schooling, by
investigating either conscripts or bridal couples. But we might also take a
measurement closer to what actually goes on in school, by looking at the
performance of school-leavers. The only material available to us on a
national scale for this purpose is supplied by Duruy's surveys conducted in
the 1860s.[23] The figures cover all children who left school in the 1863 school
year and who never went back. We find that in half of the *départements*,
15% of these children could neither read nor write (whereas the national
average was 13.9%). In seventeen *départements*, the figure was over 20%.
Lozère held the record, with 41.2% illiterates or semi-literates (they are
amalgamated here, because children able to read only were recorded as
illiterate).

The map established on the basis of these figures (Map 6.15) once more
reproduces Maggiolo's France and the backward triangle. The striking
feature is that mid-way through the century, and thirty years after the
passage of the Guizot Act, the school had still by no means smoothed over
the disparities; it continued still to reproduce the situation handed down to
it by history and economic structures. In the backward regions, only a
minority of children attended school, and what is more, even they did not
all leave school literate: which made it doubly élitist.

Now what we would like to know is whether this relative failure of the
school, which affected nearly one schoolchild in five on average, is
attributable to the school alone. To find out, we may return once more to
the indicators of quality and the material conditions of teaching, and
correlate them with schoolchildren's performance in 1863.

Only five *départements* show a positive correlation between regularity of
attendance and the immediate results of schooling (Lozère, Vienne,
Aveyron, Cantal and Puy-de-Dôme): irregular attendance could account

for the relative failure of schooling. On the other hand, mediocre school performance can coexist with quite respectable attendance rates (as in Corrèze, Haute-Vienne, Cher, Morbihan, Seine-Inférieure, Eure, Somme, Nord, Bouches-de-Rhône, Ardèche) or even with very good rates (Vendée, Var, Gard and Allier). Nor does correlation of teaching methods employed or of teachers' incomes with school performance reveal any decisive link. In fact the only indicator whose profile may coincide with that of school results is the existence of schoolhouses: which is tantamount to laying the chief burden upon economic factors (which, as we have already seen, are crucial in the acquisition and upkeep of school buildings) to the detriment of institutional factors.

These disappointing correlations do at least draw attention to the cultural attainments of children just as they leave school. How are we to gauge the resistance of this uneven, patchy education to the passage of time? What can have lasted over a man's lifespan? To couch the question in these terms is implicitly to postulate that this education could not remain intact. But is this demonstrable?

No source broaches this topic directly. To do so we would need to be able to trace a generation from its schooldays to its death and to measure its literacy at regular intervals. In the absence of data that precise, we have taken the 1901 census, which indicates the percentages of illiterates (people unable to read or write, and those able to read only) for each age-group (in five-year intervals): this is the first histogram in which, obviously, we find the proportion of illiterates rising as we go further and further up the age-scale (from 6% for the 20–24 year-olds to 35% for the over-75s). We have also used the conscription statistics, which indicate the percentage of young men unable to read or write at age 20.[24] We then went on to compare each age-group in 1901 with the corresponding intake of conscripts: the 85–89 age-group with the group of 20 year-olds between 1832 and 1836; the 80–85 year-olds in 1901 with the group of 20 year-olds between 1837 and 1841; the 75–80 year-old age-group in 1901 with the group of 20 year-olds between 1842 and 1846; and so on. In this way, we may observe the same generation at two very different points in time.

Comparison of these two photographs of a single generation holds a surprise in store for us (see graph): the second picture, far from revealing any erosion of school learning and hence a rise in illiteracy, is actually more optimistic than the first picture. Thus, the 85–89 year-old veterans, born between 1812 and 1816, were 47% illiterate when aged 20, but only 38% illiterate in 1901. This progress is less clear-cut for later generations, but it is observable all the same, suggesting that there was no loss of elementary education (referring to the group as a whole, needless to say) over a lifetime. There seems, therefore, to have been some learning of reading and writing

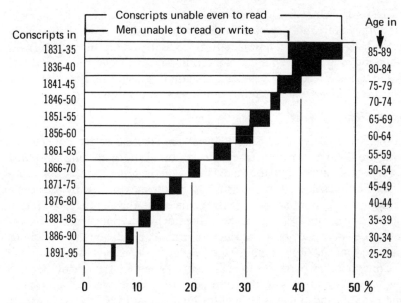

The education level of 19th-century conscripts compared with the 1901
census

outside the age limits and places laid down by society. It is worth
remembering that, since our two criteria of illiteracy are not identical, there
is in fact a slight difference between the two groups. To make the two
populations absolutely identical, all we need to do is to add to the
percentage of illiterate conscripts those 'able to read only' that had been
counted among the 'literates', or alternatively to subtract the percentage of
those 'able to read only' from the 1901 age-groups. This adjustment would
merely serve to emphasize the progress made in each generation and
confirm our hypothesis.

   Now all that remains for us to do is to deal with an objection of a
demographic order. Since illiteracy affects the socially and economically
disadvantaged sections of the population, differential mortality would
consequently eliminate the illiterates first of all. Consequently, instead of
measuring the progress made by a given generation, our method would
draw attention to a manifestation of social selection: members of the older
generations who survived in 1901 would be those who also happened to be
most literate to begin with. Even so, at the present state of our knowledge, it
does not look as if differential mortality rates entirely cancel out the
progress that we have observed within a given generation. The process of
accumulating knowledge which makes each generation more literate than

the last (for France as a whole, literacy never once receded in the course of the 19th century) also operated inside each generation, even though a few individuals might forget how to write (or, less frequently, how to read). So, while individuals are bound to forget, this factor, when transposed into group terms, was offset by belated education in regimental schools, adult education classes, classes run by employers, and so on.[25]

## Adult literacy classes

In the Army, to begin with. The official commenting on the 1866 census, compares figures on male literacy rates for the army, on the one hand, with those for the entire population aged over 5 on the other hand, and is struck by the results achieved by the army: 'the ratios discovered by the census being more favourable than those deduced at the moment of recruitment';[26] he attributes this progress to the work of the regimental schools.[27] A decade later, the official statistics on primary education include among 'auxiliary means of instruction' the 'regimental and naval schools'.[28]

Contemporary observers were already spotlighting the rôle of the army in the literacy process in the 19th century. The image of the army as purveyor of education was born of the Revolution; the Convention had, in its time, contemplated using the army to improve the education of the citizenry: 'On board each vessel of the Republic carrying twenty cannon or more, there shall be a teacher responsible for giving to the young citizens aboard these same ships lessons in reading, writing, arthmetic and even, wherever possible, for holding classes in the rudiments of the theory of navigation.'[29]

Like many of the Revolution's intentions, this was to remain a pious wish; but not without posterity. From the very earliest years of the Restoration, parallel to the upsurge of mutual teaching, this concern once more arose among the ranks of the army.[30] Senior officers belonging to the 'Society for the improvement of elementary instruction' worked, starting in 1816, to found 'regimental schools' in the barracks, for the benefit of illiterate recruits (who at the time accounted for substantially more than half the annual intake of around 80,000 youngsters). These first saw the light of day in the region of Nord, then spread to the rest of France; the Minister of War, Marshal Gouvion-Saint-Cyr, sought to furnish every unit with such a school: in 1821, at the zenith of the mutual school, some 175 regimental schools were practising its methods.

On 21 October 1818, Gouvion-Saint-Cyr ordered all divisions and guards corps to dispatch to Paris, on 15 November, an officer and a non-commissioned officer to attend a teacher-training course in mutual teaching methods, so that they might subsequently employ this method in their own units.

In 1827, however, Benjamin Appert, founder of the first mutual schools in the army, prisons and almshouses, wrote a vigorous pamphlet criticizing the attacks launched by the ultra-reactionaries and the 'congregation, celebrated for its crimes' against the mutual regimental schools and their outcome, namely that by 1827 barely half a dozen of these schools survived. Still, Appert points out, in less than three years, during Gouvion-Saint-Cyr's ministry, nearly 100,000 men received elementary instruction at these schools.

Even so, the rapid decline of mutual teaching did not compromise the educational movement inside the army. Article 47 of the Parliamentary Act dated 21 March 1832 enshrined the principle of elementary instruction, to be given in their units, to illiterate young men drafted into the army. The *Compte rendu sur le recrutement de l'armée pour 1833* enumerates the benefits accruing from this decision. It would provide a nursery of potential non-commissioned officers; furthermore, it was expected to spread its beneficial contagion into the home, which would 'profit from the instruction received under the colours'.[31] In fact the Act did speed up the development of regimental schools, and by 1831 these had more than 27,000 pupils; by 1831, moreover, they had theoretically been made compulsory for all illiterate soldiers. The Army Regulation issued on 28 December 1835 laid down instructions for the organization of these schools, and further reorganizations occurred in 1869, 1875, 1879, 1901, and so on.

The 1835 Regulation provided for the establishment, in each corps, of one 'first degree' school for the teaching of reading, writing and arithmetic, and a 'second degree' school for the further education of non-commissioned officers. The Regulation issued on 31 July 1879 instituted a 'field primary school' for illiterates, and a 'preparatory course' for non-commissioned officers, corporals and privates having some rudiments of education and who wanted to gain promotion to the rank of sub-lieutenant, whether on the active or the reserve list. F. Buisson added: 'In so far as is possible, a session of at least one hour shall be spent in the company school each day; the length of the session may be increased to two hours in wintertime.'[32]

In the Navy, primary schools aboard ship were instituted by Ordinance in 1829 and in 1836, while 'divisional schools' were set up in the five naval ports in 1828. The Regulation issued on 25 May 1870, by Admiral Rigault de Genouilly, made attendance at elementary school compulsory for illiterate sailors.

Presumably, though, the reason why attention is so frequently drawn to the compulsion to attend for illiterate soldiers is because it was not applied very strictly: even in 1910, Ferdinand Buisson expressed the hope that the new law establishing a proper examination for conscripts[33] 'would result in stricter application of the obligation for illiterate recruits to attend primary classes, whether held inside or outside the barracks'.[34]

Even were we to acknowledge that compulsory attendance was not strictly enforced, the annual figures supplied by the Ministry of War point to the efficiency of these regimental schools in improving literacy among men past school age. Thus between 1844 – the first year for which figures concerning the results of these regimental schools are available[35] – and 1869 (i.e. in twenty-six years) over 1,150,000 young men who had joined the army illiterate had at least learnt to read.[36] After a three-year statistical hiatus (1870-72) due to war, the results for 1873 to 1889 are once more available. In all, in less than half a century, the army brought literacy to more than two million men.

These are impressive figures. Let us take another look at the first period. Over 1,150,000 young men are supposed to have undergone elementary instruction in the army between 1844 and 1869, and are supposed to have learnt at least to read. Now, the 1872 census returns tell us that scarcely more than 8 million men aged over 20 were able at least to read. So the regimental schools account for a considerable portion of this educated cohort.

Does this mean that we ought to rush to praise the army's educational rôle? There are grounds for tempering our enthusiasm, namely that, for many young soldiers, education apparently stopped at learning to read. If we now analyse these 1,150,000 soldiers supposed to have learnt *at least* to read in the regimental schools, we find that 440,000 learnt *only* to read. In other words, over 38%, which is very high compared with results obtained in school or with 1866 and 1872 census data. Yet it is confirmed by the again very high rate of people 'able to read only' indicated on educational records of the regular army, which are available for the whole of this period in the *Comptes rendus*. On 1 January 1867, for instance, out of the 325,554 non-commissioned officers and other ranks in the regular army, 33,423, i.e. 10.3%, (all of them privates) could read only.

We are only concerned here with that part of the army which is recruited by the call-up system. The remainder, excluding the *gendarmerie*, is not very numerous (barely 6% of total manpower in 1844 and in 1864) and is made up of special corps such as the African Light Infantry Batallion, the disciplinary companies, veterans, the foreign regiment, native African corps (Algerian sharpshooters, spahis), etc.

The 1866 census indicates a figure of 314,732 men for that year, of whom 9.31% could read. So the two figures and both percentages are very similar.

At the same moment, however, only 2.53% of the conscripts in the class of 1866 could read only. This contrast runs like a leitmotif throughout the entire period for which we have figures: in 1844, 12.75% of other ranks in the regular army could 'read only', compared with 4.27% for the class of that year; in 1854, 12.13% in the army, and 3.66% for the class of that year.

What is more, we find this contrast between adult males and conscripts in the country at large. Thus, at the time of the 1872 census, 8.1% of the male population aged over 20 could 'read only'; now, by aggregating figures for conscripts in the years 1827 to 1872, the average percentage 'able to read only' comes to—only 3.68%. Yet, among these men aged over 20 in 1872, we find aggregated (excluding those deceased, obviously) all the ex-conscripts of the previous forty-five years!

To clear up these little mysteries, we may envisage two hypotheses. First, that the forms indicating real educational levels were filled in more conscientiously in the army or at census time than at draft board inspections: in which case the percentage of those 'able to read only' could be under-estimated in conscripts' own declarations. Secondly, that the teaching dispensed in the regimental schools really did turn out a high proportion of people able to read only. This is what produces such a high percentage of people in this category in the regular army. These may also go some way towards explaining the distortion between the high rate of males able to 'read only' in the 1866 and 1872 censuses and the slender percentages of males in the same category among conscripts recorded over the previous three or four decades.

But what matter? After all, being able to read only still means being literate. At least, that is how people saw things until very late into the second half of the 19th century: an 'illiterate' was someone who could neither read nor write, and the ability to read only was in fact regarded as an elementary, though decisive, stage of literacy. By turning out a relatively high proportion of men able to read only, among its 'pupils', the army may therefore be considered an essential agent of male literacy in the 19th century.

In a survey conducted a few years ago, a schoolteacher in the Manche *département*, born in 1883, questioned about his father's education, replied: 'My father learnt to read and write when doing his national service, in 1868', before becoming a customs officer, and later customs inspector.

One cannot say as much for adult education courses, in spite of their renowned advocates, from Jean-Baptiste de la Salle to Condorcet.[37] For they figured more heavily in speeches than in substance. Apart from the surge that occurred in the 1860s, when their guiding motives tended to be charity and surveillance, 'lifelong education' affected only a tiny margin of the population: 2.18% on average. The percentage of the population reached by these adult education classes exceeded 3% in twenty *départements* only, while for women it was derisory:

*Pupils in adult education classes*[38]

|        | men     | women   |
|--------|---------|---------|
| 1837   | 36,964  |         |
| 1843   | 90,451  | 4,613   |
| 1850   | 73,800  | 7,003   |
| 1863   | 115,673 | 9,974   |
| 1866   | 747,002 | 82,553  |
| 1869   | 678,753 | 114,383 |
| 1872   | 539,978 | 101,616 |
| 1876–77| 500,053 | 105,710 |

Were these classes at least attended by the illiterate fringes of the population? 'At the classes that we hold', wrote Perdonnet, 'we have as many shop-assistants, clerks and stitchers as genuine workers, and the results leave much to be desired.'[39] Anthime Corbon noted the preponderance of comfortably-off craftsmen at these evening classes.[40] It is hard to imagine workers flocking to night school after the kind of long and taxing day that was then their lot. One had to have uncommon constancy of purpose; perhaps, too, one had to have had some slight taste of education already in one's life. At rate, Duruy's figures show that in 1866–67, 13.1% of pupils attending adult education classes were illiterate, and that 9.5% were able to read only. So the majority of pupils came to night school not so much to learn to read and write as to learn arithmetic and to tackle subjects that had been optional in elementary school.

And yet, when publishing *Statistique de l'instruction des adultes* in 1865, the Ministry of Education passed the following comment on the table indicating the annual progress of education among 20 year-olds between 1833 and 1865:

> What emerges from the table below is that, from the point of view of education of conscripts, the best results in terms of rapidity of progress were achieved in the years 1839 and 1847 on the one hand, and in 1865 on the other.... Now it so happens that these three exceptional years, 1839, 1847 and 1865, correspond to the moment at which adult education classes first began (1837 and 1838) and to the years when attendance reached its peak (1847 and 1865).[41]

Not only did these adult classes fail to attract the men and women for whom they had been intended, their record in teaching illiterate pupils to read and write was also very mediocre: 44.8% of the illiterates that did attend came out either illiterate as before, or just about able to read (Map 6.16) (the figure rises to 53.4% for women).[42] This failure of supplementary education affected more than half the pupils in twenty-five *départements*. Apart from Eure and Yonne, these were *départements* labouring under an accumulation of handicaps, all of them lying south of the Maggiolo line, as if a southern illiterate was no match for a northern illiterate, even when both took to attending school.

As for the schools established at the initiative of employers, for both adults and children, bearing the great names of industry such as Dollfus, Koechlin or Peugeot, their purpose was less to eradicate illiteracy than to spread knowledge that would be 'advantageous' to industrial efficiency. Even so, these philanthropic, paternalist undertakings were confined to certain towns and industries only. In 1868, they affected slightly fewer than 2% of school-age children: 99,212 children still subject to the 1841 Act, plus another 28,509 children in factories of less than twenty workers, whom the Act did not cover. Much of the time, the obligation to produce a school certificate was a dead letter for this group, and the child-labour surveys present a pitiful picture of these children's conditions.

The 1841 Act referred to factories with over twenty workers and to children aged 8 to 16. It restricted children between the ages of 8 and 12 to 8 hours' work a day, and those between 12 and 16 to 12 hours, prohibiting night work. This Act was generally regarded as a praiseworthy attempt at philanthropy, though detrimental to industry, and was poorly applied. One can quite believe Jules Simon when he writes:

> Talk to schoolmasters: they have no trouble picking out the child who has spent six hours in the factory and the one who has spent eight hours. This schoolchild, who is only so in name, will know his alphabet when he leaves school, but he won't be able to read; he will be able to sign or copy a letter, but he won't know how to write.[43]

So the impact of employers' schools on literacy proper is hard to gauge. We can say as much for the 'evening reading classes', 'public classes', 'working men's classes', 'working men's faculties': all those ephemeral schools which were aimed at a public which, if not cultivated, was at least literate already.

## The alternative school

So far we have discussed the school without once spotting a friar's habit or a nun's wimple. And yet, in traditional societies, where literacy is pursued not for its own sake but as a by-product of some design for moral, political or religious education, we could hardly fail to find the Church in school. As the State used the school to cement national unity – depending on circumstances, children were taught to cry 'Long live the Republic', 'Long live the Emperor', or 'Long live the King' – so the Church pursued its evangelization—in school. There can be no question here of entering into the controversy between clericalism and non-denominationalism, for which the bibliography is already weighty enough. What we are concerned to find out is whether the congregational school was a carbon copy of the non-denominational school in regions where religious observance still throve. If it was, then its exact denominational shading is of secondary importance to use, and the rôle of the Church in literacy may be regarded as analogous to that of the school in general. If not, then we should have to ask ourselves whether educational disparities between regions and the sexes were not sustained by the Church's grip on the school system, and on girls' schools in particular. National statistical sources are ill-suited to questions as complex as this one. Still, we can at least try to address it by comparing the geography and evolution of the congregational school with religious observance and literacy rates.

At first glance, the statistics on congregational schools[44] reveal two very different situations in this respect: for girls were indeed brought up in the lap of the Church (41.6% of girls' schools were congregational in 1850, compared with only 5% of boys' schools). So the problem raised here concerns one-third of all children in school, and is above all associated with the female sex.

Since we already know that the number of schools is an indirect parameter of literacy, the map of congregational schools ought to be the first thing to hold our attention: it reflects the Church's rôle in the development of the school system, independently of the density of that system. In 1850, congregational schools for boys form a very loose point-illist network, representing a tiny proportion of the total number of schools, though concentrated in two rather well-defined areas, one in Brittany (Côtes-du-Nord, Morbihan, Ille-et-Vilaine, with 33%, 21% and 19.3%), the other in the Rhône Valley (Loire, Rhône, Vaucluse, Ardèche and Haute-Loire, with 46.6%, 18%, 14.5%, 13% and 11.6%). The map of congregational schools for girls at the same date presents a very different picture (Map 6.39), and the manner in which it slices up France no longer coincides with the Maggiolo line. The line still starts out from Saint-Malo, but this time in the direction of Provence, contrasting eastern France, where most of the girls' schools were congregational, with western France where, despite some notable exceptions,[45] and contrary to all expectations, this is not the case.

Did this network alter at all between 1850 and 1896, under the impact of changing political and legislative circumstances? There was no upheaval among the boys' schools (Maps 6.42, 6.43 and 6.44), other than the strengthening of the Breton and Rhône Valley bastions right up to the end of the century; and these remained well delineated. As for the girls (Maps

6.39, 6.40 and 6.41), on the other hand, the geography of the congregational school was completely recast under the impact of the Falloux and Ferry Acts. In 1896, under the pressure of secularization, the map of congregational girls' schools altered to match the map of religious observance: the main beneficiaries of this process in which the congregational schools took root in the most religiously observant areas were, obviously, western France and the south-eastern part of the Massif Central (Map 6.45). Thus it goes without saying that, all things considered, the patterns of distribution of boys' and girls' congregational schools were far more similar than in 1850.

But it is not only the number of schools that counts; it is also the clientele that they draw (6.46 to 6.51). The table below indicates a proportionally greater clientele of pupils than one might have supposed from the number of schools: three times greater for boys in 1850, twice as many in 1867 and 1896; and in all cases slightly more for girls.

This apparently bizarre state of affairs may be partly accounted for by the way the congregational schools were organized: monks never went around alone. The 'Frères de la doctrine chrétienne' (Brethren of Christian doctrine) went around in threes, while in most of the congregational institutions they went around in pairs. So their schools could accept more pupils than the lay schools and spread them over several classes. But this advantage cut both ways, for to justify this 'heavy equipment', there had to be a social demand capable of supporting it. So it is easy to understand why those regions in which attendance at congregational schools was proportionally greater than the normal school system were also those in which the Church profited greatly from its hold on the population (Maps 6.54 and

|  | BOYS<br>% congregational<br>schools | %<br>attending<br>school | GIRLS<br>% congregational<br>schools | %<br>attending<br>school |
|---|---|---|---|---|
| 1850 | 5.0 | 16.3 | 41.6 | 44.2 |
| 1867 | 9.9 | 20.7 | 52.3 | 55.2 |
| 1896 | 9.5 | 18.6 | 42.0 | 53.4 |

6.55). And the reverse was also true, obviously. This means that we can predict the long-term development of the congregational schools from differences between the maps of schools and school attendance in 1850 (Maps 6.52 and 6.53). Regions with a shortfall in 1850 (those where attendance was proportionately lower than the school network itself would suggest) are also those in which congregational schools declined in the second half of the century. Conversely, regions with a surplus in 1850 (those where school attendance was high relative to the school network) were also those in which heavy social demand helped the congregational schools to take lasting root: these were the bastions of Catholicism.

Even so there is no immediate correlation between the impact of congregational education and religious observance, since in 1850 there was no such correlation at all in the case of girls, and only an imperfect one for boys (Maps 6.56 to 6.61). This was because, prior to the assumption by the State of responsibility for education, the congregational school simply grew up wherever the environment was receptive to school of any kind. Everything changed once the secular State took the school in hand, and this is what accounts for the new geographical distribution of congregational schools (Maps 6.52 and 6.53). The Church beat a retreat first in areas where literacy was most widespread: where the school system was functioning most smoothly and was most receptive to the solicitations of the State: among men in general, and in the north-eastern regions for women. On the other hand, as the secular school's official rival, the congregational school waxed strong or grew up where the ground was doubly receptive, because both poorly-educated and with a high degree of religious observance. In the case of boys, there was little room to manoeuvre, and so it merely strengthened its positions in its Breton and Rhône Valley bastions. When it came to girls, it carved out a veritable empire for itself, for the very reason that there had been so few schools previously; there was however a very significant slide from the more literate regions, whether observant or not, towards regions where schools were sparse, but only provided these happened to be regions where religion was strong. In contrast with 1850, we may assert that in 1896 there arose between the congregational school and religious practice a bond stamped with the features of defeat.

What we still need to see is whether, through this geographical shift, the Church actually played a dynamic rôle in the literacy process. If we are to credit Duruy's figures for the year 1863, the results achieved by the congregational schools were often inferior to those of the secular schools: 6% of children left the State-aided congregational schools totally illiterate, compared with 4.8% of those leaving the secular State schools, while for 'reading only' the respective figures were 19% and 16.1%, giving us respectively 25% versus 20.9% illiterates or semi-literates. In fact, though, these averages are probably less demonstrative than the geographical breakdown of performances (Map 6.62). Barring a handful of exceptions (Vendée, Deux-Sèvres, Dordogne and Aube, where the results obtained by the congregational schools were distinctly inferior to those of the secular schools), the educational attainments of children leaving school in 1863 seems to be independent of the type of school attended and relates more directly to the customary hierarchy of *départements*: in the north-east, the congregational schools produced as few illiterates as the secular schools; the schools with poor results, whether congregational or secular, tended to lie south of the Maggiolo line. So it was not the congregational character of the teaching which accounted for disparities in school results, but once again the deadweight of socio-economic and cultural factors; so this is not the place to look in order to appraise the rôle of the Church. From this point of view, the Church's specific contribution to French literacy in the 19th century was the founding of girls' schools in those regions that were *simultaneously* strongly religious and backward.

One commonplace has surely been exploded in this chapter, as we have scrutinized the different indicators of schooling, namely the assumption that the school played the decisive rôle in the spread of literacy. Of course we are not criticizing the school as such, except where its teaching was patently ineffectual; what interests us is to see it in its relations with a whole host of other factors, to investigate by means of a kind of sedimentation of economic factors (communal resources), geographical factors (climate, access to school), cultural factors (linguistic differences) and psycho-sociological factors.

Indeed, as if additional proof of the inadequacy of the school – literacy sequence were required, we might seek it in the application of a regression analysis to the full range of scholastic variables (Table 2). When, in 1830 for instance, we take the educational level of conscripts as an indicator of literacy, all our variables taken together account for 84% of the variance. When we take men's signatures at marriage, they account for 78% of the variance; and for women, 81%. From this we are forced to conclude that at all events at least 20% of the literacy process is not attributable to school. And that, at whatever date we happen to consider, amounts to a constant residuum.

From all this we may gather that while the growth of school did speed up the literacy process, it was also a response to it. Although the school was one sign – and sought to appear to be its symbol – it did not give the signal for access to written culture.

Table 6.2– *Regression analysis with three dependent variables (education of conscripts, men's signatures, women's signatures) and schooling variables (density of school network, children's enrolment and attendance in school, adult education classes, workers' education classes, congregational schools, etc.) at three intervals: the years 1830–34, 1860–66 and 1890–96.*

| | Explanatory variable<br>% of variance explained<br>(educational level of conscripts) | | Explanatory variable<br>% of variance explained<br>(marriage signatures, men) | | Explanatory variable<br>% of variance explained<br>(marriage signatures, women) | |
|---|---|---|---|---|---|---|
| 1830 | All variables | 84% | All variables | 78% | All variables | 81% |
| | 1. % of children enrolled/ attending school | 75% | 1. % of children enrolled/ attending school | 69% | 1. % of girls enrolled/ attending school | 66% |
| | 2. Communes with no school | 79% | 2. Communes with no school | 72% | 2. School per 100 children enrolled | 70% |
| | 3. Total schools | 80% | 3. Total schools | 73% | 3. Total schools 'communes with no girls' school' come 10th | 73% |
| 1866 | All variables | 86% | All variables | 83% | All variables | 85% |
| | 1. % of children enrolled | 80% | 1. % of children enrolled | 75% | 1. % of girls enrolled | 85% |
| | 2. Workers' education classes success | 82% | 2. Total schools | 79% | 2. Workers' education classes success | 78% |

3. Communes with no girls' schools — 83%

1896 All variables — 75%
1. % of girls enrolled — 33%
2. Workers' education success — 44%
3. % of girls in congregational schools — 54%
4. Schools per 100 children enrolled — 60%

3. Workers' education classes success — 81%

All variables — 80%
1. % of girls enrolled — 43%
2. Children in nursery school — 54%
3. Schools per 100 children enrolled — 60%
4. Women in adult education classes — 67%

3. % congregational schools — 79%

All variables — 78%
1. % of girls enrolled — 38%
2. Workers' education success — 52%
3. % girls in congregational schools — 59%
4. Schools per 100 children enrolled — 64%

Communes with no school

::: 45.78  ::: 91.45    137.18    182.91  ::: 228.64

::: 274.36 ::: 320.00 ::: 365.82 ::: 411.54 ■

**1837**

6.1

■ > 20 %    ≡ 10 à 20 %    ::: 7 à 10 %

**1850**

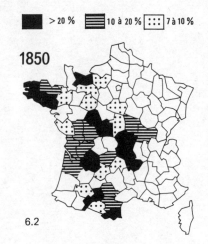

6.2

Mixed schools

::: 8.92  ::: 16.06  ::: 23.20  ::: 30.35  ::: 37.49

::: 44.63 ::: 51.78 ::: 58.92 ::: 66.06 ■

**1834**

6.4

::: 7.01  ::: 11.88  ::: 16.75  ::: 21.62  ::: 26.50

::: 31.37 ::: 36.24 ::: 41.11 ::: 46.98 ■

**1866**

6.5

State schools/total

::: 27.76   ::: 35.55   ::: 43.34   ::: 51.14   ::: 58.93

:x: 66.72   ::: 74.51   ::: 82.31   ::: 90.10   ▬

6.3

Special girls' schools

::: 8.59   ::: 12.70   ⊤ 16.82   ::: 20.94   ::: 25.05        ::: 13.22   ::: 16.60   ::: 19.98   ::: 23.36   ::: 26.74

:x: 29.17   ::: 33.29   ::: 37.40   ::: 41.52   ▬        ::: 30.12   ::: 33.50   ::: 36.89   ::: 40.27   ▬

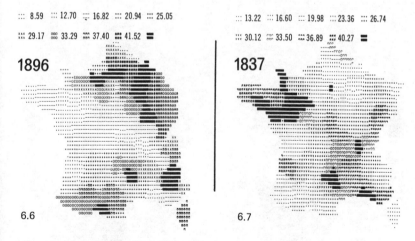

6.6                                     6.7

Geographical distribution of the school system (6.1–6.7)

**1850**

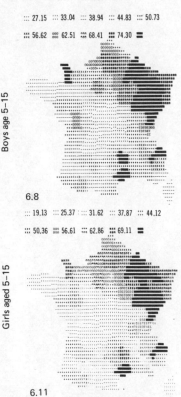

::: 27.15   ::: 33.04   ::: 38.94   ::: 44.83   ::: 50.73

::: 56.62   ::: 62.51   ::: 68.41   ::: 74.30 ▬

Boys age 5–15

6.8

::: 19.13   ::: 25.37   ::: 31.62   ::: 37.87   ::: 44.12

::: 50.36   ::: 56.61   ::: 62.86   ::: 69.11 ▬

Girls aged 5–15

6.11

Children enrolled in schools of all types

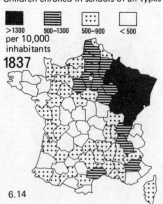

>1300   900–1300   500–900   < 500
per 10,000
inhabitants
**1837**

6.14

School-leavers unable to read or write

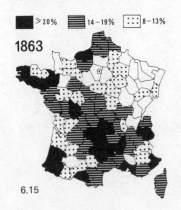

≥ 20%   14–19%   8–13%

**1863**

6.15

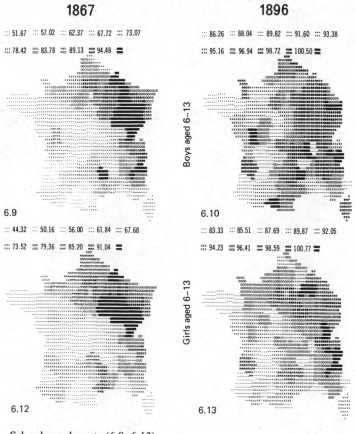

## 1867

::: 51.67  ::: 57.02  ::: 62.37  ::: 67.72  ::: 73.07

::: 78.42  ⸜⸝⸞ 83.78  ⸘⸘ 89.13  ▓▓ 94.48  ▬

## 1896

::: 86.26  ::: 88.04  ▬ 89.82  ::: 91.60  ::: 93.38

::: 95.16  ⸜⸝⸞ 96.94  ⸘⸘ 98.72  ▓▓ 100.50  ▬

**Boys aged 6–13**

6.9

6.10

::: 44.32  ::: 50.16  ::: 56.00  ::: 61.84  ::: 67.68

::: 73.52  ⸜⸝⸞ 79.36  ⸘⸘ 85.20  ▓▓ 91.04  ▬

::: 83.33  ::: 85.51  ▬ 87.69  ::: 89.87  ::: 92.05

::: 94.23  ⸜⸝⸞ 96.41  ⸘⸘ 98.59  ▓▓ 100.77  ▬

**Girls aged 6–13**

6.12

6.13

School enrolments (6.8–6.13)

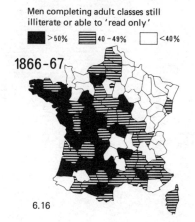

Men completing adult classes still
illiterate or able to 'read only'

■ >50%   ▤ 40–49%   □ <40%

1866–67

6.16

Literacy in 1866–7 and school enrolments in 1850

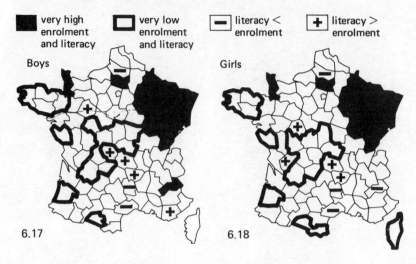

6.17    6.18

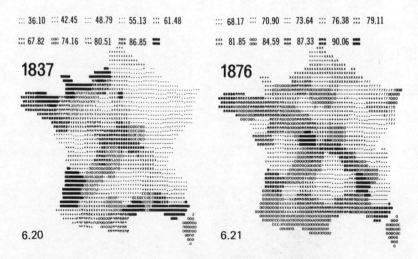

6.20    6.21

Pupils enrolled in summer per 100 enrolled in winter (6.20–6.22)

'Seasonal' and 'annual' attendance rates

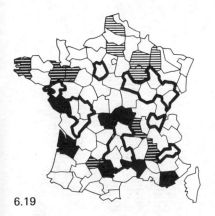

CORRELATION :

'seasonal' attendance > 85%
'annual' attendance > 55%     ■

'seasonal' attendance < 80%
'annual' attendance < 45%     □

ABSENCE OF CORRELATION

'seasonal' attendance > 85%
'annual' attendance < 45%     ▤

'seasonal' attendance < 80%
'annual' attendance > 55%     ▥

6.19

Correlations (6.17–6.19)

6.22

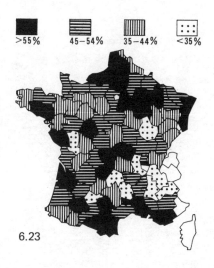

6.23

Proportion of pupils having attended school for 10 months or more in 1865 (6.23)

**Existing in 1833 as proportion of optimal number**

::: 14.39  ::: 23.69  ::: 32.99  ::: 42.29  ::: 51.59

::: 60.89  ::: 70.19  ::: 79.49  ::: 88.79  ■

6.24

**partial shortage of books and other articles**

::: 20.48  ::: 27.25  ::: 34.01  ::: 40.78  ::: 47.55

::: 54.31  ::: 61.08  ::: 67.84  ::: 74.61  ■

6.25

**housed by the commune**

:: 14.33  ::: 26.03  ::: 37.74  ::: 49.45  ::: 61.15

::: 72.86  ::: 84.56  ::: 96.27  ::: 107.98  ■

6.27

**with fixed wage**

::: 14.92  ::: 27.28  ::: 39.64  ::: 52.00  ::: 64.37

::: 76.73  ::: 89.09  ::: 101.45  ::: 113.81  ■

6.28

**totally inadequate (classroom conditions and teachers housing conditions)**

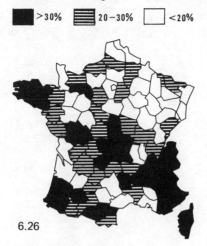

6.26

Schoolhouses (6.24–6.26)

**Average fixed wage**

6.29

Teachers (6.27–6.29)

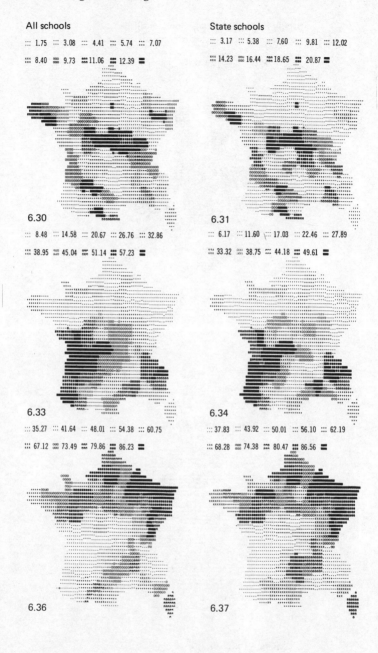

**All schools**

::: 1.75   ::: 3.08   ::: 4.41   ::: 5.74   ::: 7.07

::: 8.40   ::: 9.73   ::: 11.06   ::: 12.39 ▬

6.30

::: 8.48   ::: 14.58   ::: 20.67   ::: 26.76   ::: 32.86

::: 38.95   ::: 45.04   ::: 51.14   ::: 57.23 ▬

6.33

::: 35.27   ::: 41.64   ::: 48.01   ::: 54.38   ::: 60.75

::: 67.12   ::: 73.49   ::: 79.86   ::: 86.23 ▬

6.36

**State schools**

::: 3.17   ::: 5.38   ::: 7.60   ::: 9.81   ::: 12.02

::: 14.23   ::: 16.44   ::: 18.65   ::: 20.87 ▬

6.31

::: 6.17   ::: 11.60   ::: 17.03   ::: 22.46   ::: 27.89

::: 33.32   ::: 38.75   ::: 44.18   ::: 49.61 ▬

6.34

::: 37.83   ::: 43.92   ::: 50.01   ::: 56.10   ::: 62.19

::: 68.28   ::: 74.38   ::: 80.47   ::: 86.56 ▬

6.37

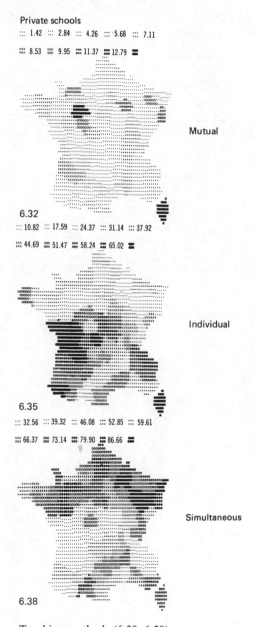

Private schools

::: 1.42  ::: 2.84  ::: 4.26  ::: 5.68  ::: 7.11

::: 8.53  ::: 9.95  ::: 11.37  ::: 12.79  ≡

Mutual

6.32

::: 10.82  ::: 17.59  ::: 24.37  ::: 31.14  ::: 37.92

::: 44.69  ::: 51.47  ::: 58.24  ::: 65.02  ≡

Individual

6.35

::: 32.56  ::: 39.32  ::: 46.08  ::: 52.85  ::: 59.61

::: 66.37  ::: 73.14  ::: 79.90  ::: 86.66  ≡

Simultaneous

6.38

Teaching methods (6.30–6.38)

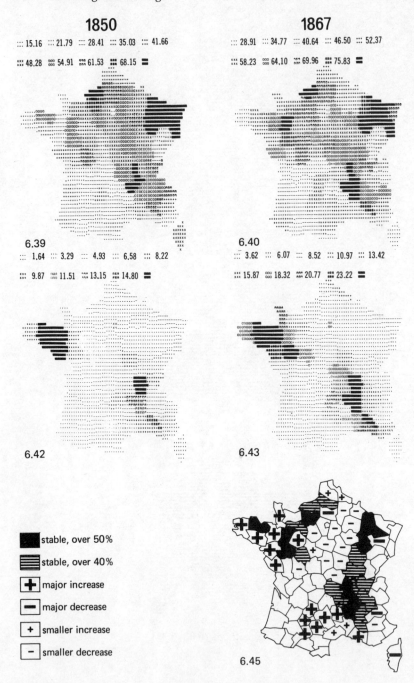

Evolution of congregational schools for girls between 1850 and 1896 (6.45)

## 1896

::: 25.62   ::: 29.79   ▦ 33.85   ::: 37.92   ::: 41.99

::: 46.06   ꜱꜱꜱ 50.13   ꜰꜰꜰ 54.20   ꜱꜱꜱ 58.27   ▬

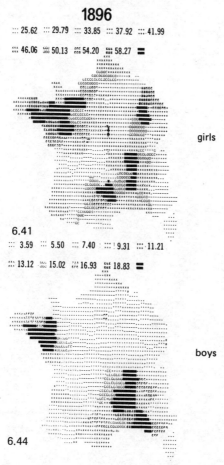

girls

6.41

::: 3.59   ::: 5.50   ▦ 7.40   ::: 9.31   ::: 11.21

::: 13.12   ꜱꜱꜱ 15.02   ꜰꜰꜰ 16.93   ꜱꜱꜱ 18.83   ▬

boys

6.44

Congregational schools (6.39–6.44)

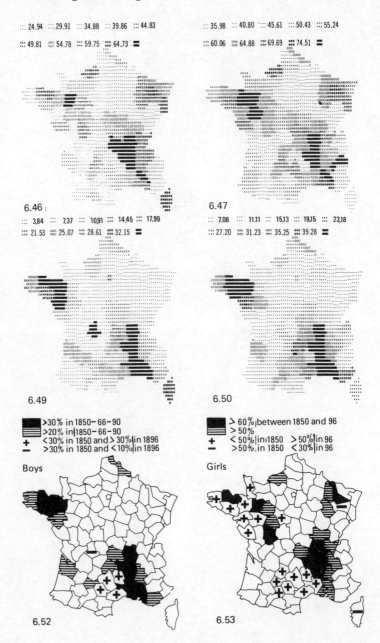

::: 24.94 ::: 29.91 ::: 34.88 ::: 39.86 ::: 44.83
::: 49.81 ::: 54.78 ::: 59.75 ::: 64.73 ■

6.46

::: 35.98 ::: 40.80 ::: 45.61 ::: 50.43 ::: 55.24
::: 60.06 ::: 64.88 ::: 69.69 ::: 74.51 ■

6.47

::: 3,84 ::: 7,37 ::: 10,91 ::: 14,45 ::: 17,99
::: 21.53 ::: 25.07 ::: 28.61 ::: 32.15 ■

6.49

::: 7.08 ::: 11.11 ::: 15,13 ::: 19,15 ::: 23,18
::: 27.20 ::: 31.23 ::: 35.25 ::: 39.28 ■

6.50

■ >30% in 1850−66−90
▤ >20% in 1850−66−90
+ <30% in 1850 and > 30% in 1896
− >30% in 1850 and <10% in 1896

Boys

6.52

■ > 60% between 1850 and 96
▤ >50%
+ < 50% in 1850  > 50% in 96
− >50% in 1850  < 30% in 96

Girls

6.53

Evolution of attendance at congregational schools (6.52−6.53)

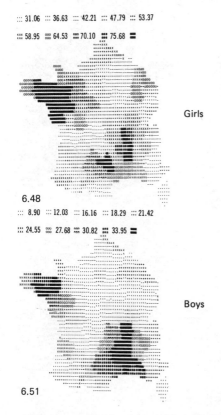

::: 31.06   ::: 36.63   ::: 42.21   ::: 47.79   ::: 53.37

::: 58.95   ⁈ 64.53   ⁈ 70.10   ⁈ 75.68   ■

Girls

6.48

::: 8.90   ::: 12.03   ::: 16.16   ::: 18.29   ::: 21.42

::: 24.55   ⁈ 27.68   ⁈ 30.82   ⁈ 33.95   ■

Boys

6.51

Children enrolled in congregational schools (6.46–6.51)

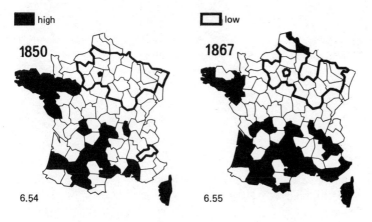

■ high      ☐ low

1850

1867

6.54             6.55

Attendance proportionally high or low in relation to the network of
congregational girls' schools (6.54–6.55)

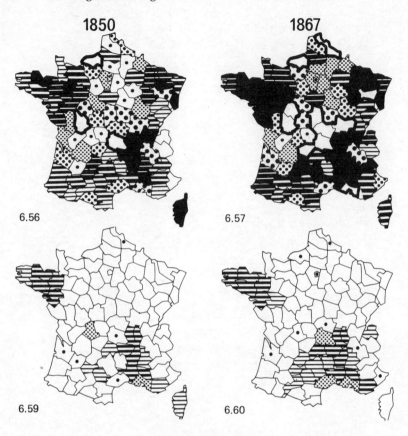

1850

1867

6.56

6.57

6.59

6.60

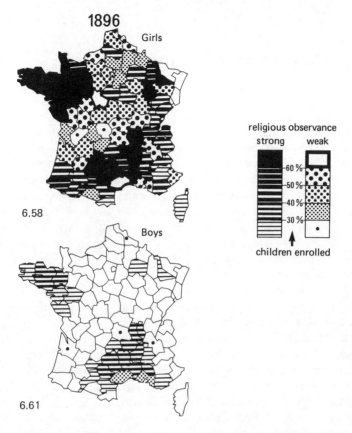

Religious observance and enrolment in congregational schools (6.56–6.61)

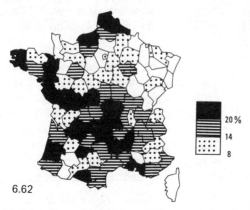

School-leavers (boys and girls) unable to read or write (6.62)

# 7

## READING AND WRITING IN FRENCH

Did the coexistence of a native regional tongue with the French language – and their inevitable competition – in any way retard the spread of literacy? This is a vast problem, which has been brought to the attention of the French nation by the revival of the regionalist movement over the past decade. It is an elusive problem, warped by impassioned subjectivism and by systematic reference to the responsibilities of the central authorities. Yet we cannot evade it, for three observations bring us face to face with it: first, the raw data provided by our sources on the history of elementary education; next, by first-hand accounts; and last, the interpretations put forward by contemporary historians.

The first piece of evidence is provided by 19th-century statistics, according to which several (partially or totally) non-French-speaking *départements* persistently lingered around the bottom of the league table, whether for marriage signatures, for educational levels on the occasion of census (1866 and 1872) or for conscripts' literacy rates. These laggards include the three Breton-speaking *départements* together with Corsica, Pyrénées-Orientales and several *départements* belonging to the Occitan nebula (Ariège, Corrèze, Haute-Vienne, Dordogne, Landes). Again, on the occasion of the 1901 census, the nine *départements* with the lowest levels of education – those we have just enumerated, with the exception of Pyrénées-Orientales – had at least partially non-French-speaking populations.

According to Charles Robert, Permanent Secretary of the Ministry of Education (1867), nearly one-third of conscripts did not normally express themselves in French. He wrote:

> At the request of the Minister of Education the Minister of War verified, two years ago, at the moment of the draft (by lots), whether each young soldier registered with the draft board spoke French or not. It was discovered that out of 321,981 conscripts, only 220,522 (61.1%) normally spoke French; 32,658 spoke no French at all, speaking only patois; 65,879 had only a smattering of French, since they spoke patois most of the time; there was no information available for the remaining 12,922 conscripts.

Now, and this is the second observation, contemporary writers unhesitatingly seized upon the language barrier in their efforts to explain the backwardness of elementary education in the non-French-speaking *dé-*

*partements*. The administrators of Revolutionary France before them had ascribed to 'the peculiar idiom of the inhabitants of our countryside' the difficulties that they were encountering in spreading enlightenment.

'The peculiar idiom of the inhabitants of our countryside, the Breton language, will long stand as a tremendous obstacle to the spread of enlightenment and education.'[1]

Throughout the 19th century, investigators – Guizot's part-time inspectors, and later the *inspecteurs primaires*, and the *inspecteurs d'Académie, recteurs* and inspectors-general – returned to this theme. The Inspector for the *arrondissement* of Perpignan pointed his finger at Catalan, his counterpart in Quimper blamed Breton; their colleague in Pau divided the blame between topography – the old refrain of the mountain people's rejection of enlightenment – and the 'idiom of the land'. Much later on in the century, on the occasion of the competition organized by Rouland in 1860 to discover the needs of rural schools,[2] schoolteachers (who had adopted this sweeping accusation) tried to list the difficulties with which their pupils had to cope and to assess their degree of backwardness. In Noordpeene, a Flemish-speaking commune in the canton of Hazebrouck, the teacher confessed his embarassment at finding himself confronted with a classroom of children walled up within their language: 'The only way to cope is by using their language to translate and put across the explanations I am obliged to give in French.' Breton teachers reckoned that their pupils needed one year of schooling to learn to speak French 'fairly well': at Riantec, the 'newcomers' suffered a one-year handicap right from the word go.[3] Which is no mean handicap when one considers that children scarcely spent more than two or two and a half years in school altogether.

A book published in 1905 bluntly sums up these educational observations. This was a manual of elementary French published by Delagrave, based on a direct method that aimed at associating the object directly with the corresponding French word:[4] the sub-title of *Le français par l'image* explained that this book was intended not only for deaf-mute children, but also for 'the children in our patois-speaking provinces, to the young natives in our colonies, as well as for children learning French abroad'.

Finally, our last observation, namely the hypothesis that linguistic exoticism was a factor obstructing education, is favoured by the best historians of non-French-speaking France. 'Without doubt', says Jean Meyer, 'the late dates [of education in Lower Brittany] may largely be accounted for by the language barrier.'[5] André Armengaud, studying populations in Eastern Aquitaine in 1845, most of whom then spoke practically nothing but Languedoc or Gascon dialects, also saw in this an obstacle to the spread of elementary education.[6]

Faced with such a convergence, it might be tempting to leave it at that and conclude that low literacy rates are plainly bound up with the existence of a regional language, were it not for a number of immediately obvious examples showing the exact opposite: in the mid-19th century, in the *département* of Nord, the two largely Flemish-speaking *arrondissements* (Dunkirk and Hazebrouck) were among the leading *arrondissements* in the *département* where marriage signatures were concerned, for both men and women. Dunkirk came second and Hazebrouck third, ahead of four French-speaking *arrondissements*. And then, needless to say, there is north-eastern France, which achieved literacy so early on, even in its German-speaking areas: in 1865, Bas-Rhin and Haut-Rhin lay respectively sixth and ninth in the ranking of French *départements* for conscripts' education, and in the 1866 census, Bas-Rhin had the lowest rate of illiteracy of any *département*.[7] As early as 1833, one of Guizot's inspectors had remarked on the apparent paradox of this province, 'where out of a given number of individuals' one finds 'the fewest able neither to read nor to write', and the 'greatest number unable to read or write the national language'.[8]

Leaving aside for a moment the good reasons that spring to mind to account for this contrast, we shall concentrate on those factors encouraging us to take a closer look at the spectacular educational backwardness in certain non-French-speaking regions. The first task, before even looking for causes, is to try to measure accurately the correlation between backwardness in literacy and the presence of a regional language. There are unfortunately a number of considerable obstacles to any such investigation (Map 7.1). For there are few *départements* in which it is possible to compare – all other things being equal – the educational level of French-speaking inhabitants with that of their fellow citizens who usually speak a non-French regional language (not to mention patois or dialects, for which it would be practically pointless to look for any true frontiers).

**The Breton border: the edge of instruction?**

For this reason, we decided to begin with an experiment in Brittany, where the dividing line between French and the regional tongue was relatively clear-cut and familiar in the 19th century (Map 7.2). This means that we can compare educational levels on either side of the language boundary. A recent study of education in Morbihan in the 18th century,[9] moreover, has made this *département* an obvious choice. The author, Augustin Cariou, examines the level of instruction as indicated by godfathers' and god-mothers' signatures at baptism (made compulsory by royal ordinance in 1667 and confirmed in 1736). For each parish and 'trève' (branch chapel of the parish church) in Morbihan, Cariou scrutinizes the hundred baptismal certificates immediately prior to 31 December 1789, recording the names of godfathers and mothers[10] and their signatures where these exist. In all, for 26,100 baptismal certificates examined in 261 parishes and 'trèves' (out of the 264 making up the future Morbihan in 1789), 45,719 different men and women had been called upon to sign and 21.2% of godfathers and 7.5% of godmothers proved capable of fulfilling their obligations.[11] But the most interesting thing about this study is not contained in these depressing figures; it lies in the distinction that the author draws, among these parishes and 'trèves', between the 'gallaises' (French-speaking people in 'Gallo' country) and the Breton-speakers, who shared the future *département* more or less evenly, 117 for the former, 144 for the latter. By classifying these 'signature' data according to linguistic criteria, we obtain the following results:

|  | Men | Women |
|---|---|---|
| Gallo-speaking district | 23.7% | 6.5% |
| Breton-speaking district | 19.3% | 8.3% |

So there were distinctly more men signing in Gallo country than in Breton-speaking parts ( + 4.4%), while female signatures were slightly more numerous ( + 1.8%) in Breton-speaking country. But the disparities are slight as a whole. So we also need to bear in mind the fact that there were considerably more urban parishes (where people had far more occasion to sign) in Breton-speaking than in Gallo country. If we concentrate solely on rural parishes and 'trèves', the difference almost vanishes for women (0.2%) and becomes worse for men (6.6%):

|  | Men | Women |
|---|---|---|
| Rural parishes and 'trèves' in Gallo-speaking areas | 21.3% | 4.2% |
| Rural parishes and 'trèves' in Breton-speaking areas | 14.7% | 4.4% |

It is also worth noting that, at least where men were concerned,[12] there was an additional contrast in Breton-speaking country: while male educational levels in Gallo country were more or less evenly distributed from the north to the south of the *département*, the situation was very different in the Breton-speaking part, where the coastal population signed a good deal more than did the inland folk.

Such are the observations that emerge from A. Cariou's study of the situation at the end of the 18th century (Map 7.3). For the 19th century, we ourselves have examined the lists of conscripts for 1850 and 1890, and we have had access to data concerning the education of conscripts between 1853 and 1872, collected by a Morbihan scholar.[13] Doctor Fouquet's concerns were primarily those of a specialist in public hygiene,[14] and it was precisely because of this that his attention was attracted by the singular convergence of high rates of physical disability or sickness and low levels of education in the different cantons, which he distinguished according to linguistic and geographical criteria. From his figures, which he published in 1874, it emerges (Map 7.4), that:

1. The sixteen cantons catalogued as purely Breton-speaking between them constitute the tail-end of the list of thirty-seven Morbihan cantons; in all of them, the illiteracy rate is higher than the departmental average (56.55% unable even to read). The least illiterate ones are the cantons lying on the language boundary and are even chipped away by it (Saint-Jean-Brévelay 58.47%; Elven 61.25%); one canton with an administrative and urban centre (Pontivy 56.88%); one maritime canton (Port-Louis 59.27%).

2. The thirteen entirely French-speaking cantons, those making up the Gallo district, have illiteracy rates lower than the departmental average (with one not very significant exception: Questembert, which is only 0.23% over the mark at 56.78%).

3. The six best-educated cantons (with fewer than 40% total illiterates: from Lorient-I with 10.2% to Sarzeau with 36.7%, via Vannes-Ouest, Belle-Ile, Vannes-Est and Quiberon) all happen to have mixed populations – French and Breton – and to lie along the coast (at this period, none of Morbihan's maritime cantons was exclusively French-speaking); further, it was here that the two main towns, Vannes and Lorient, were situated and where, even in a Breton-speaking region, French was far more widely used than in the countryside.

4. The six most backward cantons, three-quarters illiterate or more (Plouay 87.3%; Pluvigner 81.2%; Le Faoüet 79.9%; Cléguérec and Gourin 76.4%; Guémené 74.7%), were all entirely Breton-speaking, lay inland and were rural.

These facts show that, in Morbihan, the use of Breton in everyday life in a canton went hand in hand with a low, or very low, rate of literacy. Even in the case of two otherwise very similar cantons (in terms of situation and activity), the disparity in literacy rates is considerable when they happen to speak different languages, as in the case of Plouay and Allaire. Both are rural, both are inland cantons, but the Breton-speaking canton of Plouay lags 28 points behind in educational terms. Port-Louis and Sarzeau furnish another example: both are coastal, both live to a large extent off maritime activities, but the Breton-speaking Port-Louis lags 23 points behind.

Our last set of figures comes from our perusal of the conscription lists for 1850 and 1890, from which we have recorded, in addition to figures relating to education for each conscript, his residence and his stated occupation. To obtain adequate samples, we have had to confine ourselves to dividing conscripts into two crudely-drawn categories, one of which embraces farmers and farmworkers,[15] the other shopkeepers and artisans,[16] always bearing in mind the distortions that arise when one lumps together rag-and-bone men with clocksmiths and cabinetmakers.

Let us now take a look at the figures for farmers and farmworkers in the inland rural cantons (Map 7.5). For the thirteen inland cantons classified as Breton-speaking by Dr Fouquet in 1874, 17.6% of farmers and farmworkers were literate; for the sixteen inland cantons in Gallo country, the corresponding figure was 35.3%, exactly double. These averages in fact conceal some quite impressive discrepancies. 7% of the peasant conscripts from the Breton-speaking cantons of Plouay or Faoüet were literate; 44 and 47% of those from the Gallo cantons of Mauron and Guer were. In fact, the average score for the Breton-speaking cantons is arrived at with the aid of the four cantons lying along or even astride the linguistic frontier: 25.4% in Grandchamp, 24.4% in Locminé, 28.4% in Saint-Jean-Brévelay, and 28.6% in Elven. Peasant conscripts in the French-speaking areas were distinctly more literate than in the west of the *département*.

The second point of comparison, again in 1850, and again with reference to the inland cantons, concerns conscripts stating artisan or commercial occupations. For the Breton-speaking cantons as a whole, the literacy rate for 20 year-old artisans and shopkeepers was 41.2%, whereas in Gallo country this rate already stood at 55.4%. Here too, the disparities between the most backward Breton-speaking cantons (15% in Plouay, 22% in Guémené) and the most advanced Gallo cantons (63% in Malestroit and 74% in La Gacilly) was quite considerable.

The samples are comparable in size, containing 323 individuals in the Breton-speaking one, and 267 in the Gallo-speaking one. While the main town plays no rôle in the Gallo area (if we leave out the canton of Ploermel the average rate remains unchanged), the reverse holds for Breton-speaking country, where removal of the canton of Pontivy brings the score down to 36.9%.

Scrutiny of the maritime and semi-maritime[17] cantons yields very similar contrasts within the different socio-occupational categories. The figures for farmers and farmworkers are, give or take minor variations, identical to those inland: 17.7% of conscripts were literate in the Breton-speaking area, while 33% were literate in Gallo country. Among shopkeepers and artisans, the disparity is analogous (15.1% compared with 14.3% for the inland cantons), but at a much higher level, with 51.6% in the Breton-speaking cantons and 67.1% in the 'Franco-Breton' district (although admittedly this does contain Vannes and Lorient).

We come across the same contrasting literacy rates in Breton-speaking and French-speaking cantons – so blatant in Morbihan – in the Breton *département* lying astride the language frontier, Côtes-du-Nord, at the same moment in time (1846) and according to the same sources, i.e. conscription lists. Overall, the French-speaking part of Côtes-du-Nord is by far the more literate. For an equivalent number of conscripts,[18] the Breton-speaking cantons were 73% illiterate, while the French-speaking (or Franco-Breton) ones were only 56.2% so. Although slightly less pronounced than in Morbihan (17.8 versus 22.1%), the discrepancy is still spectacular. Out of the twenty-seven entirely or partially French-speaking cantons, only seven had a literacy score of less than the departmental average of 35.46%, and four of those came close with over 30%. The most literate Breton-speaking canton, Paimpol, scored only 45%, whereas six French-speaking ones topped 60%.[19]

When we now distribute conscripts from the cantons of Côtes-du-Nord according to the geographical characteristics of their place of residence (inland, maritime or semi-maritime), the disparities are similar to those found in Morbihan if we take language into account: the inland cantons scored literacy rates of 21.9% in the Breton-speaking areas, and 42.9% in Gallo country (a disparity of 21%, compared with 18.5% in Morbihan); the coastal cantons score respectively 31.4% and 57% (a disparity of 25.6%, compared with 19% in Morbihan). Even then, these averages conceal enormous discrepancies here too. Close on 80% of the conscripts from the Gallo-speaking canton of Pléneuf were at least able to read, whereas their counterparts from the Breton-speaking canton of Maël-Carhaix rated only 14% on the same scale.

When classified according to socio-occupational and language criteria, as with Morbihan, conscripts from Côtes-du-Nord present a similarly contrasting picture, whichever criterion we choose. For Breton-speaking cantons as a whole, 20.1% of farmers and farmworkers were literate, while 36.3% of these same categories were literate in Gallo country (a disparity of 16.2% in the Gallo-speakers' favour); for artisans and shopkeepers, the corresponding figures were 39.1% and 61.7% (giving a disparity of 22.6% in the Gallo-speakers' favour).

Finally, even when we confine ourselves to a homogeneous geographical zone, we still come up with the same contrasts. Take, for example, the maritime cantons: among Breton-speakers, 27.5% of farmers and farmworkers were literate, compared with 45.8% in Gallo country (a disparity of 18.3% in favour of the Gallo-speakers); the figures for artisans and shopkeepers were 37.7% and 73.1% respectively (+ 35.4%). And now take a look at the inland cantons: + 17.8% for Gallo-speaking farmers and farmworkers, and + 11.8% for shopkeepers and artisans. To conclude this welter of figures, it is worth noting that most of the disparities recorded in Côtes-du-Nord were very close to those found among Morbihan conscripts (to within 0.1% for peasants in the inland cantons!).

This, then, is the picture we have been able to reconstruct of how Breton conscripts were educated on either side of the linguistic frontier in the middle of the 19th century. How did this picture alter in the course of the second half-century? Not surprisingly, between 1850 and 1890 Morbihan's conscripts worked hard to make good their backwardness (cf. Map 7.6). In forty years, the proportion of those 'able at least to read' increased from

36.75% to 76.54%. But the crucial phenomenon here is not so much this overall progress of close on 40%. Rather it is the fact that the French-speaking (or partly French-speaking) region, which had already opened up a big lead by mid-century, still continued to progress more rapidly than the departmental average (+ 41.54%). Compared with this average, the Breton-speaking cantons slipped still further behind (with + 35.59% only). Contrary to expectation, the disparity between the two zones widened instead of narrowing: it rose from 22.1% in 1850 to 28.1% in 1890. And of the fourteen cantons in which literacy spread more rapidly than the departmental average, ten were French-speaking or Franco-Breton.

If we employ the same distinctions as in 1850, we can readily observe that this worsening of the disparity between the two linguistic zones is due entirely to the situation in the inland Breton-speaking cantons, and in particular to the peasant conscripts falling still further behind (together with day-labourers and domestic servants, although they had become relatively much less important). To be sure, the educational level of day-labourer and farmer conscripts in the Breton-speaking region had improved considerably (+ 33.7%); but in Gallo country it had improved still more (+ 40.2%). So the Breton-speakers' relative position had worsened in forty years. For the other main category distinguished by us, namely shopkeepers and artisans, literacy spread at the same pace on either side of the linguistic frontier: in these same inland cantons,[20] there was a 33.7% rise, on both sides of the line. Here, the Gallo-speakers maintained their 1850 lead (+ 14.3%), but they were unable to increase it.

The bald facts are, without a shadow of doubt, that for a mid-19th century conscript, regardless of his social category (peasant, domestic servant, day-labourer, shopkeeper or artisan), and irrespective of place of residence (inland, semi-maritime or maritime), the fact of being a Breton-speaker meant that he was considerably less likely than his French-speaking counterpart to be literate. In the second half of the century, when everywhere else people were fast making good their handicaps (sexual, social, geographical), Breton-speaking conscripts experienced a marked deterioration in their relative position whenever they also happened to be peasants, farm labourers, domestic servants or day-labourers.

What interpretation are we to put on this twofold observation, in which illiteracy is so persistently bound up with the fact of speaking another language? And how precisely did this factor exert its pernicious influence? One's first thoughts, obviously, are of the repressive rôle played by the school:[21] from the word go, the State primary school in France was synonymous with the French-speaking school. No sooner was Roussillon annexed to France in 1659 than the royal administration began supplanting Catalan by French; for the sons of the bourgeoisie and minor nobility, a Jesuit college was opened in Perpignan, while the Benedictines of Béziers took care of the girls' education. As for the children of the people, for whom this operation took on its full significance, an attempt was made to enforce upon them some manner of compulsory education, long before its time. In 1672, the *intendant*, Carlier, suggested to the Consuls of Perpignan that they 'invite', under threat of sanction, the sons and daughters of the people to attend the elementary schools spread among the four parishes of the town: there they would learn to read and write until they had become familiar with the French language. To make sure no one would slip through this French-speaking net, the schools would be given a monopoly of education and their teachers would be paid by the town.[22] The plan came to nought, for want of money and goodwill, but there can be no doubt as to its ultimate goal at least.[23]

There are plenty of similar examples down the centuries. The best known is the Decree of 8 Pluviôse Year II, which the Convention passed on the motion of Barère: this required the establishment within 10 days – but this breathless Decree was never put into effect – of a French-speaking schoolteacher in every rural commune in the non-French-speaking *départements*.[24] Four decades later, on 28 October 1838, Salvandy sent out a circular once more drawing the attention of the *recteurs* to those children in primary schools who 'speak a local idiom' and firmly reminding them of the dogma of national homogeneity: one language, one education for all the people of France.

Would we be justified in thinking, therefore, that the French school was the sole factor to blame for illiteracy among children speaking a regional language and, in the case we have been examining, among Breton-speaking children? Things are not quite as simple as that, for established practice long put up a determined resistance to these endlessly reiterated plans for unification. There were star Breton-speaking pupils who were nevertheless honoured with the civic palm and the 'fraternal accolade of the citizen-president', like the pupil from the republican schools of the commune of Plouagat-Guerraud, crowned for having recited a Breton translation of the Declaration of the Rights of Man on the occasion of the feast of the King's death.[25] There were teachers who went on using Breton in class, like the one Jules Simon recalls, who in his school in Morbihan taught French 'like a foreign language'.[26] In 1863, a survey conducted by Duruy confirmed the fact on a national scale, observing that in many schools teachers used both dialect and French to make themselves understood by their pupils, the newcomers especially.

This was so in 87% of Corsican schools; 76% of schools in Bas-Rhin and 76% in Finistère too (where 6% taught exclusively in Breton); 48% in Haut-Rhin; 45% in Côtes-du-Nord; 44% in Moselle; 40% in Morbihan, and so on.[27]

In the meantime, presumably, the administrators and inspectors of education continued to rail against the 'detestable Breton idiom'. Still, we must dismiss the notion of a school uniformly and obstinately determined to stigmatize the use of regional languages.

Indeed, in our example, it is the absence rather than the presence of schools that is to be blamed, and this alone should suffice to demonstrate the need, while not altogether ruling it out, to look beyond the problem of the school's responsibility. For in 1845-46, the least literate *arrondissement* in Morbihan, Pontivy, was also the one with the least adequate school network:[28] only three-fifths of the population lived in communes with schools (by which we mean boys' schools, needless to say); to make matters worse, these were generally communes spread over a wide area, which meant that even when they were fortunate enough to have schools, distance was an obstacle to attendance, and among the different factors of absenteeism from school, 'distance of the child's home from school' and 'natural obstacles' were at their peaks here, scoring 18% (compared with only 10 to 15% in the other Morbihan *arrondissements*).

At the same date (1844), the situation in Côtes-du-Nord was comparable to this. The two entirely Breton-speaking *arrondissements* came bottom of the list of communes having a communal school for boys: 53% for the *arrondissement* of Guingamp and 60% in the *arrondissement* of Lannion. The three fully or partially French-speaking *arrondissements* came top: 69% for Saint-Brieuc, 63% for Dinan and 62% for Loudéac.[29]

Forty years on, in 1884-85, the situation regarding primary schools points in the same direction. The eight cantons having the worst boys' school attendance rates were all Breton-speaking ones lying inland (30.7%–53.5% of boys aged 6 – 13 were in school).[30] Six out of the eight were again in the *arrondissement* of Pontivy where, in spite of the presence of the *arrondissement chef-lieu* (the school enrolment rate in the canton of Pontivy itself was 87%), the average rate had only managed to haul itself up to 58%. A few years later, in 1890, these eight under-schooled cantons were those with the highest conscript illiteracy rate for the entire *département*. The cantons with high school enrolments, on the other hand, mostly (seven out of ten) lay in the far-eastern part of the *département*, nudging Ille-et-Vilaine. In 1890, *all* of them ranked among the leaders in terms of conscript literacy.

If the line running through Côtes-du-Nord and Morbihan, from Plouha to Muzillac, divided the area up into French and Breton-speaking districts only, we would probably be forced (since we have already established that it also defined two separate levels of literacy) to acknowledge the existence of a one-way relation of cause and effect between illiteracy and a minority language. Once this frontier ceases to be exclusively linguistic, though, everything changes, or least becomes more complicated. Now, as we have just seen, this frontier also represents a scholastic front, and more besides, for André Siegfried's studies have familiarized us with the contrast between the 'feudal' structure of the Breton-speaking west, with its large estates and hierarchical society dominated by the local 'lord', and the patchwork structure of Gallo country, with its preponderance of small farms and holdings. That this dichotomy may also affect cultural attitudes is a hypothesis at least worth investigating.

It so happens that the famous linguistic frontier also marked the limits of religious fervour in the 19th century (cf. Map 7.7). It separated an area of high religious observance (the French-speaking region in the east, with its marches), from one of little religious practice more or less coincident with the Breton-speaking west. Claude Langlois has established this incontrovertibly for the Morbihan.[31] This was so in the late 18th century, when the supervision of the parish clergy clearly favoured the Gallo-speaking region; and for the early 19th century, when the region was still much better supplied with priests and when – and this is an unequivocal sign of the clergy's grip – the tithe still persisted in many cantons, at a time when this practice had become unusual in the Breton-speaking areas. It was so again at the end of the 19th century, when the distribution of pupils in congregational schools (State or private) also reflected the religious divide (the congregational school played little part in the Breton-speaking west, whereas in Gallo country it backed up the work of the clergy). This was enough to make the Breton-speaking west, with its low literacy rate and poor school system, and an under-Christianized region to boot: a 'zone of religious indifference'.

Claude Langlois' book suggests yet another contrast, namely the political aspect of this division of the *département*. The present-day voting patterns in Morbihan shows the red cantons as lying in the western part of the *département*: Baud, Cléguérec, Hennebont, Pont-Scorff, Le Faouët and Gourin. According to Claude Langlois, this politically more 'advanced' behaviour has a long history: the western regions welcomed the constitutional, and later the concordat, clergy especially warmly; in Year X, and later in Year XII, rejection of the Life Consulate and subsequently the Empire crystallized around the little Breton-speaking towns of Pontivy, Baud, Hennebont, Lorient and Port-Louis: under the Revolution they were 'patriotic', while the Restoration considered them 'liberal'. In 1881, moreover, the Prefect of Morbihan noted in a report that, for Brittany as a whole, the French-speakers were far from being more 'enlightened' than the Breton-speakers (the epithet needs to be interpreted in terms of political psychology), and awarded the prize for 'republicanism' to the totally Breton-speaking *département* of Finistère. The runners-up were the rural areas of the Breton-speaking *arrondissements* of Morbihan, which were 'more republican that the French-speaking countryfolk of Ploermel and Loudéac'.

In a letter dated 18 January 1881 addressed by the Prefect to the Director of Primary Education, discussing the report on education in Morbihan submitted by an Inspector-General which the Minister of Education had passed on to him (A.D. Morbihan), the Prefect notes that the 'Gallos are not more enlightened than the Breton-speakers', that the 'parts of the former Brittany which seem most refractory to political progress are those nearest to the capital (the *arrondissements* of Vitré and Chateaubriant)'. For him, the entirely Breton-speaking Finistère was 'the most republican of the *départements* in Brittany'; and, in Morbihan, the *arrondissements* of Lorient and Pontivy.

The picture is even more clear-cut in Côtes-du-Nord. Here, to the west of the 19th-century linguistic frontier, almost all the cantons voted red, whereas only a minority did so in Gallo country. Still more so than in Morbihan, we find a Breton-speaking, not very Christian, west which favoured movement, contrasting with the French-speaking, clerical east, upholding the established order: a now-familiar contrast.[32]

Rather than a linguistic frontier, what we ought to speak of is an accumulation of boundaries: of an east/west dichotomy so ancient and so multifarious that it rules all simple explanations out of court, whether these draw a direct connection between linguistic differences and illiteracy or establish the school as the sole mediating agency between one or the other. What the case of Brittany in fact suggests is, on the one hand, the existence of a cultural desert, since not only did the western parts of both *départements* not speak French as a general rule, they also lacked priests and schools, as well as those middlemen, the smallholders and small farmers through whom the processes of social imitation operate. Perhaps on the other hand, in addition to the absence of these different factors, we ought also to record the existence of a kind of mechanism of rejection. There is, in the Breton-speaking west, if not a capacity for revolt, at least a tendency to resist both political directives and cultural injunctions.

> In the east, there is a passive population which *accepts* a social structure that still has lingering overtones of an hierarchical past, a structure which, while fairly egalitarian, engenders poverty while remaining in thrall to a clergy that exploits its fear of hell from which it hands down its political directives. In the west, a proud race has shaken itself free of a social and agrarian structure with typically hierarchical tendencies. Or, where still under the yoke, it *rebels*, its first spontaneous revolt being to emigrate, which serves to bolster its conscious desire for liberation.[33]

**Beyond Brittany**

In the other regions speaking minority languages or regional speech-forms and dialects, we have had to confine ourselves to sample surveys for the 19th century.[34] From an extreme variety of situations, our findings no more suggest that illiteracy arises, ipso facto, from the presence of a regional language than they did in Brittany, nor that the Jacobin school bears sole responsibility for any case of backwardness.

First: as in Brittany, one can point to examples where the map of illiteracy does appear to coincide with some regional language. In Basses-Pyrénées, for example, where in the early 19th century more than one Basque conscript in two was illiterate, even in the towns. In the mountains, the proportion sometimes exceeded two-thirds or more in certain bastions of Basque tradition: 75.5% in Saint-Jean-Pied-de-Port; 79.2% in Iholdy; 84.6% in Baigorri. These figures contrast spectacularly with those of adjacent Béarn. The Basque towns themselves, leaving aside slightly less god-forsaken Bayonne, stood some thirty-odd points below the departmental average, countryside included. As for the Basque – Béarn contrast, this persisted despite the leap forward in Basque literacy rates in the last decades. All through the century, we may say of the Basques, as a Commissioner of the Executive Directorate noted with melancholy in Year VI: 'They seem to form a separate people.'

We find the same results in the Mediterranean south, judging from the conscripts in Hérault in 1846-47. Not that there was any linguistic frontier properly speaking here. Even so, we have been able to draw a line through the *département*, perpendicular to the coast, separating the south-western cantons, where people generally spoke patois, from those to the north-east, where people more usually spoke French. These French-speaking cantons enjoyed a substantial lead of 22% for 'able at least to read' among farmers and of 11% among artisans.[35]

Even in Lorraine, in the developed north-east, standing in the forefront of the elementary educational process, detailed analysis can still detect the advantage enjoyed by the French-speaking cantons. Even here, we find more totally illiterate conscripts in the German-speaking cantons studied. In the 1841 intake, for instance, 25.1% compared with 6.6% in the French-speaking cantons.[36]

Yet still we cannot conclude from these facts that there is a constant link between illiteracy and the existence of a regional language. The rule that French-speakers enjoyed an advantage is not applicable everywhere. In Alsace, for instance, where in mid-19th century we find no significant disparity between French-speaking and German-speaking cantons. Or in Nord, where as early as the late 18th century many Flemish-speaking cantons stood near the top of the literacy league table, ahead of a mass of French-speaking ones.

In 1828-29, for the Flemish-speaking *arrondissements* of Hazebrouck and Bergues (later renamed the *arrondissement* of Dunkirk), eight cantons (out of fourteen) had conscript literacy rates of over 50% (three of them over 60%), i.e. above average for the *département*; and none of the six others figured among the tail-end cantons of Nord. At the end of the century, in 1892-93, eleven out of fourteen had conscript literacy rates of over 90%. So the position of the two Flemish-speaking *arrondissements* relative to the rest of the (otherwise French-speaking) *département* was at least as good as it had been three-quarters of a century beforehand.

There was a comparable case in the Dordogne, where the most illiterate cantons were those where the Oil patois was spoken (the Nontronnais in the north of the *département*), whereas the 'Perigordian' cantons, where Oc patois predominated, were more literate.

Faced with this diversity, it behoves us, as in the case of Brittany, to shun over-hasty conclusions. As in the case of Brittany, also, we should not be too quick to pin the blame on the demanding character of primary school education. For not only was the compulsion to speak French very unevenly enforced from one region to the next, above all its results seem by no means unequivocal. Take, for example, two regions in which the use of the minority language was, officially or semi-officially, tolerated. The Basque country, where, in 1874, the 'Regulations adopted by the Higher Board for Public Schools of the Département of Basses-Pyrénées' were tolerant in tone: schoolteachers were instructed to hold daily exercises in translation, oral and written.[37] Flanders, where the *Ancien Régime* teachers traditionally taught reading and writing in Flemish,[38] and where not until the second half of the 19th century was Flemish (still permitted in catechism) forbidden in primary education – forbidden in principle that is, although enforcement of the prohibition seems to have been fairly lax.[39] It is tempting to make this liberal policy a causal factor. But how? To do so, one would have to claim that a single policy could have opposite effects, generating literacy in Flanders and illiteracy in Basque country.

In Alsace, the curriculum of the Strasbourg teacher training college, founded in 1810, included classes in French and German throughout the three-year course. In Lorraine, regulations governing the State primary schools of Meurthe, published in 1852, stipulated that 'in the German communes, children shall learn to read in both languages and to translate both from German into French and from French into German';[40] in Moselle, the new regulations adopted in 1870 stipulated that 'practice of the German language shall be maintained to a reasonable degree, either as a necessary means of communication between master and pupil in the lower and elementary divisions, or by means of exercises in translation and conversation in the intermediate and upper classes'.

We come now to two regions in which a fierce war was waged on use of the local language. Béarn, where the same 1874 Regulations which recommended translation exercises in the Basque schools stipulated that 'the use of patois is explicitly forbidden in the Bearnais schools; all exercises shall be done in French'. Landes, as illustrated by the answers

296 Reading and writing

given in the 1860 competition, where the teacher at Montfort, for example, could write: 'All idioms foreign to the French language being strictly forbidden in our schools, the various branches of teaching are studied in the mother tongue [sic] which no French man or woman may, under any pretext, be excused from learning.' Here again, there can clearly be no question of attributing identical results to repressive policy, since the backward Landes stand in contrast to the literate Béarn.

At the conclusion of our journey through non-French-speaking France, we find ourselves much less assured that the use of French in schools attended by non-French-speaking pupils was a decisive obstacle to the spread of literacy. Indeed, the accounts of those obliged to bow before this strange educational practice are themselves more mitigated than might commonly be supposed. A schoolteacher in Morbihan was satisfied, in 1843, that even with non-French-speaking pupils, nine months sufficed to teach them to read.[41] A primary school inspector for the *arrondissement* of Hazebrouck, unconvinced that the use of Flemish among his pupils hampered them in acquiring the first rudiments of instruction, noted: 'It has been said that the pupil who is able to read one language will be able to read the other after a few weeks' practice', and he adds: 'People even say that Flemish represents no greater obstacle to the spread of education than does the patois of Lille, and this does seem to be true in many cases.'[42]

### Poor France, oral France, rebellious France

The negative – murderous, many people all over France are now inclined to say – rôle of the French school in non-French-speaking regions cannot, therefore, be the correct answer to our question. If, inside non-French-speaking France, we have managed to identify such considerable differences between Béarn and Lower Brittany, between German-speaking Alsace and Lorraine, or between Flemish-speaking Flanders and Basque country, it is surely because while linguistic peculiarities are reflected in low literacy rates, they either encompass or tie in with other differences or singularities.

Sometimes the factor may quite plainly be one of unequal prosperity, as in Lorraine, where the contrast between the poor German-speaking zone and the rich French-speaking zone was taken for granted by the middle of the 19th century. From this stemmed, according to the observations of the school inspectors, the readiness of the more prosperous French-speaking populations to make 'sacrifices' for schooling and to assent to the ideology of the school.

In 1856, the Inspector of the *Académie* of Moselle recorded that, in the French part of his *département*, 'families are better off and are more inclined to make sacrifices for their children'; they kept them in school longer, bought them everything they needed for their school work, etc.

We could easily show for inland Brittany too, that the most easterly bastions of the Breton tongue and illiteracy – where Breton and ignorance combined encroached upon the land of Gallo-speakers – that these too were outposts of poverty, such as the particularly god-forsaken Landes of Lanvaux.

Now it is also necessary to focus upon another yet more crucial factor, namely the oral character of culture in many under-literate non-French-speaking regions. These were generally dominated by oral tradition, their languages having no popular written culture to underpin them; they were non-élitist (unlike the German and Flemish-speaking north-east, those two atypical examples which keep recurring, the explanation for which is doubtless to be found here). So, in these regions of oral tradition then, there was no mediating factor between written French culture and unwritten language, the instrument of group solidarity and shared intimacy. There was nothing to attenuate the strangeness of written culture and mitigate the sensation of a considerable gulf, which yawned all the wider because the minority tongue resembled no language of civilization. It was this gulf, regardless of the language of teaching and civilization, regardless too of the repressive zeal ascribed to teachers and the pressures of the school, which formed the decisive obstacle to the literacy process. One can scarcely learn to read and write in a patois, in a language either very little written or not at all. Learning to read bears no relation even to some collective need, since all written documents are in French, i.e. in a language that is neither used nor even understood by the great majority of the lower orders. This is the case, for instance, in many regions of Occitania. It was so in the Basque country, where the community assemblies showed little concern to set down their vernacular tongue in writing, as if the consensus here were sufficiently deep-seated to give force of contract to public speech and audition. This was what happened in French Catalonia where, once the élites had become gallicized in the 18th century, a chasm spread between the Catalan-speaking people and the keepers of written culture, henceforward French.

In all these regions, the primary factor accounting for low literacy rates was this distortion between spoken culture and written culture, which hindered – or even dammed up entirely – social demand for education, since of necessity this could only be satisfied in written language. When we bear this hypothesis in mind, we are less likely to encounter those intractable examples with which the traditional explanation of illiteracy had to cope. It no longer comes as a surprise, for instance, to learn that there were more and better-attended schools in Gallo-speaking Brittany than in the Breton-speaking part, for from our newly-adopted standpoint, the school ceases to be the cause and becomes the consequence of a good level of education, in other words a form of prior consent to written culture.

Even so, low levels of education may also reflect a much more visceral, more sweeping rejection of a culture, going way beyond mere rejection of literacy in a language that is felt to be foreign. Seen thus, low levels of literacy in certain regions where minority languages were spoken may be viewed as an expression of resistance first to monarchic centralization, later to Jacobin unification, as the rejection of that ideology of a homogeneous humanity which was the cement of the national community. Of this total rejection, illiteracy was one sign among others, such as emigration abroad and disobedience in Basque country. What is important here, for us, is that one manifestation of this rejection was the non-demand for written culture and indifference, hostility even, towards its temple, the school.

The contrast between Béarn and Basque country may illustrate this hypothesis.[43] Though non-French-speaking, Béarn, which began writing very early on, also achieved literacy at an early date, both in French and in Béarnais (it was already widespread in the 18th century). The people of Béarn welcomed the school in the 19th century, for their desire for upward social mobility in the French establishment – through admission to the State machine and the civil service in particular – implied acceptance of the social and cultural values of the nation and of the ideal of progress through education. The lower orders of the Basque community, on the other hand, without writing in its own language, found in that language no reason, *a fortiori*, to make the effort to acquire French written culture, and rejected integration out of hand: like emigration, illiteracy was a manifestation of this collective rejection.

Can we stretch the reflections that this example inspires to the whole of France? What is remarkable is that in the 'integrated' parts of France, which also happened to be the educated parts of France where concern for education was widespread, the existence and use of purely oral patois (lower Normandy, Picardy, Lorraine) no more significantly hindered the literacy process than did the truly foreign languages such as Flemish or Alsatian. In regions which early on demanded – or accepted – education and schooling (as in Alsace, Flanders and Normandy), the presence of a minority language, a dialect or a patois presented little or no obstacle to literacy. In backward France, on the other hand, the existence of a patois or non-French language tended to aggravate the educational backwardness: but this was also the France of rejection, rejection of the school included.[44]

One might, in that case, speak of a situation felt – rightly or wrongly, this is not our problem – to be 'colonial' in type. A recent book on elementary education in French Algeria under the Third Republic records – in a genuinely colonial situation – a comparable rejection. The 'natives', repugnance towards the education offered by the 19th-century colonialists, regardless of the form that this might take – schools modelled on the metropolitan pattern, Arabo-French schools, traditional schools controlled by the army, or even the native schools founded in 1883 – is interpreted here not as a sign of indifference or passiveness, but as the symptom of outright cultural rejection. This is attested by the countless empty schools mentioned in the reports sent in by administrators, who, seeing these deserted premises, concluded that the population must be hostile. 'The schools of the M'Zab', wrote the *Recteur* of Algiers in 1906, 'are generally poorly attended because the Mozabites are hostile to French education, as to everything that is foreign.'[45] Comparison with the situation in parts of metropolitan France is artificial in appearance only moreover: as evidence in support of its plaintive analyses of the difficulties encountered in educating Algerian children, the *Bulletin de l'enseignement des indigènes*, in 1888, cites reports written in France on the problem of non-French-speaking children, and in particular Breton children.

In 1888, the *Bulletin de l'enseignement des indigènes* published a report by Inspector-General J. Carré:

> One still finds in France regions in which the inhabitants neither understand nor speak the French language, the very language in which their obligations as men and citizens are prescribed for them; I am referring to the Flemings, in part of the *arrondissements* of Dunkirk and Hazebrouck, the Basques in the Pyrenees, and particularly to the Bretons in Lower Brittany (the whole of the *département* of Finistère and roughly half those of Côtes-du-Nord or Morbihan, less, however, the townspeople and the seamen along the coast . . . We need Frenchmen to Frenchify the Bretons, for they will not become French of their own accord.)[46]

Poor France; oral France; rebellious France. The non-French-speaking part of France did not always combine all these features at one and the same time. And when it did not, however non-French-speaking it may have been, this did not necessarily mean it was illiterate. Out of their combination was born, not as a kind of negative inertia but rather as positive rejection, stubborn resistance to that new-fangled form of social integration, literacy.

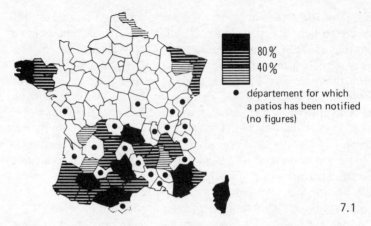

7.1

Percentage of commune populations unable to speak French in 1863

Morbihan.

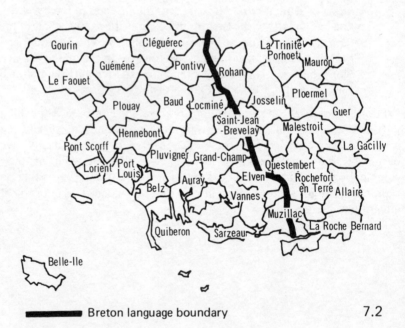

━━━━━ Breton language boundary

7.2

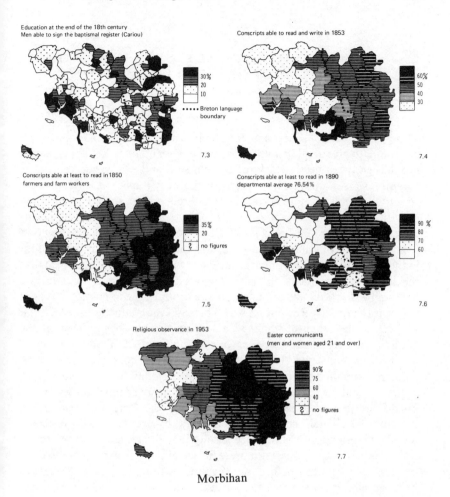

Education at the end of the 18th century
Men able to sign the baptismal register (Cariou)

30%
20
10
•••• Breton language
boundary

7.3

Conscripts able to read and write in 1853

60%
50
40
30

7.4

Conscripts able at least to read in 1850
farmers and farm workers

35%
20
? no figures

7.5

Conscripts able at least to read in 1890
departmental average 76.54%

90 %
80
70
60

7.6

Religious observance in 1953

Easter communicants
(men and women aged 21 and over)

90%
75
60
40
? no figures

7.7

Morbihan

# CONCLUSION: THREE CENTURIES OF CULTURAL CROSS-FERTILIZATION

Thus, literacy is not schooling, and the history of the school by itself will not suffice to give a full account of the progress of literacy. Yet if this central link has so often been held to be self-evident, and if it has served as the common subsoil implicit in so many of the struggles in the 19th and 20th centuries, this is because through it the French have shared in an interpretation of their history. Marx, in *The Holy Family*, characterized this interpretation as the 'illusion of politics': the conviction that all change flows from the conscious action of people, and that human destiny is therefore in the hands of educators and legislators. It was hardly surprising then that the school, as the focus of such voluntarist belief, became the strategic fulcrum for the fashioning of minds, and a central issue in political struggle.

It was the French Revolution which brought the conflict to a head, but it was not at the origin of the issue. For from the very beginning Catholic Church had viewed the school as an instrument of social and intellectual control and, consequently, as a source of power whose exercise must be neither abandoned nor even shared. When the monarchic State intervened, particularly at the end of the 18th century, it was not so much to demand its portion as to set the seal, at the expense of the Protestants, upon the concept of a Catholic school whose task was to extirpate heresy once and for all; its intention was to place throughout the kingdom, down to the tiniest parish, a schoolmaster representative of the Revocation of the Edict of Nantes. A century before the Revolution, then, the school lay at the heart of religious conflict, as the instrument of one party against the other. So it is hardly surprising that the Revolution in its turn should have made it its standard against the old world, focusing upon it its hopes of changing the minds of men; it turned against the Church the very weapons of the Church, its educational beliefs and practices, for all were agreed that the minds of the young were utterly malleable, and that therefore the school could never be neutral. The Republic wanted its school to be republican, and for a century and a half made it the centre-stage its battle with the Church.

Two sorts of confusion arose thereby. For a start, the history of the school, over-burdened with ideological and political significance, has always been regarded as central to the history of literacy: people have viewed it either as the victory of enlightenment over obscurantism, or alternatively as that of the Church beset by republican persecution. As for the history of literacy itself, which has been a long, slow process of evolution and putting-down of roots, subject to a high degree of social inertia, people have confused it with the history of ideas about the school and its ideological rôle: but these clearly do not proceed at the same pace, nor are they subject to the same gravitational pulls.

Our inquiry becomes meaningful only if it has managed to set this history back on its feet; if it has succeeded in focusing attention on literacy itself, as a gateway to written culture; if it has restored to society itself the chief credit for this change. The Church, the State, the School are mere dramatis personae or agents.

The sequence of events, as shown in the first place by Maggiolo's survey, and as pinpointed by our supplementary surveys, by and large reveals – regardless of local or regional variations – a series of trends that are utterly independent of major political events, including the most important one, the French Revolution. The great battle that was then joined between Church and State for control of the schools appears to have had no decisive (nor even a particularly noteworthy) impact on the evolution of literacy scores. The reason for this, as we have seen, was that decisions taken by the Revolutionary Assemblies wrought no lasting change in the traditional school system, and still less so the periods of Terror in 1793 and 1797, whether Montagnard or Fructidorian. Which is evidence that this school system, far from being an institution imposed upon society from above, by government, was on the contrary the product of social demand for education, swelling in step with the gradual spread of a cultural model. This demand germinated and burgeoned in institutions other than the school – such as the family. In the last resort, also, it determined the distribution of schools, their type, their methods and their curriculum. By the time, a century after the Revolution, Jules Ferry fulfilled the Jacobin dream by establishing the republican, secular, free and compulsory school, the French were practically fully literate. The reason was that, in the previous two or three centuries to which Ferry was – unwittingly and unwillingly – heir, the communities of France had founded, run and financed schools of their own.

That is why both the chronology and the geography of French literacy are dependent less on the evolution of the school network than on the social history of France. The consequences of this are many and heavy. The obligation to gain admission to written culture was democratized first by Protestantism, and subsequently by the Counter-Reformation; but more than a condition of salvation, and for much longer, it represented the key to entry to the cultural model of the upper classes. Wherever we look, in every period, social stratification presides over the history of literacy. By the 17th century, the élites of the old kingdom of France could read, write and count, while the peasantry was still massively illiterate. Most of the spectacular progress made in the 18th century occurred among the middle ranks of the old society: merchants, shopkeepers, artisans, tenant farmers and rich peasants. Wage-labourers, especially in the countryside, formed a kind of residual though substantial stock, undented by progress in the surrounding milieu. It was only in the 19th century that they too became caught up in the general movement towards universal literacy, the timing of the process keeping pace with its gradual 'trickling down' through society.

The contrast between town and countryside, from this point of view, refers to much the same state of affairs: the reason why the towns achieved literacy earlier was that their population contained more lawyers, merchants, artisans, and fewer peasants or journeymen. So much so that in the 19th century, the mushrooming towns that grew up as a result of 'English-style' industrialization suffered a drop in average literacy rates owing to the massive influx of new wage-labourers. The *Ancien Régime* town, on the other hand, growing up and reigning over its peaceful countryside as market town and administrative centre, taking pride in its law-courts, its high school and its seminary, was a pole of literacy *par excellence*: not only because by definition it contained more 'bourgeois', in the old sense of the term, here foreshadowing the other, but because as a result of this they wielded greater influence over the rest of the population. The smaller towns, with a literate élite, thus enjoyed a decisive advantage: the élite was more important than elsewhere, and the example it set was visible to everyone. The urban history of literacy shows just how much importance old French society attached to admission to written culture, several centuries prior to the triumph of industrial capitalism. Seen from this angle, the French Revolution merely celebrated one of the great certainties of the *Ancien Régime*.

Finally, social development conditioned the spread of literacy with respect to regional disparities. The maps included in this book, which illustrate a France divided in two, reiterate and partially transpose the geographical distribution of social inequalities and disparities in socio-occupational structures. But they show too that the spread of literacy by and large conformed to the laws of uneven economic development:[1] literate France was, both globally and in detail, open-field France, with high farm productivity and well-to-do villages and peasant communities. The spread of literacy was born of the market economy, which contributed to the division of labour and to the growth of written communication, from the pinnacle of society downwards. The great religion of the Book, Protestantism, soon to be joined by the Counter-Reformation, could probably have made do with a modicum of reading ability on the part of the faithful, as in Sweden. But the market economy, backed by and relying upon the machinery of the centralized state, expanded the rôle of writing as a necessary condition of modernization. In fact, the true subject – and the mystery – of our inquiry is the transition from the religious to the 'modern' age.

So the descriptions and analyses contained in this book lead us less to a conclusion in the true sense than to further questions. For something lies beyond the language of figures and maps, namely the questions it enables us to ask.

Literacy: what a deceptive term that is if taken to imply a beginning – when no one can read or write – and an end – when everyone can! Down the two or three centuries whose history we have sought to reconstitute, what it suggests rather is a process in which, between the 17th century and the 1914–18 War, the French made their entry into written culture. But this long submerged history is not the story of a radical substitution of written for oral culture. For writing had pre-existed this collective acculturation; the oral tradition, meanwhile, has survived right into the middle of the 20th century.

Probably the most useful concept in seeking to understand the point at issue is that of restricted literacy, as defined by the English anthropologist Jack Goody.[2] What happened in France between Louis XIV and Jules Ferry is not, properly speaking, the spread of literacy among the French people; rather it is the transition from restricted to mass literacy. The reasons for restricted literacy may be chiefly technical, as in China, where non-phonetic writing was so difficult to learn and master that a small number of literati enjoyed a monopoly of it. Mostly, though, it is rooted in privileges relating to the handling of some sacred text by a specialized clergy trained for the purpose: the job of the masses here is to listen and commit to memory. In either case, however (technical or religious), the fact of having a monopoly over writing gave its possessors immense political and social power.

Now the civilization of the Christian Middle Ages was characterized by restricted literacy. It was associated with a book-centered religion, whose sole depositees and interpreters were the clergy; it was associated too with mass preaching, aimed at the ignorant crowd, which was expected to listen, memorize and chant. Writing, that secret of secrets, that language for initiates, that power of the clerks, existed solely for translation into the oral register. Scarce, fragile, confidential, it was inseparable, even for those who knew how to write, from the complementary exercises of memory and eloquence, as can be seen from the way rhetoric was taught in the Middle Ages. For the dominance of writing had not yet become the dominance of administrative rationality, which was then in limbo, it was still that of belief, which summoned up collective emotions, interpersonal and concrete transmission of the message: a dominance in which the book was still contaminated by commentary or litany, voices, or the murmur of men.

The history of the introduction of written culture to Tahiti,[3] as described by the members of the London Missionary Society at the beginning of the 19th century, is a perfect illustration of the functions performed by this culture in the history of Europe, of its chief agents, and of the mechanisms by which it established itself. This tardy, exotic laboratory for a transplanted. European culture offers us a caricature of the brutal import of writing into the Society Islands by the West, in which the local authorities aquiesced under pressure. In those waxworks of European history, the colonial institutions, we can just about make out the strange features, distorted by their extension in space and their contraction in time, of a civilization that seems natural to us because familiar.

The first missionaries sent out by the London Missionary Society settled in the Island of Tahiti in 1797, under the protection of King Pomaré I, whom they backed against his rivals. By 1805, Tahitian had become a written language, thanks to their intercession: a letter from the Roman alphabet was attributed to each sound to simplify learning, so that to spell a word was to pronounce it. Writing thenceforward became the twin banner of power and Christianity against oral culture and the rivals of the Pomaré dynasty. After his victory in 1815, Pomaré II founded a Catholic kingdom, whose subjects embraced the new religion. The book having been the vehicle for this conversion, the missionaries set themselves up as printers and schoolmasters; the press established in 1817 published all the books required for this dual process of literacy and catechization: spelling books, selected readings from the Old and New Testaments, uplifting stories from the Scriptures, religious booklets, sermons and prayer books. As well as being a vehicle for Christianization, written culture served as an instrument for the regulations, laws and codes inseparable from the 'civilization' of these islands. A touching 'European-style' family occasion took place in 1824, when the English missionaries who had organized the accession of Pomaré III, aged four, placed the crown upon his head, Bible in the right hand, legal code in the other. Lo and behold, writing was queen of the isles!

The missionaries seem to have been surprised by the aptitudes, and above all the extraordinary memories, of their new catechumens: in one year, adults learned to read the New Testament fluently, and were able to quote whole chapters by heart. The performance was an ambiguous one, though, for the pupils recited rather than read: some knew their spelling books thoroughly, but held them upside down; they all loved the hymnals, with their familiar metrical forms. In a word, the transition from oral to written culture occurred, in the first place, through memorization. Learning by rote was the heart of the old system of education, and it could serve as a useful stepping stone to the new one. The Tahitians reveal the same ambiguity of being able to 'read only' as characterized the literacy process in Europe. It is all the easier to spot here for having been introduced abruptly from without, imposed from above, with the result that written culture enjoyed even greater prestige here than among French peasants in the 18th and 19th centuries. It is more than just a sign of upward social mobility: it represents the superiority of the colonial world over the world of the natives. This accounts for the excessive devotion to the book, for the crush of local inhabitants around the printing presses, those flotillas of canoes laden with their cargoes of learning, and in many cases, probably, a symbolic simulation of reading, which was indispensable for the appropriation of the new object.

To this extent, 'reading', based on memorization, of religious texts amounted to no more than a veneer of colonial Christianity, coexisting with the more permanent traditional oral culture, which still held sway in the minds of the people. At this basic level it did not even imply a gradual transition towards another cultural world: rather it was the instrument for the substitution of one form of worship for another, of one form of domination for another, in which writing was worshipped as an image of secrecy, not of learning. That probably explains why it was reversible, not as in European history: the work of the missionaries in the Society Islands apparently did not survive the demise of the Pomaré dynasty, and an amateur anthropologist who visited the islands twice, in 1829 and 1830, the American consul 'to the Oceanian islands', recorded the 'retrograde' movement of the natives, their rapid backsliding from 'civilization' to their 'primitive state'. There were, to be sure, churches and schools in Tahiti, but no society to want or found them.

It was in the Renaissance that the European West rediscovered the conditions that had made possible the miracle of Greece and Rome, namely the phonetic alphabet, and the absence of a religious monopoly with a unique book. Even so, the advantages which Graeco-Roman civilization derived from the tolerance of its priests tended instead to be mirrored in Europe by competition among its clergy: once the book was open to more than one interpretation – although remaining, by mutual consensus, the key to salvation – the faithful now found themselves called upon to judge for themselves. Whereas Erasmian humanism had produced a secularized version of a culture revitalized by the model of Antiquity, for the use of the élite, Protestant heresy, on the other hand, democratized writing for the masses. The dissipation of the secret of the clerks spelled the end – in the long run – of a restricted literacy society. Paradoxically, writing came to Western Europe through religion, and doubtless throughout the learning process it retained its superstition of Latin, the language of the Church.

As early as the end of the 16th century, the post-Tridentine Catholics agreed with their Protestant rivals that literacy ought to be universal. That was the great revolution, the dividing line between two epochs, two kinds of relation between individuals and the written word. Beforehand, in the restricted literacy society, the text had been sacred, and contained truth. To approach it demanded endless coded study: because it was constantly repetitive, like some interminable genealogy, whose enigmas the scholar strives to decipher in order to winkle the truth out of them. In material terms, writing was a copyist's art, a form of drawing, a collective exercise in symbolism, in the same way as reading was an exercise in chanting. Recopying and repetition illustrate writing's dependence on the oral tradition; the rôle of the former was merely to pin down the latter and prevent it from getting lost. But things were very different once everyone was able to read and write. The individual's relation to the written text underwent complete transformation: the function of the cultural mediator had no further justification, and from having been collective, the conditions of communication became individual. Writing now concealed an 'I' and no longer a 'he'; reading revealed a content, and no longer a mere remembrance.

This mutation – of which the invention of printing merely furnished the technological condition – was thus inherent in the heresies of Protestantism, which from the moment of their victory introduced pluralism into reading (i.e. turned it into an individual exercise). In fact, though, this did not happen quite as swiftly as the principle suggests. All it did was to usher in a period in our history – the one that forms the subject of this book – during which the whole of society made its entry into written culture. It did so at very different paces, and had to overcome lengthy resistance on the part of traditional culture, which was founded on speech. The information we have gathered perhaps allows us to advance a number of hypotheses on these long centuries of cross-fertilization between the oral tradition and the written word.

For a long time, the distinction between reading and oral communication was unclear. In the school curriculum it was merely the first, quite distinct, step in the literacy process: the most universal, but also the most rudimentary. This reflected the Church's long-held view of reading as, principally, the means of ensuring collective celebration of Church ritual. Reading, which was learned first of all in Latin – at school, in church or at home – only gradually became dissociated from the act of memorization; where it was not linked with ability to write, it amounted more to a mnemonic for an illustration than a means of deciphering a text. It did not change the individual's relation to culture: it confirmed it. Morally speaking, it was innocent, confining itself to the reception – generally collective (i.e. public) – of the divine message. It implied neither the autonomy of the individual, nor the obligation to exercise at least a modicum of intellectual freedom, nor again the beginnings of an inner break with the restraints of the community. Writing means being able to communicate in secret, individual to individual. Reading by itself is merely a passive activity: the fact of receiving the message does not really ensure admission to the new cultural circuit. This is presumably what a peasant in Quercy was trying to say when he told the author that until recently many of the girls in his canton had been able to read only, not write: 'The nuns didn't want them to be able to write to their sweethearts.'[4]

In so far as residual data for the 19th century allow us to assume, it is quite probable that there was in ancient France, and especially in that part of France where the school was least securely established, a very widespread semi-literacy based on reading, organized by the Church and in the home, and chiefly intended for girls: this phenomenon would tend to be evidence of religiosity rather than of any concern for modernization. Until sometime in the 19th century this rudimentary, lopsided, education did nothing to alter the traditional means of communication among the rural population: this concession on the part of the Church to the spirit of the times served to consolidate the power and the prestige of written religion over these regions and folk with their oral culture.

In 1709, one Jean-Baptiste de Guigues, priest at Tourettes, in the diocese of Vence, was accused by the ecclesiastical court of owning Jansenist books and of allowing his flock to read them.[5] In fact, several witnesses testified that the priest lent his books not only to men but also to women, far more of whom were implicated in the case. Honnorade Isnard, 'wife of Etienne Curel, labourer on the land', had read *La Vie mystique de Jésus Christ, L'Instruction à la pénitence* and *La Conduite chrétienne*, which de Guigues had lent her. She had read the services written by the priest on the grandeur of Jesus, the Child Jesus and the name of Jesus. Among these devout women was a schoolmistress, Louise Gazagnaire. She had read two volumes of the *Testament nouveau avec des Réflexions* and *Savoir sur l'Epître de saint Pierre et sur l'Evangile de saint Jean*, belonging to the lady of Tourettes and lent by de Guigues. She too had read the priest's services. Yet she was unable to sign her name. Indeed, none of the women who gave evidence at the trial were able to sign their names. Thus Jansenism, that learned devotional form, with its bookish refinement, trickled down to the lower classes through reading, whose sole purpose was to receive the word of God. Men and women who could not read listened to others reciting it, or learned to chant it from memory. This was the function of the 'social evenings' so heavily criticized at the priest's trial; far into the night, the 'congregation' of women in the parish would gather at Louise Gazagnaire's. They often sang or chanted until midnight, 'which created a big scandal in the neighbourhood'. It was at these meetings, according to one witness, that de Guigues would hold readings of Amelot's *Le Nouveau Testament* and *L'Imitation de Jésus Christ*.

Another witness stated that these social gatherings had taken place prior to the arrival of the Jansenist priest, and we have every reason to think that in the France of the past they often served as a place of religious socialization, for women especially. Through them, books were annexed to the tradition of community culture, based on rote learning and oral communication.

Writing represented modernization, modernity. What transformed the act of reading into a silent, internal, individual exercise was the conquest of writing. Without writing, reading was powerless to withstand the group pressures which the oral tradition exerted on the individual. Alone, the democratization of the art of writing paved the way for a new kind of relation with the social and natural world, thereby transforming the conditions of reading. It was this that triggered the transition from 'restricted literacy' to general literacy (in the two senses of intellectually complete and socially widespread). To be sure, this transition did not occur in the space of a single generation, nor even in one century: in the case of France it took three centuries, and dating is made all the harder by the fact that the spread of general literacy throughout society long assumed the features of the previous period, that of restricted literacy. For example, until the French Revolution, most people learned to read in Latin. Again, right up to the mid-19th century, the technique of writing retained its bewildering formal complexity, with the variety of handwritings testifying to its status as a rare and learned art.

For the spread of writing presupposed the divulgence of a corporate secret, an exclusive form of power: that of being able to communicate beyond the control of the group, i.e. beyond the control of tradition. The upshot was that the whole of society now gradually found itself splitting into autonomous units (or at least more or less independent of the collective voice, which is the wisdom of the ages). This transformation of the dominant mode of communication even modified the social fabric itself, breaking up the group in favour of the individual. Oral culture is public, collective; written culture is secretive and personal. It is a great silence, inside which the individual carves out a free private space for himself.

It establishes a new relation between time and space, for the benefit of those able to master its economy. Indeed, specifically historical sensibility begins with writing. Before, no one ever records the sequence of men and events; it is viewed exclusively through an original matrix, which is assumed to reproduce the same thing over and over again, as though the present was at all times absorbing all of the past, in an endless process of repetition. By setting down on paper markers to record the passage of time, births and deaths for example, writing frees individuals from the tyranny of the present; it enables us to establish the 'pastness of the past' (J. Goody). This activity, which is infinitely more abstract than speaking or listening, also detaches the writer from what he is writing: time can be related. It is the present which, in a sense, has ceased to exist, since even the thing that pins it down constitutes a past.

This transition from repetitive time (i.e. non-time) to linear time in individual consciousness is accompanied, in the group, by the preservation and selective appropriation of this past through writing: archives contain what amounts to its *available* memory, as distinct from the real memories of its different members, whereas oral culture indiscriminately mingles both sorts of memory handed down by word of mouth, from one generation to the next, of the secret of the community's origins. This process of transforming the past into a heritage by means of writing thus establishes the difference between history and religion: the group possesses a specific time of its own, which is punctuated by identified and recorded events.

Of course, this time, although pinned down and appropriated by the written word, may yet remain religious in character, created and governed by a transcendental being such as the biblical God. In that case it serves as a universal, model time, a tale of the Beginning written down once and for all, around which all particular histories of humanity revolve. Even so, it is still *history*, in other words a time-vector, open to the creative, cumulative activity of mankind and its societies. It helps us to distinguish the past from the beginnings, and consequently from the present: in a word, it constitutes that present.

The written word is in that case the legatee of this past. It allows it to exist both in terms of the ego and in terms of the group. The archivist and the historian are its specialist guardians, but in fact every member of the community can have access to this collective memory, which is both more reliable and above all older than their own. The recording of events, the fact of relating them and celebrating them, tends to supply the group with a foundation that is simultaneously secularized and particularist. Now comes the time of the history of the City, which in Europe's case was to become the history of the nation. Even when much in this history has come down from the oral tradition or mythology, it is obliged, merely because it is written down, to rationalize the passage of time. Herodotus paved the way for Thucydides.

In the process, the written word binds the individual to a human entity vaster than the group with which he shares the community's oral tradition. Face-to-face discussion presupposes close neighbourliness, whereas the written word multiplies and standardizes information for an intellectually individualized, geographically scattered, world. It would be more accurate to say that the first thing the written word did was to break down relations between the individual and the fragile group formed by oral communication, transferring those relations to a broader, different community. Speech is no longer inseparable from the empirical moments out of which it springs; it is abstract, general, cumulative, presupposing a minimum number of recipients capable of understanding it, necessarily on its level of abstraction, generalization and knowledge. What now underwrites relations between individuals is no longer the immemorial utterances of old men, acting as guardians of local jurisprudence, but the dual authority of the market and the State, sealed in writing and embodied in contract and law. As money is the general equivalent of commodities, so the contract is the general form given to the will of the individual. For two groups to exchange goods or women, all that is needed is for them to live stably in geographical proximity, and for there to be an oral tradition between them, regulating these exchanges, which are programmed for the two communities. But for two individuals to perform the same operation, they first need to be constituted as such, i.e. as free, abstract units, acting in their own right: freed from group and geographical constraints, and founders of a new code to regulate the market in individual wills. The written word is alone capable of pinning down the *particular* terms agreed upon in discussion, the signature of each contracting party guaranteeing performance. Witnesses, those depositees of agreements concluded, cease to exist save at marriage ceremonies: the group likes to keep an eye on exchanges of women. But the exchange of goods is consigned to the secrecy of the contract, which is constitutive of free and equal individuals, in other words, of the market. To sign one's name is to step over the frontier.

The other guarantee backing dealings between individuals is the State. But the State too is the written word. A contract is meaningless except in terms of the law. Without writing, after all, there can be no general law sufficiently abstract to be applicable to the multitude of different cases imaginable. Without writing, all that would remain would be tradition, or custom, preserved and handed down by old men, whose knowledge derives not from what they have learned but from what they have seen: they are the collective memory of the group's experience. Now when this tradition or custom is consigned to paper, through the intermediary of the notary (for civil law) or the lawyer (for public law), it escapes simultaneously both the concrete experience and the arbitration of the old: it hands down principles and doctrine, of which jurisprudence is an illustration. The written law is an abstract universal. The emergence of the State is the fruit of the obedience and even the respect due to it.

When it comes to obedience, the State has the means to constrain people to it, physical violence being the most blatant of these. Writing is another, though more subtle, and perhaps more fundamental: it is the written word which establishes direct communication between State and individual, 'liberated' from the tyranny – or the protection – of the group; it is through the written word, as it short-circuits the barriers erected by the oral community, that each subject or citizen is recorded and defined by his social co-ordinates: born on such-and-such a date, of this father and that mother, in the town of X, occupying some specific profession, and so on. The tax rolls were the first manifestation of this political individualization; this was the condition of State rule, which is probably why, independently even of the monetary contribution it heralds, this so often aroused the hostility of traditional communities, from the parish to the assemblies of the nobility.

At a later phase in the development of the State, the accumulation and storage of these written biographical traces made possible the process of statistical aggregation, which is a method of envisaging the collective through, and on the basis of, the individual. This is a central paradox, one that has always been crucial to European political philosophy, and statistics are the modern State's operational response to it, its thirst for knowledge being inseparable from its desire to manipulate people. It was the abstract thought of distinct individuals that supplied the intellectual groundwork for statistics, and it was the fact that these individuals were themselves recorded and noted down which made the operation technically feasible; statistics then organized them into comparable, interchangeable units, and henceforward subject to calculated probabilities (this speciality too made its appearance around the same time), in other words, definable in terms of what is identical in their behaviour and rôles. The outcome was a mechanical vision of society, subject precisely to the laws of its constituent mechanism: no longer a group consciousness, but a form of knowledge-cum-domination.

Seventeenth-century English political arithmetic, Prussian political arithmetic in the 18th century and French mercantilism in the same age, were doctrines of national might and head-counting techniques: the strength of the modern State was measured in terms of the number of its subjects. From this, military strength was derived, of course, but it was rooted in economic and monetary wealth: the counting of men and their incomes yielded a tax base and thus defined the resources of the State. Before becoming one of the values of our civilization, the individual was an accounting unit: more important than the honour accorded him by society is the fact that he is manipulated by the State; before representing the image of freedom and equality in the form of inner consciousness, he is first defined externally by his measurable characteristics and by what he shares with all his fellow men. The egalitarian function of State centralization precedes the egalitarian religion of individualist philosophy. The former imposes the written word through obedience to the temporal power, whereas the latter internalizes its implied values.

This is because it is not enough merely to obey the written law; it demands respect as well, in other words internal acceptance. Now this, however, is only lastingly acquired through a minimum of access to the intellectual world that makes the very notion of law meaningful. At the simplest and most factual level, 'ignorance of the law excuses no man', which implies a minimum of literacy; in any case, in his everyday life the individual is increasingly hemmed in by the State and its laws, so much so that ignorance is turning into a kind of social handicap. Even when, being unable to read or write, the individual cannot know the law, he must at least internalize the spirit of it, and however ignorant he may be he must accept this new form of socialization: the secret of good conduct soon passed out of the hands of the old – who had been its trustees because they had lived through so much – and into those of the schoolmaster, the notary, the magistrate – because they had read everything. The parish priest, who represents a kind of half-way figure between the oral tradition and writing in our history, gradually ceased to embody written civilization as the triumph of the latter spread. General literacy claimed two sets of victims, the parish priests and old people, by robbing the former of the secret of their prestige and the latter of the utility of their memory.

What they lost was reinvested in the abstract community, and in its symbol the State: what we now call 'politics' – i.e. the sphere of dealings between individuals and the State, and of the struggle for power as such – does after all presuppose the existence of a broadly dominant written civilization. In oral or restricted literacy societies, politics never manages to establish organizations of its own: struggles for power do take place, but they are waged by traditional communities according to their own view of themselves based on oral consensus, and hence enveloped in religion or rooted in changeless tradition.

By engendering the individual in his social context, the generalization of writing threw up a new problem, that of how to integrate the individual into the community, posing this as a distinct, abstract question: it substituted ideology for religion, assuming we are prepared to apply the word ideological to the new manner of envisioning society in secularized terms, in such a way as to re-establish a correspondence between individual and society in written culture. Ideology is a representation of social life in terms of the historical action of individuals; it presupposes the collapse of the traditional community and of oral transmission of information. It places the individual in a new vision of society by means of the representations or values of written culture, which society is then supposed to embody, attain or accomplish through the free activity of its members.

Laurence Stone[6] notes that the three great revolutions of modern times, in 17th-century England, in France at the end of the 18th century and in Russia at the beginning of the 20th, all coincided with a moment at which half the male population had achieved literacy. If we are to read into this similarity anything other than coincidence, then it is precisely the fact that as a modern political phenomenon revolution is characterized by the emergence of a new kind of relation between State and individual, going hand in hand with the development of written culture: this relation confirms both the autonomy and the importance attached to the individual as the bases of the new political civilization, and his egalitarian integration into the nation-State through ideology. From these two standpoints, destructive and reconstructive, disintegrating and reintegrating, this relation presupposes that writing is widespread in the population: how, for instance, could we conceive of the explosion and the dissemination of Jacobinism between 1789 and 1793 without this prior acculturation, or without the availability of this means of transmission?

Of course, this is not to say that Jacobinism was confined to the literate section of the population: there are a certain number of 'bridges' between oral and written culture, such as the reading of newspapers in public, by members of the *clubs populaires* – but this is tantamount to saying that a phenomenon such as Jacobinism was an expression of an already-dominant written culture even among the masses. It was a culture that was at great pains, moreover, to repress minority languages as symbols of the past, as symbols of an impoverished form of communication, of a community that was not 'national'.[7]

By modifying the system of communication and the transmission of information, writing transformed social relations in their entirety; at the same time, it was through it that the new relations became firmly established. The notary's deed, or the deed merely made official by a commissioner for oaths, is to the private sphere what the constitution is to the public: it institutes rights, property and status, and stands guard over them. It supplants ritual in celebrating the events of people's lives: one's signature, crucial evidence that one can write, now bears witness to the key moments in life and is the sole guarantor of their permanence. The traditional wedding ceremony, for instance, with its carefully coded exchange of gestures and words, tends to be supplanted by the bridal couple's signatures; the participation of the community in the event, and its sanction, gradually give way to the symbolic presence of witnesses. The marriage 'deed', once a collective representation, has become a slip of paper. It is as if in literate societies writing played the part performed by collective rituals in oral civilizations: it incarnates the very existence of that society, endowing it with foundations in a specific space-time which thenceforward dominates all social behaviour.[8]

It is significant, from this point of view, that it was the French Revolution which most intransigently insisted on the benefits of written culture as opposed to the pernicious influence of oral tradition: this belief, which the Revolution bequeathed to republican generations throughout the 19th century, is part and parcel of its constituent ideology, according to which its function is to wrench communities from their past in one blow, in order to point the way to *another* future. The written word is conceived of as instrumental in breaking with the everyday life of the *Ancien Régime* and as a means of instituting new customs and habits, which alone might assure the long-term survival of the public weal embodied by the Revolution.

The conception, which was inseparable from that of Jacobinism as a 'life-renewing' force, was particularly clear-cut in the Directory period, when it shone forth in all its institutional transparency: the Jacobins no longer enjoyed the dynamic, organized support of the *clubs populaires*, and to counter the royalist upsurge they were obliged to lash the Revolution to whatever mooring point – legislative or imaginary – they could find in the institutions. As witnessed by the report submitted by a deputy for Maine-et-Loire to the Council of the Five Hundred, J-B. Leclerc, on 16 Brumaire Year VI.[9] This was just after the coup of 18 Fructidor: its aim was to wean citizens away from the bad habits upon which the royalist reaction fed; to put a stop to what he termed 'this retrograde development', the rapporteur proposed to intervene in the 'private morals' of the citizens, i.e. in their family life, by instituting a 'family book' which would serve both as its written memory and an instrument for the celebration of a private cult, guaranteeing public morality.

The family book (or album or commonplace book) was to contain certificates of birth or adoption, civil registration, marriage, guardianship, wardship, and death. These certificates would accumulate in the natural order of the events they were supposed to record, and would be separated by a blank space to be filled in by lists of prizes won on different occasions, either in the State schools or public festivities. There would in addition be room for a record of occasions when one had acted as witness in a marriage, and adoption or any other civil deed, as for those when one had the misfortune to lose a child, a relative or a friend. There would also be space to mention public posts achieved, either by election or by governmental appointment. These records entered into the family book would differ from official records in the sense that they would concentrate on the moral aspect of events marking the chief moments in life, not forgetting the purely civil forms in the case of the most important occasions, knowledge of which is necessary to facilitate settlement of family interests and disputes. This book would be brought out at all occasions connected with the civil register, and each deed would be authenticated by the same signatures as those required for the public records. There would be very stiff penalties for forgeries or the entering of information other than what was prescribed by the law, as well as for deliberate damage to or defacement of a family book, whether one's own or someone else's: everything, even mere disrespect for this institution, was to be severely checked.

On the death of the two spouses, the book would pass to their eldest child, or to their closest heir. Its preservation was to be a sacred duty. Its owner would be bound to communicate it to all other members of the family, who would be entitled to sue in the event of refusal, damage, defacement or forgery; he would also be duty bound to present it to the magistrate-inspector of public schooling, who would be empowered to lay charges against anyone breaking the laws relating to this book.

Nobody could apply for civil registration without a family book, nor could anyone be entitled to one until deemed fit to own one by his education and his morality. Immediately after the civil registration ceremony, the individual's birth certificate would be entered into the book, along with any prizes he might have won, and the book would accompany him through all the events of his life.

Thus the institution of a family record would perform a function at once civil, moral and political. It would contain the civil records (birth, marriage, etc.) as well as deeds relating to the interests of the family, so as to furnish each family with precise information about itself. But it would relate this private history in moral terms, so that the record of it might serve as an example and a matter for celebration. Lastly, it would at all times serve the Republic, since this instrument of what Leclerc termed 'domestic surveillance' also helped to ensure public morality. As an infallible substitute for individual recollection, as the principal repository of virtue, elevated into a ritual, the written word was given the task of reconstituting republican society from its basic units upwards; the family had become the focus of the beneficial commemoration which the written word made possible: unable to contemplate a collective past sullied by the Terror, the Republic now envisaged a future founded upon these archives of private virtues.

The written word is, simultaneously, the basis for the new morality, i.e. respectability, the means through which it is perpetuated, and the means whereby the 'familial' may be re-aggregated with the 'social', through shared celebration. The 'lonely crowd'[10] of families thus rediscovers communion with the Republic through a book that recounts its virtues.

The Thermidorian dream of using this family book of examples to build an entirely new and utterly good society was merely a transposition into family terms of the Jacobin belief in the virtues of written culture: for the men of 1797, as for those of 1793, the dichotomy between oral and written was coterminous with the temporal opposition between old and new, barbarity and enlightenment, good and bad behaviour, which gave meaning to the revolutionary upheaval and to the order it was now creating; whether transmitted through the school or through the family, writing was both a vehicle for and a symbol of the advent of civic and private virtue, and at the same time an instrument of republican surveillance.

The elements of this ancient belief date back to Protestantism, before the Catholic Reformation took them over, until finally, in a secularized, radicalized form, they emerged as the favoured breeding ground of republican mythology. For only the written word lent plausibility to the idea of a complete break with the past, following the example of the

Revolution itself: an end to tradition, the emergence of a humanity reconciled with reason and morality. However illusory, this should not blind us to its constant, profound insight, namely that the spread of writing throughout the entire nation had generated a new tissue of social communication, subjecting people's behaviour to the arbitration of a new 'reason'. Stendhal, an attentive, critical observer of this cultural revolution, was the first to sense the ambiguity of the effects of access to this 'reason' – the key to what the Enlightenment had called 'civilization', which had thereby acquired universal prestige. He was one of the first to grasp the fact that it wrenched the individual from the profounder life of the instincts and the passions. Several times, in his travels through France,[11] Stendhal notes the backwardness of the south compared with the north, but especially that of the south-west, Aquitaine. Already, apparently ignorant of Brittany's problems, he guessed that it was here, increasingly, that peasant illiteracy had come to lodge in 19th century France. Like a worthy son of the Enlightenment (in its Jacobinized version), he deplored this illiteracy. But at the same time, he could not help extending to the south of France his sensual affection for Italy and the intellectual blessings which he bestowed upon these lands of sun and passion, reservoirs of natural energy, and hence of superior men. 'A Minister of the Interior,' he wrote in *Henry Brulard*,[12]

> concerned to do his job rather than intrigue with the King and in the Assemblies, like M. Guizot, would do well to request a subsidy of two millions a year to raise, to bring up to the level of education of the rest of the French people, those who live in the fatal triangle stretching between Bordeaux, Bayonne and Valence. They believe in witches, they cannot read and they do not speak French in these parts. They may, by chance, produce a superior being such as Lannes, or Soult, but in general . . . they are unbelievably ignorant.

Yet the very next sentence, without warning, contradicts that 'by chance':

> I think that because of the climate, and the love and the energy with which it fires the [human] machine, this triangle ought to produce the greatest men in France. Corsica makes me think so. With 180,000 inhabitants, this island has given eight or ten men of merit to the Revolution, and the *département* of Nord, with its 900,000 inhabitants, scarcely one. And even then, I could not say who that *one* was.

Finally, without transition, he reverts to his initial pessimism:

> It goes without saying that the priests are all-powerful in this fatal triangle. Civilization runs from Lille to Rennes and stops around

Orléans and Tours. To the south-east, Grenoble is a shining outpost.

Was it so fatal, this triangle, or was it providential? Was it a sanctuary of clerical obscurantism, or a nursery of future Bonapartes? What is interesting in this Stendhalian contradiction is not so much its mistaken conception of the Church's part in the acculturation of the Occitanian peasantry (since the said Church was very unevenly represented in this 'triangle' and because where it was strong, as in the Velay or the Rouergue, it acted as a force for basic literacy, either through the school or directly): this erroneous view was consonant with his Jacobin convictions. The interesting thing about this incoherent judgement, pronounced by an otherwise acutely perceptive man, was his very modern insight – expressed in his quirky statistical computation of great men – into the ambiguous benefits of written culture: the emergence of a nationality that left no room for witches, but at the same time the impoverishment of powerful spirits through the censorship which it imposes upon individual *furia*. Just as he loved the people yet could not stand contact with it, so he advocated instruction for the people while regretting the passing of all that the old world had allowed in the way of freedom of instinct and passion. For this aristocrat of democracy, the literary vision of a natural, sensual Midi, where rationalization or standardized behaviour are unknown, counterbalances his political conviction of the virtues of 'civilization'. In this, Stendhal speaks less to the reader of 1880, to whom he was ostensibly addressing himself, than to the present-day reader, to whom he still sounds like a brother.

This is because the transition from one culture to another is a slow, partial process, like a long, endless rending asunder. As we can see from the figures, it took three or four centuries: which means that over a very long period (differing from one geographic zone to another, possibly lasting right into the early years of this century in the more backward parts of France) the cultural level of the country was one of restricted literacy. Restricted to certain provinces; restricted to men, to the exclusion of women; restricted to certain social groups, to the exclusion of the poorest peasants; restricted too to the bare minimum, which means that writing was not always taught, and that the age-old loyalty to the subjective ties of solidarity found in oral tradition did not always disappear. Even in northern France and north-eastern France, which had achieved high thresholds of literacy by the 18th century, it is clear that cultural traditions still lived on in the villages, even where, as we have seen in the childhood of Monsieur Nicolas, these gradually mingled with book culture. What is more, the combination of upward social mobility and emigration, which schooling provided for the more gifted country children, helped to preserve oral traditions through the agency of the mass of those who stayed behind, although these oral traditions had become tinged with regret and, soon, discredit. In the latter half of the 19th century, the south of France, fast catching up educationally and culturally, furnished the Third Republic with its officials, yet this did not transform village life in the south. By offering a chance of escape, and even merely by embodying the image of employment of another kind, the school raised a barrier between the community and its potential 'modernizers'; it helped to entrap the community in its traditions, even though these were now felt to be residual.

This long history of the spread of literacy in France is therefore an integral part of a dialectical to-and-fro between institutions and society. Its roots lay in the dominance of written culture, which from very early on both society and the State had embraced, encouraged and cultivated as a harbinger of progress; but for a very long time, and even now, the business of learning and the practice of this culture is intimately bound up with oral communication. For centuries, as he was slowly being torn from his roots, the French peasant was a cultural half-breed. So much so that this book will some day have to be rewritten, using other sources and facts, looking behind the figures and hypotheses given here to examine the history of this anthropological mutation.

# NOTES

## 1 The spread of literacy in France, a one-way ride

1     M. Fleury et P. Valmary, 1957.

2     Maggiolo, 1874, 1875, etc.

3     Ch. Dupin, 1827.

4     Published sources, 19th-century education, II, 1.

5     Priests had been obliged to sign marriage proceedings in the parish registers since the Ordinance of Villers-Cotterets, 1539. But it was not until the Ordinance of 1667 (commonly known as the 'Code Louis') that the newly-weds themselves were ordered to sign the proceedings, together with four witnesses. Article 10 under Heading XX even stipulates: 'If none of them knows how to sign, they shall declare it so and shall in consequence be reprimanded by the vicar or priest, and this shall be recorded.' (Jacques Levron, 1959)

6     Published sources, 19th-century education, I, 1.

7     Published sources, 19th-century education, 1, 4, vol. II.

8     Leaving aside more than forty articles in Ferdinand Buisson's *Dictionnaire de pédagogie*, Maggiolo published a further fifteen or so books and articles after 1880, covering education in Lorraine and on the Revolutionary 'fêtes', on the Abbé Grégoire and François de Neufchâteau, etc. In 1889, he announced ('if God give me life') for the following year, the second and third parts of his book on schools in Lorraine, and a major study of the life and work of François de Neufchâteau.

9     The Statistical Commission for Primary Education was set up in March 1876 by the then Minister of Education and Worship, Henri Wallon. Its chairman was E. Levasseur, Member of the Institute, Professor at the Collège de France and at the Conservatoire Nationale des Arts et Métiers. The commission had seventeen members, including Ferdinand Buisson, who was in charge of primary education at the Ministry of Education, and Octave Gréard, *vice-recteur* of the *Académie* of Paris.

10    The only 19th-century population censuses containing information as to people's educational levels were those of 1866 and 1872. Not until 1901 was further such information sought. The type of information on education furnished by the 1866 and 1872 censuses is discussed below, p. 14.

11    Ministerial letter dated 9 January 1865.

12    According to E. Lavasseur, who signed this report of the Statistical Commission on Primary Education, the two prime architects (of the report) were Ferdinand Buisson, 'who, together with the Chairman, worked out the main lines of the Report', and Octave Gréard 'who discussed it in detail and, with his great competence in the matter, revised the draft'. (Published sources, 19th-century education, I, 4, vol. II.)

322 Notes to pages 11–32

13   The simultaneous teaching of reading and writing spread slowly through the French school system in the course of the 19th century. Introduced by the mutual schools under the Restoration, this novelty was adopted by the 'Statute' of 25 April 1834: basing itself on the 1833 Guizot Act, this required that the different subjects – in particular reading, writing and arithmetic – be taught simultaneously 'from Form 1' (pupils aged 6 to 8). But it took some decades for this reform to be applied in full in all schools.

14   R. Schofield, 1968.

15   F. Furet and W. Sachs, 1974.

16   M. Fleury and P. Valmary, 1957 (note 15, p. 77).

17   *Ibid.* (p. 80).

18   J. Houdaille, 1977.

19   M. Vovelle, 1972.

20   These investigations were conducted by a team of researchers from the Centre de Recherches Historiques (VIth Section of the Ecole Pratique des Hautes Etudes), and the main findings are published in the second volume of this book (not published in English). These refer to Muriel Jeorger's study of Normandy, Véronique Nahoum's work on Champagne, and studies by Marie-Laurence Netter on Brie, Yvonne Pasquet on Vienne and by Marie-Madeleine Compère on Languedoc. To these we have added contributions by Pierre Lévêque on Burgundy, Paul Butel, Guy Mandon and Jean-Pierre Poussou on Aquitaine and the south-west, also published in the second volume of this book. Lastly, in her doctoral thesis on the history of literacy in Haute-Garonne and Yonne, Marie-Laurence Netter obtains the following results, reproduced below with her kind permission:

| | 1686-1690 | | 1786-1790 | | 1816-1820 | |
|---|---|---|---|---|---|---|
| | M | W | M | W | M | W |
| HAUTE-GARONNE | | | | | | |
| Less Toulouse | 12.9 | 4.7 | 19.8 | 8.1 | 27.3 | 10.1 |
| With Toulouse | 16.5 | 6.2 | 26 | 10.6 | 39.2 | 19.4 |
| Maggiolo | 7.5 | 2.3 | 18 | 5.3 | 45 | 13.1 |
| | | | | | | |
| YONNE | | | | | | |
| Less Avallon | 27.9 | 11.2 | 34.9 | 14.4 | 47 | 20.3 |
| With Avallon | 28 | 11.4 | 36.9 | 16.6 | 50.5 | 25.6 |
| Maggiolo | 32.9 | 15 | 48.4 | 22.3 | 56.6 | 30.5 |

   The greatest discrepancy between M.-L. Netter's surveys and Maggiolo's figures concerns male scores in Haute-Garonne in the aftermath of the French Revolution. In both cases, literacy spread rapidly during the Revolution and under the Empire, but Maggiolo's figures amplify this progress by comparison with those established by M.-L. Netter.

21   We have considered urban areas of over 2,000 inhabitants as towns.

22   Substitution of marriage signatures taken from the *Statistique générale de la France*, from 1854 onwards, leads to a relative over-estimation of scores by comparison with Maggiolo's figures, since those contained in the

*Statistique générale de la France* are complete and therefore include urban marriages, which Maggiolo's survey had neglected. But this over-estimation refers to a period when rural scores had already drawn considerably closer to urban ones, so it only amounts to a slight exaggeration. It is inevitable, in any case, since Maggiolo himself very probably drew his own figures for 1866 from the *Statistique générale de la France*.

23   In addition, thirteen *départements* had comparable rates of growth for men and women alike. The others are those missing from Maggiolo's survey.

24   See the article by W.S. Robinson in the *American Sociological Review*, 15(3), 1950, p. 351.

25   Manuscript sources, '*Institut pédagogique national*'.

26   Pierre Chaunu, 1971 (p. 150). This Lower-Norman chronology is based on figures cited in several dozen M.A. theses.

27   Jean-Claude Perrot, 1975.

28   In 1883, at the request of the *Société Archéologique*, and with encouragement from Ferdinand Buisson, the Inspector of the *Academie* of Limoges, L. Galliard, had the teachers of his *département* carry out the survey which we have commented on here. The results were presented and discussed by Louis Guilbert in a booklet printed in Limoges in 1888, under the meaningful title: *L'instruction primaire en Limousin sous l'Ancien Régime*.

## 2   The school, the *Ancièn Régime* and the Revolution

1    Allain, 1883.
2    D. Julia, 1972.
3    L. Stone, 1969.
4    F. Buisson, 1882. E. Johansson, 1974.
5    Allain, 1883.
6    C. J. Hefele, Vol. x, 1938.
7    A. Artonne, L. Guizard, O. Pontal, 1969. The list of Synodal statutes used is given in the bibliography of 'Printed sources'.
8    *Statuts et ordonnances du diocèse d'Angers.*
9    *Statuts et ordonnances du diocèse d'Amiens.*
10   Groethuysen, 1939.
11   See note 8.
12   Allain, 1883.
13   Chartier, Compère, Julia, 1976.
14   *Ibid.* p. 37.
15   *Ibid.* p. 37.
16   *Ibid.* p. 38.
17   *Ibid.* p. 39.
18   J.-J. Rousseau (1761), 1969.
19   Chartier, Compère, Julia, 1976.
20   Yves Poutet (1654), 1963, 1970.
21   Tocqueville (1856), 1963.
22   See chapter 1.
23   A. de Rohan-Chabot, 1969.
24   L. Borne, 1957.
25   L. Perouas, 1964.

26     M. Laget, 1971, 1972.
27     M. Vovelle, 1975.
28     Y. Poutet, 1970. Robillard de Beaurepaire, 1872.
29     A. de Rohan-Chabot, 1969.
30     Emile Souvestre, 1860. Jean Meyer, 1974.
31     Martin Nadaud (1895), 1948.
32     *Ordonnances et règlements synodaux pour le diocèse de La Rochelle.*
33     *Actes de la province ecclésiastique de Reims, 1842–44. Lettre rélative aux écoles du diocèse d'Amiens, 1641.*
34     N. Restif de la Bretonne (1796), 1959.
35     Muriel Jeorger.
36     Published sources, 17th-and 18-century education, *L'Escole paroissiale,* 1654.
37     Yves Poutet.
38     An elementary school where Latin was taught.
39     *Statuts et ordonnances du diocèse d'Angers,* 1680.
40     Yves Poutet, 1960, 1962.
41     Jean Meyer, 1974.
42     George Sand (1854–55), 1968.
43     Yves Poutet, 1970.
44     Quéniart, 1975.
45     Jean-Baptiste de la Salle, 1720.
46     Michel Foucault, 1975.
47     Quéniart, 1975.
48     Le Roy Ladurie, 1972.
49     Charles Dupin, 1827.
50     Gabriel Compayré (1879), 1970.
51     Maurice Gontard, 1959.
52     Certeau, Julia, Revel, 1975.
53     'Plaine' was the name given to the uncommitted 'Moderate' deputies in the Convention (1792).
54     Speech delivered on 1 August 1793, concerning the Lepeletier plan presented by Robespierre on 13 July. *Archives parlementaires,* Vol. LXX, Ist. series, p. 83.
55     'The mountain' was the Jacobin faction in the Convention, so-called because they occupied the high seats at the back of the Assembly.
56     A.D. Loir-et-Cher, L 765.
57     The departmental archives (A.D.) consulted for this period of our history of the school are listed under *Enquêtes révolutionnaires sur l'école* (series L).
58     Octave Gréard, 1889–1902, Vol. I, p. 134.
59     A.D. Gers, L 392.
60     A.D. Charente, L 420.
61     A.D. Aisne, L 1454.
62     A.D. Bas-Rhin, I L 1515.
63     A.D. Seine-et-Marne, L 536.
64     A.D. Gers, L 392.
65     Yves Poutet, 1970.
66     These figures are reprinted by kind permission of Jean-Pierre Bardet.
67     A.D. Seine-Maritime, L 1152.
68     *Ibid.*

| | |
|---|---|
| 69 | *Ibid.* L 1153–1154. |
| 70 | 'Instruction publique', *Annuaire des cinq départements de l'ancienne Normandie*, Ist year, 1835. |
| 71 | A.D. Seine-Maritime, L 1152. |
| 72 | *Ibid. passim.* |
| 73 | A.D. Maine-et-Loire, 1 L 928. |
| 74 | A.D. Maine-et-Loire, 1 L 928. |
| 75 | A.D. Gers, L 392. |
| 76 | The 'décadi' was the tenth day, designed to replace the *Ancien Régime* Sunday. |
| 77 | A.D. Pas-de-Calais, III L 130. |
| 78 | A.D. Nord, L 4803 and A.D. Bas-Rhin, I L 1515. |
| 79 | Cf. for example the Decree of 13 June 1793 ordering the holding of a competition for the writing of new textbooks. |
| 80 | A.D. Seine-Maritime, L 1152. |
| 81 | A.D. Gers, L 392. |
| 82 | A.D. Seine-et-Marne, L 536. |
| 83 | A.D. Bas-Rhin, I L 1515. |
| 84 | A.D. Charente, L 420. |
| 85 | A.D. Maine-et-Loire, 1 L 928. |
| 86 | A.D. Seine-Maritime. |
| 87 | A.D. Maine-et-Loire, 1 L 928. |
| 88 | A.D. Charente, L 420. |
| 89 | *Ibid.* |
| 90 | *Ibid.* |
| 91 | *Ibid.* |
| 92 | *Ibid.* |
| 93 | See for example B. Bois, 1908; F. Autorde, 1888. |
| 94 | A.D. Seine-Maritime, L 1152. |
| 95 | *Ibid.* |

## 3 School, society and State

| | |
|---|---|
| 1 | On the subject of these statistics, see J.-C. Perrot, 1976. |
| 2 | The replies sent in by the Commissioners of the Executive Directorate for each canton are contained in the 'Tableaux décadaires', in compliance with the Circular of 21 Fructidor, Year V. Viz. for instance the reply sent in by the canton of Montréjeau, Haute-Garonne: '[Public instruction] is badly neglected. True, in most communes one finds citizens who get the children to read and write, but confining their instruction to this, they in no way develop in the minds of their pupils that love of liberty which must be the underlying strength of an infant Republic' (C. Aulard, 1887). |
| 3 | Guizot, vol. III, 1860. |
| 4 | On 28 February 1813, the *Journal de l'Empire* reported 31,000 primary schools and 900,000 pupils, out of a total school-age population of four million (approx. 22.5%). |
| 5 | Between 1789 and 1801, the percentage of men able to read and write in Haute-Vienne increased from 7.8 to 8%. In another example, the Morbihan, the sub-prefect of Pontivy wrote, in reply to a survey of the state of education ordered by Chaptal on 12 Brumaire, Year X: 'in 1789, 90, 91, fathers had the occasion to feel the need for learning, and the |

number of schoolchildren increased prodigiously' (in *Notices, Inventaires et Documents* of the 'Comité des travaux historiques et scientifiques', Paris, 1914).

6    Fourcroy demanded a whole series of facts and figures: name of teacher, accomodation, number of pupils, salary, etc.

7    Circular of May 1809, addressed to prefects by Fontanes, *grand-maître* of the University.

8    Quoted by A. Rivet, 1964.

9    A.D. Maine-et-Loire, 52 T 5.

10   Ambroise Rendu, 1827.

11   Baron Charles Dupin, 1827.

12   The western Pyrenees (Basses-Pyrénées and Hautes-Pyrénées), Languedoc and the Alpine region.

13   René Masson, born 1812 in northern Finistère, at Porspoder, who himself became captain of a coastal tramp, wrote the tale of his youth in 1878 (published in *les Cahiers de l'Iroise*, 1956, no. 3, under the title: 'René Masson, capitaine au cabotage').

14   René Masson points out – and this is interesting for all those regions with a high proportion of 'read only' – that: 'The eldest of the aunts used to say that when one could read the mass one was already fairly smart.'

15   A.D. Maine-et-Loire, 52 T 5 (Mayors' replies).

16   Gadebled, 1838.

17   A.N. $F^{17}$* 98.

18   Grimmert, 1956.

19   A.N. $F^{17}$ 9370.

20   Quoted by André Thuillier, 1974.

21   For the whole of the *département* of Maine-et-Loire in 1832, the figures refer to recorded clandestine teachers – excluding itinerant teachers – while there were roughly 200 officially-recognized ones (J.-Ph. David, 1967).

22   Cited by A. Rivet, 1964.

23   R. Boudard, 1959.

24   M. Rebouillat, 1964.

25   A. Rivet, 1964.

26   Minutes of the Jargé municipal council (A.D. Maine-et-Loire, 52 T 5).

27   'Monographie sur l'instruction primaire à Souligny' (monograph on primary education at Souligny), written in 1861 by the village schoolmaster (communicated by the C.D.D.P., Troyes).

28   A.N. $F^{17}$* 126, Haute-Marne.

29   M. Gadebled, 1838.

30   G. Cholvy, 1965.

31   'Receveur-buralist', in fact combined postmaster and tobacconist (trans.).

32   A.N. $F^{17}$* 98, Creuse: Moustier-Rozelle, the teacher 'sometimes went to the masons, in other words, he emigrated to the Périgord'; another was absent several days each week: his other job was bailiff!

33   Quoted by M. Gontard, 1959.

34   A.D. Gironde, 24 T 3 (quoted by Paul Butel).

35   In Haute-Marne (A.N. $F^{17}$* 126).

36   Erckmann-Chatrian, 1873.

37  Royal ordinance of 28 February 1816.
38  It is true, however, that there was a high proportion of suitably-qualified teachers here: 46% in Haute-Marne, 40% in Côte-d'Or (compared with 18%, for example, in Creuse).
39  The request was supported by a letter and a petition from the mayor and the members of the municipal council (see J.-Ph. David, 1967).
This letter is so riddled with errors of syntax and spelling mistakes that it is hardly necessary to render them all to convey the author's illiteracy (transl.).
'Je soussigné, René Narcisse Oreau, ex-militaire né à Baugé le 16 mai 1793 prie monsieur de recteur de bien vouloir Bien à voir la Bonté de Me faire recevoir instituteur pour la commune de juigné sur Loire ou Mon épouse est institutrice; je le prie de Voulloir bien à voir égard à un Brave Militaire éyant plusieurs Blécure et sang retraite fait à juigné sur Loire le 14 juillet 1831.'
40.  The distinction was not abolished until 1850, when it was replaced by two age-groups, which were themselves done away with in 1862 (M. Sacx, 1970).
41  According to the municipal records of Jouy, reproduced in *Histoire locale, Beauce et Perche*, 1965.
42  'Once one could read a little, or mumble rather, one began to write, which meant drawing large letters, two or three centimetres high, on a slate or on paper': such was the curriculum around 1835 in a country school at Saint-Aubin-d'Arquenay, in Calvados (C.D. Férard, 1894); the teacher always began reading with Latin.
43  *Journal d'éducation*, 1845.
44  M. Herpin, 1835.
45  Quoted by R. Tronchot, 1972.
46  A remarkable description of a traditional rural school in the 1830s is given in the memoirs of the entomologist J.H. Fabre (J.H. Fabre, 6th series, 1899).
47  *Rapport au Roi* (signed F. Guizot), 1834.
48  'I became aware', wrote Guizot, 'that the real state of primary education in France, and everything connected with it, was so incompletely, so vaguely, so imprecisely known that the higher authorities were constantly acting in the dark, and most of time obtaining from its actions, for want of a sure light to guide them, but the most ephemeral, or very imperfect, result.'
49  I.e. boys' and mixed schools.
50  Grammar school heads and principals, mainly, but also inspectors of *académies*, wardens, vice-principals and teachers of *collèges royaux* (lycées), directors and teachers at primary-school teacher training colleges, etc.
51  Guizot, vol. II, chap. XVI, 1860.
52  P. Lorain, 1837. Paul Lorain was editor of the *Manuel général de l'instruction primaire*, at the time the official organ of the Ministry of Education.
53  A.N. F$^{17}$* 126 (Haute-Marne).
54  The text is taken from the monograph on the 'pen-ty' of Lower Brittany (*arrondissement* of Quimper), in *Les Ouvriers européens*, 1885.
55  F. Guizot, vol. III, Paris (1860), 1969.

56    Chancelier Pasquier, vol. 5, 1894. This text is cited by Pierre Zind in his remarkable study: *Les nouvelles congrégations de Frères enseignants en France de 1800 à 1830.*

57    From the reports of primary school inspectors and *recteurs* (1837), quoted by André Armengaud, 1961.

58    E. Guillaumin (1943), 1974.

59    Taine, vol. III, 1901.

60    Cardinal de Diepenbrock was the Prince-Bishop of Breslau. In E. Rendu, 1855. Guizot quotes this anecdote in his *Mémoires* (vol. III, 1860).

61    See Pieyre fils, Year X. The prefect insists on the importance of reading and writing, and adds: 'It is more important to have teachers everywhere, [even if their] teaching [of] reading and writing is imperfect, than to have fewer, though better-equipped and more intelligent, teachers.' Which leads him to recommend entirely free education, with more rather than better schools. The prefect of Meurthe, for his part, declares that: 'Most of the working-class children lack the wherewithal to attend fee-paying schools, remain deprived of all education and acquire the wretched habit of idleness and insubordination' (M. Marquis, prefect, Year XIII).

62    Departmental Council of Hérault, June 1816 Session (A.N., F$^{17}$ 1395).

63    Departmental Council of Bas-Rhin (A.N., F$^{17}$ 1395).

64    Abbé Affre, 1826.

65    On this revival of the teaching congregations, see P. Zind, 1969. See also: canon A. Garnier, 1933.

66    P. Zind, *op. cit.* This was the 'Société pour l'Instruction élémentaire'.

67    F. Guizot, 1816.

68    F. Guizot, vol. III, 1860.

69    Abbé Doyotte, 1876.

70    F. Guizot, 1860.

71    Destutt-Tracy, Year IX.

72    P. Vilar, 'Niveaux de culture et groupes sociaux', 1967.

73    F. Courtois, 1893.

74    R. Oberlé, 1961.

75    See Georges Dupeux's reply to Pierre Vilar, in 'Niveaux de culture et groupes sociaux', 1967.

76    A.P. Deseilligny, 1868 (quoted by J. Bouvier, in G. Duby, 1972). At the same time – October 1871–the Northern district of the *Société de l'industrie minérale* undertook a survey of coalmining companies in the region. In its circular, it proclaimed its desire to describe the sacrifices made by these companies to provide schools for the children of miners: the chief aim, the Society pointed out, was to demonstrate the practical results thus achieved in the 'moralization' of working people through instruction (E. Vuillemin, 1872). The reader is also referred to Louis Mazoyer, 1934. Lastly, Richard Johnson (University of Birmingham) has studied the 'moralization' of the English working class – albeit slightly too schematically in our view – in a recent unpublished communication: 'Notes on the Schooling of the English Working Class, 1780–1850', Maison des Sciences de l'Homme, Paris, 1975. See also his article in *Past and Present* (1970), which he concludes thus: 'Supervised by its teacher, surrounded by its playground wall, the school was to raise a new race of working people – respectful, cheerful, hard-working, loyal, pacific and religious.' For Germany, see P. Lundgreen's article (1974).

77   J. Simon, 1873. These pages, the Preface points out, 'were written in 1870, before the war'.
78   Reply to the Commissioner of the Executive Directorate for the cantons of Verfeil, on the *Tableaux décadaire*, in application of the Circular dated 21 Fructidor, Year V. Quoted by F.A. Aulard, 1887.
79   Erckmann-Chatrian, 1873.
80   Ch. L. Chassin, 1875.
81   G. Dupeux, in 'Niveaux de culture et groupes sociaux', 1967. During the course of the same symposium, Christine Mora cited a circular of the *Ligue de l'enseignement* (League for education) dated 15 October 1871: 'After the Prussians, and then the Commune, the crusade against ignorance is more than ever necessary and must redouble its efforts.'
82   L.A. Meunier, 1838.
83   Cited by Henri Forestier, 1959.
84   Jean Moreau (pseudonym of Jean Macé), 1848.
85   In the period 1846–1850, 36.54% of conscripts could neither read nor write.
86   A good third at the time of the 1866 census . . . and over 15% at the 1901 census!
87   The expression is taken from Victor Clavel, Professor at the Faculty of Letters at Lyon, in his preface to J. Janicot, 1891.
88   Jules Simon, 1873: 'You cannot call someone who does not even know what the piece of paper he's putting into the ballot box is an elector or a citizen.'
89   Philippe Ariès, 'Problèmes de l'éducation', in *La France et les Français*, 1972.
90   Jules Simon, 1865.
91   Roger Thabault, 1945.
92   Shawl-weaver employed by the Paris urban collective mill (1857 survey). This monograph is included in 1st series vol. I, of *Les, Ouvriers des deux mondes*, 1858.
93   Quarryman in the Paris region (1856 survey). In *Les Ouvriers des deux mondes*, 1st series, vol. II.
94   Coalminer in Pas-de-Calais (1893 survey). In *Les Ouvriers des deux mondes*, 2nd series, vol. V.
95   Master-launderer in the Paris suburbs (1852 survey). In *Les Ouvriers européens*, 1885.
96   Emile Guillaumin, 1973.
97   Bonnaire, Prefect, Year IX.
98   Published sources, 19th-century education, I, 2, *Etat de l'instruction primaire en 1864*, 1865, vol. I.
99   See for the Ossau Valley, L. Soulice, 1873; and also Ch. Chopinet, 1886.
100  Guillaumin, 1973.
101  Coastal fisherman, master of an Etretat vessel (1861 survey). In *Les Ouvriers des deux mondes*, 2nd series, vol. II.
102  Steel-tool fitter in the Hérimoncourt factory (1858 survey), *ibid*. 1st series, vol. II.
103  Quarryman in the Paris region (1856 survey), *ibid.*, Ist series, vol. II.
104  N. Delacroix, 1835. The 'regimental schools' must have played an important part in the elementary education of men from the 1830s, moreover, and there is as yet no systematic study of it (cf. below, chapter 6).

105    People believed luck and a good harvest would come from jumping on the hay in summer (trans.).
106    Published sources, 19th-century education, I, 2.
107    *Ibid.* I.
108    Norbert Truquin, 1888. Born in 1833 in the Somme, Truquin took part in the June 1848 *Journées*, then left with his family to settle in Oran, in Algeria.
109    Peasant and soap-boiler in Lower Provence (1859 survey). In *Les Ouvriers des deux mondes*, 1st series, vol. III.
110    Linen-maid in Lille (1858 survey). *Ibid.*
111    Iron worker in Paris (1878 survey). *Ibid.* 1st series, vol. V.
112    Tinsmith at the Commentry factory (1889–1890 survey). *Ibid.* 3rd series, vols I–II.
113    A.N. F$^{12}$ 3109.
114    G. Duveau, 1947.
115    Published sources, 19th-century education, I, 2.
116    F. Guizot, 1816.
117    Ch. de Villers, 1808.
118    In 1811, the naturalist Georges Cuvier, of the University Board, visited schools in Holland and Lower Germany in company with Board-member Noël, Inspector-General of the University (cf. G. Cuvier et M. Noël, 1812). Later, Victor Cousin visited schools in Germany, Prussia especially, and sent in reports to Montalivet (V. Cousin, 1833).
119    In Holland, teachers had to have a diploma (ranked in four grades).
120    Thus several founders of the Society for Elementary Education: Alexandre de Laborde (Member of the *Institut*), Benjamin Delessert, Jomard (another member of the *Institut*), the Abbé Gaultier, Jean-Baptiste Say, etc. On this problem, as on all other aspects of mutual education in France, see first R. Tronchot's work of reference (1972) and secondly Pierre Lesage's IIIrd cycle doctoral thesis (René-Descartes University, Paris V): *L'enseignement mutuel de 1815 aux débuts de la IIIe République* (contribution to the study of the teaching of reading and writing in mutual schools).
121    Several were to become the first heads of mutual schools in France.
122    E. Quinet, 1858.
123    Quoted by R. Tronchot, 1972.
124    Initially placed in one of 8 grades on the basis of their reading ability, pupils were soon divided according to their reading *and* writing abilities.
125    P. Bayaud, 1964.
126    *Ibid.*
127    These are the very terms used by J.-M. Robert de Lamennais, Vicar-General of the Diocese of Saint-Brieuc (1819).
128    Gadebled, 1838.
129    Lamennais, 1819.
130    Sarazin, 1829.
131    M. Foucault, 1975.
132    True, Lammenais did criticize mutual teaching methods for trying to make learning for children fun: 'Making education an amusement, what a pity!'
133    L. Bourilly, 1895.
134    V. Duruy, vol. I, 1901.

135     Octave Gréard's *Organisation pédagogique*, 1868.

136     Even at the very end of the 19th century, *Organisation pédagogigue et plans d'études* drawn up in compliance with the legislation (1907), laid down the following objectives for writing: in the lowest forms, 'large, medium and small writing', for the intermediate forms, 'ordinary cursive writing'; and for the upper forms, 'cursive, round and bastard' writing!

137     In *Nos Fils* (1869) Michelet said that writing ought to precede reading, and that the 'drawing of living subjects ought to precede that of letters'.

138     Article 23 of the 1850 Act provided for the same range of compulsory subjects as the 1833 Act; and the 'model regulation' of 1851, issued in application of the 1850 Act, mostly reiterated the terms of the 1834 Statute, without being any more specific or more restrictive.

139     In 1868 in *Organisation pédagogique des écoles communales de la Seine.* The Gréard plan was the culmination of a spontaneous movement which, for some fifteen years, had seen inspectors of *académies*, primary-school inspectors and teachers in several *départements* collaborate in commending a methodical classification of the pupils, a more strict use of time, the keeping of a 'classroom diary', etc.

140     In November 1871, the Minister of Education confined himself to advising inspectors of *académies* to introduce a classroom organization analogous to that of Gréard.

141     *Organisation pédagogique*, 1882. (Published sources, 19th-century education, V.)

142     In 1831, Montalivet noted that the poverty and anarchy of schools in so far as textbooks were concerned was 'one of the chief factors holding up progress in education'; and he began to order the distribution of elementary textbooks in schools, paid for out of State funds.

143     At the same time, Guizot asked *recteurs* to submit their elementary textbook requirements for the start of the 1834 school year, reminding them to count only 'the very poor pupils, the only ones to whom the provision of free textbooks is justifiable' (Circular to *recteurs*, 2 June 1834).

144     M.-A. Peigné was Guizot's secretary until 1838. His tables study in turn consonants and simple vowels, then their different combinations, and lastly the syllables (see M.-A. Peigné, 1832).

145     R. Thabault, 1945. In 1854, the municipal council of Mazières noted that 'the premises now being used as a school, and for which the commune pays a very high rent, are utterly ill-suited, inadequate and very uncomfortable', and that it was therefore 'absolutely essential' to build a 'schoolhouse' with State aid.

146     See p. 113 above.

147     When the Education Boards transferred the setting of pay scales from the municipalities to the prefects, these scales now being based not on the subjects studied but on the age of the children.

148     On men's and women's teacher training colleges, see: E. Jacoulet, 1889; and M. Gontard, 1962.

149     Not to mention the novitiates of the Christian Brethren's schools or the teacher training college of Year III. As well as pioneering experiments such as the 'teacher training' classes in Oise under the First Empire (see H. Quignon, 1905).

150     M. Garcia, undated.

151    F. Guizot, vol. III, 1860.
152    'Each *département* shall maintain a primary teacher training college, either on its own or by combining with one or more neighbouring *départements*. The departmental councils shall vote the resources necessary to the upkeep of primary-teacher training colleges.'
153    E. Laigneau, 1897; P. Bailly, 1953; B. Julien et J. Naudan, 1936.
154    Gadebled, 1838.
155    Article 16 of their 1832 Regulations invited them to do so, moreover.
156    F. N. Nicollet, 1896.
157    D. Mallet, 1889. Inaugurated in 1838, the further training courses held in Aix were attended by *all* practising teachers in these *départements* in the space of four years: each attended a two-week course, was housed at the school, and followed courses of lectures and practical exercises.
158    E. Laigneau, 1897. In Troyes, as early as 1833, groups of thirty teachers were admitted at a time as non-resident students (with a monthly stipend).
159    Between 1832 and 1848, the Manche teacher training college ran annual further training courses for groups of approximately 10 teachers (L. Deries, 1931).
160    Gadebled, 1838.
161    Like the teacher from Tarn who, having attended a course at the teacher training college in Albi at its foundation in 1831, then went on to open a small 'teacher training class' for teachers from the communes lying close to his own: 'He explained to them and helped them to understand the new methods of reading and writing and the metric system' (see A. Combes, 1834).
162    J. Chollet (1975), who has studied primary-school teachers in the Orne under the Second Empire on the basis of the 'Registre matricule du personnel' (roll of personnel), concluded that at that time 'there were teachers, but as yet no homogeneous corps of teachers'.
163    A. Thuillier, 1974.
164    J. Vallée, 1901.
165    In 1886–87, the women's teacher training college in Haute-Loire was offering 22 places to ... 20 candidates.
166    But we must bear in mind that, on the eve of the Third Republic, many teachers had entered primary schooling before all these changes. As, for example, the country schoolmaster in Eure – born in 1800, started teaching in 1820–described by Le Play's investigator in 1860 (*Les Ouvriers des deux mondes* 1st series, vol. III, 1861).
167    The Brethren ran only two men's teacher training colleges out of 77, and one teacher training class in six (another was run by a priest).
168    96% for secular teachers alone.
169    12% of the secular schoolmistresses had no diploma, while 95% of the *congregational* mistresses had none!
170    23rd December, 1880; A.N.F[17] 9269.
171    Jules Ferry, vol. III, 1893.
172    The *Statistique de l'enseignement primaire* for 1861 show, for example, that 12% of schoolchildren at that time were aged over 13. One observer notes in 1873, for Jura, that many pupils were aged between 14 and 16, especially in the mountain areas, and that they were the hardest-working and most mature. In Calvados, according to Gabriel Désert (1974), school attendance rates under the Second Empire were swollen by the presence of pupils aged 13–15.

173 2,316,000 girls and 2,401,000 boys.
174 Five in the west (Morbihan, Finistère, Côtes-du-Nord, Loire-Inférieure, Mayenne); four in the centre (Indre, Haute-Vienne, Corrèze, Haute-Loire) and Landes. Even in 1880 (A.N., F$^{17}$ 9269), in Morbihan, only 56% of the children aged 6–13 registered with their respective town halls actually attended school.
175 In 1868 alone, for example, 44 communes in Côte-d'Or requested permission to introduce free schooling.
176 After Jules Simon's November 1871 Circular.
177 The educational press published model teaching methods and rules, curricula and lessons. By 1876–77, the *Bulletins départementaux de l'enseignement primaire*, founded in 1865, numbered 70. Furthermore, the 'commercial' educational press began to develop, with the *Manuel général* – the father of them all – which lost its official character in 1840; the *Journal des instituteurs*, from 1858 onwards; the *Revue pédagogique*, founded in 1878, etc.
178 In 1878, a teacher-delegate to the Universal Exposition from Nord waxed lyrical over a model school: 'I saw', he reports, 'a type of school whose classrooms are designed to accomodate only 56 pupils: now that is surely a great step forward' (A.N., F$^{17}$ 10799).
179 Inspector of primary schools for the *arrondissement* of Melle (see A. Léger, 1880).
180 In 1882, the Inspector of primary schools and cantonal delegate for Issoudun (Indre) declared in a report: 'We have no hesitation in holding deplorable the method generally employed (for reading), which consists in gathering a certain number of children about a blackboard and, there, having them spell simultaneously' (A. Boucher and E. Thevenin, 1882).
181 According to Duruy, the percentage of 'academic duds' was 1.2% in Bas-Rhin, but 41.2% in Landes.
182 81% of all schoolchildren attended a State school: over 91% of the boys, and over 70% of girls.

## 4 The Peasant: from oral to written culture

1 Muriel Jeorger.
2 Jean-Paul Giret, 1973. Alain Corbin, 1975.
3 Vovelle, 1975.
4 Published sources, 19th-century education, II, 4.
5 Cf. chapter I. pp. 34–5.
6 *Statistique agricole décennale de 1852. Movement de la population en 1854.*
7 Emile Guillaumin (1905), 1973.
8 Siegfried, 1913.
9 Gabriel Désert, 1974.
10 Published sources, 19th-century education, II, 2.
11 Guizot, Published sources, 19th-century education, I, 7.
12 Jean-Paul Giret, 1973.
13 Conversation between F. Furet and M. Grenadou, farmer at Saint-Loup (Eure-et-Loir).
14 Corbin, 1975.
15 See note 20, p. 322.
16 See note 20, p. 322.
17 See the second volume of this book.

18    See note 20, p. 322.
19    Alain Corbin, 1975 (*Revue d'histoire économique et sociale*).
20    Martin Nadaud (1895), 1948.
21    Louis Guilbert, 1888, p. 38.
22    Chapter 1, graphs A and B.
23    Canon Boulard, 1966.
24    Egil Johansson, 1974.
25    A.D. Aveyron, 1866 census, series *M*.
26    These figures were kindly communicated to us by Gérard Cholvy, professor at the University of Montpellier.
27    In Normandy, for example.
28    Dunglas, 1865.
29    Le Play, 1861.
30    Auguste Rivet, 1964.
31    Interviews of old people in the *département* of Haute-Loire, conducted by Muriel Jeorger in 1975.
32    Dunglas, 1865.
33    Report submitted by the Prefect Chèvremont, A.N.F[1] CIII, Haute-Loire (5).
34    L. Lempereur, 1906.
35    R. Chartier, M.M. Compère, D. Julia, 1976, p. 23.
36    H. Affre, 1903.
37    L. Lempereur, 1906.
38    R.P. (Reverend Father) Clément Leygues, 1959.
39    Interviews conducted by Muriel Jeorger in Haute-Loire in 1975.
40    A.D. Seine-Maritime (series M).
41    A.D. Seine-Maritime, JJ 1–8 (1876–80). See Chaunu *et al.*, 1976.
42    Private document (J. Ozouf).

## 5   City lights

1    A.N. F[1] C III, Isère.
2    Jean Quéniart, 1975; Jean Meyer, 1974; Michel Vovelle, 1975.
3    The bulk of the study of towns in Nord was published in 1976 in the *Journal of European Economic History*. We gratefully thank its editor, Professor Luigi di Rosa, for having kindly authorized us to reprint here the figures and maps illustrating them.
4    E. Fontaine de Resbecq, 1878.
5    The towns (Lille, Avesnes, Douai, Valenciennes, Hazebrouck, etc.) were at the time divided into several cantons: we have therefore attributed a uniform rate to the cantons belonging to a single town.
6    See Raoul Blanchard, 1906.
7    On this point, see Jules Flammermont, 1907.
8    M.A. thesis, 1973, University of Lille III, supervised by P. Deyon.
9    On the development of the coalmining industry see A. Lequeux, 1936.
10    In the *arrondissement* of Avesnes, however, the differences were very small, and the rule giving the advantage to built-up areas over the surrounding countryside was inoperative here, although the contrary did not hold either. Out of eight cantons, five gave the advantage to the countryside (Avesnes, Berlaimont, Landrecies, Maubeuge and Solre), while three favoured the main town (Bavai, Le Quesnoy and Trélon).

11    M. Sanderson, 1968. On the same subject, see Thomas W. Laqueur and Michael Sanderson, 1974.

12    Marcel Lachiver, 1969.

13    J.-C. Perrot, 1975.

14    Forty years later, we find considerably more conscripts able at least to read than men able to sign the marriage register: 78% (in 1867–1871) against 69.5% (in 1866).

15    Dr Louis-René Villermé, 1840.

16    Bridegrooms were not necessarily of conscript age: in 1863, for example, 40.2% of the 1,119 men getting married in Lille were aged over 30 (13.5% were actually over 40), as were 28% of the women.

17    Coornaert, 1971. On this point, see also A. de Saint-Léger, 1900, especially pp. 340 f.

18    According to Maryvonne Leblond's M.A. thesis (*La Scolarisation au XIXe siècle dans le Nord*, Lille, 1968). The school attendance rate is the relation between the total number of children enrolled in all the primary schools in a given year and the number of school-age children in the same year (i.e., for reasons of statistical convenience, children in the 5–14 age-group).

19    P. Pierrard, 1965.

20    E. Vuillemin, 1872.

21    'Enquête parlementaire sur les conditions du travail en France', *3e questionnaire*, 'Situation intellectuelle et morale' (A.N. C 3019) (Parliamentary inquiry into working conditions in France, 3rd questionnaire, 'Intellectual and moral conditions' (National archives)).

22    David Wardle, 1971.

23    The Inspector of the *Académie* of the Nord wrote, in 1864: 'In a region where labour shortages have raised salaries considerably, it is difficult to prevent admission of children to the factories' (Published sources, 19th-century education, I, 2).

24    19th-century statistics show that, for the rudimentary cultural apprenticeship which was what literacy amounted to, the *fact of having been* to school, i.e. school attendance (even of short duration), was far more important than the actual *length* of school attendance in the course of a year.

25    'It is not our agricultural cantons which furnish the greatest number of illiterates; for in agriculture, no matter what one does, even with the diversity of crops which I have mentioned (for Nord), there are still certain periods of less intensive labour; there is the long idleness of the really bad season, which is put to good use by attending classes...' (E. Anthoine, *inspecteur d'Académie*, 1878).

26    F. Chapelle, 1870.

27    Pierre Lévêque's monograph in the second volume of this book (not translated into English).

28    A. Corbin, 1975.

29    R. Oberlé, 1959.

30    R. Oberlé, 1959, table II, p. 105.

31    Paris Chamber of Commerce (Published sources, 19th-century education, V, 1851). And: Paris Chamber of Commerce (Published sources, 19th-century education V, 1864).

32    F. Chapelle, 1870.

33    Rolf Engelsing (1973) notes that in Germany, in the first phase of industrialization, with the development of weaving looms and the building industry, economic growth tended rather to hinder the elimination of illiteracy, on account of the rising demand for uneducated workers. He reckons that the situation began to change in the second half of the century, with the emergence of a skilled working class.

34    In the 1872 census, a total of 373 towns were surveyed (Published sources, 19th-century education, II, 3).

35    For these two examples, see again Pierre Lévêque's monograph.

36    Men and women, of all ages.

37    I.e. the whole of the *département*, less all the towns counted, regardless of size.

38    The general average for the *départements* is 61.3%.

39    General average for the whole of Finistère: 55.2%.

## 6    The rôle of the school: the computer's verdict

1    For the material for this chapter, we are deeply indebted to Cécile Dauphin, Pierrette Pézerat and Danièle Poublan, whom we thank most warmly.

2    At a seminar held in Grenoble, in May 1968, on *La scolarisation en France depuis un siècle* (1974), P. Chevallier could still remark: 'The 19th century seems to have been the chief period of development of primary education. *Its spread explains* (our italics) the steady fall in the number of illiterate bridegrooms.'

3    The succeeding volumes of the *Statistique de l'enseignement primaire* published from 1875 onwards by the Ministry of Education; and singularly the retrospective volume (vol. II) covering the period 1829–77 (Published sources, 19th-century education I, 4).

4    *Rapport au roi*, 1834 (Published sources, 19th-century education, 1, 7).

5    It was only late in the 19th century that the State and the *départements* began financing a portion of school expenditures.
     Percentage of expenditure covered by the State:

     In 1834 : 22.7
     In 1866 : 14.2
     In 1896 : 67.2

6    Figures show that there were exactly 119 communes with a population of over 10,000 in 1836, out of a total of 37,252 communes, giving 3,764,187 'city-dwellers' for a total of 33,540,910 French people (Published sources, 19th-century education, II, 4).

7    With the familiar important qualifications: communes were not *obliged* to maintain a girls' school, any more than the *départements* a teacher training college for women.

8    In many girls' schools, 'non-teaching' *régentes* or supervisors taught their pupils sewing and embroidery while giving them instruction in the Catholic religion.

9    Pupils in *all* primary schools, State and private.

10   The first population census to take age into account dates from 1851, so it is impossible to calculate earlier percentages. For 1850 and 1860, we have referred to children aged 5–15 appearing in the 1851 and 1866 census

returns; for 1896, children between 6 and 13 shown in the returns for that year.

11 The three series (years 1830, 1860 and 1890) describing the same indicator are combined into a single variable.

12 It should be remembered that the absence of girls' schools associated with a high percentage of mixed schools should be interpreted, paradoxically, as a sign of literacy. This bias accounts for the higher correlations with this parameter, even though they are not actually significant.

13 In 1837, indeed, the school network was particularly inadequate in these same *départements* (over 40% of the communes in Charente, Ariège, Haute-Vienne, Indre, Allier, Corrèze, Puy-de-Dôme, Côtes-du-Nord, Finistère and Morbihan had no school).

14 I.e. a break in continuity through education. See Margaret Mead, 1943: 'Primitive education was a process by which continuity was maintained between parents and children... Modern education includes a heavy emphasis upon the function of education to create discontinuities – to turn the child ... of the illiterate into the literate.'

15 See note 9.

16 We shall not refer again to the first points, which are discussed at length in chapter 3.

17 Guizot, 1834: Published sources, 19th-century education, I, 7.

18 Except Seine-Inférieure, which merely rented them.

19 Durkheim, in F. Buisson, 1911.

20 Published sources, 19th-century education, I, 2.

21 An argument frequently raised in discussions connected with the introduction of free schooling.

22 In the case of foundations, the teacher's income was no long dependent on fees and hence on the number of pupils present.

23 Published sources, 19th-century education, I, 3 (p. 46).

24 Until very late in the 19th century, conscripts able to read only were not included among illiterates but among the 'literate'.

25 Apart from these 'crammers', there were also various forms of informal, individual or occasional teaching: the private family tutor, the education garnered by the self-taught, by burning the midnight oil, or the benevolent employer's efforts on behalf of his apprentice; then there were chance – or deliberate – meetings between the ignorant and the lettered, there was the Church wanting to catechise its faithful: in a word, all those crumbs which statistical analyses include, only to dismiss them as falling within the margin of error.

26 In the army, total illiterates (unable to read or write) numbered 18.73%; 24.37%, or almost 6% more, for the class of 1865.

27 Published sources, 19th-century education, II, 2.

28 Published sources, 19th-century education, I, 4 (vol. II).

29 According to the *Statistique de l'enseignement primaire* (vol. II), the provision of primary education aboard Government ships was instituted by the 16 Plûviose Year II Act (4 February 1794).

30 Cf. R.R. Tronchot, 1972 (1st part, vol. I).

31 Published sources, 19th-century education, IV (1833).

32 F. Buisson, 1882 (1st part, vol. I).

33 *Examen annuel de l'instruction primaire des conscrits et écoles régimentaires des corps de troupes de toutes armes* (Published sources, 19th-century education, V).

34      F. Buisson, 1911.
35      In four categories:
        'knowing nothing or, having only the rudiments of education, have learnt
        to read;
        knowing nothing or, having only the rudiments of education, have learnt
        to read and write;
        knowing nothing or, having only the rudiments of education, have learnt
        to read, write and count;
        unable to read or write, but able to count'.
        In 1863, the terms 'knowing nothing or, having only the rudiments of
        education' were supplanted by 'knowing nothing'. Finally, in 1873:
        'Among those men knowing nothing at the moment of admission to the
        elementary class, have learnt to read', etc.
36      For the two years missing from *Comptes rendus* (1858 and 1859), we have
        taken the average for the four years on either side (1856 and 1857, and
        1860 and 1861).
37      In his report to the Assembly (20–21 April 1792), Condorcet declared that
        the educational process 'ought not to abandon individuals just as they
        leave school: it ought to embrace people of all ages. . . This second
        education (further public education) is all the more necessary when that
        received in childhood has been squeezed between the narrowest
        horizons . . . On each Sunday a public lecture would be held, attended by
        working men of all ages . . . We might then at last show them the art of
        teaching oneself' (quoted by B. Cacérès, 1964).
38      Figures published in the retrospective volume of *Statistique de l'en-
        seignement primaire* (vol. II, 1829–1877).
39      Perdonnet, 1867.
40      A. Corbon, 1859.
41      Published sources, 19th-century education, I. 4.
42      Too few women attended adult classes to furnish a sufficiently reliable
        statistical base for region-by-region analysis.
43      Jules Simon, 1867.
44      Schools run by religious orders.
45      West of the 'boundary', only Côtes-du-Nord, Mayenne, Maine-et-Loire,
        Indre-et-Loire and Vienne show above-average proportions. There are
        very few exceptions to the east of it also: Nord, Pas-de-Calais, Doubs,
        Jura, Haute–Saône and Manche.

## 7 Reading and writing in French

1       Report of the Commissioner of the Executive Directorate at Vannes, 1
        Pluviôse Year VI (A.N. F$^1$ CIII, Morbihan 6).
2       Reports, classified by *académies*, on 'the needs of primary education in
        each commune, from the three points of view of the school, the pupils and
        the master', to be completed amongst themselves by the teachers by 12
        December 1860 (A.N. F$^{17}$ 10757 to 10798).
3       As early as 1819 the Prefect of Morbihan cited 'the Breton language'
        among the principal causes which had hindered the progress of elemen-
        tary education since the Revolution (Report of 28 May 1819, A.N. F17
        11778).
4       A. Boyer, 1905.

5    J. Meyer, 1974.
6    A. Armengaud, 1961.
7    5.44% of the population over 5 were illiterate.
8    A.N. F[17]* 140 (*Enquête sur la situation des écoles primaires*, 1833).
9    Augustin Cariou, 1955.
10   Counting only once the names of people appearing several times.
11   These figures are appreciably higher than those indicated by Maggiolo for
     marriage signatures in 1786–90: 9.7% for men and 6.8% for women. But
     the 'population' studied is not quite the same: the whole *département* is
     covered, whereas Maggiolo's sample (2,830 marriages in 1786–90) is, as
     elsewhere, mainly rural.
12   For women, the figures are too small for reliable analysis of the
     differences.
13   Dr Fouquet, *père*, 1874.
14   Dr Fouquet was originally particularly concerned with the study of
     disabilities and illnesses which, between 1853 and 1872, had given rise to
     exemptions from military service; and he remarked that the cantons
     where exemptions were most numerous were generally those which had
     the lowest level of education.
15   The sample covered 1,032 peasant conscripts in Breton-speaking and 767
     in Gallo-speaking country.
16   We have excluded categories with very small numbers (such as industrial
     workers) and those that are fully literate (lecturers, students, teachers,
     landowners, etc.).
17   With two reservations: 1. none of the cantons is purely Gallo-speaking, all
     are of mixed language; 2. Franco-Breton-speaking cantons (10) are here
     much more numerous than Breton-speaking cantons (3).
18   2,577 in Breton-speaking and 2,915 in Gallo-speaking country (it appears
     that only the conscripts have been able to improve their level of
     education).
19   Of which only two were urban cantons, those of Dinan-Est and Dinan-
     Ouest (60.6%); the others (Pléneuf 79.4%, Ploubalay 69.4%, Saint-Jouan-
     Caulnes 65%, Evran 66%) contained no urban centre.
20   Those which, moreover, provided a major part of the annual contingent
     of conscripts from Morbihan: around two-thirds both in 1850 (66%) and
     in 1890 (63%).
21   Phenomena which still today raise questions on the rôle of the school in
     literacy in areas of French-speaking black Africa.
22   Cited by A. Brun, 1922.
23   In contrast, the long regulation governing the 'poor school' of Cassel,
     founded in 1738, contained in the letters patent of approval by Louis XV,
     is written in Flemish (C. Looten, 1924).
24   These are listed: Morbihan, Côtes-du-Nord, Finistère, Loire-Inférieure,
     Haut and Bas-Rhin, Corsica, Moselle, Nord, Mont-Terrible, Alpes-
     Maritimes, Basses-Pyrénées.
25   Report of the Commissioner of the Executive Directorate, 2 Pluviôse Year
     VII (A.N. F[1] CIII, Finistère 4).
26   Jules Simon (1873) describes here a school founded in Morbihan under
     the law of 1833. In Nord, school-work continued in Flemish in the
     Flemish-speaking communes (E. Coornaert, 1971).
27   A.N. F[17]* 3160.

28       In the three other *arrondissements* of Morbihan, four-fifths or more of the resident population of the communities had at least a boys' school (A.N. F¹⁷ 12203).

29       R. Sancier, 1952 and 1953.

30       A.N. F¹⁷ 10625, *Etats de situation des écoles primaires publiques et libres et des écoles maternelles* (Morbihan, 1884–85).

31       Claude Langlois, 1974.

32       A. de Vulpian, 1951.

33       *Ibid.*

34       These surveys have been made by Marie-Thérèse Bouissy, Danièle Poublan, Muriel Jeorger, Marie-Madeleine Compère, Véronique Nahoum, Yvonne Pasquet and Cécile Dauphin. As in Brittany, they have for the most part even identified socio-occupational categories.

35       We have taken as patois-speaking the cantons of Saint-Pons, Olonzat, Saint-Chinian, Olargues, Capestang, Senian; and as non-patois-speaking those of Mauguio, Les Matelles, Lunel, Castries.

36       For Alsace, see J.-P. Kintz, 1973.

37       Published sources, 19th-century education, V (République Française, Préfecture des Basses-Pyrénées, *Recueil des Actes Administratifs*, 1874, no. 15).

38       A. de Saint-Léger, 1900. See also C. Looten, 1919–21.

39       E. Coornaert, 1971.

40       *Académie* of Meurthe, *Règlement pour les écoles primaires publiques du département, approuvé par le Conseil supérieur de l'Instruction publique,* 1852.

41       Enquiry of the primary school inspector for Morbihan on the teaching of reading and writing, 1843 (A.D. Morbihan, T 419).

42       A.N. F¹⁷ 9330 (Inspection des écoles primaires, année 1855–56, Nord).

43       For the figures on this contrast, see L. Soulice, 1873 and 1880–81.

44       Rejection of national integration here. But this could also be a rejection of social integration: as with those Nottingham schools which, at the height of industrialization, remained partly empty (see David Wardle, 1971).

45       *Bulletin de l'enseignement des indigènes*, 1906 (cited by Fanny Colonna, 1975).

46       Fanny Colonna, 1975.

**Conclusion**

1        Nothing has changed in this respect: A. Darbel's remarkable article (1967) on regional and social inequalities in school enrolment rates concludes that 'geographical inequalities are fundamentally of the same nature as social inequalities'.

2        J. Goody, 1968.

3        G. Duverdier, 1971.

4        R. Cagnac, a peasant at Lugagnac (Lot), interviewed by F. Furet (Jan. 1976). The strictest interpreter of this notion that for women to remain submissive and innocent was to exclude them from written culture was Restif de la Bretonne, who 'even' looked askance at reading: 'All women should be prohibited from learning to write and even read. This would preserve them from loose thoughts, confining them to useful tasks about the house, instilling in them respect for the first sex, which would be all the

more carefully instructed in these things for the second sex having been neglected.' See Restif de la Bretonne, 1777.

5 This example, and the passage that follows, is taken from a doctoral thesis prepared by M.-H. Froeschlé: *Les dévotions populaires dans les diocèses de Vence et de Grasse, 1680–1750* (unpublished thesis, presented in June 1976 at the University of Paris-Sorbonne).

6 L. Stone, 1969.

7 Certeau, Julia, Revel, 1975.

8 This analysis of the secularization of rites through writing is based on an unpublished study by Véronique Nahoum.

9 This report by J.-B. Leclerc (*Rapport au Conseil des Cinq-Cents sur les institutions relatives à l'état civil des citoyens, Séance du 16 Brumaire an VI*, n.d.) was brought to our attention by Mona Ozouf.

10 To borrow David Riesman's expression.

11 Stendhal (1838), 1928.

12 Stendhal (1890), 1929.

# SOURCES AND BIBLIOGRAPHY

## Manuscript sources

### National archives

The archival sources cited here have not, needless to say, been analyzed in full. We have selected and studied the registers relating to specific *départements* which were of particular interest in the course of our work, and which are frequently cited throughout the book.

C 943 to 969: Enquête sur le travail agricole et industriel prescrite par le décret du 25 mai 1848.

C 3018 to 3024: Enquête sur la situation des classes ouvrières, 1872–1875.

C 3326 to 3373: Enquête sur la situation des ouvriers en France (3° Législature, 1881–1885).

$F^1$ CIII: Esprit public et élections (par département, notamment rapports décadaires et mensuels des Commissaires du Directoire).

$F^9$ 150 to 261: Recrutement (par département).

$F^{12}$ 3109 to 3124: Exposition Universelle de 1867. Rapports des délégués ouvriers.

$F^{17}$* 80 to 160: Enquête sur la situation des écoles primaires, 1833 (enquête Guizot).

$F^{17}$* 3158 to 3160: Statistiques de l'enseignement primaire sous le ministère Duruy (entre 1863 et 1869).

$F^{17}$ 1395: Voeux des Conseils généraux relatifs à l'instruction publique, 1815–1842.

$F^{17}$ 9251 to 9278: Inspection Générale, 1847-1893.

$F^{17}$ 9306 to 9320: Rapports des inspecteurs primaires sur les écoles primaires, 1832–1855.

$F^{17}$ 9321 to 9349: Inspection des écoles primaires, 1855–1860.

$F^{17}$ 9351 to 9352: Résumé de l'inspection des écoles primaires, 1835–1837.

$F^{17}$ 9367 to 9372: Rapports des recteurs sur l'enseignement primaire, 1811–1837.

$F^{17}$ 10350 to 10355: Règlements scolaires départementaux, 1851–1882.

$F^{17}$ 10368 . . . etc.: Etats de situation des écoles primaires . . . (à partir de 1808).

$F^{17}$ 10757 to 10798: Mémoires, classés par académies, sur 'les besoins de l'instruction primaire dans une commune rurale, au triple point de vue de l'école, des élèves et du maître', présentés par les instituteurs du concours ouvert entre eux par arrêté du 12 décembre 1860.

$F^{17}$ 10799: Rapports d'instituteurs du département du Nord sur l'Exposition de 1878.

$F^{17}$ 11752 to 11780: Enseignement mutuel, 1815–1824. Affaires générales et dossiers classés par académies.

$F^{17}$ 12203: Etat des enfants en âge de recevoir l'instruction, qui ne fréquentent pas l'école, 1847.

$F^{17}$ 12317 to 12323: Degré d'instruction des conscrits, 1866–1904.

$F^{17}$ 14270: Etats numériques par départements et cantons des conscrits, avec indication de leur degré d'instruction, 1899.

$F^{20}$ 154 to 275: Mémoires statistiques, ou description, ou tableaux topographiques... tableaux statistiques... (1793–1813).

#### Departmental archives
*Enquêtes pastorales*
AD Seine-Maritime JJ 1-8 (1876–80).
*Enquêtes révolutionnaires sur l'école* (série L)
AD Aisne L. 1454 – AD Charente L. 420 – AD Gers L. 392 – AD Loir-et-Cher L. 765-66 – AD Loire-Atlantique L. 614-615 – AD Maine-et-Loire 1 L. 928 – AD Pas-de-Calais III L. 130 – AD Puy-de-Dôme L. 2171 – AD Bas-Rhin I L. 1515 – AD Seine-Maritime 1152–1154, 3422 et 5098 – AD Seine-et-Marne L. 536 à 539.
*Instruction publique* (série T)
AD Gironde: 24 T 3.
AD Dordogne (Series T was being classified in 1975).
AD Maine-et-Loire: 52 T 5.
AD Morbihan: T 1, T 419.
*Registers of conscription* (série R)
AD Côtes-du-Nord: années 1846 et 1890.
AD Dordogne: années 1867–1881.
AD Meurthe-et-Moselle: années 1841.
AD Morbihan: années 1851 et 1890.
AD Basses-Pyrénées: 1863.
AD Moselle: année 1841.
AD Haut-Rhin: année 1841.
*Censuses* (série M)
census of 1866: AD Eure-et-Loir (une cote par commune) – AD Seine-Maritime: 6 M 184 *bis* à 6 M 228 – AD Aveyron: 29M,
census of 1872: AD Seine-Maritime 6 M 229 *bis* à 6 M 239.

#### Diocesan archives
Bishopric of Rodez: Records of the diocesan visitations (1872–1896) undertaken at the instigation of Cardinal Bourret: 1 volume yearly.

#### Institut pédagogique national
*'Etudes manuscrites faites par les instituteurs du département de Seine et Marne, rassemblées par Château, inspecteur primaire à Meaux, et addressées par lui à de Resbecq, au Ministère de l'Instruction publique, le 22 mai 1875.'*

#### Published sources

#### Synodal statutes
*Statuts synodaux du diocèse d'Alet, faits depuis l'année 1640 jusqu'en 1674, renouvellés et publiés dans le synode tenu à Alet les 20 et 21 mai 1670. Encore dans le synode tenu le 17 et 18 avril 1674*, Paris, 1674.
J.M. Miolano, *Actes de l'Eglise d'Amiens*, Amiens, 1848–49.
*Statuts du diocese d'Angers depuis environ l'an 1240 jusqu'en 1679, recueillis par l'ordre de Henry Arnauld, évêque d'Angers*, Angers, 1680.
*Recueil des règlements et ordonnances du diocèse d'Arras*, Arras, 1746.
*Ordonnances synodales de Nos Seigneurs les Illust. et Révér. évêques d'Autun* (Collected ordonnances from 1706 to 1740), Autun, 1783.

*Recueil des Ordonnances synodales de Mgr André Colbert, évêque d'Auxerre, publié au synode tenu à Auxerre, le 4 mai 1695,* Auxerre, 1699.

*Ordonnances synodales de Mgr l'Illustrissime et Révérentissime évêque d'Auxerre, publiées dans le synode tenu au palais épiscopal d'Auxerre le 18 et 19 juin 1738 et homologuées en Parlement par arrêt des 3 et 5 septembre 1741,* Paris-Auxerre, 1742.

*Statuta seu decreta synodalia Bisuntinae Dioecesis, publicata ab anno 1480 ad Annum 1707,* Besançon, 1707.

*Ordonnances synodales de Mgr F.J. de Roye de la Rochefoucauld...,* Bourges, 1738.

*Statuts, ordonnances, mandemens, règlements... imprimés par ordre de Mgr L.A. de Noailles...,* Châlons, 1693.

*Ordonnances et statuts synodaux du diocèse de Comenge par ... Hugues de Labatut, évêque de Comenge,* Toulouse, 1642.

*Statuts synodaux publiés dans le synode général tenu à Mende les 22 et 23 octobre 1733 par Mgr Gabriel Florent de Choiseul-Beaupré évêque de Mende,* Mende, 1739.

*Statuts et ordonnances synodales de l'Eglise et diocèse de Noyon,* Noyon, 1694.

*Statuts et règlements synodaux publiez dans le synode général tenu à Quimper le mercredy, trentième jour d'avril 1710 par Mgr François Hyacinthe de Ploeux, évêque de Quimper,* Quimper, sd.

*Ordonnances et règlements synodaux pour le diocèse de la Rochelle,* La Rochelle, 1711.

*Statuts du diocèse de St-Brieuc, imprimés par l'ordre de Mgr l'Illustr. et Révérent. Messire Pierre Guillaume de la Vieuxville, évêque et seigneur de St-Brieuc,* Rennes, 1723.

*Ordonnances synodales du diocèse de Rodez, imprimées par ordre d'Illustr. Gabriel de Voyer de Paulmy,* Rodez, 1674.

*Ordonnances et statuts synodaux du diocèse de Saint-Flour,* Saint-Flour, 1760.

*Ordonnances synodales du diocèse de Soissons, publiées au synode tenu le 17 mai 1673 par Mgr Charles de Bourlon et au synode tenu le 17 mai 1700 ...,* Soissons, 1769.

*Statuts synodaux de feu Messire Jacques de Fieux avec les ordonnances synodales faites par Messire Henri de Thiard de Bissy et François Blouet de Canilly,* Toul, 1712.

*Recueil des ordonnances du diocèse de Viviers renouvellées et confirmées par Mgr François Reynaud de Villeneuve,* Bourg Saint-Andéol, 1734.

### 17th- and 18th-century education

J. Cossart, curé de Dormans, *Méthode pour apprendre à lire, écrire, chanter le plain-chant et compter,* 1633.

Charles Demia, *Règlements pour les écoles de la ville et du diocèse de Lyon,* sd.

*L'escole paroissiale ou la manière de bien instruire les enfants dans les petites escoles par un prestre d'une paroisse de Paris,* Paris, 1654.

M. Helie, *Nouveaux principes de lecture, d'écriture, d'orthographe et d'arithmétique, également utiles aux maîtres et maîtresses d'école et à leurs élèves,* Caen et Paris, 1784.

*Quelques maximes touchant la première instruction des enfants,* mid-17th century, cited by Y. Poutet, 1962.

S. Roux, *Méthode nouvelle pour apprendre à lire parfaitement bien le latin et le français,* Paris, 1694, Y. Poutet, 1962.

J.B. de la Salle, *Conduite des Ecoles chrétiennes divisée en deux parties*, Avignon, 1720.

### 19th-Century education

I. *Ministère de l'Instruction publique:*
1. *Statistique rétrospective. Etat récapitulatif et comparatif indiquant, par département, le nombre des conjoints qui ont signé l'acte de leur mariage aux XVIIᵉ, XVIIIᵉ et XIXᵉ siècles.* Documents provided by 15,928 teachers, collected and classified by Maggiolo, *recteur honoraire*, on the commission of the Minister of Education (extract from the *Statistique de l'instruction primaire*, vol. II). Undated.
2. *Etat de l'instruction primaire en 1864*, based on the official reports of the *Inspecteurs d'Académie* (supplement to the *Statistique* of 1863), Paris, 1866, 2 vols.
3. *Statistique de l'Instruction primaire pour l'année 1865*, situation at January 1866, Paris, 1867.
4. *Statistique de l'Enseignement primaire*

| vol. | I | 1876–1877 | Paris | 1878 |
|---|---|---|---|---|
| vol. | II | 1829–1877 | Paris | 1880 |
| vol. | III | 1881–1882 | Paris | 1884 |
| vol. | IV | 1886–1887 | Paris | 1889 |
| vol. | V | 1891-1892 | Paris | 1895 |
| vol. | VI | 1896–1897 | Paris | 1900 |
| vol. | VII | 1901–1902 | Paris | 1904 |
| vol. | VIII | 1906–1907 | Paris | 1909 |

5. *Annexe à la Statistique de l'Enseignement primaire. Degré d'Instruction des Adultes*, 1833–66, Paris, 1866.
6. *Statistiques des cours d'adultes:*

| situation | at 1 April | 1866-n.d. |
|---|---|---|
| situation | at 1 April | 1867-n.d. |
| situation | at 1 April | 1868-n.d. |
| situation | at 1 April | 1869-n.d. |

7. *Rapports au Roi:*
*Rapport au roi par le ministre secrétaire d'Etat au Département de l'Instruction publique sur l'exécution de la loi du 28 juin 1833, relative à l'instruction primaire* (signed F. Guizot), Paris, 1834.
*Rapport au roi . . . sur la situation de l'instruction primaire* (signed Salvandy), Paris, 1837.
*Rapport au roi . . . sur la situation de l'instruction primaire* (signed Villemain), Paris, 1840.
*Rapport au roi . . . sur la situation de l'instruction primaire* (signed Salvandy), Paris, 1843.

II. *Statistique générale de la France:*
1. 2nd series—vol. IV—*Population, mouvement de la population pendant l'année 1854*, Strasbourg, 1858.
2. 2nd series—vol. XIII—*Population, résultats généraux du dénombrement de 1861 comparés aux Cinq Dénombrements antérieurs*, Strasbourg, 1864.
3. 2nd series—vol. XVII –*Population, résultats généraux du dénombrement de 1866*, Paris, 1869.
4. 2nd series—vol. XXI—*Population, résultats généraux du dénombrement de 1872*, Paris, 1875.

5. 2nd series—vol. XVI—*Agriculture, résultats généraux de l'enquête décennale de 1862*, Strasbourg, 1870.

III. *Ministère de l'Industrie, du Commerce, des Postes et Télégraphes*
*Résultats statistiques du recensement général de la population effectué le 24 mars 1901*, 4 vols. Paris, 1904.

IV. *Ministère de la Guerre*
*Comptes présentés en exécution de la loi du 18 mars 1818 sur le recrutement de l'armée pour l'année 1818*, Paris, 1819 (published annually thereafter).

V. *Recueils de règlements, décrets, statistiques, . . . etc.*

Chambre de Commerce de Paris, *Statistique de l'industrie à Paris, résultats de l'enquête faite par la Chambre de Commerce pour les années 1847–1848*, Paris, 1851.

Chambre de Commerce de Paris, *Statistique de l'industrie à Paris, résultats de l'enquête faite par la Chambre de Commerce pour l'année 1860*, Paris, 1864.

*L'Administration de l'Instruction publique de 1863 à 1869*, Ministère de Son Excellence M. Duruy, Paris, 1870.

*Circulaires et instructions officielles relatives à l'Instruction publique*, Ministère de Son Excellence M. Duruy, 1863–1870, Paris, 1870.

*Examen annuel de l'instruction primaire des conscrits et écoles régimentaires des corps de troupes de toutes armes* (Loi du 29 juillet 1910, Décret du 8 septembre 1912, Instruction du 21 septembre 1912, Arrêté du 23 septembre 1912), Paris, 1912.

O. Gréard, *La Législation de l'Instruction primaire en France depuis 1789 jusqu'à nos jours. Recueil des lois, décrets, ordonnances, arrêtés, règlements, décisions, avis, projects de lois. Avec introduction historique et table analytique*, 7 vols. Paris, 1889–1902.

République française, Préfecture des Basses-Pyrénées, *Recueil des Actes Administratifs*, 1874, no. 15.

*Organisation pédagogique, plans d'études et programmes des écoles primaires publiques, arrêtés le 27 juillet 1882.* Paris, 1882.

*Organisation pédagogique et plans d'études*, Paris, 1907.

A. Rendu, *Code universitaire des lois et statuts de l'université royale de France*, Paris, 1827.

### Books and articles

A.C.T. 'De l'instruction publique en France', *Revue des Deux Mondes*, 15 Sept. 1838.

Abbé Affre, *Nouveau Traité des Ecoles Primaires ou Manuel des Instituteurs et des Institutrices*, Paris, 1826.

H. Affre, *Dictionnaire des Institutions, moeurs et coutumes du Rouergue*, Rodez, 1903.

Abbé E. Allain, *L'instruction primaire en France avant la Révolution*, Paris, 1883.

Abbé E. Allain, *Construction à l'histoire de l'Instruction primaire dans la Gironde*, Bordeaux, 1895.

Abbé A. Angot, *L'instruction populaire dans le département de la Mayenne avant 1790*, Paris, 1890.

E. Anthoine, inspecteur d'académie, *Rapport sur l'exposition universelle de 1878*, Lille, 1878.

Ph. Ariès, *L'enfant et la vie familiale sous l'Ancien Régime*, (1960) Paris, 1973.

Ph. Ariès, 'Problèmes de l'Education', in *La France et les Français*, Encyclopédie de la Pléiade, ed. François, Paris, 1972.

A. Armengaud, *Les populations de l'Est-Aquitain au début de l'époque con-temporaine; recherches sur une région sous-développée, vers 1845—1871*, Paris, 1961.

J.-P. Aron, P. Dumont, E. Le Roy-Ladurie, *Anthropologie du conscrit français*, based on the registers of army recruitment (1819–26), Paris-La Haye, 1972.

A. Artonne, L. Guizard, O. Pontal, *Répertoire des Statuts synodaux des diocèses de l'ancienne France*, Paris, 1969.

L. Audiat, 'L'instruction primaire gratuite et obligatoire avant 1789', *Archives Historiques de la Saintonge et de l'Aunis*, XXV, Paris-Saintes, 1896.

A. Aulard, 'Etat de l'instruction primaire dans un département français en l'an VI', *La Révolution française*, vol. XIII, 1887.

F. Autorde, 'L'instruction primaire avant la Révolution (dans la Creuse)', *Mémoires de la Société des sciences naturelles et archéologiques de la Creuse*, vol. VI, 1888.

A. Babeau, *L'instruction primaire dans les campagnes avant 1789, d'après des documents tirés des archives communales et départementales de l'Aube*, Troyes, 1875.

P. Bailly, 'A.R. Bellissant (1811–1897), premier "major" de l'Ecole Normale d'Instituteurs de Melun', *Bull. de la Société d'études historiques, géographiques, et scientifiques de la région parisienne*, 1953, no. 79.

Abbé L. Baraud, 'L'instruction primaire dans le Bas-Poitou avant la Révolution', *Revue du Bas-Poitou*, 1908 and 1909.

P. Bayaud, 'L'enseignement mutuel dans l'Académie de Paris (1817–1822)', *Actes du 88ᵉ Congrès des Sociétés savantes, Clermont-Ferrand*, 1963, Paris, 1964,

A. Bellee, *Recherches sur l'instruction publique dans le département de la Sarthe, avant et pendant la Révolution*, Le Mans, 1875.

R. Beteille, *La vie quotidienne en Rouergue avant 1914*, Paris, 1973.

M. Blanc, *Essai sur l'instruction primaire avant 1789* (Basses-Alpes), Forcalquier, 1954.

R. Blanchard, *La densité de population du département du Nord au XIXᵉ siècle*, a study of ten censuses, Lille, 1906.

B. Bois, 'Recherches historiques sur l'enseignement primaire en Anjou des origines jusqu'à nos jours', *Revue de l'Anjou*, Oct., Nov., Dec. 1908, March, June, July, 1909.

Bonnaire, Préfet, *Mémoire au ministre de l'Intérieur sur la statistique du département des Hautes-Alpes*, Paris, Year IX.

B. Bonnin, 'L'alphabétisation des classes populaires rurales en Dauphiné au XVIIᵉ siècle', 'Le XVIIIᵉ siècle et l'Education', supplement to no. 88 of the *Revue Marseille*, 1st quarter 1972.

H. Boon, *Enseignement primaire et alphabétisation dans l'agglomération bruxelloise de 1830 à 1879*, Louvain, 1969.

M. Bordes, 'Contribution à l'étude de l'enseignement et de la vie intellectuelle dans le pays de l'Intendance d'Auch au XVIIIᵉ siècle', *Bull. de la Société archéologique du Gers*, 4, 1957 and 1-2-3, 1958.

L. Borne, *L'instruction publique en Franche-Comté avant 1792*, Paris, 1957.

A. Boucher and E. Thevenin, *Situation de l'enseignement primaire dans la ville d'Issoudun et son canton Nord*, Châteauroux, 1882.

R. Boudard, 'L'enseignement primaire clandestin dans le département de la Creuse entre 1830 et 1880', *Mémoires de la société des sciences naturelles et archéologiques de la Creuse*, vol. 33, part 3, 1959.

Canon F. Boulard, *Premier itinéraire en sociologie religieuse*, Paris, 1966.

Canon F. Boulard, *Pratique religieuse urbaine et régions culturelles*, Paris, 1968.
A. Bourgeois, 'Le clerc d'église et l'enseignement en Artois avant la Révolution', *Bulletin de la société académique des Antiquaires de la Morinie*, vol. XVIII, 1954.
L. Bourilly, 'L'instruction publique dans la région de Toulon', *Bulletin de l'Académie du Var*, vol. XVIII, 1895.
M.J. Bowman and C.A. Anderson 'Human capital and economic modernization in historical perspective', in *4° Conférence internationale d'histoire économique (Bloomington 1968)*, Paris, 1973.
A. Boyer, *Le Français par l'image, manuel pratique pour le tout premier enseignement du langage oral et écrit à l'image des écoles d'enfants sourds-muets, convenant également aux enfants de nos écoles patoisantes, aux jeunes indigènes de nos colonies ainsi qu'aux élèves des classes de français à l'étranger*, Paris, 1905.
A. Brun, *L'introduction de la langue française en Béarn et Roussillon*, Paris, 1922.
F. Buisson (ed.), *Dictionnaire de pédagogie et d'instruction primaire*, 5 volumes and 2 supplements, Paris, 1882–93.
F. Buisson (ed.), *Nouveau Dictionnaire de pédagogie et d'instruction primaire*, Paris, 1911.
B. Cacères, *Regards neufs sur les autodidactes*, Paris, 1960.
B. Cacères, *Histoire de l'Education populaire*, Paris, 1964.
A. Cariou, 'L'instruction dans le département du Morbihan à la veille de la Révolution de 1789', *Mémoire de la Société historique et archéologique de Bretagne*, vol. XXXV, 1955.
T. Cauvin, *Recherches sur les établissements de charité et d'instruction publique du diocèse du Mans*, Le Mans, 1825.
M. de Certeau, D. Julia, J. Revel, *Une politique de la langue: la Révolution française et le patois: l'enquête de Grégoire*, Paris, 1975.
Dr Chabrand, 'De l'Etat de l'instruction primaire dans le Brianconnais avant 1789', *Bull. de l'Académie delphinale*, 3rd series, vol. XVI, 1893.
J. Champion, *Les langues africaines et la francophonie; Essai d'une pédagogie du français en Afrique Noire par une analyse typologique des fautes*, Paris-La Haye, 1974.
F. Chapelle, *Statistique de l'ignorance dans le département de la Loire, avec carte teintée*, Saint-Etienne, 1870.
A. de Charmasse, *Etat de l'instruction primaire dans l'ancien diocèse d'Autun pendant les XVIIe et XVIIIe siècles*, Autun, 1876.
R. Chartier, M.M. Compère, D. Julia, *L'éducation en France du XVIe siècle au XVIIIe siècle*, Paris, 1976.
Ch. L. Chassin, *Projet de Cahier du délégué de commune aux élections sénatoriales*, Coll. of 'L'Instruction républicaine', New series, no. 20, Paris, 1875.
P. Chaunu, *La civilisation de l'Europe des Lumières*, Paris, 1971.
P. Chaunu et al., 'Mentalités religieuses dans la France de l'Ouest au XIXe siècle et XXe siècle, Etudes d'histoire sérielles', *Cahiers des Annales de Normandie*, No. 8, Caen, 1976.
P. Chevallier (ed.) *La scolarisation en France depuis un siècle*, no. conference held at Grenoble in May 1968. Paris-La Haye, 1974.
Joseph Chollet, 'Notes sur l'enseignement primaire dans l'Orne sous le Second Empire', *Annales de Normandie*, 25th year, no. 3, October 1975.
G. Cholvy, 'Etat de l'instruction primaire dans l'Hérault vers 1833', *Actes du 89e Congrès national des sociétés savantes, Lyon, 1964*, Paris, 1965.
G. Cholvy, 'Le catholicisme en Rouergue aux XIXe et XXe siècles: première approche', *Actes du Congrès d'Etudes de Rodez*, 1974.

G. Cholvy, 'Une chrétienné au XIX^e siècle: La Lozère', *Fédération historique du Languedoc méditerranéen et du Roussillon, XLVI^e Congrès, Mende 1973*, Mende, 1974.

Dr Ch. Chopinet, 'Etude statistique de l'état de l'instruction dans la subdivision militaire de Saint-Gaudens', *Revue de Comminges*, vol. II, 1886.

E. Choron, 'Recherches historiques sur l'instruction primaire dans le Soissonnais', extracts from the *Bulletin archéologique, historique et scientifique de Soissons*, 1865–66, 1875, 1879.

C.M. Cipolla, *Literacy and development in the West*, Londres, 1969.

F. Colonna, *Instituteurs algériens, 1833–1839, Travaux et recherches de sciences politiques*, no. 36, Paris, 1975.

A. Combes, *Statistique de l'arrondissement de Castres*, Castres, 1834.

G. Compayre, *Histoire critique des doctrines de l'éducation en France depuis le XVI^e siècle* (1879), Geneva, 1970.

G. Compayre, 'Charles Démia et les origines de l'enseignement primaire à Lyon', *Revue d'Histoire de Lyon*, 1905.

E. Coonaert, 'Flamand et Français dans l'enseignement en Flandre française, des annexions au XX^e siècle', *Revue du Nord*, April-June 1971.

A. Corbin, *Archaïsme et modernité en Limousin au XIX^e siècle, 1845–1880*, Paris, 1975.

A. Corbin, 'Pour une étude sociologique de la croissance de l'alphabétisation au XIX^e siècle. L'instruction des conscrits du Cher et de l'Eure-et-Loir (1833–1883)', *Revue d'histoire économique et sociale*, vol. 53, no. 1, 1975.

A. Corbon, *De l'enseignement professionnel*, Paris, 1859.

F. Courtois, 'Les écoles du Creusot, 1787–1882', *Mémoire de la Société Eduenne*, New series vol. XXI, 1893.

V. Cousin, *De l'instruction publique dans quelques pays de l'Allemagne et particulièrement en Prusse*, Paris, 1833.

G. Cuvier et M. Noel, *Rapport sur l'Instruction publique dans les nouveaux départements de la Basse-Allemagne, fait en exécution du décret impérial du 13 décembre 1810*, Paris, 1812.

A. Darbel, 'Inégalités régionales ou inégalités sociales? Essai d'explication des taux de scolarisation', *Revue Française de Sociologie*, vol. VIII, special number, 1967.

F. Darsy, *Etude historique sur l'instruction publique: les écoles et collèges du diocèse d'Amiens*, Amiens, 1881.

P. Dauthuille, *L'école primaire dans les Basses-Alpes, depuis la Révolution jusqu'à nos jours*, Digne, 1900.

P. Dauthuille, *L'école primaire dans les Deux-Sèvres depuis ses origines jusqu'à nos jours*, Niort, 1904.

J.-Ph. David, *L'établissement de l'enseignement primaire au XIX^e siècle dans le département du Maine-et-Loire (1816-1879)*, Angers, 1967.

Decap, 'L'instruction publique dans le diocèse de Rieux en Languedoc avant la Révolution', *Comité des travaux historiques, Notices, inventaires, documents*, vol. III, Documents on local history, MM. Decap, de la Martinière et Bideau, Paris, 1914.

N. Delacroix, *Statistique du département de la Drôme*, new edition, Paris, 1835.

L. Deries, 'La naissance de l'Ecole Normale d'Instituteurs de la Manche (1833–1848)', *Notices et documents publiés par la Société d'agriculture et d'archéologie de la Manche*, 1931, vol. 43.

A.P. Deseilligny, *De l'influence de l'Education sur la moralité et le bien-être des classes laborieuses*, Paris, 1868.

G. Desert, 'Les progrès de l'instruction primaire dans le Calvados (xix-xx$^e$ siècles)', *Cahiers d'histoire de l'enseignement*, no. 2, 1974 (Public records of the C.R.D.P. of Romen).

Destutt-Tracy, *Observation sur le système actuel d'instruction publique*, Paris, Year IX.

M. Dieudonne, Préfet, *Statistique du département du Nord*, Douai, Year XII, 1804.

Ronald Doré, *Education in Tokugawa Japan*, Berkeley, 1965.

Abbé Doyotte, *Manuel du Délégué cantonal*, Paris, 1876.

G. Duby (ed.), *Histoire de la France*, Paris, 1972.

M. Dunglas, *Notice sur les Béates de la Haute-Loire*, Rodez, 1865.

J. Dupaquier, *Les écoles de paroisse dans le Vexin français* au XVIII$^e$ siècle, Pontoise, 1966.

G. Dupeux, 'La croissance urbaine en France au xix$^e$ siècle', *Revue d'histoire économique et sociale*, no. 2, 1974.

Baron Ch. Dupin, *Forces productives et commerciales de la France*, Paris, 1827.

V. Duruy, *Notes et souvenirs*, vol. I, Paris, 1901.

G. Duveau, *La vie ouvrière en France sous le Second Empire*, Paris, 1947.

G. Duverdier, 'La pénétration du livre dans une société de culture orale: le cas de Tahiti', *Revue française d'histoire du livre*, 1971. 'L'école rurale sous la Restauration (règlement de 1819)', *Histoire locale, Beauce et Perche*, no. 20, 1965.

N. Elias, *La civilisation des moeurs* (1939), Paris, 1973.

R. Engelsing, *Analphabetum und Lektüre, Zum Sozialgeschichte des Lesens in Deutschland zwischen feodaler und industrielle Gesellschaft*, Stuttgart, 1973.

Erckmann-Chatrian, *Histoire d'un sous-maître*, Paris, 1873.

J.H. Fabre, *Souvenirs entomologiques*, 6th series, Paris, 1899.

P. Fayet, *Les écoles en Bourgogne sous l'Ancien Régime*, Langres, 1875.

P. Fayet, *Pièces d'archives et documents inédits pour servir à l'histoire de l'instruction publique en Lorraine*, Nancy, 1875.

P. Fayet, *L'enseignement dans le Berry avant 1789*, Paris, 1879.

P. Fayet, *L'enseignement en Auvergne avant 1789*, Châteauroux, 1879.

P. Fayet, *Recherches historiques et statistiques sur les écoles et communes de la Haute-Marne*, Paris, 1879.

P. Fayet, *La rétribution scolaire et la gratuité de l'enseignement primaire, étude historique*, Paris, 1886.

C.D. Férard, *Mémoires d'un vieux maître d'école*, Paris, 1894.

J. Ferry, *Discours et opinions*, vol. III, Paris, 1893.

J. Ferté, *La vie religieuse dans les campagnes parisiennes (1622–1693)*, Paris, 1962.

J. Flammermont, *Histoire de l'industrie à Lille*, Lectures by M.A. de Saint-Léger, Lille, 1907.

M. Fleury and P. Valmary, 'Les progrès de l'instruction élémentaire de Louis XIV à Napoléon III d'après l'enquête de L. Maggiolo (1877–79)', *Population*, Jan.-March 1957.

C. Fohlen, 'Instruction et développement économique en France au xix$^e$ siècle', in *4th Conférence internationale d'histoire économique (Bloomington 1968)*, Paris, 1973.

E. Fontaine de Resbecq, *Histoire de l'instruction primaire dans les communes qui ont formé le département du Nord*, Paris, 1878.

H. Forestier, *L'Yonne au XIX$^e$ siècle*, Auxerre, 1959.

M. Foucault, *Surveiller et punir*, Paris, 1975.

Foulques de Villaret, *L'instruction primaire avant 1789 à Orléans et dans les communes de l'arrondissement d'après des documents inédits*, Orléans, 1882.

Dr Fouquet, père, 'Du recrutement dans le Morbihan au point de vue de l'instruction primaire', *Bulletin de la société polynmathique du Morbihan*, 1874.

F. Furet and W. Sachs, 'La croissance de l'alphabétisation en France' *Annales E.S.C.*, no. 3, May-June 1974.

M. Gadebled, 'Aperçu statistique sur l'instruction primaire dans le département de l'Eure depuis la loi du 28 juin 1833', *Recueil de la société libre d'agriculture, Sciences, Arts et Belles-Lettres du département de l'Eure*, vol. IX, 1838.

M. Garcia, *L'école normale primaire d'instituteurs du Cantal, 1831–1880*, report on teaching edited by M. Silvert, Clermont-Ferrand, undated.

Canon A. Garnier, *Au temps de l'Empire et de la Restauration: L'Eglise et l'éducation du peuple*, Paris, 1933.

J.-P. Giret, *La vie scolaire et les progrès de l'instruction populaire en Eure-et-Loir*, report on teaching typewriting, Faculté des lettres et sciences humaines de Tours, 1973.

M. Gontard, *L'enseignement primaire en France de la Révolution à la loi Guizot (1789-1833)*, Paris-Lyon, 1959.

M. Gontard, *La question des Ecoles normales primaires, de la Révolution de 1789 à nos jours*, Toulouse, 1962.

M. Gontard, *L'Ecole primaire de la France bourgeoise (1833–1875)*, Toulouse, 1964.

M. Gontard, *L'oeuvre scolaire de la III<sup>e</sup> République: l'enseignement primaire en France de 1876 à 1914*, Toulouse, nd.

J. Goody (ed.), *Literacy in traditional societies*, Cambridge University Press, 1968.

J. Goody, I. Watt, 'The consequences of literacy' in *Comparative studies in society and history*, vol. v, no. 3, Cambridge, 1963.

Harvey J. Graff, 'Towards a meaning of literacy: Literacy and social structure in Hamilton, Ontario, 1861', *History of Education Quarterly*, Fall, 1972.

*Grandes villes et petites villes, Démographie et croissance urbaine—Démographie et scolarisation*, National conferences of the C.N.R.S., Lyon, St-Etienne, Grenoble (22–26 April 1968), C.N.R.S., Paris, 1970.

O.Gréard, *Organisation pédagogique des écoles communales de la Seine*, Paris, 1868.

G. Grimmert, 'Livret d'instituteur ambulant', *Le Vieux papier*, 1956.

B. Groethuysen, *Les origines de l'esprit bourgeois*, Paris, 1927.

A.M. Guerry, *Essai sur la statistique morale de la France*, Paris, 1833.

J. Guibeaud, 'Notes statistiques sur l'instruction publique à Perpignan, 1684–1891', *Société Agricole, Scientifique et littérature des Pyrénées Orientales*, vol. XXXIV, 1893.

L. Guibert, *L'instruction primaire en Limousin sous l'Ancien Régime*, Limoges, 1888.

E. Guillaumin, *La vie d'un simple (Mémoires d'un métayer)* (1905), Paris, 1973.

F. Guizot, *Essai sur l'histoire et sur l'état actuel de l'instruction publique en France*, Paris, 1816.

F. Guizot, *Mémoires*, Paris, 1860.

C.J. Hefele, *Histoire des Conciles,* trad. H. Leclercq, T.X. *Les décrets du Concile de Trente*, Paris, 1938.

M. Herpin, *Sur l'enseignement mutuel, les écoles primaires des campagnes et les salles d'éducation de l'enfance*, Paris, 1835.

Ch. Hiegel, 'Problème scolaire et linguistique à Mainvillers en 1745', *Cahiers Lorrains*, July 1970.

'Instruction publique', *Annuaire des cinq départements de l'ancienne Normandie*, 1st year, 1835.

J. Houdaille, 'Les signatures au mariage de 1740 à 1829', *Population*, 1977, 1.

E. Jacoulet, *Notice historique sur les écoles normales d'instituteurs et d'institutrices*, Paris, 1889.

E. Jaloustre, *Les anciennes écoles de l'Auvergne*, Clermont-Ferrand, 1882.

J. Janicot, *Monographie des écoles communales de Lyon (1828–1891)*, Lyon, 1891.

E. Johansson, 'Studying literacy in the Swedish church examination registers', *Rapport de recherche inédit, juin 1974*, favourable report by Prof. Johansson, University of Umea.

E. Johansson, 'The History of Literacy in Sweden, in comparison with some other countries', *Education Reports Umea*, no. 12, 1977.

R. Johnson, 'Educational policy and social control in early Victorian England', *Past and Present*, 1970.

R. Johnson, 'Notes on the schooling of the English working class, 1780–1850'. *Communication inédite* on the *Journée d'Histoire sociale européene sur* 'Les problèmes de la formation du prolétariat au temps de la première Révolution industrielle', held by the Maison des Sciences de l'Homme, Paris, 1975.

J. Jovenet, *Opinion relative aux moyens à employer pour la propagation de l'enseignement mutuel dans les écoles civiles et les écoles régimentaires*, Paris, 1817.

D. Julia, 'L'enseignement primaire dans le diocèse de Reims à la fin de l'Ancien Régime', *Annales historiques de la Révolution française*, April-June 1970.

D. Julia, 'L'enseignement primaire dans le diocèse de Reims à la fin de l'Ancien Régime', *Actes du 95ᵉ Congrès des sociétés savantes, Reims, 1970*, Section on modern and contemporary history, 1974.

D. Julia, 'La réforme post-tridentine en France d'après les procèsverbaux des visites pastorales: ordre et résistance', in *La Sociéta religiosa nell'etâ moderna, Atti del convegno studi di storia sociale e religiosa*, Capaecio-Paestrum, 18–21 May 1972.

B. Julien and J. Naudan, *Histoire des Ecoles Normales de l'Aveyron*, Rodez, 1936.

Kaestle and M.C. Vinovskis, 'Quantification, Urbanization and the History of Education: an Analysis of the Determinants of School Attendance in New York State in 1845', in *Historical Methods Newsletters*, vol. VIII, no. 1, Dec. 1974.

J.-P. Kintz, 'Instruction et lectures populaires à la fin du Second empire', in *L'Alsace en 1870–1871*, Faculté des Lettres de Strasbourg, 1971.

J.-P. Kintz, 'Recherches sur l'instruction populaire en Alsace à l'aube du XIXᵉ siècle', in *Mélanges Reinhardt*, Paris, 1973.

M. Lachiver, *La population de Meulan du XVIIᵉ au XIXᵉ siècle* (about 1600–1870), Study of historic demography, Paris, 1969.

E. Lafforgue, *L'instruction primaire en Bigorre*, Tarbes, 1924.

M. Laget, 'Petites écoles en Languedoc au XVIIIᵉ siècle', *Annales, E.S.C.*, Nov.-Dec. 1971.

M. Laget, 'Ecoles paroissiales et Révocation dans le diocèse de Montpellier', *Le XVIIIᵉ siècle et l'Education*, Supplement to no. 88 of the *Revue Marseille*, 1972.

E. Laigneau, *Monographie de l'Ecole normale primaire de Troyes*, Troyes, 1897.

J.-M. Robert de Lamennais, *De l'enseignement mutuel*, Saint-Brieuc, 1819.

C. Langlois, *Un diocèse breton au début du XIXᵉ siècle: le diocèse de Vannes, 1800–1830*, Paris, 1974.

Th. W. Laqueur and M. Sanderson, 'Debate: Literacy and Social Mobility in the Industrial Revolution in England', *Past and Present*, no. 64, August 1974.

A. Laveille, *L'instruction primaire dans l'ancien diocèse d'Avranches avant la Révolution*, Evreux, 1891.

M. Leblond, *La scolarisation au XIX^e siècle dans le Nord*, Mémoire de maîtrise, Lille, 1968.

A. Léger, 'Etude sur les principales causes des valeurs non-scolaires et du peu de progrès des enfants dans les écoles', *Annuaire de la société d'émulation de la Vendée*, 1880.

N. Lemaitre, *Tradition et continuité aux confins de l'Auvergne: Ussel et son pays (1680–1789)*, Thèse de III^e cycle, 1975.

R. Lemoine, *La loi Guizot, 28 juin 1833, son application dans le département de la Somme*, Paris, 1933.

R. Lemoine, *L'enseignement mutuel dans le département de la Somme sous la Seconde Restauration*, Abbeville, 1933.

L. Lempereur, *Etat du diocèse de Rodez en 1771*, Rodez, 1906.

A. Lequeux, 'L'évolution de l'industrie houillère dans la région du Nord', *Bulletin de la société de géographie de Lille*, nos. 7 and 8, 1936.

E. Le Roy Ladurie, 'Ethnographie rurale du XVIII^e siècle: Restif de la Bretonne', *Ethnologie française*, nos. 3–4, 1972.

F. Le Play, *Les Ouvriers européens, études sur les travaux, la vie domestique et la condition morale des populations ouvrières de l'Europe, précédées d'un exposé de la méthode d'observation*, Paris, 1885.

*Les ouvriers des deux-mondes, Etudes sur les travaux, la vie domestique et la condition morale des populations ouvrières des diverses contrées et sur les rapports qui les unissent aux autres classes*, published in the form of monographs by the 'Société internationale d'études pratiques d'économie sociale', three series, eleven volumes, Paris, 1857.

P. Lesage, *L'enseignement mutuel de 1815 aux débuts de la III^e République* (contribution à l'étude de la pédagogie de la lecture et de l'écriture dans les écoles mutuelles). Thèse de doctorat de III^e cycle, Univ. R.-Descartes, Paris V.

J. Levron, 'Les registres paroissiaux et l'Etat Civil en France', *Archivum*, vol. 9, 1959.

R.P. Leygues, *Histoire de la province de Rodez* (unedited publication of the Congrégation des Clercs de Saint-Viateur, supplément 1959).

F. L'Huillier, 'L'enseignement primaire en Alsace à la fin du Second Empire' in *l'Alsace en 1870–1871*, publication of the Faculté des Lettres de Strasbourg, Strasbourg, 1971.

K. Lock Ridge, *Literacy in colonial New England: an enquiry into the social context of literacy in the early modern west*, New York, 1974.

C. Looten, 'La question du flamand', *Bulletin du Comité flamand de Flandre*, 1919–21.

C. Looten, 'La pauvre école de Cassel', *Bulletin du Comité flamand de Flandre*, 1924.

P. Lorain, *Tableau de l'instruction primaire en France d'après les documents authentiques et notamment d'après les rapports adressés au ministre de l'Instruction publique par les 490 inspecteurs chargés de visiter toutes les écoles de France à la fin de 1833*, Paris, 1837.

P. Lundgreen, 'Industrialization and the educational formation of manpower in Germany', *Journal of social history*, 1974.

L. Maggiolo, *Pièces d'archives et documents inédits pour servir à l'histoire de l'instruction publique en Lorraine*, Nancy, 1874.

L. Maggiolo, *L'instruction publique dans le district de Lunéville, 1789 à 1802*, Nancy, 1875.

L. Maggiolo, *Les archives scolaires de la Beauce et du Gâtinais*, Nancy, 1877.

L. Maggiolo, *De l'enseignement primaire dans les Hautes-Cévennes*, Nancy, 1879.

L. Maggiolo, *Pouillé scolaire du diocèse de Toul*, Nancy, 1880.

L. Maggiolo, *Les écoles dans les anciens diocèses de Châlons et Verdun avant 1789*, Arcis-sur-Aube, 1881.

L. Maggiolo, *Pouillé scolaire du diocèse de Verdun*, Nancy, 1882.

L. Maggiolo, *Historique de l'instruction publique dans les Vosges avant et après 1789*, Nancy, 1889.

L. Maggiolo, *De la condition de l'instruction primaire et du maître d'école en Lorraine avant 1789*, Paris, 1889.

L. Maggiolo, *Les écoles avant et après 1789 dans la Meurthe, la Meuse, la Moselle et les Vosges*, Nancy, nd.

L. Maitre, *L'instruction publique dans les villes et les campagnes du Comté nantais avant 1789*, Nantes, 1882.

D. Malet, *Monographie de l'Ecole normale d'instituteurs d'Aix depuis son origine jusqu'à nos jours*, Aix, 1889.

M. Marquis, Préfet, *Mémoire statistique du département de la Meurthe*, Paris, Year XIII.

L. Mazoyer, 'Rénovation intellectuelle et problèmes sociaux: la bourgeoisie du Gard et l'instruction au début de la Monarchie de Juillet', *Annales d'Histoire économique et sociale*, vol. VI, 1934.

M. Mead, 'Our Educational Emphasis in Primitive Perspective', *American Journal of Sociology*, XLVIII, 1943.

Ch. Metais, *Les petites écoles à Vendôme et dans le Vendômois*, Orléans, 1886.

L.A. Meunier, 'Obstacles qu'apportent aux progrès et à l'amélioration de l'enseignement primaire la plupart des familles qui envoient leurs enfants dans les écoles', *Recueil de la société libre d'agriculture, sciences, arts et belles-lettres du département de l'Eure*, 1838.

J. Meyer, 'Alphabétisation, lecture et écriture. Essai sur l'instruction populaire en Bretagne du XVI$^e$ au XIX$^e$ siècle', *Actes du 95$^e$ Congrès des sociétés savantes, Reims, 1970*, Section on modern and contemporary history, vol. I, Paris, 1974.

J. Michelet, *Nos fils*, Paris, 1869.

J. Moreau (pseud. de Jean Macé), *Lettres d'un garde national à son voisin*, Paris, 1848.

M. Nadaud, *Mémoires du Leonard, ancien garçon maçon* (Bourganeuf, 1895), Paris, 1948.

F.N. Nicollet, 'Etat de l'enseignement primaire dans le département des Hautes-Alpes', *Bulletin de la Société d'étude des Hautes Alpes*, 1st quarter, 1894.

F.N. Nicollet, 'Notice historique sur l'Ecole normale d'instituteurs des Hautes Alpes', *Bulletin de la société d'études des Hautes-Alpes*, vol. XV, 1896.

'Comité des travaux historiques et scientifiques', *Notices, Inventaires et Documents*, Paris, 1914.

R. Oberlé, 'Etude sur l'analphabétisme à Mulhouse au siècle de l'industrialisation', *Bulletin du musée historique de Mulhouse*, vol. LXVII, 1959.

R. Oberlé, *L'enseignement à Mulhouse de 1798 à 1870*, Paris, 1961.

M. Ozouf, *L'Ecole, l'Eglise et la République*, Paris, 1963.

M.A. Peigne, *Méthode de lecture, ouvrage adopté par la société pour l'instruction élémentaire*, Paris, 1832.

A. Perdonnet, *De l'utilité de l'instruction pour le peuple*, Paris, 1867.

J.-Cl. Perrot, 'L'âge d'or de la statistique régionale (an IV à 1804)', *Annales Historiques de la Révolution française*, no. 224, April-June 1976.

J.-Cl. Perrot, *Genèse d'une ville moderne: Caen au XVIII<sup>e</sup> siècle*, Paris-La Haye, 1975.

L. Perouas, *Le diocèse de la Rochelle de 1648 à 1724, Sociologie et pastorale*, Paris, 1964.

P. Pierrard, *La vie ouvrière à Lille sous le Second Empire*, Paris, 1965.

P. Pierrard, '*L'enseignement primaire à Lille sous la Monarchie de Juillet*', in *Revue du Nord*, no. 220, Jan.-March 1974.

Pieyre fils, Préfet, *Statistique du département du Lot-et-Garonne*, Paris, Year X.

Dom P. Piolin, 'Les petites écoles jansénistes dans l'Anjou au XVII<sup>e</sup> siècle', *Revue de l'Anjou*, Jan.-June 1876.

Ch. Portal, 'L'instruction primaire dans le Tarn au XIX<sup>e</sup> siècle', in *Revue Historique, Scientifique et littéraire du Département du Tarn*, vol. 23, 1906.

Y. Poutet, 'L'enseignement de la langue française est-il redevable à Saint J.B. de la Salle de l'existence d'un nouveau syllabaire', *Mémoires de la société d'agriculture, commerce, sciences et arts de la Marne*, vol. LXXV, 1960.

Y. Poutet, 'Une phase scolaire de la querelle des Anciens et des Modernes: la dispute des syllabaires', *XVIII<sup>e</sup> siècle*, no. 43, 1960.

Y. Poutet, 'Une victoire de l'enseignement du français par le français: "Le syllabaire français" de J.B. de la Salle (1698)', *Le Français moderne*, no. 4, 1962.

Y. Poutet, 'La compagnie du Saint-Sacrement et les écoles à Marseille', *Provence historique*, vol. XIII, Oct.-Dec. 1963.

Y. Poutet, 'L'auteur de l'Eschole paroissiale et quelques usages du temps (1654)', *Bulletin de la Société des bibliophiles de Guyenne*, a. 32, no. 77, 1963.

Y. Poutet, *Le XVII<sup>e</sup> siècle et les origines lassalliennes, Recherches sur la genèse de l'oeuvre scolaire et religieuse de J.B. de la Salle*, Rennes, 1970.

Y. Poutet, 'L'enseignement des pauvres dans la France du XVII<sup>e</sup> siècle', *XVII<sup>e</sup> siècle*, nos. 90–91, 1971.

J.E. Puiseux, *L'instruction primaire dans le diocèse ancien de Châlons-sur-Marne avant 1789*, Châlons-sur-Marne, 1881.

M. Quantin, *Recherches sur l'instruction primaire du temps passé principalement dans les diocèses de Sens et d'Auxerre*, Auxerre, 1876.

M. Quantin, *Histoire de l'instruction primaire avant 1789 dans les pays qui forment le département de l'Yonne*, Auxerre, 1878.

J. Queniart, *Culture et société urbaine dans la France de l'Ouest au XVIII<sup>e</sup> siècle*, Thèse de doctorat d'Etat, University of Paris I—Panthéon Sorbonne, le 20 juin 1975.

J. Queniart, 'Les apprentissages scolaires élémentaires au XVIII<sup>e</sup> siecle: faut-il réformer Maggiolo?' *Revue d'histoire Moderne et Contemporaine*, Jan.-March 1977.

H. Quignon, 'Le centenaire des cours normaux primaires de l'Oise, 1804–1807', *Bulletin de la société d'Etudes historiques et scientifiques de l'Oise*, vol. I, 1905.

Ed. Quinet, *Histoire de mes idées*, Paris, 1858.

M. Rebouillat, 'L'instruction publique dans le département de Saône-et-Loire sous le Consulat et le Premier Empire', *Actes du 88<sup>e</sup> congrès national des sociétés savantes, Clermont-Ferrand, 1963*, Paris, 1964.

E. Rendu, *De l'Education populaire dans l'Allemagne du Nord et de ses rapports avec les doctrines philosophiques et religieuses*, Paris, 1855.

'René Masson, capitaine de cabotage', *Cahiers de l'Iroise*, no. 3, 1956.

N. Restif de la Bretonne, *Les Gynographes ou Idées de deux honnêtes femmes sur un projet de règlement proposé à toute l'Europe pour mettre les femmes à leur place et opérer le bonheur des deux sexes*, Paris, 1777.

N. Restif de la Bretonne, *Monsieur Nicolas ou le coeur humain dévoilé* (1796), Paris, 1959.

A. Rey, 'L'école et la population de Saint-Prix (canton de Montmorency) depuis 1668', *Mémoire de la Société de l'histoire de Paris*, vol. V, 1879.

A. Rey, 'Enseignement primaire et instruction publique dans les états pontificaux de France et les régions qui ont formé le département du Vaucluse', *Mémoires de l'Académie du Vaucluse*, 1892.

A. Rivet, 'Aspects et problèmes de l'enseignement en Haute-Loire pendant la première moitié du XIXᵉ siècle', *Actes du 88ᵉ Congrès National des sociétés savantes, Clermont-Ferrand, 1963*, Paris, 1964.

Ch. Robert, *De l'ignorance des populations ouvrières et rurales de la France et des causes qui tendent à la perpétuer*—Information provided by state primary-school teachers and assembled by M. Charles Robert, maître des Requêtes au Conseil d'Etat, Montbéliard, 1863.

Ch. Robert, *De l'ignorance*, Paris, 1867.

Ch. Robert, *Notice sur l'enseignement donné à Morcenx par la Compagnie des Chemins de fer du midi*, Paris, 1873.

Ch. de Robillard de Beaurepaire, *Recherches sur l'instruction publique dans le diocèse de Rouen avant 1789*, Evreux, 1872.

L. Robin, *Les petites écoles et leurs régents en Saintonge et Aunis avant la Révolution* (1685–1789), La Rochelle, 1968.

W.S. Robinson, 'Ecological correlations and the behaviour of individuals', *American Sociological Review*, 15(3), 1950.

A. de Rohan-Chabot, *Les écoles de campagne en Lorraine au XVIIᵉ siècle*, Paris, 1969.

J. Rohr, *Victor Duruy, ministre de Napoléon III, Essai sur la politique de l'instruction-publique au temps de l'Empire libéral*, Paris, 1967.

J.-J. Rousseau, *La nouvelle Héloïse* (1761), *Œuvres complètes*, vol. II, Bibliothèque de la Pléiade, Paris, 1969.

J.-J. Rousseau, *Emile ou de l'Education* (1762), *Œuvres complètes*, vol. IV, Bibliothèque de la Pléiade, Paris, 1969.

M. Sacx, 'L'enseignement primaire dans une commune basque: Bidart, 1715–1885', *Bulletin du Musée Basque*, no. 50, 1970.

A. de Saint-Léger, *La Flandre maritime et Dunkerque sous la domination française (1659–1789)*, Paris, 1900.

R. Sancier, 'L'enseignement primaire en Bretagne de 1815 à 1850', *Mémoires de la Société Historique et Archéologique de Bretagne*, 1952 and 1953.

G. Sand, *Histoire de ma vie* (1854–55), Paris, 1968.

M. Sanderson, 'Social change and Elementary Education in Industrial Lancashire, 1780–1840', *Northern History*, III, 1968.

Sarazin, *Manuel pratique des écoles élémentaires ou Exposé de la méthode d'enseignement mutuel*, Paris, 1829.

E. Schmidt, 'L'instruction primaire à la campagne en Lorraine, il y a cent ans, d'après l'enquête de 1779', *Revue chrétienne*, April-May 1880.

R. Schofield, 'The measurement of literacy in pre-industrial England', in *Literacy in Traditional Societies*, J. Goody ed., Cambridge University Press, 1968.

C. Schuwer, *Quelques mots sur l'instruction primaire en Corse avant et depuis la Révolution*, Corte, 1880.

M. Serurier, 'L'instruction primaire dans la région des Pyrénées occidentales et spécialement en Béarn, depuis la fin du XVI$^e$ siècle jusqu'en 1789', *Bulletin de la société des sciences, Lettres et arts de Pau*, vol. III, 1873–74.

A. Siegfried, *Tableau politique de la France de l'Ouest sous la III$^e$ République*, Paris, 1913.

J. Simon, *L'ouvrier de huit ans*, Paris, 1867.

J. Simon, *L'instruction gratuite et obligatoire*, Paris, 1873.

L. Soulice, 'Statistique de l'ignorance dans le département des Basses-Pyrénées', *Bulletin de la société des sciences, lettres et arts de Pau*, 1873.

L. Soulice, 'Notes pour servir à l'histoire de l'instruction primaire dans les Basses-Pyrénées, 1835–1880', *Bulletin de la société des sciences, lettres et arts de Pau*, 1880–1881.

E. Souvestre, *Souvenirs d'un bas-breton*, Paris, 1860.

Stendhal, *Mémoires d'un touriste* (1838), Paris-Le Divan, 1928.

Stendhal, *La vie d'Henry Brulard* (1890), Paris-Le Divan, 1929.

L. Stone, 'The educational revolution in England 1560–1640', *Past and Present*, July 1964.

L. Stone, 'Literacy and education in England, 1640–1900', *Past and Present*, Feb. 1969.

H. Taine, *Les origines de la France contemporaine* (vol. III. *Le régime moderne*), Paris, 1901.

H. Tartière, 'De l'instruction publique dans les Landes avant la Révolution et spécialement en 1789', *Société des Lettres, Sciences et Arts du département des Landes*, 7th bulletin, July 1868.

R. Thabault, *1848–1914, L'ascension d'un peuple, mon village, ses hommes, ses routes, son école*, Paris, 1945.

A.G. Thuillier, *Economie et société nivernaises au début du XIX$^e$ siècle*, Paris-La Haye, 1974.

A.G. Thuillier, *Pour une histoire du quotidien au XIX$^e$ siècle en Nivernais*, Mouton, Paris-La Haye, 1977.

A. de Tocqueville, *L'Ancien régime et la révolution* (1856), Paris, 1963.

Toreilles and Desplanques, 'L'enseignement élémentaire en Roussillon avant 1789', *Bulletin de la société agricole, scientifique et littéraire des Pyrénées-Orientales*, vol. XXXVI, 1895.

L. Trenard, 'Les instituteurs en France à la veille de 1848', *Actes du 90$^e$ Congrès national des sociétés savantes, Nice, 1965*, Paris, 1966.

L. Trenard, 'Culture, alphabétisation et enseignement au XVIII$^e$ siècle', *XVIII$^e$ siècle*, 1973.

R. Tronchot, *L'enseignement mutuel en France de 1815 à 1833, les luttes politiques et religieuses autour de la question scolaire*, Thèse de doctorat d'Etat, Paris, 1972.

Canon Ch. Urseau, *L'instruction primaire avant 1789 dans les paroisses du diocèse actuel d'Angers*, 2nd edition, Angers, 1893.

J. Vallée, *L'Ecole normale d'instituteurs de Vesoul, monographie*, Vesoul, 1901.

P. Vilar, 'Enseignement primaire et culture populaire en France sous la III$^e$ République' in 'Niveau de culture et groupes sociaux', *Actes du Colloque réuni du 7 au 9 mai 1966 à l'Ecole Normale Supérieure*, Paris-La Haye, 1967.

Dr L.R. Villerme, *Tableau de l'état physique et moral des ouvriers employés dans les manufactures de coton, de laine et de soie*, Paris, 1840.

Ch. de Villers, *Coup d'oeil sur les universités et le mode d'instruction en Allemagne protestante*, Paris, 1808.

M. Vovelle, 'Maggiolo en Provence: peut-on mesurer l'alphabétisation au début du XVIII^e siècle?' in *Le XVIII^e siècle et l'Education*, supplement to no. 88 of the *Revue Marseille*, 1st quarter 1972.

M. Vovelle, 'Y a-t-il eu une révolution culturelle au xviii^e siècle? A propos de l'éducation populaire en Provence', *Revue d'histoire moderne et contemporaine*, Jan.-March 1975.

E. Vuillemin, *Enquête sur les habitations, les écoles et le degré d'instruction de la population ouvrière des mines de houille du Bassin du Nord et du Pas-de-Calais*, Arras, 1872.

A. de Vulpian, 'Physionomie agraire et orientation politique dans le département des Côtes du Nord, 1928–1946', *Revue française de science politique*, 1951.

D. Wardle, *Education and society in Nineteenth Century Nottingham*, Cambridge, 1971.

J. Willm, *Essai sur l'éducation du peuple ou sur les moyens d'améliorer les écoles populaires et le sort des instituteurs*, Strasbourg, 1843.

P. Zind, *Les nouvelles congrégations de Frères enseignants en France de 1800 à 1830* (Centre d'histoire du catholicisme français de l'université de Lyon), 2 vols., 1969.

# SUBJECT INDEX

adult literacy classes, 254–9; army and navy, 254–7; adult education classes, 257–9; employers' schools, 259
*Ancien Régime* and schooling, 1, 7–8, 58
army, literacy in the, 128, 254–7
attendance at school, 88–9, 96, 103–4, 146–7, 155, 244–6, 291

*Béates*, 106, 109, 178–80, 182
bocage (mixed woodland and pasture) and literacy, 152–66

catechism, 74, 93, 154, 175, 182–3, 191, 295
Catholic Church and schooling, 1, 60–3, 97–8, 100–1, 109, 120–1, 145–6, 259–63, 302; and written culture, 58–60; and reading, 174–8
child labour, 219, 259
Christian School Brothers/Frères des écoles chrétiennes, 78–80, 113–15
clergy, civil constitution of the, 84
Counter-Reformation, the, 60–1, 65–6, 69–70, 78, 80, 149, 167, 178–9, 182–3
counting, the learning of, 77
curriculum, 74–82, 93, 112–15, 137–42

demand for education (from society), 66–8, 82, 96–7, 99, 101, 117–30, 154, 159, 162, 164–5, 303
distance from school, 155, 182

elementary schooling and literacy, 2, 68, 147–8, 233–63
elementary schooling surveys; Maggiolo, 5–34; French Revolution, 86–99; Guizot, 116–17
elementary schools (1): 'foundation' schools, 67, 70, 167; rural, 69–71, 103, 105–9; 'little' schools, 69, 72; state *v.* private, 83–4, 88–9, 96–8, 248–9; clandestine, 106–8, 146; 'congregational', 179–82, 260–3; employers', 259
elementary schools (2): demand for establishment of, 58–68; rules of, 73–4; objectives of, 61–3, 66, 71–3, 120;

universal, free and compulsory, 83–4, 125, 129–30, 136, 138; communes without, 234–5
enrolment figures (elementary schools): under the Directory, 89–90; nineteenth century, 103–5, 146–7, 217, 291; correlation with number of schools and with literacy rate, 237–44
erosion of school learning in later life, 252–3

financing of schools by communes, 156–7, 249–50
free schooling, 250–1
French-speaking in schools, 289–91, 294–5

girls' education, 67, 70, 71–3, 89, 109, 116, 136, 138, 144–6, 178–9, 236–7, 260–1

history and geography, 139, 154

ideology of the school, 1–3, 60–5, 81–99, 120–30, 135, 148, 179–80
illiteracy, residual, 46–7, 150–1, 162, 320
industrialisation and literacy, 4, 203–6, 207–8, 210–25

kindergartens, 170

Latin, reading in, 75–6, 80, 113, 137, 308, 310; for the 'sixième' (First form), 77–8
legislation on education, 62–3, 83–6, 136, 138
literacy, chronological distribution, 27–31, 35–47, 303; reading only, 172–4
literacy, geographical distribution, 25–7, 35–47, 104–5, 152–66, 304–5; reading only, 171–89; disparities between town and country, 199–206, 217, 222–3
literacy, sexual distribution, 32–4, 36–44, 46–7, 199–211, 214; reading only, 171–2
literacy, restricted or mass, 305, 307–8
Lutheran Church and reading, 175

mass education, opposition to, 63–5, 118, 135
Middle Ages, 59, 151, 305

*359*

# INDEX OF PLACE NAMES

# INDEX OF PERSONAL NAMES